Warsaw - Birthplace

Warsaw Ghetto - From Nov. 15, 1940

Wlodzimierz Agricultural School
July 1938 - Sept 1939

Lublin - Sept. & Nov. 1939

Visits 1941, 1942

Bychawa - Country estates
June 1941, - Feb.1942

Bielany Luftwaffe Camp
July - Nov. 1942

6 Okecie Luftwaffe Camp
  Jan. 1943 - May 12, 1943

7 Budzyn SS Camp
  May 1943 - March 1944

8 Majdanek Conc. Camp
  March 1944 - April 1944

9 Plaszow Conc. Camp
  April 1944 - Oct. 1944

10 Flossenbuerg Conc. Camp
   Oct. 1944 - April 1945

Scale - Approx. 0   25 Miles

Bydgoszcz

Plock

Treblinka

Warsaw

SOVIET

UNION

1945 Boundary

Lodz

POLAND

Lublin

Majdanek

Vladmir
Volynsk

Czestochowa

Zamosc

Plaszow

Krakow

Auschwitz

Ostrava

Boundary

LOVAKIA

Presov

Transport Route from
Plaszow to Flossenbuerg

R.R. Trip from School
Destination Warsaw

Evacuation march, Flossenbuerg - Liberation, April 23,
1945

Transports to Lublin
Majdanek, Budzyn, Plaszow

The Iron Furnace

The Iron Furnace

A HOLOCAUST SURVIVOR'S STORY

George Topas

THE UNIVERSITY PRESS OF KENTUCKY

Copyright © 1990 by The University Press of Kentucky
Scholarly publisher for the Commonwealth,
serving Bellarmine College, Berea College, Centre
College of Kentucky, Eastern Kentucky University,
The Filson Club, Georgetown College, Kentucky
Historical Society, Kentucky State University,
Morehead State University, Murray State University,
Northern Kentucky University, Transylvania University,
University of Kentucky, University of Louisville,
and Western Kentucky University.

Editorial and Sales Offices: Lexington, Kentucky 40506-0336

Library of Congress Cataloging-in-Publication Data
Topas, George, 1924-
    The iron furnace : a Holocaust survivor's story / George Topas.
        p.   cm.
    Includes bibliographical references.
    ISBN 0-8131-1698-8 (alk. paper)   :
    1. Holocaust, Jewish (1939-1945)—Personal narratives.   2. Topas,
George, 1924-   .   I. Title.
D804.3.T67   1990
940.53'18'092—dc20
[B]   90-11905
                                                                        CIP

This book is printed on acid-free paper meeting
the requirements of the American National Standard
for Permanence of Paper for Printed Library Materials. ∞

Contents

Illustrations follow page 246

To the unfortunate victims of baseless hatred and inhumanity;
to my parents, Eugenia and Abraham Henry Topas,
and my brothers Shimon and Meir,
who were consumed in the flames of the Holocaust;
and to my fellow survivors,
whose ordeal I was fated to share.

It is my cherished hope that this book
will speak for the myriads of people
whose tongues were silenced.

Preface

When the warm rays of the sun burst through the rainclouds in April 1945 and I could count myself among the living, a free man, a survivor, I was at first too enchanted with life to look back upon the world—on my world—that had burned to the ground. To recall those visions of destruction would compel me to face the reality that from my entire immediate family, I alone was left.

So, one day after my liberation, I volunteered to serve with the U.S. Army, where I found friendship and an opportunity to strike back at my oppressors. I was soon totally absorbed in and preoccupied with my new environment and role as a soldier. Bearing arms, participating in raids, acting as an interpreter (in one instance an entire Panzer division heard its orders and terms of surrender from me), sharing in the elation of V-E Day, the heady feeling of being part of the victorious armed forces—all these added up to an exciting new life for me. It lasted a little over a year.

But even during this brief time things were changing. As soon as the war ended, the discovery of concentration camps, gas chambers, crematoria, and piles upon piles of unburned corpses sent shock waves around the world. The somber face of General Eisenhower during an inspection tour expressed outrage at this evidence of unspeakable evil. At first the U.S. occupation authorities in Germany were intent on bringing the perpetrators to justice. But as soon as the original authority was replaced, the attitude changed, and a process of deemphasis of Nazi crimes began to pervade the lower echelons of command, including the U.S. Military Government posts throughout Germany. Thus the whitewash began. The ostensible reason was that the Cold War with the U.S.S.R. had changed the official U.S. perception of the Nazi enemies to that of potential allies. The "ex"-Nazis sensed the new trend and began to portray themselves as merely good German soldiers who had "only obeyed orders." We have since learned that our own State Department was instrumental in helping Gestapo officers and high-ranking Nazis to disguise their identity in order to evade capture.

So when I received an affidavit from my grandmother, who fortunately had journeyed to the United States just before the outbreak of the war and had thus survived, I was ready to leave for the New World, where I tried civilian life for a while. I found it difficult to adjust, and consequently, in less than a year, I was back in the Army again. This time, I told myself, it was in order to acquire the credentials for going to school under the GI Bill of Rights.

It was while I was stationed at Fort Dix, New Jersey, in 1947, scarcely two years after the war, that I first began to make notes of the events that I had been fated to experience during the five and a half years of my life under the German occupation. I did this because—just as my forefathers had been commanded not to forget their slavery in Egypt—I wanted to make sure that I would never forget mine. And there was this irresistible urge to record it for posterity.

Soon after I got out of the army in 1948, I married, went to technical school under the GI Bill, started both my own business and a family, and in the evenings rewrote the collection of my notes and put them in some sort of order. It wasn't until 1963 that I completed a full draft and showed it to a publisher, whose senior editor encouraged me to edit and resubmit. But I was busy during those years, rebuilding my life and concentrating on my growing construction business. I let the manuscript gather dust. With the voluminous Nuremberg War Crimes trial records providing massive evidence of the Nazi crimes and atrocities, there seemed to be no urgent need to add my own testimony.

Unfortunately, few books on the Holocaust made any real impact, and when books began to appear denying the authenticity of the Holocaust, I lost my complacency. I had thought the history of that epic tragedy would remain on the record unchallenged and undistorted for eternity. Not so. The revival of anti-Semitism brought with it the attempt to falsify the Holocaust.

A very good friend of mine told me about a recurring dream in which he sees himself standing behind barbed wire, a prisoner in a concentration camp. Outside, pedestrians walk along the adjoining thoroughfare, fine people with smiling faces, but they do not see him. He cries out: "Look! We are still imprisoned and oppressed! Help us!" But they ignore him and do not seem to hear him at all—it's as though he did not exist.

In 1967, two decades after the war, I was called to Germany to testify at a trial of SS concentration camp guards. The trial made me realize that the events of the Holocaust were already receding into history; because of the lapse of time, even those who had lived through it could not remember the details of their ordeal with certainty. This made it all the more urgent for me to preserve my own eyewitness account, based on the notes I had made soon after the end of World War II.

Perhaps it was my writings and my desire to improve them that led me to the next step, or perhaps it was my experience at the trial, which gave me the impetus to learn more in order to get a better perspective on past events. In any event, in 1970, at the age of forty-six, I entered college as an evening student. In the course of twelve years I earned my master's degree from Rutgers University. In my last year of undergraduate study, my memoir had formed the basis of my senior thesis.

During that time I also began to give talks on the Holocaust in colleges and high schools, and in the process I found a real interest among the young to know how people their age had lived, coped with, resisted, and survived the conditions of life imposed on them. At one college lecture I was asked, "Why do some writers try to deny the Holocaust?" I felt challenged by the question. "I think," I replied, "that anti-Semites find the enormity of the Holocaust a formidable obstacle in winning a following because a lot of thinking people feel that since rabid anti-Semitism led to the Holocaust, it could happen again. Therefore, those who want to re-create the past must first delegitimize—deny—the authenticity of the Holocaust, absolve the perpetrators from responsibility, and accuse the Jews of fabrication, in order to create a climate conducive to fomenting anti-Jewish sentiment." Some students, after hearing of my experiences under the Nazis, found it very difficult to comprehend the terrible things that had been done to the Jewish people. As one student expressed it, "How could a man act that way?" That kind of hatred really is difficult to explain. You would have to have felt it to understand it. I cannot say that I can now answer that question. I suppose that hatred of others has to be fed to you from the very beginning.

The significance of the life of an individual human being is dwarfed by the events of the Holocaust. The total picture may never be seen in its full enormity, but its composite images may be fitted together like fragments of a mosaic from the testimonies of eyewitnesses. In presenting my fragment, I felt that it was not enough to tell about the ordeal of the battle for survival and about some of its casualties; I had to describe scenes from the way of life that was ultimately extinguished. Thus, I have attempted to take a small part of history out of the realm of cold statistics that list casualties in the millions and in so doing depersonalize this human catastrophe.

I hope I have told a story with which both young and old can somehow identify. My fervent prayer is that my testimony will help people not only to appreciate the value of freedom and the many blessings that those who did not suffer often take for granted but to recognize the importance of tolerance and the need for a constant vigil against the spread of causeless hatred.

And Jacob was left alone; and there wrestled a man with him until the breaking of the day—Genesis 22:26

Jacob will have to contend until Night wanes from the earth. Throughout the whole of the struggle at night, Jacob's opponent tries to take the ground from under his feet, to give him no standing at all, to have no claim to exist at all on earth.—Samson Raphael Hirsch

Prologue: Witness against Persecution

The Lufthansa 707 jet roared down the JFK runway and lifted up into the evening sky. We were airborne. I reclined in my seat and pulled out some papers that had a direct bearing on my reason for making this journey.

Being a pilot myself, I am in the habit of paying attention to the performance of another pilot—but not on this flight. This was no ordinary business or vacation trip. I had been summoned to give testimony at the trial of three German SS guards in Kiel, Germany. The prosecution expected me to testify as to the complicity of these guards in the shipment of Jewish children from Plaszow concentration camp, near Krakow, to Auschwitz for liquidation.

The papers in my lap were memoirs that I had drafted soon after the end of the World War II. I had brought them along to help me recall the events about which I would testify. But I could not concentrate. As the muffled noise of the engines droned on, I became immersed in revisiting the past that sprang to life from the pages of my recollections. Muted voices, familiar faces, and pleading eyes emerged from my inner consciousness. I had the premonition that this trip would rekindle memories which, from a purely selfish point of view, would be better left undisturbed. Taking the path of least resistance, however, would in this matter be tantamount to a betrayal of the people who had perished. And so I continued reading, and it must have been quite late when I finally closed my eyes and tried to get some sleep.

It was a misty morning on 28 August 1967 when the plane touched down at Hamburg Airport. The next day I boarded a train for Kiel. This was my first opportunity to see Germany after an absence of twenty-one years. When I left Europe in 1946, after having served with the U.S. Army of Occupation, Germany was in ruins. The people then were somewhat subdued and almost reverent toward the American military authorities and personnel. Perhaps they had feared retribution, believing that the Allies would demand accountability for the crimes committed during the war. It soon became apparent to me that all this had changed. The cities had been rebuilt. There were no ragged children on the streets, no *Fräuleins* seeking to consort with American GIs. Indeed, there was no evidence left of the war damage. The people's air of self-assurance was reminiscent of the days when Germany had been victorious.

The only other occupant of my train compartment was a young, blond German naval officer. Looking at him with curious eyes, I wondered how present members of the military establishment differed from their wartime counterparts. When he put his paper down and returned my gaze, I took it as a cue to start a conversation. "I thought that modern missile warfare had made the navy obsolete," I said, for an opener.

"Not as long as there are oceans," he replied gingerly, with a good command of English.

We continued talking, switching back and forth between English and German. I asked him what he thought about the relatively new German military code. One of its clauses forbids soldiers to obey orders to kill unarmed civilians. He thought that it was a rather silly law. "Who is going to decide whether an order should be obeyed or not?" he said heatedly. "A sergeant?"

"Well," I said, " a sergeant or a private, the low in rank are usually those charged with executing orders."

He considered such a regulation contrary to the logic of military discipline, which places decision-making authority in the hands of senior officers.

I then mentioned a news item about a naval ship recently named after Colonel Claus von Stauffenberg, the German officer who had been the key man in the unsuccessful attempt to kill Hitler in 1944. This too he thought a foolish thing: "It can only have a demoralizing effect on our people. Naming a ship after Karl Doenitz makes sense because he was a hero, whereas Stauffenberg was a traitor—at that time—and if you honor someone for rebelling against authority, you encourage anarchy," he said emphatically.

I steered the conversation in another direction. "When I served with the U.S. Army in Bavaria, I noted that the people there seemed more relaxed and easygoing than the people here up north," I said.

"The people down there are like the Italians—but here you have people you can rely on. If one tells you something, you can believe him," he said with a glint of Teutonic pride.

Although he could not have been more than a teenager when the war had ended, it was apparent that for this man the past survived as seeds saved from a disastrous harvest. The army that followed Hitler, killing millions without ever disobeying orders, would have been proud of this model of a naval officer.

As the train pulled into the Kiel railroad station, we parted company. I took a taxi to the hotel, one of two selected for trial witnesses because of their proximity to the high court (*Schwurgericht*—literally, the court that takes sworn testimony). My hotel was small, clean, unpretentious in its plain decor, and by American standards second-rate. A clerk at the registration desk examined the letter of "admission" issued by the German judicial authorities who had paid the bill. Behind the facade of her dutiful manner, I could detect an air of disdain.

In the lobby I met another witness who had just arrived. We tried to recognize each other, without success.

"My name is Moshe Bejski," he said. "I was in Plaszow from 1943 to 1945. What is yours?"

"Mine is Topas. I was in Plaszow in 1944, from April through October."

A man of short stature, with an air of self-assurance that more than made up for his height, Dr. Bejski was now an Israeli judge. In Plaszow he had worked in the camp's records office. Before we discussed the trial, he told me a fascinating story about a German named Schindler who had actually tried to save "his" Jews, those who had worked for him in his plant. He went to great lengths to inflate the importance of the defense-related work performed by the prisoners under his authority in order to circumvent or delay their deportation to Auschwitz. After the war he fell on hard times, but the handful of surviving Jews who had worked in his group kept in touch with him and helped him. A unique story indeed: it was later told in the book *Schindler's List*.[1]

Bejski had talked with other witnesses who had already testified. According to them, the jurors seemed weary and bored; they had already listened for several months to a continuous flow of witnesses who repeated many of the same terrible happenings that they had all experienced. Especially sad were the witnesses whose children Franz Joseph Mueller, one of the defendants, had killed personally at the Bochnia camp before he came to Plaszow concentration camp. Unfortunately, many witnesses had gotten mixed up and had had difficulty remembering and matching the time frames with the crimes committed by the guards. The resulting doubts favored the accused, who seemed to be in good spirits and who smiled when witnesses were tripped up. To overcome this disadvantage, Bejski counseled that our testimony should be brief, specific, and accurate; above all, we should exclude any part that we did not clearly remember.

Bejski, well informed on the workings of the German trial process, explained to me that the court consisted of three judges and six laymen—jurors—working jointly, with one judge presiding. The prosecution acted not as an adversary of the defense but as a "friend" of the court, seeking the truth and theoretically taking no sides. In this trial the three SS men were defended by two state-retained lawyers. The witnesses could be questioned by the judges, cross-examined by the defense lawyers, and questioned or corrected by the prosecutor.

Before I fell asleep that night, I again scanned my written recollections and came across my record of a strange occurrence involving German pilots. This gave me an idea.

Early the next morning Bejski and I met another man and a woman who were also scheduled to testify that day. As we entered the massive court building, we were directed to a clerk, who told us the order in which we were to appear. The court seemed to be a busy place. Small groups of people were standing in the hall, speaking in hushed voices. As the time for the day's session drew near, court functionaries and spectators hastily emptied the hall and went into the courtroom. I was shown to the spectators' section, and took a seat. A witness was already giving testimony.

I took a good look around. Directly in front of me the three SS men were seated on an elevated podium behind bulletproof glass. They stared impassively in the direction of the witnesses. The once dreaded killers had aged since their heyday, when they had held sway over the lives of thousands of people. Except for Mueller, whose features still retained their brutish image, they were not at first easily recognizable. I was struck by a sense of unreality: the scene I was witnessing would have been unthinkable twenty-three years earlier. In 1944 the hope that some of us would live to confront our tormentors in a court of law seemed at best very remote.

The three judges, flanked on both sides by the jurors, were seated behind a long table directly to the right of the accused. The space separating the podium from the spectators was occupied by the defense lawyers, the witness, and the prosecutor. The atmosphere was a bit tense. The first witness, a woman in her mid-fifties (named, as I learned later, Felicja Rolnicki), was giving her testimony between quiet sobs. An elderly man in a gray uniform with an armband displaying the Red Cross emblem walked over and offered her something, but she shook her head and continued nervously, barely maintaining her composure.

She was in the process of describing, in Polish, the liquidation of the Krakow ghetto. (Plaszow concentration camp, where the survivors of the ghetto had been interned, was located on the outskirts of Krakow.) She spoke in a low voice, pausing between sentences for the interpreter to translate the Polish into German. "I heard a shot . . . then a scream . . . Kunde [one of the accused SS men] shot and killed a child on Wengerska Street during the roundup action in the ghetto. The child cried bitterly before he died."

The prosecutor showed the witness a map of the city and asked her to point to the location where the killing had taken place. A discussion ensued about the relative positions of the witness, the child, and the killer. Continuing her testimony, she told of running with her own daughter. She heard shots fired, turned, and saw another woman fall and the SS men Wilhelm Kunde and Hermann Heinrich (the third defendant absent in this episode) shooting. She fell, still holding her child, thinking herself shot. Her child, she cried, was only ten years old. She went on to describe the roundup of two hundred children in Plaszow for transport to Auschwitz for liquidation. Her own daughter had been among those forcibly taken and herded onto railroad cattle cars. Desperate mothers, driven to madness, scuffled with the SS men in a vain attempt to free their children, but they were ruthlessly suppressed.

"My daughter was murdered," she cried.

"Did you actually see them kill your daughter or one of the people you refer to?" asked one of the defense attorneys, pointing to the defendants.

"Is it not enough that I know they were killed and these men took her away from me?" she cried.

"Which one of these defendants did you see taking away your daughter?"

She whispered something inaudible.

"Would you point him out."

She pointed at Mueller, but then she said something about one of the others, perhaps Kunde.

The defense lawyer jumped to his feet and declared that her testimony was invalid because the actual crime of killing had not been observed by the witness but was only presumed, and because Kunde had happened to be away that day. The woman wiped her eyes with a handkerchief and cried silently as though she had just relived the experience again. She seemed not at all interested in or conscious of the effect her testimony had on the proceedings or of the significance of the challenge just raised. Her wounds had been reopened, and she did not contest the lawyer's argument.

"Is there anything else you wish to add?" asked the presiding judge.

"She wiped her eyes again and said in a tremulous voice: "It happened to be my birthday. As the children's procession was led out of the camp, a song, 'Mamusiu, buy me a small [rocking] horse,' played through the camp loudspeakers. It was followed by another: 'Mommy, don't cry, we are all going to heaven.'" She paused for a moment, trying to overcome her grief. "I was later sent to Auschwitz myself and learned that every child in that transport had been killed."[2]

She tried in vain then to control her emotions and cried inconsolably. The passage of twenty-three years had not extinguished the painful memories. As she struggled again to regain her composure, the presiding judge thanked her for coming and for giving her testimony;

her husband, who had been sitting beside her, helped her out of the courtroom.

Later, the state-appointed lawyer addressed a man who appeared to be over seventy years old. (His name, I learned later, was Kalman Broder.) "You have said that the accused, Kunde, killed the man. Can you show us Kunde in this photo?"

The witness, after some thought, said, "No, I cannot."

The lawyer asked, "Should I remind you that during the interrogation last year you said that the accused Heinrich had shot the man dead?"

The elderly witness said, "Yes, I made an error now, for it was the accused Heinrich!"

The timely check by the defense attorney had cast doubt upon the most damaging part of the witness's testimony.

The jurors bestirred themselves from their lethargy and seemed relieved. Before the woman finished giving her testimony, it had been apparent from their wearied expressions that they were having trouble focusing their attention on the court proceedings. Judge Rausch, however, appeared alert and earnest and seemed to be aware of the historic and moral significance of the trial. The defendants exchanged smiling glances when the witness was excused, as if they had just dispensed with more testimony not very damaging to their defense.

The question of his complicity in assembling the children's transport to Auschwitz did not cause Mueller to abandon his repeated denials of responsibility. He knew all the excuses. At one point, he turned to the chairman of the court and said, "You can easily accuse me but I don't know anything."

I briefly studied the faces of these men who had held the fate of thousands of innocent people in their hands and who had destroyed so many of them. The little children were not here to complain, nor could their bereaved mothers be consoled. But their anguish began to fill me with a sense of outrage, which I forced myself to control as I had done so often during those fateful years. I decided not to testify about the children's selection and deportation to Auschwitz, as I was expected to do. I was not going to bore the court with more of what they had repeatedly heard during these proceedings. I was going to surprise them with something they would find more stimulating.

Though I still retained a measure of fluency in German, I chose to testify in English; therefore, the court assigned an interpreter to translate my testimony. After the initial formalities of the oath and establishment of identification and residence, I was asked by the presiding judge: "What is your present occupation?"

"I am a construction executive who runs his own company."

"Were you interned in the concentration camp Plaszow?"

"Yes, I was."

"During what time period?"

"From April through October 1944."

"Are you prepared to give testimony now about your experiences in the camp which bear upon any acts of these three defendants?"

"Yes, I am."

"You may proceed."

"I was brought to Plaszow concentration camp with a transport that arrived in April 1944. During one of the hot summer nights my friend Mark and I were sleeping outside the barracks, below the 'magazine' [storeroom]. It was situated near the double fence separating the inner from the outer camp, directly opposite the elevated hilly spot where a site had been leveled for the building of an SS hospital barracks."

After each sentence or paragraph I had to wait for the interpreter to catch up with his translation, correcting an occasional error. I continued.

"We were awakened by the slamming of car doors. It was barely the dawn of a new day. I watched with amazement as three SS vehicles pulled up and discharged half a dozen SS men and then two German *Luftwaffe* pilots wearing leather jackets and Iron Cross decorations, who were then tied to two poles that had been hastily set into the ground. The pilots did not protest but just stood there facing their executioners. Moments later they were killed by a short burst of automatic rifle fire. Mueller was one of the SS men in attendance."

One of the defense attorneys rose to his feet: "Are you absolutely sure that Mueller pulled the trigger?"

"No, I am not absolutely sure," I replied.

The defense lawyers turned quickly toward the judges and exclaimed, "The witness is not sure."

At this point the prosecutor made his presence felt by correcting the defense: "No, no, he did not say he was not sure; he said he was not absolutely sure."

A fine point. It should have been obvious to the judges that from a distance of fifty to one hundred feet it was not easy to see who among the SS men present had fired the shots, although all held guns. To me, the most important thing was to convey the fact that two Luftwaffe pilots were killed by the SS. Who actually had done the shooting mattered less to me than the fact that those who murdered Jewish women and children also killed their own men; this, I thought, should give the court something to think about.

There was no doubt that the court had come to life, and the jurors cast anxious glances at the SS prisoners in the dock. Mueller, visibly shaken, mumbled some denials, but Judge Rausch admonished him to behave himself in court. The judges and jurors appeared to me to have taken good notice of the accused at last and to have seen them, perhaps for the first time, as murderers who had committed heinous crimes rather than as soldiers obeying orders. Perhaps it reminded them that the first people to fall victims to Hitler's concentration-camp terror were the Germans themselves. Whatever their thoughts were, I felt that the mood in the courtroom had perceptibly changed against the three former SS guards.

When Dr. Bejski later charged Mueller with the personal preparation of the list for the shipment of the Jewish children to the death camp factory of Auschwitz, Mueller denied that he did this on his own authority, insisting that the orders had come from Berlin.

The presiding judge, Dr. Kluth was annoyed by this reply: "In response to earlier testimony, you stated that you received your orders from the camp *Kommandant*, and now you say that the orders came from Berlin. Come now, Mueller, which of your statements is true, and which would you have the court believe?"

Mueller got up and angrily snapped back, disclaiming responsibility. Bejski contested his disclaimer with a detailed explanation of Mueller's interests and his exclusive role in zealously searching the files for the names of children. Looking tense, Mueller seemed to realize that the case had turned against him. His effort to extricate himself from his bad slip failed to convince the court.

Bejski, a criminal judge himself, knew the value of specific facts, so he testified in detail about an outgoing transport of 7,000 Hungarian Jewish women to the Auschwitz extermination camp. The articulate witness spoke with tremulous voice, as only one who had shared in their agony could, describing the transport of these doomed women. When Mueller refused to admit responsibility, Bejski asked the accused in a voice charged with indignation: "Can you so easily forget something so flagrant: that you sent 7,000 women to their extermination?"[3]

Not even one woman from the May 14, 1944, transport to Auschwitz had survived.

The argument about Mueller's ability to remember brought a flicker of excitement to the faces of the small courtroom audience, as did Bejski's further testimony about shootings; about a prisoner who was torn apart by a vicious dog that had been set upon him; about corpses shipped out of the ghetto; about Jews who were hung by their hands for hours and intermittently dropped to the ground and flushed with water.[4]

Mueller denied knowledge of most of these events.

"When I came to the camp the Jews numbered 28,000 people. At the end we were 3,000. What did you do with the others?" demanded Bejsky in an angry voice.

There were no smiles on the faces of the defendants when Bejski completed his testimony.

Before leaving Kiel, I asked one of the hostesses, a Dutch girl whose job it was to put the witnesses at ease and to make them feel welcome, to mail me the newspaper account of the final findings of the court. As I boarded the train the same day for Hamburg, I reflected upon the general apathy of the people here toward the prosecution of Nazi criminals, on the general dispensation of light sentences, and on the fact that the overwhelming majority of the Nazi murderers had managed to evade justice with relative ease. Several months later I received two newspaper clippings from Kiel. One was a partial account of the testimony given on the day I appeared in court. The other reported the court's final session and its verdicts. "SIX TIMES LIFE SENTENCE IN MAXIMUM SECURITY PENITENTIARY IN KIEL TO ATONE FOR HIDEOUS ACTS OF MURDER AGAINST THE JEWS," the headline read. A close-up picture of Mueller and one of his accomplices, taken as the verdict was pronounced, showed the stunned expression on his hard face.[5]

The newspaper reported that after eleven months of hearings, the *Schwurgericht* gave its verdicts and pronounced sentences against the three defendants. The three judges and six sworn laymen sentenced SS *Hauptscharfuehrer* (a rank equivalent to master sergeant) Mueller, camp-master and "manager" of Bochnia, to six times life-long confinement in a penitentiary and the forfeiture of his civil rights. After more than ninety days of testimony, the court found him guilty in two instances of complicity in the commission of mass murders and in four instances of attempted and executed murders of individual Jews.

Judge Rausch described Heinrich and Mueller as "small wheels" (*Kleine Rädschen*) in the big (*Vernichtungs*) extermination machinery of the Nazis. "Furthermore," Rausch was quoted as saying, "as chief of the Bochnia camp, Mueller displayed a special eagerness and extreme brutality in many instances against Jewish internees." The report continued:

> The court noted that among other acts in September 1943, on the *Appellplatz* [assembly grounds] in Bochnia, he [Mueller] tore a one-and-a-half-year-old child from the arms of his mother and then threw him on a heap of pitifully crying children and he set his vicious dog upon them.
>
> In three other instances, the court was convinced, Mueller had shot Jewish men and women on his own initiative, without receiving orders from higher ups. After taking testimony from 250 witnesses, the court became convinced that Mueller had made Hitler's and Himmler's extermination

plans his own. This was demonstrated by the degree of his participation in two mass deportations during the liquidation of the two camps [Bochnia and Plaszow] where he had exercised his authority. Therefore, as an accomplice, Mueller must be brought to account.

The findings and conclusions of the court upon which it based its verdicts took a good two hours to recite, before a courtroom filled to capacity.[6]

The disposition of the cases against the other two men was mild. Heinrich, who was charged with a cumulative count of six instances of rendering "assistance" in mass murders (but apparently not volunteering it), was sentenced to six years in a penitentiary. The third man, SS *Hauptscharfuehrer* Kunde, the ghetto chief of Krakow, though characterized as *Gewaltieger* (violent), was released because of a reported heart ailment.

A detailed account was given of the other witnesses' testimony during the August 30 session, but no mention whatsoever was made of something as sensational as the killing of the *Luftwaffe* pilots by the SS. I was surprised; what was the motive for this glaring omission? Could it be that the editors were embarrassed by the incriminating fact that not only Jews and other nationals but German fighter pilots were killed by the SS as well?

Whatever the case, it was true that Mueller was just a "little wheel" in the big extermination apparatus, as the German judge had concluded, and he does not figure prominently in my own recollections. But the totality of the Holocaust and its success as a work of ultimate evil was assured by thousands upon thousands of Muellers who made the Hitler regime's extermination plans their own.

1 The Approaching Storm

As the vulture swoops down . . .
—Deuteronomy 28:49

It was at my grandparents' apartment in Warsaw that my view of the world began to take shape. Sitting by the two large windows that faced the wide and busy thoroughfare of Leszno, one of the more prominent streets of the city, I would watch the scene below and listen to its sounds. The sidewalks teeming with people, the streetcars, horse-drawn vehicles, autos, and newspaper and bagel vendors—each made a distinct sound, and together they made music that I became accustomed to hearing from morning until late evening.

Our home at Leszno 28 was in a fine four-story apartment building, a quadrangle with a courtyard in the center that was more than merely a passageway leading out to the street. There in spring and summer various peddlers, junk dealers, and glaziers carrying glass panes on their backs would announce their wares and crafts, each in the peculiar call distinct to his trade. Occasionally, when a whole traveling band entered our courtyard and played for us, not only would all the windows be filled with listeners but a following from the street would fill the courtyard—standing room only. Before the finale one of the musicians would pass among the audience accepting coins, while those on the balconies would toss their share from above.

I was the eldest of three sons. At the outbreak of the war in 1939 I was almost fifteen, Simon was eleven, and Meir was only five. My father, Abraham Chaim, called Henry, was a man of medium height with deep-set brown eyes and a short Van Dyke beard; he looked very distinguished.

He helped manage the family-owned shoe business that had been founded and was still operated by my paternal grandparents. While Grandpa was actively occupied with the affairs of the company and looked the part of a well-dressed boss, it was Grandma who was actually the driving force that had transformed a modest shoe shop into a sizable manufacturing and sales enterprise. Grandma, a tall, stately, no-nonsense kind of woman, followed two guiding principles: close attention to the business, and dedication to her family. She also scrupulously gave money to charity and lit the Sabbath candles every Friday night, even though the Sabbath was not formally observed in the house.

In fact, the business was kept open on Saturday, much to my father's chagrin; he had become religious and observed the Sabbath rest, but he could not prevail on his parents to do so. Caught up in the wave of assimilation that had swept postwar Europe after World War I, my grandparents sought economic opportunity at the expense of our tradition and its well-tested values. My father and his sister and brothers had been sent to Polish high schools rather than Jewish schools. But my father was not content with things as they were, though he initially let himself be influenced by the trappings of the "new age" and even Polonized the names of his brothers and sister and three cousins (orphans who lived with our grandparents), changing my uncle Moshe's name to Mietek and cousin Zaharia's name to Sevek.

As an adolescent my father had shown extraordinary interest in court proceedings, spending many hours in the courtroom listening to legal arguments. He was a thinking individual who eventually reached the conclusion that assimilation was a failure—a failure to appreciate our own traditional values. Perhaps the flickering light kindled by the memories of his grandparents' Sabbaths and the warmth of their home sparked in him an interest in his heritage that led him to search for and return to Jewish tradition some years later. When the change came, it was something of a revolution that placed invisible barriers between us and our nonobservant, freewheeling relatives. Some of them became distant if not altogether alienated from us.

My mother, Genia, whose maiden name was Borenstein, came from a relatively poor family, in spite of which she had won admission first to the state high school (gymnasium) in her hometown of Plock and then to the University of Warsaw. (These achievements were all the more remarkable because of her double handicap of being both Jewish and a woman under the anti-Semitic restrictions of the time.) Since she had to earn her living while attending the university as a law student, she became a tutor to the Topas sons. The oldest son Henry and the young tutor fell in love and married.

Grandpa, who was identified in every way with the growing Topas enterprise, was content to let Grandma run the main store while he divided his interests and developed a taste for the finer things in life. In my mind's eye I see him seated at the head of the massive mahogany table in our dining room, striking a confident pose as he puffs his cigar and surveys the morning paper. Above the upright clock directly behind him the sculpted face of Goethe looks across the room to Dante's bust resting upon the mantel of the fireplace. Frescoes of Roman soldiers and Praetorian guards decorate the walls over the doorways leading to the parlor and hall. The large dining room on which Grandpa had lavished so many of his artistic efforts reflected that care in every article displayed, including an elaborate imported chandelier. It was a room that had witnessed many beautiful Passover and Purim feasts attended by the entire Topas clan. It was the place where family and guests would usually gather for any special occasion.

It was at one of the family's impromptu meetings in this very room that I overheard my father plead and argue with my grandparents to move to Canada before it was too late. At the time Hitler had already annexed Austria but had not yet invaded Czechoslovakia.

"But who knows Topas in Canada?" asked my grandfather incredulously. "Do you think that these are our forefather Abraham's times, when one moved from one pasture to another?" It was obvious that those who controlled the purse strings of the Topas family were not about to embark on a new adventure. How could they foresee the consequences of their stubborn commitment to the status quo?

My father's repeated plea to his parents to sell all their possessions and leave Poland before it was too late fell on deaf ears. My grandparents scoffed at the idea of danger to the Polish Jews; the persecution of the Jews was nothing new, they pointed out, but what was happening to the Jews in Germany and Austria would not happen here. On the other hand, were we to leave a place where we were well established, we would be throwing away all the efforts and toil it had taken to build up the now well-known Topas shoe business. I recall my parents discussing one evening the then sensational plan of shipping Polish Jews off to Madagascar. The headline proposal was made by an anti-Semitic member and one of the leaders of O.Z.N. (Camp of National Unity, a Polish political party) named Col. Jan Kowalewsky. Bitterly criticized by Jewish leaders, he denied the charge of anti-Semitism; to prove his point, he said, he would gladly exchange Polish Jews for German Jews because in his opinion the German Jews made better citizens. A few days later Father read us a letter to the editor from a rabbi in a small town near Grodno in which he respectfully assured the Polish representative that every country gets the kind of Jews it deserves. A faint smile appeared on my father's face as he put the paper down.

It was that same summer of 1938 that I was sent away to an agriculture school that was supposed to prepare me for a career in farming and eventual emigration to Palestine. I did not know then that my battle training for survival would begin in this very school, where an integral part of the program of turning city boys into future farmers occurred through a toughening process that came from toil and sweat. Even as a soldier's training is to prepare him for the eventuality of battle, so too was I given a preparatory physical and mental fitness course without actually knowing then how much my life was going to depend on it.

My father's decision to send me there had been made as a result of several considerations: primarily because of his belief that the Jewish people should return to the life of agriculture that they had been forced to leave after having been driven out of their homeland, and also because of the uncertainty of any Jewish future in Poland. The probability of war gave urgency to the plan, and since he himself was unable to make the transition, he wanted to take the first step through me.

Situated near Wlodzimierz, the district's main town, the school was an overnight journey by train from Warsaw. My father accompanied me there in July 1938 and we spent the day we arrived together. As the time came for his departure, a feeling of homesickness began to overwhelm me, and I felt like bursting into tears. I wanted so much to ask him to take me back home with him, for this place seemed so remote from Warsaw and everything I had been used to. But all the arrangements had been made, and I had to make the best of it. I could see that Father probably did not feel too easy about leaving me this far away from home either. As I held on to my meager pride so that he would not think me "just a kid," he turned toward me and, as if reading my thoughts, said gently but firmly: "Jurek [pronounced Yurek, a name derived from my Polish name, Yerzy, which in English is George], you were brought here for a good reason. Here you will learn a skill that someday may help us all to leave Poland before it is too late. I have great hopes for you, and I am certain that this school, with its training, will prove to be of great help to you in the future. Perhaps it is the work of Providence that you were brought here to prepare you for an important task. Try to get along with your friends, and try to abstain from the influence of bad company."

The school was run under the auspices of Tarbut, a Zionist-oriented educational society.[1] Although the Sabbath and Jewish holidays were observed, most of the students were lax in their observance. Nevertheless, when I once joined a Saturday soccer game, several of the boys yelled, "Hey, Topas, don't you know that you're not supposed to play soccer on Shabbat?" On Friday night there was always the singing of Hebrew songs, some religious and some Zionist, and Sabbath morning services were conducted in one of the classrooms. Attendance was mandatory, and failure to show up meant forfeiture of the special dessert. When the weather was nice I would walk into the fields, where I sat by a haystack and nostalgically sang *zemiroth* (Sabbath songs) as I would have at home.

New students had to undergo an impromptu rigged initiation rite. Thus I was persuaded to ride a "tame" horse that discharged its rider unexpectedly. A fellow student named Libson washed the laundry for the entire freshman class because he was told on his arrival that it was his turn. Despite such pranks, however, there was a spirit of camaraderie among the students.

My arrival at the school coincided with the beginning of harvest time, and the work was so hard that several of the newly arrived students quit. Although I was much in sympathy with the idea of quitting and returning home, I was determined to hold out for at least a week. By making several such resolutions during succeeding weeks, I managed to get through the harvest season. Eventually I came to like the school and to do well in my studies.

The driving spirit of the school was its principal, Nachum Sienicki, an agricultural engineer and the best teacher I ever had. Mr. Sienicki demanded competent performance from his students and seldom got less. He was both feared and liked and best remembered for two words he was fond of repeating: "initiative" and "responsibility." His task was to transform city-bred boys not only into tough, efficient farmers but also into self-reliant individuals. Those of us who survived owe him a debt of gratitude. I know I do—if only for arousing my thirst for knowledge. His influence brought about a marked change for the better in my learning habits, enough to surprise my parents, who had not expected such a marked improvement; they thought of me as an intractable, wild youth without any patience or inclination for serious study. Mr. Sienicki's enthusiasm did more to improve my attitude toward school than all the pep talks from somber-faced teachers I had ever had. I sensed the change in myself and felt strengthened by it.

An unexpected visit from my father in late May 1939 for Shavuoth (holy days that commemorate the giving of the Ten Commandments and also celebrate an early harvest) was a most pleasant surprise, even though his stay of a few days seemed but a few moments. Aside from the usual admonitions, Father confided to me his strong conviction that this period of uneasy peace in Europe might not last much longer. Therefore, on my graduation in fourteen months, the family would try to emigrate to Canada because the British were closing the gates to Palestine for Jewish immigrants. Later that summer I received letters and pictures from a farm where he himself was working and learning farming during his vacations, in keeping with his plans for emigration.

In one of my very last letters from home I learned that my paternal grandmother, the matriarch of our clan, had left for the United States on the Polish liner *Pilsudski* to visit her sister and to see the World's Fair. In fact, my father had succeeded in getting her out of Poland in the hope that she might be able to help us somehow before it was too late.

Rumblings of war marked the end of the Polish harvest in the summer of 1939. While the brilliant August sun and clear skies gave a reassuring picture of a peaceful countryside, invisible clouds were gathering a menacing strength. In the midst of a growing though deceptive optimism that "all will yet be well," Poland began to mobilize. It was high season for the press and radio, and they worked overtime. One day's headlines featured Chamberlain's declaration of "PEACE IN OUR TIME," followed by "PRAGUE'S DAY OF SORROW." Then, racing after each other, came "CHURCHILL WARNS CHAMBERLAIN" . . . "HITLER DECLARES HE DOES NOT WANT WAR" . . . "DANZIG QUESTION TO BE SOLVED THROUGH DIPLOMATIC CHANNELS" . . . "POLISH CORRIDOR TO BE DECIDED BY PLEBISCITE" . . . "BRITISH WILL NOT STAND IDLE IN THE EVENT OF GERMAN AGGRESSION" . . . "GERMAN ULTIMATUM" . . . "POLAND WILL NOT YIELD TO GERMAN THREATS."

Not quite fifteen then, I was in my second year in agricultural school, some 340 kilometers (about 210 miles) from Warsaw. The frequent talk of war generated much excitement among the students; the mere sound of the warlike news drowned out all other subjects and made routine schoolwork drab by contrast: who wanted to know how to cultivate and save plants or flowers from parasites when the whole country might soon need saving? In the bright light of day, the imminent war seemed more like a movie adventure than a time of real danger and destruction. But at night, as I lay awake in my dormitory, I felt depressed by foreboding visions. Pictures of Jews being forced by the Nazis to wash the streets in Vienna after the *Anschluss*[2] or of refugees carrying bundles of personal belongings appeared with increasing frequency in the newspapers, disturbing my comforting illusions of relative security.

Events were about to draw the curtain on schoolday reflections and to disrupt many pursuits. Walking back to my dormitory late one afternoon, I paused on the side of the road and gazed westward across emptied fields. The beautiful sunset differed somehow from all I had seen before. The golden sun turned crimson, blood-red against a background of darkened red-flaming skies. There was something ominous in this spectacle. Pawelczak, the school's young driver and handyman, stopped by and wiped his forehead. He had happened to be walking back to his home when the same sight arrested his attention. Born and raised in these parts, Pawelczak knew quite a lot about farming without ever having attended an agricultural school, or perhaps any other school.

"Look at that sun," he exclaimed, and on his face there was an expression of fear. Crossing himself, he whispered as he moved his hand: "Young fellow," he said, without turning or distracting his gaze but slowly shaking his head in disbelief, "that big bowl of fire—it's bad. It's a sign of war." Such a prophecy was really no longer an improbable revelation, but this extraordinary sunset gave an illusion of blazing fields all along the horizon, suggesting something even more foreboding and awesome than mere talk of war.

Then, on Friday morning, September 1, 1939, despite all assurances to the contrary, the inevitable happened: Hitler attacked Poland—the war was on in earnest. The news we heard over the radio at breakfast time was so startling that there was an unusually solemn quiet in the mess hall. Warsaw had been bombed that morning, the communiquě said. The event seemed more sensational than real, but reality was beginning to settle in.

On Saturday we were informed that as of Monday all school studies would be temporarily suspended. The following day, Sunday, the news that England and France had declared war on Germany was broadcast with hysterical enthusiasm, and predictions of victory were repeated amid march music: "God Save the King," the "Marseillaise," and the Polish national anthem. The next morning a regiment of the Polish Army arrived at our school to occupy some of the buildings, causing quite a stir of excitement among the admiring students. The school authorities announced that with the exception of students from Warsaw (which was under bombardment), all were to go home until "the end of hostilities." Those of us from the Warsaw area, however, grew anxious and demanded permission to go home too. Eventually, our insistence prevailed, and we began to pack immediately.

As though going home for vacation, I put on my dashing school uniform with its visored, octagonal, green velvet cap, navy blue jacket with mandarin collar, riding pants, and high riding boots. I remembered that, soon after my enrollment, obtaining full uniform and boots had seemed very important to me, and so I wrote home, asking my father again and again to send me riding boots. He soon got angry and asked me not to "bombard" him with constant demands for boots— then one day a large package from home brought a pair of the most elegant boots I had ever seen. My new boots gave me a feeling of prominence. When you are a young man, your appearance and self-image are very important. The last time I had worn my full school regalia was to go home for the Chanukah winter vacation, when the country was still at peace. Now, in September 1939, youthful hopes and boyish curiosity about war were giving way to a feeling of sad awareness that whether this war was won or lost, whenever the world resumed where it left off, our lives would not ever be the same again. I was about to leave the place that had been my home for the past fifteen months. It meant a separation from teachers and friends who had become part of my life.

But foremost in my thoughts was fear for the safety of my family, with Warsaw under aerial attack. Anxious to rejoin them, I was relieved to be finally allowed to set out for home. So in the evening of September 9 six students from Warsaw walked through the blacked-out town of Wlodzimierz heading for the railroad station and the approximately 340-kilometer ride to Warsaw. The Polish people, I thought, were really remarkable; what they lacked in military skill and armaments they made up for in pride and spirit. From the beginning the radio newscasters had sounded overconfident; on the fifth or sixth day, after making allowances for German Air Force bombings, they declared that the Polish cavalry was fighting like "wild lions," and it would not be long before they would take Berlin. If someone heard news at one end of town that three German planes had been shot down, by the time this information reached the other end of town, the figure might have grown to three hundred!

Moving through the darkened streets, under blackout, we finally reached the railroad station. How different it looked from the way I remembered it. What a lively and cheerful place a railroad station usually is in peacetime—especially before winter recess when the waiting room is brightly lit: people in high spirits mill around buying magazines and sweets for their trip, saying farewell to those who escorted them to the station, sitting at canteens enjoying a snack, chatting with traveling companions, occasionally singing. Now the place I had associated with the happy memories of Chanukah and Pesach trips home was dark, quiet, and almost deserted. Two Polish gendarmes (military police) asked for our school identification papers, and then we stood and waited for the train to Warsaw. I recall being asked by the cashier whether I would like a ticket to the East Bank Station or the Main Station in the heart of the city—the difference being another fifty cents. I requested one for the Main Station, oblivious of the possibility that we might not reach either destination.

The train carried few people, perhaps fifty passengers, and because of the blackout and a conspicuous silence, the mood was somber and depressing. We moved slowly and by the next morning had traveled barely ninety kilometers, to the town of Zamosc. The train was detained at Zamosc for a good part of the morning, and when it finally moved, it did not go very far—because the tracks ahead had been bombed out.

Before we had an opportunity to realize the seriousness of our predicament or to think about getting some food, the roar of an airplane engine stirred up a commotion; as the sound drew nearer and became more pronounced, we realized what it was, abandoned the train, ran down the track embankment, and made for a nearby field. No sooner had we hit the ground than the sound of exploding bombs nearly shattered my eardrums. Instinctively putting my hands over the back of my head, I looked sideways and saw through black clouds of dust that the invader was a single-engine plane with the red and white Polish emblem, apparently flown by a German pilot. In a moment it was gone.

As the noise of the departing plane faded, a great scream could be heard from a woman shocked to see a man's hand severed and hanging from his wrist by a small piece of skin. He held his torn and bleeding hand in his good one. It was a terrifying sight—my first taste of war. Fragments of shrapnel had wounded others, too, and there were wails and lamentations coming from all directions.

My school friends and I soon decided that if we were ever going to get anywhere near Warsaw, we would have to depend on the oldest mode of transportation—walking. We decided to make Lublin (about seventy-five kilometers away) our first destination. If we had had any sense or experience, we would have known that marching should be done under cover of night and that railroad tracks and cities spell trouble because they are prime bombing targets. But we were as green as the wooded forests around us, as green as the green-clad soldiers we saw wandering the country roads and smelling of new uniforms. Still, somehow, walking and hitchhiking for two days and a night and sleeping in the fields, we made it to the outskirts of Lublin, sighting the city at dawn on September 12.

Even through the morning mist we could see that the town already bore many pockmarks and bomb craters. Here and there, Polish soldiers were manning machine guns on the roofs of buildings. No sooner had we entered the town than the air raid raid sirens wailed and people hastily began to clear the streets. Some hurriedly made their way into the backyards of tenements; others scrambled into the trenches that had been dug alongside the sidewalks. We spotted a bomb crater in the middle of the street and jumped into it to hide. What had started with the expectation of a sensational war adventure, unreal and distant at first, had turned into a real-life experience, with whole city blocks set ablaze and tall buildings crumbling to bury the trapped dwellers under a heap of rubble.

The noise of low-flying planes was broken by the shattering explosions of bombs and the sound of collapsing buildings. Bricks, glass, and debris were thrown in every direction. At intervals one could hear the rattle of machine guns strafing the streets. In a few minutes it was all over, yet in this small fragment of time, hundreds of people had been killed and wounded, and many others were buried under the debris of tenement houses that had been reduced to rubble. Billows of smoke blocked the sun. The militia was recruiting volunteers on the street to help dig people out from the debris. Stretcher-bearers emerged from damaged buildings and carried the wounded to first-aid stations. Fire engine bells rang out and then faded as the engines sped away. Around the heaps of ruined buldings, people were frantically looking for relatives, friends, and personal belongings. A city that had taken centuries to be built and that only yesterday had stood proudly erect now lay defenseless at the mercy of the ruthless enemy.

We headed toward the center of town, where we hoped to find a refugee center that would give us temporary shelter and some basic necessities. We did not know then that nearly everything in Poland was in a state of chaos—except the advancing German army. Bewildered but determined, we reached the main junction of Lublin, Lubartowska Street and Krakowski Boulevard. The municipal building was at the far corner and behind it the large, unoccupied market square, now zig-zagged by trenches.

It must have been close to noon on this sunny day when the air raid sirens sounded again. We took cover in one of the trenches on the square and watched as the German planes, practically unopposed, came in low, strafing and bombing the buildings in their path. Suddenly, before our very eyes, a bomb dropped on the municipal building, slicing it vertically in half. The side of the building facing us came tumbling down, while the other side stood firm. When the dust finally settled, one could see in the half of the building still standing the assembly hall on the second floor, its even rows of chairs still in place. The floor below exposed a wall bedecked with portraits. This kind of sight was to become a familiar one.

That afternoon, at the suggestion of a friendly stranger, we entered a small synagogue that occupied part of the ground floor of an apartment house several blocks down Lubartowska Street. Here, we students, far away from home and family, experienced a very special Jewish hospitality. Most of the tenants of this apartment building sat in the courtyard between air raids, and every family in the building took a special interest in one or more of the refugees who happened to be there. Since we were very young, we attracted considerable attention, and it was my good fortune to be befriended by the Rosenbaums.

Mr. and Mrs. Rosenbaum appeared to be in their fifties. Their daughter, about my age, was with them, and it was apparent that she was the only child of their "old age" and obviously all the more precious to them. Melech Rosenbaum, who was originally from Radom, was a thin, bespectacled man of medium height, with delicate features and a fair complexion. He spoke in a low voice as though not in the best of health. Mrs. Rosenbaum, by contrast, appeared robust; she had a ready smile, spoke with abundant energy, and seemed to enjoy talking to people. Their daughter Gina was a very pretty girl with a pleasant manner who more closely resembled her father than her mother.

I told them the story of our adventures and explained that we were cut off from our families in Warsaw.

"How could the school authorities have permitted you to wander by yourselves, and in time of war, without anyone to take care of you?" asked Mrs. Rosenbaum with a pained expression on her face.

"They actually did not want to allow our group from Warsaw to leave, but we insisted on going home—so here we are."

"How old are you?" asked Gina.

"I will be fifteen in November."

"Mother, they are not little kids," Gina protested.

"Fourteen- or fifteen-year-old boys should have been under the care of an adult," Mrs. Rosenbaum insisted.

"What is the point of complaining about something that has already happened?" Mr. Rosenbaum reasoned. Turning to me, he added, "Don't worry, the war will soon be over, and all of you young men will be reunited with your families."

"And in the meantime," Mrs. Rosenbaum counseled, "it is best that you stay here."

"We don't seem to have much choice."

"Well, at least here you will be among friends," concluded Mr. Rosenbaum, setting the matter to rest. What a comforting thought!

In the evening the tenants returned to their apartments, and we refugees to the synagogue. Besides our small group from the agricultural school the synagogue was sheltering a number of other Jews from out of town who had flooded Lublin when they ran away before the advancing German army. Soon, a young dark-haired, personable, friendly-looking man wearing a Hassidic cap brought us food. Although it was a modest meal of herring, bread and butter, and tea, there was something very special about Chaim and the way he tended to us. He brought our meal not as a do-gooder performing a charitable deed but as a kind host, trying to put his guests at ease. Three times a day he would come down to the synagogue with food, and sometimes one of the women would also assist and bring us soup.

The following morning, September 13—the day before Rosh Hashanah, the Jewish New Year—a refugee who like ourselves was living at the synagogue brought in a newspaper report that the Germans were outside Annopol—about eighty kilometers from Lublin. He deduced that they would be in Lublin in a matter of hours and advised us to flee together toward the east, where the Russians were rumored to be ready to move in.[3] My five fellow students were all in favor of such a move, reasoning that they could go back to the school. I was the sole dissenter, opposed not so much because of the danger as because by going, we might separate ourselves permanently from our families in Warsaw.

Unable to yield to each other's advice, we decided to separate, and so at dusk I accompanied my friends to the edge of town, where I said goodbye to Libson, Reichert, and the others. As I headed back, thoughts of school ran through my mind. Libson and I had started school at about the same time, and although we had not been close friends, he was a good companion; so were the others, and I regretted that we had to part.

That evening, the first night of Rosh Hashanah, an incredible incident occurred. As the time for the evening prayer was at hand and the small synagogue had filled up with people, a violent argument suddenly erupted between a couple of the members of the congregation over the choice of a *Sheliach Tzibur*—the individual who leads the worshippers in prayer—and a fight broke out. Fearful of what such disrespect for a place of worship might bring as a consequence, I forced myself between those engaged in the scuffle and demanded that they stop the quarrel and consider the folly of fighting among themselves in a house of worship, in a city under bombardment, on the eve of a sacred holiday. My outburst must have stirred their consciences because they stopped abruptly, perhaps embarrassed by my youth, and the services started with the familiar melody of the holy day. But the chanting was mixed with the sounds of artillery bombardment not far distant. The mood was subdued; people were choking back tears; and I thought of my family far away and prayed fervently for their safety.

Friday, September 15, was a day I am not likely to forget. Just before dusk, a friend of Gina's who apparently knew my name told me that another person from Warsaw named Topas was temporarily residing only a few blocks away. I hastily made my way there, but when I reached the address the girl had given me, I found no one who knew anyone by the name of Topas. As it was now getting late and it was time for the Sabbath and holy day services, I returned to the synagogue somewhat disappointed and puzzled.

According to our tradition, all decrees are inscribed on Rosh Hashanah, the New Year, and sealed on Yom Kippur, the Day of Atonement. There was dire need for prayer, then, and so I was moved to pray fervently for a safe reunion with my family and for an end to this cruel bombing. As I stood engrossed in meditation and prayer, I glanced sideways and caught sight of a familiar face that also was absorbed in prayer. At first I thought I was daydreaming. Then, suddenly, our eyes met—it was my father! According to religious observance, one must conclude the service of *Shemone Esrei* (eighteen blessings) before one may speak out. The next few minutes seemed like eternity. Completing my prayer, I waited for a moment for Father to finish, and then we ran to meet, embracing each other, choked up and on the verge of tears. Held in his embrace, I felt secure. For a moment I could not speak, so overwhelmed was I at this meeting. There was no need for words; it was sufficient that we were together again. I felt mystified by what had just happened. Considering the odds, our meeting in a large city under enemy fire, so far from home, was extraordinary. Imbued as I was with biblical teachings, I considered this reunion with my father to be a good omen, and I was grateful to God.

Some of the people in the synagogue watching this reunion between father and son broke into quiet sobbing, so deeply moved were they by this moment. Because occasions like this were rare in a city crowded with fleeing masses of refugees torn from their families and homes, everyone wished us well. The Rosenbaums came over with Gina and greeted my father. There were many who marveled at this unusual meeting taking place in the midst of confusion and displacement. One man claimed credit for the remarkable event because, as he said, he had advised me not to leave the town or the synagogue. Several people, in a spirit of friendship, offered us room in their apartments. Eventually, Father promised to move in with a family residing in the same building as the synagogue. I left my shelter and went to share this place with him.

Walking back from the synagogue, I related to him how I happened to be in this town, and he told me how he happened to be there too. On the eve of September 6, 1939, the Germans had seized a Polish radio station outside the capital and had issued orders in Polish and in the name of the Polish authorities to all able-bodied men to leave Warsaw at once and head east, where they would be mobilized across the Bug River.[4] By the time the Polish authorities were able to expose and denounce this hoax, thousands of men had marched out of the city, leaving their families behind. As is now all too well known, the enemy, with typical ruthlessness, attacked the marching procession of civilians on the highway, killing many with bombs and machine-gun fire. Father and his two younger brothers had left home together, but because of the chaos that characterized the marching multitude, he had become separated from them. When he heard, as I had, that someone with the name of Topas was in Lublin, he had expected to find one of my uncles. (Father and Uncle Mietek had both been in military service; Uncle Ben, the youngest, was a university student almost up to the time of the war.)

The intensity of the Lublin bombing reached its climax on the second day of the Jewish New Year. The service was interrupted by numerous explosions. We had moved in with a Hassidic family named Grynszpan, who had invited us to stay there along with two other men. Father slept on a cot, while I put several chairs together to make a bed. But we did not get much sleep because that night we all had to go down to the courtyard during an artillery barrage that rocked the town. Some of the people sat in the basement, others in the vaulted entranceway to the backyard. We saw the Polish soldiers retreating through Lubartowska Street. A noncom with a drawn pistol commanded all uniformed personnel to move out—possibly, as Father explained, to discourage soldiers from deserting. In the descending darkness we watched truckloads of uniformed men pass through the streets. They were clad in bluish uniforms and must have been POWs— the first ones I had seen.

Finally, the barrage toned down and we went to sleep, only to be awakened the next morning in time for the morning prayer by a commotion in the apartment. People looked out of their windows and saw a deserted street. In a moment a German on a motorcycle, with another one sitting in a sidecar holding an automatic rifle, drove past our place toward the end of the street. The driver, wearing a green raincoat and a steel helmet with goggles, a rifle hanging across his back, swung the motorcycle in a sharp U-turn and drove away. The next time he came around, there was a civilian militiaman wearing a white armband with him, shouting that all windows must remain closed and that people must remain inside their homes. All this took place at about 6:30 A.M. By eight o'clock the invading soldiers were in the city, several in each apartment house. The famous first words of our captors were *"Frauen bleiben, Maenner heraus!"* (women remain, men get out).

Without being given a moment even to take some food, we filed out onto the street. The Germans were forming columns of the men they had rounded up. Someone asked where we were being taken and was told that we would "soon know." Another German looked over the bewildered faces of the people and, in an apparent gesture to subdue anxiety, shouted, *"Habt keine Angst"* (have no fear). The assembled multitude was marched down Lubartowska Street, Father keeping silent most of the way. As we reached Krakowski Boulevard, the smoldering Polish army barracks could be seen, and it was here in a grassy, fenced-in area that the Germans interned us. A ranking infantry noncom motioned for all of us to sit down on the ground. About midday a procession of women carrying food in baskets began to trickle in, each seeking out her relatives. It was really surprising to see how quickly the private "relief" operation had been organized by these seemingly unafraid women. Refugees in town, of course, did not have anyone to care for them, but by afternoon one sergeant had begun to confiscate some of the food that came across his path and divide it among those seated near his post, benevolently trying to feed those to whom no one brought food at the expense of the others.

Through the fence, we saw a lot of activity; German mechanized formations were passing through. Their petrol fumes had a peculiar odor, different from anything we had known. Aside from curiosity, I felt hunger. Father seemed concerned and was probably as hungry as I was. Speaking fluent German, he asked one of the rifle-carrying guards for permission to speak to his superior. The guard nodded and pointed the way to the man in charge, who was standing by a field kitchen not far off. My father approached him and explained that we were refugees and had received nothing to eat since that morning; he wondered if they would let me go, since I was barely fifteen. I must say that my one year of high school German was only enough to cause me to be fascinated by my father's command of the language.

In response, our "host" claimed that he had no authority to release anyone, but he gave us half a loaf of bread from one of the German field wagons. Encouraged by this gesture, Father asked why and how long we were going to be kept here. He was told that we would be held for a few days to assure the safe-conduct of the German forces through the city. In the town of Czestohowa the Germans had been fired upon from buildings while passing through, and they were making sure this would not happen again.

Shortly after we had shared our free meal, darkness fell, and it became apparent that the only accommodations for our sleep that night was the bare ground. Using whatever clothing we were wearing for cover, we lay down for the night. While some, still bewildered, spoke in subdued voices, and here and there a tiny cigarette glow could be seen against the chilly September night, sleep came fast to me.

Awakened at dawn by mounting noise in the camp, I stretched my limbs and looked at Father, who was already up. I noted that more women and some young boys were hauling baskets filled with food to their menfolk. A plan occurred to me, and I asked Father's permission to try it. When he reluctantly consented, I asked one of the women for an empty basket. She gave me one, and I headed for the gate, mixing in with the women and boys who were leaving. At the gate stood two pairs of guards, the pair on one side examining the baskets of the incoming women and the other pair checking those who were leaving. I do not recall any difficulty at the gate, and I managed to slip out, my first mission accomplished.

Since I did not know what lay ahead, I could only reflect later that a paratrooper starts his training by jumping from a three-foot height first. Once outside, I drew a deep breath, and felt renewed hope that all would yet end well.

There is nothing more exhilarating about walking than walking away from trouble. Yet I knew what I had to do and wanted to do: I must get food and blankets and take them back for my father.

Again, it was a sunny day, typical of that whole month of September, even though September in Poland is usually marked by the beginning of the rainy season. This year, however, the weather was warm and dry, favoring the German troops, whose mechanized armor depended on good roads. Rain would have turned the roads to mud and thus bogged down the enemy's advance. Indeed, before the German invasion people had knowingly said, "Let them come and let's see how far their tanks will get on our roads." Well, even the weather was against the Poles.

This second day of occupation was bustling with activity as an endless flow of *Wehrmacht* vehicles and motorcycles moved through the streets. Townspeople lined up at the edge of the sidewalk quietly watched the procession of the clean-shaven, mechanized aggressors. While the Germans had good reason to be jubilant, the faces of the onlookers expressed sadness and surprise. After all, the press and radio had assured them of a gallant victory; instead, it had been a crushing defeat. Young men in *Luftwaffe* uniforms, identified by the wing insignia on their field caps, were roaming the streets and entering restaurants to demand service. Some sounded loud and boisterous. Some paid and others did not. When a Polish shopkeeper did not understand an order, one of the Germans looked into a little pocket dictionary and ordered *Pivo*, beer. Chocolate was also near the top of the list of commodities the victors were after.

The influx of motor vehicle traffic in Lublin, which was more accustomed to horse-drawn transportation, created problems, and some pedestrians were hurt. The German drivers, used to discipline, were furious with people who did not know that crossing the moving German columns and convoys, or even standing on the pavement, was contrary to the rules of the "New Order." One woman, carrying two chickens in a basket, started diagonally across the street ahead of a truck convoy led by two motorcycles. About two-thirds of the way across she hesitated and then turned back, causing one of the Germans on a motorcycle to turn sharply toward the curb. The woman, now frightened and confused, ran forward again, forcing the other motorcyclist to hit the curb, bounce back, and fall. He turned off the motor, picked himself up and brushed the dust from his sleeves, then yelled angrily at the woman, "*Ihr seid doch ganz primitiv!*" (you are quite primitive). The woman ignored him and ran. Repeating his insult, he kicked the pedal with his heel and started the motorcade.

Finally back in the building that had been our refuge, I grabbed a blanket, underwear, and bread, and hurried out. Making my way back to camp, I tried to think of getting this food and clothing to my father and of nothing else. As I approached the gate, I opened the basket before the guard and deliberately lingered so that I might be remembered coming in.

Father was pleased to see me, and the fact that he was somewhat dependent on my ability to perform this little task made me feel very grown up. I wanted to remain with him overnight, but he insisted that I leave; in order not to make me feel that he considered me too young, he reasoned that it was important to have someone on the outside.

The next morning marked the release of most of the people interned the first day, my father among them. It was good to see him get out. It was then that he made me realize the full meaning of his captivity. All those interned had really been hostages; any overt act by a Polish civilian might have brought death to hostages as a consequence. In fact, rumor had it that the Germans had executed some of the three hundred men they had retained. It should be noted, however, that with some exceptions the *Wehrmacht* did not at the beginning harass the people, as did the administrative, SS, and Gestapo units that followed on their heels.

On this third day, the people of Lublin saw even more Germans than they had the first two. When we reached the corner of Lubartowska and Krakowski Boulevard, I observed some visitors inside the half-destroyed municipal building, and German officers sat outside the building at tables covered with maps. They seemed busily occupied with the business of running their war from this outdoor cafe–style headquarters. These Teutonic knights seemed to enjoy their work and projected the pride of their military superiority. Their high polished riding boots gleamed in the sun. Sharp visor caps, epaulets, spurs, medals, monocles, belts, pistols, field glasses—these were their credentials, their tools of the trade. The sidewalk where they sat was roped off. Down on Lubartowska Street we saw a column of Polish horse cavalry prisoners on their mounts, escorted by German cavalrymen. Each of the prisoners was leading one or two horses without riders. They looked sad and weary.

After they disappeared in the distance, a convoy of German troops moved along. A typical vehicle looked like a convertible command car with a driver and three men, their rifles stacked in the middle of the car. The soldiers looked clean, and most of them smoked. They looked at the people whose army they had whipped, and in return the Polish people, stunned by their defeat, eyed their foreign intruders.

About that time we heard the sound of a band, and turning in that direction we saw a marching formation of men wearing brown uniforms. Most of them were blond, and all were tall specimens. Men, women, and children, drawn by the sound of music, lined the sidewalks to watch this parade. There were many outspoken reactions. A man wearing an apron stood in front of his shop to survey the goose-stepping Germans: "Look at them—a real picture of power. How can anyone oppose them?" But he was contradicted by an elderly man in a gray felt hat, who retorted, "This is sheer propaganda. They were fattened upon food they stole in Czechoslovakia and have been hand-picked to impress our people."

Then my father said something that I would not forget. "Take a good look at these men," he said, "for someday you will witness their defeat. Their confidence gone, they will be a bewildered-looking lot." Seeing them as they were then, basking in glory, it was difficult to imagine that the swagger that distinguished them as much as their uniforms did could be taken out of them like starch.

That evening we listened to the German news broadcast in Polish. After the military communiqué, the announcer continued: "Singers Jan Kiepura and Martha Eggerth sailed today from Italy for England.[5] A man who has Germany to thank for his career has left. His Maciek has died and will rise no more!" The reference was to a folk song that depicts the gaiety and vitality of the Polish spirit, personified by Maciek, who dies and is laid out on a board. But if you will play him a tune, he will yet jump and dance, because (the verse continues) Maciek's soul is such that music will always stir him to dance. Jan Kiepura had sung this song on the streets to cheering crowds. Hence the cynical German improvisation that Maciek, symbolizing Polish independence, would rise no more.

The days that followed were spent waiting for the end of hostilities. The now German-controlled local newspaper headlined the "news" that the Russians were advancing in eastern Poland in order to share in the spoils with their German allies—a fact that had already been known for some time. Meanwhile, as the fight narrowed down around the capital, Warsaw and its people were enduring incessant bombing. They city's fate was sealed, but it was still holding out.

On Yom Kippur the people worshipped in their synagogues. Muted sobs mixed with the sad melodic sounds of the liturgy and permeated the holiday service at the Lubartowska Street synagogue. Men covered themselves with their prayer shawls, turned their devotion to God, and asked his forgiveness. When the prayers reached their high point and the cantor was about to recite the words of one of the most solemn prayers of the High Holy Day service, many men tearfully tried to suppress their emotions and hide the terror in their souls. During the chant that begins "On Rosh Hashanah everyone's destiny in creation is inscribed, and on Yom Kippur it is sealed," we could hear the sound of women's weeping. As the cantor chanted, "How many shall pass away? Who shall live and who shall die? Who shall come to a timely end and who to an untimely end; who by fire and who by sword; who by beast and who by hunger?" the words suddenly assumed an ominous reality. Nevertheless, the reunion with my father had made me feel confident that somehow we would survive the scourge of this war.

At the end of the service in the small *shul* that had served as our shelter, several young German soldiers walked in and stood at the doorway. Most of the people had already left when one of the soldiers asked, "What is this place?" After my father informed them that it was a place of worship and prayer, they asked, "Who do you pray to?" "To God," was Father's reply. "Have you heard this?" continued the one who had done the talking, with a cynical intonation. "They worship God! What can He do for you? Ha!"

I expected that such a profanation would meet with drastic retribution, but nothing happened just then. Showing surprise that there were still people with such antiquated, useless ideas, the German added, "Our faith is Adolf Hitler; our religion is Adolf Hitler; our god is Adolf Hitler!" After this momentous revelation to these "backward people," they abruptly left. How strange, I thought, that they should put so much stock in a religion whose converts had made Adolf Hitler their god only since 1933!

The Rosenbaums, who always made us feel welcome, had invited us for the meal after the fast. There was warmth and light in their home, and Gina would occasionally play the piano during our visits. I felt enchanted by it all, ignoring for a moment the stark reality outside.

But while I was living in this strange dream, Warsaw fell. As soon as permissible, we were going to return home.

The holidays of Succoth, which took place the following week, were celebrated in a subdued fashion, made conspicuous by the absence of the merriment that usually accompanies especially the last day, Simchas Torah (rejoicing in the Torah).

The last evening before our departure, Gina had tears in her eyes as we said our goodbyes, and I realized that she was as deeply affected by our parting as I was.

2 Return to Warsaw

And all thy labors shall a nation
which thou knowest not eat up.
—Deuteronomy 28:33

It was early in the morning of Sunday, October 25, when we started out for Warsaw in an open two-horse wagon. As trains were off limits to civilians and probably the tracks required repairs anyway, Father had engaged the driver the preceding day, and there were three more passengers, making a total of six. Warsaw was approximately 175 kilometers (over one hundred miles) away, and it would take us at least two days to make the trip.

The countryside was strewn with soldiers' graves, each marked by a helmet, its style denoting the nationality. Unexploded bombs and shells were roped off by white tape. Polish military vehicles and cannon stood silently in woods still filled with the smell of smoke. Passing by, I sensed the terrible and hopeless ordeal that those who had manned these positions must have gone through. Many buildings along the highways were reduced to rubble. This was the face of Poland in her hour of grief; it was a mournful sight.

The highway we traveled was the same one that Father had used before. It was here that the Germans had massacred scores of able-bodied men when the radio broadcast from what they believed were Polish authorities caused him and thousands of men of military age to leave Warsaw and head east.

A town called Garvolin appeared to have been almost entirely razed. We slept there on our second night on the straw-bedded floor of an inn. The following day we reached Warsaw from the eastern approach, crossing the river Vistula from Prague, the east bank suburb. Passing Prague reminded me of the good times when we had gone there to visit the zoo. Now we learned that with no one to feed the animals, many had died during the fighting.

Warsaw had fought to the last. The little-publicized fact is is that after the Polish capitulation, the Germans refused to enter the city for fear of an epidemic. They waited two days until the Poles had buried all their dead and the carcasses of dead horses as well.

It appeared to us that the people of Warsaw had begun to recover from the blitz. Women were carrying water in buckets from the Vistula because the utilities were not yet fully repaired. Past the palace on the west bank of the river was a familiar landmark, the monument of the Swedish king who had ruled Poland. When finally the wagon turned into Leszno, our street, our anxiety rose. Standing up in the wagon, I strained my eyes to see as far as I could. "Well," said Father, "what do you see?"

"I see our building standing up!"

Closer examination proved this correct, although the fourth floor and roof had been damaged by artillery shelling. We were soon reunited with the family. Mother cried as she exchanged embraces with us. My little five-year-old brother, Meir, and Simon, nearly twelve, clung to Father. They all looked pale and undernourished. There had been no word from my two uncles, Mietek and Ben, who had left with Father.

Nevertheless, despite war scars on our building, it felt good to be home—our home. After paying respects to Grandpa and seeing Aunt Bella and cousin Lila, who lived in the same building, we settled down for a long family evening and learned of their ordeal firsthand. Mother spoke quietly, describing one aerial attack when a bomb fell in the center courtyard, spraying fragments all around. Those tenants who had stood at the entrance of the stairway instead of going down into the cellar were killed. Mr. Prussak, the kind man who owned the drugstore and had had a way with the children, giving out candy liberally, had run across the street during the raid; fire from an incendiary bomb had turned him into a torch. But the people in our building were fortunate in that most of them had survived the first trial by fire. Father commenced repairs to the building the following week. Jewish carpenters from Otwock, a father-and-son team, were hired to make repairs before winter set in. Grandpa retained me as a helper for two *zlotych* per day. (A *zloty*, a unit of Polish currency, was then worth approximately twenty cents at the prewar rate of exchange.)

Sometime in November several German trucks arrived at our place. The chief gendarme wanted to see the owner of the shoe store.[1] Grandpa did not want to talk to them and so my father opened the store, which had been closed since the war started. I tagged along.

"Is this the Jacob Topas Shoe Manufacturing and Sales Enterprise?"

My father answered, "Yes."

"Are you Jacob Topas?"

"No, he is my father."

"Go call him then. We want to ask him some questions."

Father went upstairs and came back with Grandpa.

"Is this your father—the Jacob Topas?"

"Yes."

"We have an order to confiscate your merchandise. You will get a receipt."

This formality dispensed with, they proceeded to empty the store, insisting that Grandpa help. The man who had worked hard to build this business was now forced to help liquidate it. It was a sad sight to see Grandpa's humiliation as he carried stacks of shoeboxes from the store to the police trucks. The Germans caught people off the street to help empty our store and warehouse, work that took several hours. Later I heard conversations between Father and Grandpa estimating that the confiscated stock was worth perhaps as much as the equivalent of $50,000 (in prewar American currency).

With the shoes gone and restrictions getting tougher, my father had to find a new way to make a living. So in partnership with Linder, one of our longtime employees, and another man, he started an illegal bakery. In order to elude the authorities, it was situated on the fourth floor in one of the vacant, war-damaged apartments. The wood to be used for the oven had to be carried up three flights of winding stairs, and the bread was brought down to our apartment, from which it was distributed. The bakery became a viable business—dangerous, but profitable to the extent that it kept us fed.

There was a great deal of talk around that people could go to the Russian zone to escape the growing German terror. Though I did not want to leave my family, I proposed to go to Lublin and from there to set out for the Russian zone.[2] My parents were at first reluctant to let me go, but finally, in early November I bought a ticket on a bus to Lublin.

No sooner had the bus reached the bridge on the river Wieprz than it was stopped by German army engineers. Two of them entered the bus, faced the passengers, and ordered all Jews to get off.

A few passengers rose and reached for their baggage, but they were ordered to come out without it. Then the Germans began to search each face. I said a short prayer, without moving my lips, but I was not about to volunteer. Without premeditation, this became my instinctive form of resistance toward the German authorities. They seized someone at the front of the bus and hauled him off, and then they got another man who protested that he was not a Jew. Apparently they thought he looked Jewish and took him off anyway. At last they motioned the bus to pass. I remained aboard undetected. As we started very slowly across the bridge, I saw bearded Jews standing in cold water, shoulder deep, working on the construction or dismantling of an adjacent pontoon bridge. It was a depressing sight, and I wondered how many of them could work or survive more than a day under these conditions.

As we moved away from this place, my thoughts turned to Lublin, and as I began to recognize the Lublin streets, my heart seemed to beat a faster rhythm. When the bus came to a stop, I asked the driver to hold on to the luggage of those who had been pulled off the bus; I hoped that the men would return to claim their belongings when the Germans let them go.

It did not take long before I was knocking on the door of the Rosenbaums' home. Helen, the Jewish maid who had lived with them since her youth—through her marriage and the birth of her child— opened the door. She motioned to me to be quiet and called out, "Gina, who do you suppose just came in?" Instead of answering, Gina emerged from the back of the hall, looking somewhat more surprised than pleased. It was an awkward moment. Perhaps I had expected a hero's welcome; if so, I was disappointed. Nevertheless, at the invitation of her parents, I moved in temporarily until everything was ready for crossing the Russian border, which was then not very far from Lublin. I asked the Rosenbaums to direct me to a professional guide who took people across, but they sensed correctly that I lacked real determination to go on and to leave my family behind.

"You will get homesick, and who will be able to go and bring you back?" said Mr. Rosenbaum, who seemed to realize how confused I was about this whole adventure. After considering the prospect of isolation from my family, I was persuaded to return home.

For a few days, however, I enjoyed the Rosenbaums' hospitality. Once when Gina's parents sent her on an errand and I volunteered to escort her, Mrs. Rosenbaum encouraged her to take me up on it, if not only for her "safe conduct," then perhaps to give me an opportunity to make myself useful. The path we took cut across a park. Snow was falling, and there were hardly any people around—not even children, for outdoor play was not considered very safe just then. Yet a heady feeling made me momentarily oblivious to all our troubles. I was struck by the contrast between the beautiful scene around us and the grim reality of our situation. It was a rare moment. I am unable to fully describe its splendor and anguish. But then as if to break the spell, Gina rolled a snowball and made a gesture as though she were going to use me as a target. "Hey, snap out of it," she seemed to be saying. And so the magic of the moment passed.

That evening I prepared for my return trip, and the next day I made my way back home uneventfully, sadly realizing that I was not yet of age, nor was this the time for planning one's future.

My parents were glad to see me, and Father did not chide me for my failure to carry out my plan. The idea of going to the Russian zone was put to rest.

First Winter under German Occupation, 1939–40

As soon as postal services were restored (approximately in late October), we began to receive food packages from Grandma, who had left the country for a visit to the United States two weeks before the war began. She also sent a letter containing affidavits for her entire brood, which gave us hope of going to the United States. To say that we were excited would be oversimplifying our mixed feelings of fear and optimism, yet a ray of hope had entered our prospects for survival: the affidavits could mean escape from this dreary and doubtful existence. Father was going to make discreet inquiries without arousing the authorities' suspicions, for fear that the very possession of the document designed to save us might, if not handled with extreme care and caution, bring about our undoing instead. Meanwhile, our spirits were raised by the feeling that these affidavits might mean our rescue. Oh, how wonderfully exciting and nourishing to the senses were such words as "escape" and "rescue." Father reasoned that if we could get to Russia with these papers, a trip to a neutral country was a good possibility. For the moment he admonished us not to divulge the nature of our correspondence and the possibilities it offered.

The beginning of 1940 was marked not only by intense cold but also by the influx of Jewish refugees from the smaller towns of Poland. Rounded up by the Germans, they were hustled off with such belongings as they could carry and herded into Warsaw's Jewish district to share the dwellings and fate of Warsaw Jewry.

On a cold winter Saturday morning, Father, my brother Simon, and I went to the synagogue on Novolipie Street to attend services, which were then still tolerated or at least ignored by the Germans. (The great synagogue on Tlomacka Street eventually came to be used by the Germans as a warehouse and was later destroyed.) This was *Shabbat Shira*, meaning the Sabbath on which the Song of Moses is recited from the scrolls. It is a Sabbath that occurs in winter, and observant Jews traditionally feed the birds with breadcrumbs. In cold countries, when the snow covers the ground and there is no food to be found, the birds welcome this tradition.

After the services we were just about to leave when we noticed some people sitting beside their belongings in the entrance hall of the synagogue. The elderly man, thin and pale, with a gaunt face and graying beard, was Mr. Abramowicz, the father of the family. With him were his wife, his mother-in-law, two grown sons, and a daughter. They were tailors by trade and had been forced to leave their hometown in the Lomża-Plonsk Region. All were wearing glasses, and their faces revealed a great sadness. Quiet and shy, they had not turned to any of the relief agencies that were then still functioning. Father asked

Mr. Abramowicz to be our guest for the Sabbath, but he only thanked him for the invitation and pointed to his large family who he thought would be a burden. After some persuasion, however, the Abramovicz family came to share our Sabbath meal, thankful and deeply moved by the genuine hospitality. They returned to the synagogue for the night, but the following morning we helped them move into our vacant upstairs dormer. Father secured a sewing machine and pressing iron for our new tenants and gave them much of our own clothing for various alterations. In each apartment building, a house committee had been established to aid needy tenants; as the elected president, Father informed the committee that we had on our premises a tailor who could use work. Thus he helped this gentle family to resettle and support themselves in this time of crisis.

A letter from Gina Rosenbaum informed us of the death of her father, but she asked us not to worry; she and her mother would carry on her father's wholesale shoemaking supply business. Mr. Rosenbaum had been only in his fifties, and news of his passing brought added sadness to the daily crop of bad news. Regrettably, the current restrictions for Jews prevented our paying a *shivah* call (a visit to comfort the mourners).

Spring and Summer 1940

Spring of 1940 was filled with bad news but for one exception—the appointment of Winston Churchill to lead his country; his reputation inspired confidence and hope. Otherwise, all we heard was that the Germans were conquering country after country.

As the swastika stretched across the continent, so did a reign of terror. In Warsaw any German military agency in need of workers would drive its trucks into the Jewish districts and pick men up off the streets. Alertness and quick thinking paid off then. The thing to do was to watch out for slow-moving vehicles; they were usually stalking their prey. Or if one saw people were running, it was time to get off the street and hide, a time to ask no questions.

On Purim day Uncle Mietek and Uncle Ben came home;[3] they had for a while been in the Russian occupation zone. The day they returned, the Germans incited hooligan gangs, consisting of an assortment of Polish hoodlums, to run through the streets of the Jewish district, looting and hitting every man and woman in their path. Looking out from the window of our apartment, I saw them turn into Karmelicka Street. While the main body of the gang ran on, breaking windows in the Jewish shops, four of them cornered a husky young man standing in front of a closed entranceway. He wore a brown leather jacket and riding boots. With his back to the door, he began to defend himself with remarkable courage and skill, inflicting blows on his opponents. For a moment this unequal fight resembled something from the movies. He disarmed one of the hoodlums, wresting a long wooden club away from him; unable to prevail, they yelled for help, but the rest of the gang was too far ahead to hear them, so they fled. The main body needed help itself after running into the Jewish porters' quarter on Novolipie Street. It was there that the riot ended and the group dispersed and fled. The porters, or *traigers* as they were called, had a reputation for being brawling ruffians—just the antidote the hoodlums needed but had not expected. It impressed upon me the lesson that the only effective way to stop hoodlum gangs or hoodlum governments was by ruthless counteraction. A nation-sized hoodlum gang, with world-scale ambition, now had to be reckoned with because it had not been stopped at the street level.

Economic garroting, the confiscation of property, restrictions on travel, curfews, shipping people off to camps, deportation of refugees from the provinces into Warsaw, mass arrests, beatings, and executions, the closing of schools and places of worship, epidemics, quarantines—none of these delayed the coming of spring.

Spring in Warsaw when Warsaw was happy had been heady as an intoxicating beverage. Thousands of chatty pedestrians would crowd the sidewalks of wide streets like ours; the parks would resound with the laughter of children; Sunday picnics and family excursions had become a way of life for the Warsaw breed. But in spring 1940 the parks were closed, less out of malice than as a security measure. Parks induce gatherings. Parks have space to roam, and to roam in an open area gives people a taste of freedom. But freedom was now illegal, and it was not desirable to cultivate a taste for it.

Passover is reminiscent of spring and vice versa. How wonderful that it was ordained that our enslaved forefathers were liberated in the springtime. As the faded plants are regenerated, so were they. I thus conclude that spring is the ideal season for liberation. If oppressors could control the seasons, spring would have to go.

But as spring ushered in summer, we realized that it would have to be another spring for such dreams. Because the restrictions aimed at depriving the Jews of everything that makes life worth living were brought about gradually, however, there was still visible a semblance of prewar vitality among the Jews—especially the youth. The promenade (*deptak*) on the south side of tree-lined Leszno Street, extending east from Solna Street, was soon being frequented by teenagers. Young girls walked in twos or threes, glancing shyly at the young men, both groups testing the impressions they made on each other. Occasionally they would stop to chat. After curfew, several young people in our apartment building spent some time talking in the courtyard in the evenings. I was not much above average height for my age, but I was slim, which made me appear taller. I had dark brown eyes and brown hair. The field work in the agricultural school had improved my posture and my self-confidence as well.

One of the affordable luxuries in which I indulged was climbing up on the roof of our building and using it as my private solarium. It was a way to escape the constant reminder of our situation. Up there, the air seemed free, and the relative quiet made it a favorable retreat for reflections.

Then one day in June 1940 the papers put out a single-sheet "extra." It was headlined "GERMANS MARCHING INTO PARIS." Standing in front of our building, I saw people actually cry at this news. By chance I noticed Mr. Wallach, my high school history teacher, picking up a copy from the newsboy. As he read, his look of consternation changed to one of deep sadness. Then he folded the sheet, stuck it in his coat pocket, and went on. This was the man who had captured my imagination when he taught about the Greek and Roman civilizations; he had the talent of bringing history to life. He had not expected that these civilizations would be followed by the most barbaric known in the annals of humankind. For events were yet to come that would dwarf those that had preceded them in cold-blooded cruelty.

By July, England stood alone, the last hope for defending European civilization from extinction. People who claimed expertise in such matters, and there were quite a few, cited moral corruption rather than military inferiority as the cause of the fall of France.

The Unexpected Raid

Before our shoes were confiscated, unbeknownst to me at the time, my father had hidden some shoes in sacks and laid them in a false wall between the dormer and the roof above the fourth floor of our apartment building. During the first raid the gendarmes had left Grandpa about thirty pairs of shoes of the few thousand confiscated, and the receipt they gave him reflected this.

One evening a bell rang in Grandpa's apartment. When the door was opened, two armed, steel-helmeted gendarmes walked in. They claimed to have orders to search the place for hidden shoes and leather. "Is there someone here who can speak German?" they inquired.

"Yes," I replied. "My father. I shall call him." Hearing no objection, I ran to our apartment, but neighbors had already tipped off Father, and he was on his way. In such matters as these, it was my father who could handle the Germans best. His command of the German language never failed to impress them.

Upon confronting the two men Father asked what it was they

wished, to which they repeated what they had said. Father led them to the dining room. Although Grandpa was sullen and a bit shaken, he tried to maintain his dignity as he sat in his usual place at the head of the table while my father was showing the two "supermen" the original confiscation receipt. The gendarmes acknowledged the receipt and, surprisingly, were not in a hurry to proceed either way. Father asked them to sit down, which they did. Taking their helmets off, they set their weapons alongside them. Drinks and cookies were set on the table. Our "guests" did not refuse. When Father asked them what the intention of the authorities was regarding the future of the Jews, one of them replied simply, "One part will be engaged in commerce and the other will work."

Suddenly, the bell rang again, and Irka, the girl who looked after Grandpa, opened the door. Next we heard the heavy footsteps of several men in the corridor. Father grabbed the tablecloth by the four corners, bundling up everything on the table, and set the bundle down on one of the empty chairs. The guests, sensing what was up, quickly put their helmets on and stood up.

By then a group of five gendarmes and one Jewish stooge had walked in. It did not take much to guess that they had a pretty good idea of what had just happened, but they pretended to ignore the matter and asked the first two whether they had searched the building thoroughly. "No" was the reply, "we found the official receipt of confiscation." The second group then motioned to another group of gendarmes standing in the hall. The newcomers, numbering in all about twenty men, decided to look around. They called to still others who were outside to search the attic. The *Wachtmeister*, or ranking gendarme, stood in the corridor of the apartment waiting for results. Returning empty-handed, they all filed into the corridor, as disgusted as firemen by a false alarm, and began slowly to retreat.

The stooge was not with them. When he emerged from Grandpa's bedroom, where the thirty pairs of authorized shoes were stored, his jacket was bulging. I drew this to the attention of one of the original gendarmes, who immediately grabbed the man by the collar and ripped his coat open. Two pairs of shoes in his blouse fell onto the floor.

"Arrest the *Spitzbube*," yelled the one in charge. "He brought us here on a false pretext so he could steal." This kind of charge sometimes meant a death warrant, but that was unlikely as long as they had use for such a man. However, the incident had distracted their attention and having failed to find anything, they all abruptly left.

Naturally, the whole incident was widely discussed by all the tenants. My grandfather, uncles, and father must have felt relieved by the results. There were other raids, but these were less eventful except the one staged by two SS men. They took several pairs of shoes and then, seeing young Irka, were about to rape her. Father prevented this by bluffing: he said that typhoid fever had been reported in the building, a quarantine was imminent, and he certainly did not wish to assume responsibility for the consequence of not warning them. They grabbed the shoes and left. The following day, Father reported the incident to the gendarmerie at their building on Zelazna Street. The officer said, "I would not advise you to bring charges against the SS— but if you insist, I will take your complaint." The advice, by their standards, was honest, and the inference obvious. The SS would have dismissed any such charges—the word of an alien Jew was nil; a "superman" could do no wrong—and punitive action against my father would have inevitably followed.

On one occasion I came home to find that the building had just been raided again. The moment I walked in, Father asked what I had said or done to cause it. The Germans had wanted to talk to me, and since I was out, they had left word that I must report the next day to the gendarmerie building. Father theorized that they had come on the tip of an informer who, somehow, had gotten some information from me. This was unlikely, however, because at that time Father had not let anyone but my grandfather and my two uncles know where he had hidden the stock of shoes.

One of my acquaintances, a street-wise young fellow named Skorupka, was summoned to help us solve the riddle. Between two men whom we knew to be suspected informers, the most suspicion fell on one who dressed well and lived high without any visible means of support.

Uncle Ben volunteered to go with me to the police in order to act as interpreter and principally to make me appear as a minor. I was justifiably afraid the next morning when we walked into the building, because many who had walked in had not walked out again. In a little while we stood before an officer.

"This is my sixteen-year-old nephew, George, whom the authorities requested to appear here on this day," said Ben, emphasizing my age. The officer turned to the filing cabinet and pulled out a folder. He opened it and removed the contents, which consisted of one page.

"Ask him," he said to Ben, "whether he disclosed to anyone that he knows that stock is hidden in the building at Lezno 28." Ben repeated this to me in Polish, and I replied "No."

"Does he have knowledge of any hidden leather goods?" Again I replied "No." The man lit his pipe, pondered the matter for a moment, marked the paper, and closed the file. "You can go now," he said. As we reached for the door, our interrogator added, "Naturally, if we should find out that you are lying, you know what will happen to you?" We turned around and were relieved to see him point to the door.

We walked to the exit of the building without saying a word and maintained silence until we had cleared the guards. "Only God knows this was really close." I muttered my thanks for the moral support. "I can't understand where you find such friends. Did you realize what this might have caused?" Ben sounded upset. At home, the whole family was happy to see us and thankful for the outcome.

The incident stirred a feeling of guilt, for I had indeed been drawn through a friend into a circle of young men of my age and older who gathered in one or another fellows' apartments for idle talk and card playing for small change. No one in the group knew everyone. The thought that one among us was an informer did not enter my mind. But, in fact, there was one and while I could not divulge what I did not know, he may have concluded that something other than my personal means allowed me to act so improvidently. I reproached myself for conduct leading to such conclusions realizing the seriousness of my error.

Dear Uncle Ben, who had helped me with my first German lessons in high school, had ironically been put in the position of demonstrating the practice of German under the least desirable circumstances.

3 The Closing of the Ghetto

*Ye shall be gathered together within your cities; and I
will send the pestilence among you.*
—Leviticus 26:25

Food rationing was already in effect. The Jews had to wear Star-of-David armbands. Labor camps became more numerous. Beggars were competing for alms. Railroad and bus travel was altogether off limits for the Jewish population without a special permit. All places of entertainment outside the Jewish district were closed to Jews. Streetcars that ran predominantly through the district were the only means of public transportation still available to the Jews, and then only in reserved cars marked with the Star of David. The influx of deported refugees continued, causing an acute housing shortage and overcrowding: several families had to share each single dwelling. Sudden arrests and disappearances were commonplace.

Many people managed to subsist only by illicit trade. Searches for hidden goods went on relentlessly. Any furniture of quality was confiscated, but the Germans believed that great stores of goods were still hidden, and they went about their task like prospectors. They were aided by *mosrim*, or informers: Jews who performed this disgraceful service for whatever gain it brought them. Mostly young and street-bred, they were social outcasts among the other Jews and held in utter contempt.

In spite of all this and more, life was going on. Cafes were open and doing business. In the fall of 1940, however, something new was happening: the construction of a large masonry wall embracing two sections of the city was under way. Everyone wondered what the purpose of the wall was, but the German authorities never encouraged queries.

The Polish people in general, and the Warsaw breed in particular, had a way of interpreting all defeats and shortcomings in an optimistic light. They sometimes went so far as to predict a revolt by the German populace, or a military collapse because of fuel shortages: "Hitler has enough reserves of gas for ten years," they would say, "provided it's used only for cigarette lighters." You might say that the "inside news" about the wall, then, was less than completely reliable. Each apartment house had its own "general staff," who analyzed all military developments and internal matters as well. Thus, while the British were

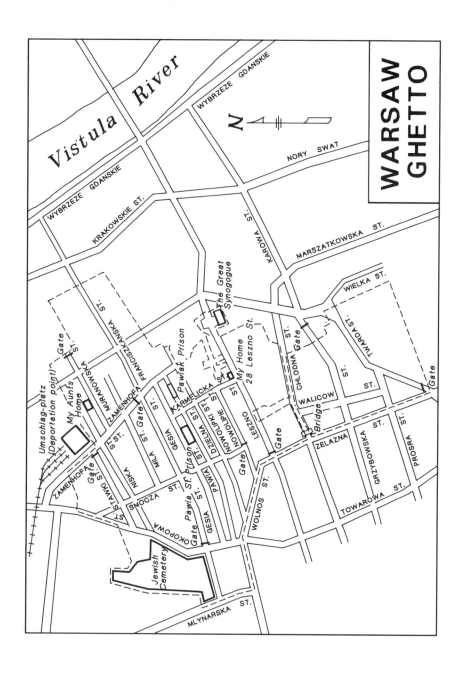

experiencing their finest hour, repelling the German invader in the sky, I was listening to a group in our courtyard arguing the purpose of the wall. One elderly man went on and on: "For those of you who have forgotten, let me remind you what happened when the Germans lost in 1918. Their return home was disorganized, and they were stripped of their arms and uniforms. Well, they are making sure that this will not happen again. When the time comes for their retreat, the wall will serve as a shield, giving them a chance to abandon the city undisturbed, because all the people will be interned within the wall."

Then the answer came: a decree of October 16 imposed a two-week deadline for all the Christians to move out of the walled area and for all the Jews to get in. A postponement allowed the scramble for apartments within the confined area to continue for two more weeks. Rolling pushcarts could be seen daily hauling furnishings and bundles of bedding all over the Jewish district. On November 15 the Warsaw ghetto became a startling reality, and the following day it was sealed off. The only way to get in or out was through guarded gates, with a pass.

Immediately, the already high prices of food shot even higher as supplies dwindled. The ration card (*bona*) issued to each person entitled a ghetto dweller to purchase—but only if he or she had the means—a pitifully meager amount of food: a Jew's ration was about two hundred calories a day, less than one-third the quantity allotted to a non-Jew.[1]

The situation bred new adventurers, mostly youngsters. Eager to carve out a living for themselves, courageous and cunning, they took up the art of smuggling. To supplement the diets of the nearly 450,000 people packed into the Warsaw ghetto, an area previously inhabited by about one-third that number, was a job that presented a challenge. Over the wall, through holes made in the wall in secluded, sealed-off streets, across the bordering cemetery, in hearses by night and often by day, the smuggling went on. The ingenuity of the smugglers was exceeded only by their courage. There were continual job openings in this line to fill vacancies that did not occur because of retirement: many youngsters were shot and killed plying their new trade. Yet when holes in the walls were bricked in, they were promptly opened up again.

Officially, order was maintained in the ghetto by Jewish police, who were disliked from the start. Corruption among them ran high. It was in the context of these events that I sought to earn some money. During the summer Uncle Ben, my brother Simon, and I were busy clearing debris from the yard, the residue of the original blitz damage. The German-installed commissar—who now collected the rents—paid us the daily dole, a small wage for our work which helped some with home upkeep. The packages from Grandma in the United States were heaven sent. We did not know it then, but I learned much later that this brave woman worked hard, tending a paralyzed woman, in order to keep those packages coming. As for our affidavits, they seemed to have arrived too late. We regarded them as hidden assets. Father did not dare apply for a visa, because that would involve going to the German authorities, and there was a rumor that such a move would result in arrest on the spot.

Although they lived in the open and could travel, could own businesses, and could hold civil service jobs, the Christian people outside the hideous wall suffered too. Those moving out of their dwellings within the designated ghetto area had to search for apartments. Many had to separate from their Jewish friends.

One large group of Christians, numbering perhaps as many as five thousand, had to live in the ghetto because they were of Jewish descent. The Nazis traced ancestors back four generations: if only one was Jewish, the subject was declared to be a Jew and was cast into the ghetto. The troubling question remains: how could the Germans have run searches on thirty-two million Poles to see how many of them had inherited Jewish blood without assistance from the non-Jewish population?

The oppression and severe harassment the Germans inflicted on the Jews openly in broad daylight was also practiced selectively on Christians at night. Hitler had vowed to liquidate the Polish intelligentsia, and he kept his word. The most awesome prison in Warsaw, called Paviak, was situated in the ghetto. Night after night, truckloads of Poles from outside the ghetto were hauled past our Karmelicka Street corner to Paviak. These were the Warsaw intelligentsia going to the slaughter. They were transferred from the prison to the nearby fortress of Modlin and machine-gunned there. Hundreds of other Warsaw Poles were awakened at night for the trip to Auschwitz; later, thousands of them were rounded up for forced labor in Germany. Many defiant clergymen were interned. The Polish people suffered at least as much as any other occupied nation of conquered Europe. Yet, allowed to work, move, trade, and own property, they were far better off than we were. If the Jewish community expected any help from their Polish neighbors, they were bitterly disappointed. Except for some individual efforts, there was very little help from our more fortunate Polish compatriots. On the contrary, despite persecution from a common enemy, anti-Semitism did not diminish.

Closing the ghetto put an end even to such conventional means of conveyance as streetcars, and taxis had long ceased to exist. A couple of dubious characters named Kohn and Heller obtained a franchise from the German authorities to run horse-drawn streetcars within the ghetto, and they had no competition. More private ways of traveling were possible by "rickshaw," a sort of tricycle with the driver sitting in the rear supplying the footpower—peddling for his piece of bread.

The Pinkert Funeral Company was already doing a booming business, and its volume in 1941, 1942, and 1943 exceeded any private competitive enterprise in the world. The firm maintained stables of horses to pull the daily payload in black hearses. The thought occurred to me that the horses had to be kept and fed in order to haul humans, most of whom had died of hunger or in the typhus epidemic. To compound the irony, the hearses were often used for the smuggling of flour through the Jewish cemetery, which happened to have good access from the adjacent Christian cemetery. The wall separating the two areas was not impenetrable, and bribes helped move goods across. Our fourth-floor illegal bakery supplemented our meager rations and kept us alive, though occasional discovery by a Jewish policeman required a bribe to keep the enterprise going.

On February 4, 1941, *Sedra Bo*,[2] my brother Simon had his bar mitzvah, which was held at home. A *Sefer Torah* was borrowed for the occasion from the rabbi of the Karmelicka Street *Shtibel*.[3] Including our family, barely a *minyan* (the required quorum of ten men) attended the services. Simon read his *sedra* flawlessly, but the surrounding circumstances presented a bitter contrast to what should have been a joyous event. Grandpa Jacob was there, but our grandmother was some 4,000 miles away in America. Still, Mother prepared a modest *seuda* (festive meal), and even some schnapps was found for the occasion. Uncle Haberman, who was married to Frania, my mother's sister, had more than his share and wandered off in his dark blue suit to the bakery on the fourth floor, where he lay down on the oven. When he got up, the back of his blue suit was flour white. On the way out he met Yankel, the young man whose job it was to carry bundles of wood for the bakery oven three stories up. Yankel, who was hard of hearing, asked, *"Vus tit ihr du?"* "What are you doing here?"

"Siz mir nish git." "I don't feel well," replied my uncle, implying that he was nauseated.

"Vus zugt ihr?" "What do you say?"

"Siz mir nish git," my uncle repeated more loudly.

"Und veym is heint git?" "And who feels well nowadays?" answered Yankel, obviously unaware of my uncle's delicate predicament.

The winter's cold added to the people's woes. The struggle for the bare necessities of life was increased by the burden of trying to find some kind of heating fuel, making the yoke of their misfortune that much more difficult to bear.

One wintry Sabbath we were returning home from services, which were then held privately in the apartment of a pious man. Before entering the vaulted entrance into our courtyard, Father lingered in front of our closed-up store, where my grandparents had done business on Saturdays in violation of our Torah law. His pensive expression suggested that he was deeply immersed in thought. My brother Simon and I also looked into the empty display window, but failed to see what had attracted our father's attention. He did not seem to be aware of our presence. Then, as he was about to turn, he nodded, uttered a deep sigh, and speaking to no one in particular, he said: "It rests for all the Sabbaths that it was open."

Coping with Life in the Ghetto

In the midst of all the confusion and agony, a man named Rubinstein added a tragicomic touch. Rubinstein was the semi-official idiot of the Warsaw ghetto. He ran through the streets of Warsaw holding one hand over his ear or rode standing-up in a horse-pulled hearse, calling out his keen observations concerning ghetto life. He would shout in Yiddish: *"Urm un reich alle gleich!"* (poor and rich are all equal); *"Schmalz hot gevoren biliq!"* (schmalz, chicken fat, has become cheap); *"Geviriim lozen zich ois!"* (the fat, rich ones are melting down). Some of the comic effects achieved by this play on the dual meaning of words is lost in the translation. But Rubinstein achieved fame characterizing the hopelessness and plight of the Jews in the ghetto.

Short and stocky wih curly black hair, Rubinstein cut a conspicuous figure with his exaggerated gestures and grotesque attire. One cold wintry day, when he was running in rags, partly exposing his bare hairy chest and wearing shoes that were really only tops, the Jewish porters pulled him off the street and provided him with shoes, winter clothes, and food. Making him their mascot, they asked, "Rubenstein, who's going to survive this war?"

Rubenstein, now encouraged, replied: *"Ich, myshugeneh* "I crazy Rubinstein, Czerniakow [president of the Judenrat, or Jewish Council] [4] who finishes everybody off, and Pinkert who buries them all." By the next day the whole ghetto had heard Rubinstein's quip. But contrary to his prophecy, he himself did not make it. When the evacuations to Treblinka's death factory began, his custodians, the porters, were shipped off. Without their daily help, Rubinstein perished.

Rubinstein's crazy mystic pronouncement imputing to Czerniakow the "finishing off" of his own brethren was far-fetched if not absurd, but as a tool of Third Reich, the president of the *Judenrat* was destined to convey German decrees to the Jewish community, of which he was the nominal head. Using Jews to aid them was part of the fiendish plan of the "New Order" to destroy the spirit and solidarity of the vanquished people. Though it was difficult to understand how our own people could act thus, hunger and the fear of death drives men to mad deeds. Here and throughout my book, I ask the reader to have compassion for those so driven.

One group of men came to be known as *hopers* (snatchers) in the streets of the ghetto. The *hoper* was always on the verge of collapse from hunger. Everything he had was spent, so he took to the streets to steal food. He would watch for a woman buying her rations or leaving a shop. Accosting her on the sidewalk, he would seize one of her packages and run. The woman would naturally scream, attracting pursuit by other men. The *hoper* would eat as he ran so that by the time they caught him, he had something in his stomach. Despite impromptu punishment, *hopers* not willing to die without a struggle persisted. Either way, they could not win.

One occurrence that stands out in my memory happened on Leszno Street, where I lived. I heard a scream and saw a *hoper* running in my direction, pursued by a civilian and a Jewish policeman. The *hoper* was having difficulty getting the package unwrapped, and the gap between the pursuing and the pursued was rapidly closing. Sensing that he had but a moment, he took a big bite right through the wrapper, and by the time they laid hands on him, he was spitting with disgust: the package turned out to contain an ordinary cake of soap. Everyone laughed except the frustrated *hoper*. His only consolation was that he was spared the punishment of a beating.

The group that created the most awesome impression on the consciences of their beleaguered brethren in the ghetto were the starving children. During the spring and summer of 1941, some men but more children would invade the streets to beg for food, with complete disregard for the penalty for being out after the eight o'clock curfew. Most of the children were sent by their parents as a last resort. With hollow cheeks and swollen legs, they would pace the streets with difficulty, looking up toward windows and chanting or wailing their familiar words: "I don't want to give up my ration cards. I don't want to give up *bona*." The expression "to give up the ration card" meant to die. My parents, heeding these cries, would toss out a piece of bread or a few cents. If there was a group, they would scramble and put up a weak fight for a fragment of bread.

I often watched people's expressions: those faces reflecting a deep longing for what they had lost and for a ray of hope; that look of fear of whatever other calamities were in store for tomorrow. Their eyes had the faraway look of those who were sinking, with no relief in sight. Even the dead lying covered with paper on the sidewalks no longer attracted the attention of any but the flies.

The spring of 1941 brought with it changes for the worse. The people in the ghetto, harassed and in a constant state of fear, had to bear the winter's bad news on the state of the war. The Germans were victorious everywhere. The name of Rommel became synonymous with the victories of the German corps in Africa. Yet many people continued to interpret all news favorably, if only to dispel the reality of their wretched condition. Another British defeat in Africa gave rise to speculation among our own tenement's "general staff."

"Did you hear the news today?" someone would throw in for an opener.

"Yes, from a German war communiqué, which as usual exaggerates their own gains," an optimist volunteered.

"Did they exaggerate when they took Paris? Did they lie when they bombed London and reduced it to rubble?" inquired the skeptic, clearly establishing an opposite point of view.

"So you interpret the fall of Tobruk as a British defeat. Thirty thousand prisoners taken. Let me tell you—don't, I repeat, don't underestimate the British or the Australians."

"If you ask my opinion" (which no one really did), continued the optimist, "you fail to see the grand strategy behind the British withdrawals. In order to move behind the British, the Germans have to throw more reserves and material into Africa to occupy territory and to maintain supply lines and communication. So only the British with their typical cleverness of losing all battles and winning the war could devise such a daring plan of drawing the Germans deeper into the trap, only to encircle them in the final hours. You will see yet," he concluded, backed up by another optimist who had the final word:

"Oh, foolish people. Don't you see that they take the Germans to the cleaners?" (literally, *"mi nemt in cheder arain,"* or "as little children are enticed to school").

This was a time when the optimist in such unscheduled debates was more popular than the pessimist because he told his audience what they yearned to hear. Perhaps this is why false prophets are often listened to and preferred over prophets who tell the truth.

One of my short-lived ventures was selling ghetto-made electric hot plates. They were in demand because many families sharing one apartment could not all use the kitchen at once. However, those to whom I sold the hot plate got very angry because they did not last long before repairs were needed. This was cause enough for me to quit and look for another venture. Joe Gothelf, a school friend of mine since childhood days, and I scraped up twenty zlotys (about $4.00), which paid for a sizable collection of postage stamps. By renting counter space in a stationery store on Solna Street, we were, so to speak, in business. Most of the customers who began to trickle in were teenagers, but occasionally an adult showed up. On rare occasions, even Germans came in to leaf through the pages looking for rare specimens. Most of them paid according to the prices marked—though one SS man did not—and this operation grossed us from ten to sixteen zlotys per day (eight to ten zlotys was the price of a small loaf of dark bread) and gave us something to do. By the spring of 1941, however, there was a sharp drop in business which reached nearly 100 percent in the closing week. By then, most people did not have enough money to buy anything but food, and many were starving.

My Uncle Ben, with the help of a small investment and a partner, Mrs. Zajs, wife of a doctor (refugees from Kalisz), converted our empty spacious shoe store into a cafe known in the ghetto by the name of *Towarzyska*, meaning "sociable." It served tea, black coffee, and miniature cakes; an accomplished pianist named Bialostocki, well known in Warsaw, performed in the afternoons. *Towarzyska* was an immediate success and favored by those still able to afford it. One may wonder how it was possible in the midst of famine, a typhus epidemic, and the scarcity of life's necessities to patronize a cafe. The answer is that there were people involved in smuggling and in illegal trade in valuables with those Poles who had passes to enter the ghetto; others were selling their valuables for income, in some instances in order to imitate the life they had once known. All of these, including people who had unusual connections with the outside world and "good" positions in the *Judenrat*, were among the patrons. I remember for instance that a Mr. Karo, who wore an Argentinian flag pin in the lapel of his overcoat, was one of the cafe's frequent visitors; he was waiting to obtain a visa from Argentina, whose citizenship he claimed, and for the German authorities' clearance. The cafe was also a place to discuss the latest ghetto rumors. In any case, thanks to my uncle's efficient management, the enterprise prospered and kept him going.

An energetic man of medium height, athletically built, with brown eyes and hair to match, a good conversationalist, Uncle Ben—my father's youngest brother—was my most interesting uncle because of his devotion to and excellence in sports and studies. Shortly before the war he had graduated from the Polytech with a degree in chemical engineering. He was only fourteen years older than I was. I remember, yet, his high school days when he and his friends would turn Grandpa's elegant dining room into a regular Ping-Pong hall. Although he was quite sharp at the Ping-Pong table and went skating at the first sign of frost, his real love was soccer, in which he excelled; sport teams were after him to join their clubs. When eventually he did join a prominent Warsaw team, it was much to his mother's displeasure, because she considered it a dangerous waste of time. But the rest of the family disagreed with Grandma. Uncle Ben soon distinguished himself in every game he played. Aunt Rose (then his fiancée) saved newspaper clippings that gave him prominent mention as the aggressive left-wing player of a prominent Warsaw soccer team.

A violin virtuoso by the name of Levin, who had once performed in the Warsaw Philharmonic, now played on the opposite side of our street, his violin case open on the sidewalk for anyone to drop coins into. The hollows under his cheekbones indicated that he might not have eaten lately. The drama of this scene was intensified by its being part of a pattern. A musician out of work was often too refined to speculate or scheme. He would refuse help at first, eventually being forced to sell everything he owned of value except his instrument. When the money was eaten up, he would stay hungry for a while, but finally he was forced to go out into the street, or die. A celebrated artist playing on the street was a sensation at first, and he would do well for a while. Then, as more and more celebrities needed help, the novelty wore off. People would be embarrassed to look at him and begin to by-pass his place. He might try a new spot and linger on for a while, but eventually, unless he was bailed out by someone, he would die in his bed or on the street—his ordeal ended.

I once looked into the eyes of a man whose shrunken face, with its patrician features, betrayed the fact that this once well-off man was gnawed by the pangs of hunger, that aside from his finely tailored but now worn-out suit he had nothing more to sell to sustain body and soul. He barely moved, supporting his fragile body on unsteady legs, his eyes fixed in a gaze of quiet bewilderment, as though already resigned to the fate that in a matter of days or hours would claim his wretched life. I was gripped to the inner depth of my heart by the anguish of seeing this gentle, undemanding man abdicate the will to live. The times were such as to remind one of the biblical prophecy: "Ye shall sell yourselves unto your enemies for bondmen and bond-women, and no man shall buy you" (Deuteronomy 28:68).

Of course, many committed suicide.

In the spring, a ghetto-based society named Toporol began to employ agronomists to teach several hundred children gardening. It organized the clearance of rubble from the 1939 blitz and utilized these areas and every available plot of ground for growing vegetables. I volunteered, and because of my agricultural school background I was accepted as an instructor. I was assigned to a debris-covered area where a prison had once stood on Gesia Street. I had a group of teen-age students assigned to me to begin clearing the grounds, a fine bunch of young people who were proud to work and eager to learn. Their efforts were remarkable, considering how little some of them had to eat. Toporol did not require tuition, and an instructor's pay was one loaf of bread per week. Of course, one could hope to share in the small harvest.[5]

We were quite pleased with our efforts when the plots started to turn green. I also helped raise crops in the Jewish cemetery. Here was an incredible contrast. At one side the corpses of the starved were dumped into mass graves; on the other side students were pruning and weeding tomato plants to preserve life. The rate of death at this time, according to Emanuel Ringelblum's diary, *Notes from the Warsaw Ghetto*, exceeded four hundred per week. Later, it was that and many more per day.

On June 22 an event occurred that took everyone by surprise. I went that day to Zamenhofa Street, where the loudspeakers blared forth the news of the German attack on Russia. Artillery had been heard earlier that morning, for the German-Russian border was less than fifty miles away. Communiqué after communiqué indicated that the Germans were making rapid territorial gains from the start. Hitler had vowed not to make the mistake that Napoleon had made when his Grand Army was stranded in Russia during the severe winter of 1812, forcing his retreat with disastrous losses. Our enemy seemed very confident. Between announcements, music came through the speakers.

In the middle of all this, a large column of refugees moved down the street, escorted by gendarmes. The new arrivals in the ghetto were from Germany, wore yellow stars, and did not appear typically Jewish. Some even yelled "Heil Hitler," but they were beaten for it by the guards. They were Germans of mixed ancestry, I concluded, or perhaps just long-assimilated German Jews who had refused to accept Hitler's view of them and the reality of their predicament.

At the height of the summer came an opportunity to get out of the hunger- and typhus-ridden ghetto. Toporol had received a request, sanctioned by the German authorities, to organize people familiar with farm work to help with the harvest on country estates situated not far from Lublin. The volunteers were to get food and lodging in exchange for work. My family discussed this possibility for me and decided on it favorably. I was glad of my parents' consent, because things were getting tighter: half of Grandma's packages were being confiscated; the bakery was hard pressed and often without flour; the season for lettuce and tomatos from Toporol's plots was over. Besides, my parents appeared to have aged. Simon and Meir, my brothers, looked pale. Simon had a touch of tuberculosis and spat blood. It was plain to see that one mouth less to feed would not aggravate the situation at home.

Out to the Country

On a bright sunny morning in July 1941 I set my suitcase down in front of the Toporol office. More than a hundred young men like me were already there awaiting roll call, and a mood of subdued expectation prevailed. At the appointed time the Jewish administration officials emerged from the building and motioned for everyone to be quiet.

"You will be taken first to quarantine," announced one, "where you and your clothes will be disinfected. You will get food rations for the trip. You will then proceed by rail to Lublin, where you will be assigned to various estates. Any questions?"

"Yes," someone said. "For how long are we going?"

The official did not seem to have a ready answer, but he replied, "That depends on how long your work will take. If I were you, I would stay as long as I could. Now, I will call the roll. When you hear your name, answer 'here' and step forward into a marching formation."

As the roll call started, I became apprehensive, wondering whether I was really on the list, but at the sound of my name my tension eased. The officials put a man in charge who later was rumored to have worked as an informer. As the column began to move up Leszno Street toward the Leszno-Zelazna gate, people looked at us, some with pity, some with mere curiosity, wondering where we were headed. Of course, they could not know that for a number of us this was a turning point, a lease on life.

From the gate the guards escorted us out to the Aryan side and to the quarantine building located at Leszno 109, where we were kept for thirty-six hours. Then, after curfew, we were led through the deserted streets of Warsaw in the quiet of night. There was something dramatic about this march out of the snare of death. The thought of leaving my dear ones dampened my spirits; nevertheless, our departure instilled hew hope.

By the light of the stars we crossed the bridge over the sandy Vistula, flowing as unconcernedly as it had for centuries. The sound of its current seemed to say to me, "Don't worry. I have witnessed bloodshed and tragedy; savage battles have raged over my long shores turning my waters red. Invaders have come and gone—and this time it will be no different." Yes, I thought, that's easy for you to say; but what about us? But the great lady, mother of all rivers in Poland, remained silent.

Reaching the eastern railway station, we were immediately ordered to board a special train already waiting. The guards got busy counting their charges as they set foot on the train. The uneventful trip ended at dawn in the Lublin station. Lublin brought a rush of memories to my mind, giving way to a feeling of expectation. A recount of heads preceded the march to a transit camp in the city. There, the guards turned us over to the Jewish administration.

Finding out that our stay would last only a few hours, I knew I had to act fast if I wanted to contact the Rosenbaums. First, I tried to get one of the Jewish policemen to escort me to their house. This he would not do, but another one promised to deliver a message. An hour passed. Then one of the typical Warsaw sharpies who knew my named called me from outside the building: "Hey, Topas, someone is here to see you."

I ran out on the porch to see if it was true. People looked on curiously as a visitor approached. Her head covered with a kerchief, Gina stood near the gate, holding a food basket under her arm. She gave me a studied look. With a faint smile and a compassionate expression, she greeted me at the entrance to the compound. Apparently the Warsaw ghetto's lean diet was reflected in my face. As I stood there in a pensive mood, Gina said, "Hey, what is all this gloom? It's not like you. Aren't you pleased to see me?"

"Of course I am. How are you; how is your mother?" I asked. "And how do you both manage to get by these days?"

Gina told me that under the circumstances, they were managing well. Lublin did not have a closed ghetto, and they were still able to keep the store. In a few minutes, though, she had to leave. She bid me goodbye and said, "Let us know where you are, if you can." The visit made me aware of the drastic change in our fortunes for the worse. When she had gone, I picked up the basket and shared the food with some of my acquaintances.

Later in the day our papers were processed, and the tour was resumed. This time we were divided into smaller groups, and mine was put back on the train for a short ride. When it came to a stop that same afternoon, it was immediately obvious that we were in real country. It was just about harvest time, and this standing army of grain was a sight I had missed for a long time. The air here was pure, carrying with it the smell of the fields. After being shut within hideous walls, used to seeing squalor and death, this was a welcome change.

We were met by the foremen of various estates, who divided us among them. A group of six picked me as their spokesman right at the station, and so we stayed together until we were told to get into a wagon. The foreman and the farmhand who handled the team of horses pulling our wagon were bewildered by the way we looked. If we had been horses, they would have exclaimed, "Look at these starved animals. Why, you can count every rib. How will they ever be fit for work?"

Soon we learned from the driver where we were going, who the boss was, and what he was like. When we reached our destination at dusk, the driver pulled the reins back and pointed to our quarters, a small barracks situated about twenty-five feet from a water mill standing on the edge of a stream. A man in an old Polish Army uniform greeted us with an air of authority. He had red hair and a reddish face to match. "All right, you guys, move into this hut, and I will see tomorrow about some food for you." Not to disappoint my friends who had made me their spokesman, I jumped off the wagon and said, "We have been in transit for two days. Could we have some food now?"

"The only thing I can get is bread and milk," said our host. I gasped in disbelief: "God, did you say milk? I don't remember when I last tasted milk." Accompanied by the music of chirping crickets, we moved into our new home, feeling a sense of unreality in our sudden good fortune. By the light of a naphtha lamp in the quiet of the night, I ate the fresh country bread and drank a lot of milk, ladled into a clay cup, feeling guilty that this could not be shared with my family.

When the others lay down on their cots, I walked out, drawn by the night smell of the meadow and the sound of the cascading water whose thrusting force powered the millstones. There I stood by the stream, listening to the sounds around me and deeply inhaling the crisp country air. Enchanted and moved by the beauty I was being allowed to enjoy, I offered a prayer of thanks and felt a lump in my throat. I cried for the sheer joy of being alive. I cried also because my folks could not share it. I cried for the reasons that prevented them and all others from living as human beings.

When morning came, it was time to see the squire, our boss. Led by the man in uniform who had constituted our reception committee, we soon stood in front of his house. Only three of us, including the guide, went in. The squire, who was lord and master over a vast stretch of land known as Bychawka, seemed cool and reserved but pleasant in manner. Young—about thirty-five—lean, and rather short, he had blue eyes and a blond mustache. The questions I asked regarding food and cooking seemed to baffle him, as though he had not given this matter any thought until now.

"You will draw bread and raw staples weekly from the storehouse, but you will have to arrange to have it cooked," he said. My suggestion of appointing one of our men to devote his time to cooking was acknowledged by a faint smile in the affirmative. "Very well, get organized and report to work when you're settled." Accordingly, a curly-haired slightly cocky, thirty-year-old fellow became our cook.

All the farmhands were curious to see us Jews show up to work the first morning. Although at the beginning they were amused by our visible lack of strength, they were soon getting a good day's work from everyone in our gang. It was good to work in the open fields . . . to prop your back against the trunk of a shady tree, to wipe the sweat off your face, to reach for slices of dark bread with real butter, to wash it down with fresh, cool milk, to gaze at the sky and have no one to oppress you. We had to work on the Sabbath (which made me feel homesick and appreciate the Sabbath more), but on Sunday we were free from work. On the first such occasion I went scouting around the neighborhood. The postmaster at the tiny post office was a very nice Polish man who assisted me in sending my first food package, a five-kilo sack of flour, to the Warsaw ghetto.

We soon became friendly with the farmhands working around the estate. There was a young fellow named Wladoszek who liked to argue with me about political matters. There was the scribe, or bookkeeper, who enjoyed the high esteem of the men because he knew how to write. A nineteen-year-old nephew of the squire, named Tadeusz, who was in charge of the storehouse, walked around the estate erect as a cadet. He would occasionally get off his high horse and speak to me, though he and his uncle maintained a distance from all their employees.

A fellow named Stephan, built like a football star, prided himself on cutting the widest swath with the scythe, but he couldn't tell time except by gazing at the sun. One of the younger workhands, he looked smarter than he was.

Once, when the men were working the edge of the field before the harvester could drive in, I took the scythe from a fellow and swung around, mowing the wheat down. There is skill to mowing: heap the stalks evenly and always away from the uncut strip of standing grain. After a few minutes of swinging, I paused for a moment, asked for a sharpening stone, and, standing the scythe upright, began to sharpen its blade. I noticed I was being watched by the help and by my migrant friends as well. No doubt they were all surprised to see a city-bred Jew doing skilled farm work. The blade sharpened, I restored the scythe to its owner and returned to binding sheaves.

"Ah, that wasn't bad, not bad at all! Where did you learn to mow?"

"In farming school," I replied, feeling pleased for a moment.

After a few weeks there was grumbling among some of the men about Curly, our cook. Felix, a tall and hefty chap, and a man called Abe complained that not all the ingredients found their way into our meals. Curly began to act like our superior, and he did not have much patience with our complaints. One evening he tried to assert his position by turning on me personally. A violent argument led to a brawl, and Curly, coming out second best, was dismissed as cook. Abe took over the job, and Curly was put back into the ranks.

Shortly after the harvest, Felix, Curly, and two others were bent on leaving for greener pastures. Abe and I wanted to stay. With only the two of us, however, one could not play the part of a cook. So I went to see the squire and asked whether he would allow my thirteen-year-old brother to keep house for us. He did not mind; after all, we worked his farm for food only. The postmaster arranged a telephone call to the Warsaw ghetto (I could have written, but this was urgent). Using the only public phone in this village, I called a paint shop opposite our house where there still was known to be a phone. The woman owner, knowing our family, ran to get my father. The first words came slowly; then excitedly, I explained the opportunity for Simon to get out of the ghetto. Yes, Father was going to get him out. Once outside, he should be able to make it: he had light brown hair and a straight short nose; he could easily pass for an Aryan. His tender age would help him avoid attracting attention. A few days later Simon stood outside the hut. He looked very thin, his face white as a sheet, reflecting his bad state of health. I rushed out and embraced his bony shoulders. His eyes showed his amazement at the change in surroundings; like one dragged out of a dark dungeon into the bright light, my brother was unable to open his eyes except to squint.

By the end of August Simon began to look better. But I began to feel that the squire did not need us as badly now that the harvest was done. Besides, Simon, a lad of only thirteen, occasionally omitted preparing a meal, which was his assigned task. This annoyed Abe and worried me. One Sunday, Simon and I went to the village general store, where I inquired for any peasant needing help—that is, needing it right away—and to our surprise we were directed to a man who needed someone to help with such chores as chopping wood, making a fire, fetching water from the well—nothing heavy.

As it later turned out, he had Simon do all this plus feed the animals and mind an infant day and night. Yet there was food, and I urged him to stay on. Father, appreciative of my care for Simon, wrote a moving letter that I wish I could have kept. In it he compared my conduct to that of Joseph in the Bible, with whom I am linked not only by ancestry but by my Hebrew name, which is Joseph.

Nevertheless, a few days before Rosh Hashanah, Simon got homesick and returned to Warsaw. When he had quit as cook, we had a problem to solve. A farm worker's family could draw extra bushels of grain and potatoes for every able-bodied man they furnished to work. In this we saw our opportunity, and after wandering around in the village, Abe got himself attached to a family that had only a small boy; they lived on the same estate where we had worked until now. I found a place to board with an honest man named Joseph Dobrowolski and reported to work as one of his hired hands. His wife and two young children made up his household. I ate at his table, but Abe and I maintained and slept in our old quarters.

A very small town named Bychawa was situated three miles away. Fewer than two hundred families were living there, of which the majority were Jewish. In this village there were no sidewalks, paved streets, plumbing, but there were a few shops, a public bath, a barber shop, and a synagogue. I needed the use of all of these facilities on the day before *Rosh Hashanah*. So my friend and I put on our best Sabbath clothes and set out for this fragment of urban civilization. According to rumors, the Germans did not consider this ramshackle town worth their while; they had not stationed any police there and raided it only on occasion.

Reaching our destination on foot, we went to the village *Judenrat* office. This agency, though under German auspices, often would care about Jewish welfare; it depended on the administrators it had. With the arrival in the area of the migrants from Warsaw, the agency in this tiny town had had more than its share of business. It was headed by one Sonabend, a tall, heavy-set man who tried to assist us.

"What about lodging during the holiday?" Abe inquired. "If you go to the synagogue," replied Sonabend, "they will take care of you. If you don't, why did you bother to come?" With our welfare assured, we proceeded to look for the barber shop before going into the bath house. Men like ourselves were pouring into town for the holiday, and the barber was working overtime, operating from his two-room apartment. A fellow facing the ceiling had just finished getting a shave, except for the final touches. The barber opened a bottle of water, poured enough in his mouth to bulge his cheeks; then, bending over, he puckered his lips, took a deep breath through his nose, and sprayed his customer's face. This professional touch brought laughter from the waiting public, but it irritated the client, who spat on the floor, apparently not used to such thoroughly personal service.

When we finally entered the small synagogue and I once again heard the familiar chant, my thoughts turned to my family shut inside the walls of the ghetto. After services an old Hasidic gentleman with a gray beard invited Abe and me to his home. Like many other towns-folk, he showed truly patriarchal hospitality.

As the cold November weather set in, the hut where we had been staying had to be abandoned. One of the farm workers gave Abe floor space to sleep on, and I found temporary quarters in the stable. The horses did not mind this intrusion. Stephan, too, set up his winter residence there. He was illiterate but friendly and proud of his strength and skill in his farm work. Fresh straw bedding in the manger may not be what you call luxurious, but it was warm. The only things that disturbed this cozy atmosphere were good-sized rats running along the walls.

Eventually I bunked in the Dobrowolskis' one-room flat on a portable straw sack stretched out on the floor. Dobrowolski and his wife slept in one bed, and his two children, a boy and a girl, in another. This kind of crowding was something I had experienced only recently, but these poor people had lived like this for generations. What's more, they seemed content; they feared only losing work, for that would force them to leave.

The squire hired these landless farmers for work by the year; if he wanted to keep them, they had to renew their agreement annually. Those hired got one-room lodgings with four walls and a roof, a baking oven, and a packed dirt floor. They would be allowed to keep one or two pigs; they had chickens roosting outside the door; and a little plot for their own vegetables provided the table with greens. The pay did not amount to one hundred dollars per year, but they drew potatoes and grain according to the number of hands they put in the field. They would get a day off to take their grain to the mill, and the women baked the bread themselves.

My hostess was up before the break of dawn. She cooked potatoes and white borscht, and then she joined the other maids to milk the estate's cows. Doing this extra chore gave them the right to keep one of their own cows in the landlord's cow barn. By the time we got up, she was back to serve us our breakfast. After the men had gone to work, she had to feed the pigs and chickens, collect the eggs, wash and mend clothes, prepare lunch and dinner, clean the place, teach the children their prayers, milk the cows again, and serve supper. On some days she also had to bake bread and churn butter. On Sunday, she would prepare something special—*pierogi*, turnovers with cheese, dunked in heavy cream. She never complained except when the children got sick. She drove herself with energy and determination to care for her household.

As for the men, theirs was no eight-hour day either; they worked sunrise to sunset, faring a little better in winter when the days were short. They too were uncomplaining. There was a quiet sort of dignity about these men. They took pride in knowing that their work—whether it was plowing a straight and even furrow or properly loading the wagon with sheaves—would be handled with competence. And they had the self-respect of men whose mission it is to grow food for living creatures.

4 Excursion to the World of the Living

There shall be no rest for the sole of thy foot.
—Deuteronomy 28:65

In late November 1941, the snow fell and blanketed the countryside, but I wasn't properly dressed for the new season. Word came from home that packages were not permitted out of the ghetto because of a typhus epidemic, which meant that I could get no warm clothing sent from there. Nor could I afford to buy any, for the cost of clothes was extremely high. Home was therefore the only place to go. I already felt the symptoms of what I believed to be a bad cold. The more I ran outside nights to the outhouse, the more often I had to run.

Then there was the question: what was our status here, now that the harvest was long past? It seemed almost certain that some of the Jews still working on the estates were doing so on their own. Thus far we seemed to have been overlooked, and we hoped to keep it that way. So, acting as though the assignment there were a permanent one, I asked the squire for a leave of absence to go home for winter clothing. Consenting, he wished me luck, and since a wagon train was due to take sacks of grain to the German authorities in Lublin, I counted myself in as one of the crew.

Early in the morning we were off. The trip might have been uneventful had it not been for the district bailiff, who was a *Volks-deutsche*,[1] a Polish-speaking German, and one of the sort that always tried to outdo their home-born brothers. Since he usually took it upon himself to dispense justice as he saw fit, the wagon drivers never knew what to expect when they pulled the convoy to a stop by the highway office before noon. An individual wagon might avoid him by taking a different road, but a convoy with an official delivery had to follow the established route lest it be suspected of smuggling.

We waited while his deputies dressed in brown sheepskin coats worked over the wagons ahead of us. With rifles slung over their shoulders, they poked the wagon straw with clubs, searching for smuggled goods or men. The notorious bailiff, whose reputation for cruelty was well known, watched from the side. So far, no one in our convoy had been beaten up or, worse, shot for smuggling food to the black market.

I sat, uneasy, while the searchers busied themselves around our wagon. As a rider sitting alongside the driver, I attracted attention, because all the others had just one man to a wagon. The bailiff's voice was crisp when he called out, "Who is the guy with you on the wagon?"

"One of our men going to town," replied the driver.

"Wait a minute. Have you got identification?"

"Yes, sir," I answered as I got off the wagon, approached him, and showed him my school card. On the card there was my picture, and it said George (Jerzy) Topas and gave the date of my birth. It only established that I was a student at the agriculture school, because this was a prewar school card, in the town of Wlodzimierz in Poland. He looked at it, then looked at me; he seemed unsure about something. I met his gaze. I was unnerved for a tense moment but tried to look confident.

"All right," he said, "get back to your wagon." The rest of the wagons having been searched, he motioned for us to move on. No sooner had the convoy started, than he ordered, "Hold it! Are you sure you're not Jewish?" He pointed his cane toward me.

"Sure," I answered, turning directly to him.

"How did you get those black eyes?" He persisted.

"From my mother—she had gypsy blood," I said half jokingly. This made him grin, and he signaled for us to go. As we drove off, I heard him say to his lackeys. "I could have sworn he was a Yid."

The moment we were out of sight, the driver crossed himself. "Oh man!" he said, "I thought he had you. You know, this guy would not have let you live." It was a close call. I was grateful that none of our men had betrayed me, but I felt too sick at my stomach to comment.

When we reached Lublin, my first thought was to visit the Rosenbaums. After parting company with the men, I went to their home, but I was so weak, I could hardly wait to go to sleep.

At that time Gina and her mother shared an apartment with another family, for conditions were such that no one seemed to live alone anymore. They were very kind, as always, and put me in a bed with clean linens. Then they disinfected and washed everything I had been wearing, which was all probably covered with lice. (The woman back at the estate had boiled our underwear practically every Sunday to kill the lice in it, and every evening before going to sleep we had to sit and pick the lice off our clothes and smash the parasites between our thumbnails).

Now, in Lublin, the Rosenbaums cared for me anxiously. As my fever began to run high and I showed spots on my face, they were worried that I might have typhus, because that would mean a quarantine. So they sent for a doctor, who, after doing the usual poking around, concluded, "I suppose he will survive. It's no more than the measles!" Everyone was relieved to hear this except me—here I was, almost seventeen years old. I remember Gina teasing me about it: "The child has measles." But I don't know anyplace where I have received such tender care. I learned that my brother Simon on his return trip had also stayed there and had gotten to know the Rosenbaums and their warm hospitality.

One morning Gina told me about a doctor whose parents lived in the same building. They had proposed their son to Mrs. Rosenbaum as a *shidduch*, or marriage match, for Gina. He was considerably older than she was, and Gina did not care for him, despite the practical advantages such an arrangement offered. I saw him once. He was a man in his mid-thirties with a somber expression who seemed to project an air of self-importance.

Although I had thought for some time that Gina was not only attractive but a very special person, I did not dare think that Mrs. Rosenbaum could consider me seriously as a potential suitor for her daughter. A young and unaccomplished youth could hardly be what she had in mind for her Gina, who deserved the best, even in the worst of times. Because the present and the immediate future of the Jews was so uncertain, very few marriages and births were taking place at this time, but having a doctor in the family would have given Gina and her mother much-needed support.

One afternoon Gina asked me, "Jurek, my mother is urging me to consider this marriage proposal. You might say it's a 'conspiracy' designed for my 'benefit'—what do you think?"

"What a question! Would my opinion really matter?" I said in disbelief.

"That depends—if I like it, it would," she said, half in jest, then added in a more serious tone, "Please tell me: what do you think?"

I was taken aback, as much by her question as by this development. A few moments passed before I could answer.

"You know, of course," I said, "that I can't be entirely unbiased in saying this, but I believe that even according to our law, a girl has the right to refuse if the man does not please her."

I felt a bit awkward.

"I like your answer. You're a true friend." She lowered her head for a moment and looked down, perhaps embarrassed by the personal subject of our conversation. Then, in an obvious effort to distract me, she asked, "And how is the patient today?"

"Much better, thanks to the Rosenbaums' excellent nursing care," I replied. Nothing more was said about the marriage matter, but my hopes of sharing my life with Gina were dashed. In the person of the doctor I recognized a formidable rival, and my youth and the abnormal times dispelled any romantic notions for the present. Still, Gina's decision, although not immediately certain, eventually left me with a ray of hope for the future.

Early Lessons in Smuggling

As I recovered, I began to scheme. I found out that Lublin, which was the center of all farming, was a place where food was comparatively abundant and—more important—much cheaper than at home. Consequently, there was considerable smuggling of goods in and food out of Lublin.

So, after rehearsing my German many times, I went to the German work office and requested a railroad pass to the Warsaw ghetto. I reported that I had been sent by the German authorities to do farm work in the estates and that now I had permission from the squire to obtain winter clothing for myself and my fellow workers. When I got the pass, I packed all the food I could possibly carry without making myself too conspicuous, and one bright morning found myself on a train heading for Warsaw. The trip in itself was uneventful, except for a shakedown in the town of Demblin, about midway between Lublin and Warsaw. There the German gendarmes relieved most of the passengers of the food they were smuggling to Warsaw, but beginner's luck was with me: as it happened I was sharing a compartment far up front, so that before the gendarmes had reached the forward end of the train, it was ready to resume its journey, and they got off.

A decree threatening Jews with the death penalty for leaving the ghetto without a pass had long been in effect, and even though I had a pass, the thought of getting through the checkpoint at the wall gave me a chill. It was a frost-biting day, however; the guards had a small bonfire going to keep them warm, and I passed into the ghetto at Zelazna Post without being searched. Walking down Leszno Street, I saw many children in rags, weeping for alms. One could become hardened to the many sights of growing evil, but the skeletonlike bodies of crying and starved children wrought utter despair in my heart and so impressed itself upon my conscience that if I live a hundred years I will never forget their plight.

To make things worse (this was apparently still possible), one of the longest, harshest winters hit Poland at the end of 1941, and many suffered not only from the scarcity of food but from the bitter cold and lack of coal. Firewood was smuggled in at high prices, but it could not be afforded by those who could stretch their money only enough to buy the meager food rations. Many apartment houses were without stair railings; they had been used for fuel.

At home I received a subdued but warm welcome; as for my

smuggling venture, it met with mixed reactions. My parents were pleased with my resourcefulness, but they worried about the risk and expressed the preference that I not repeat the venture. Encouraged by my initial success, however, I persuaded my father to let me try again. I wanted to complete the cycle by smuggling goods to Lublin and bringing back both food and money.

We now had another subtenant with whom we shared our apartment: a refugee family of four who had been evacuated from the city of Lodz made our living room their new home in exile. The father, in his forties, graying but handsome, had blue, smiling eyes, an Indian-like hooked nose, a long chin, and a pleasant disposition. He and his wife and son, who resembled the father, were all working in the infamous Toebbens shops (the teenage daughter helped with home chores). Toebbens was an ethnic German contractor employing Jewish slave labor drawn from the ghetto. His and other privately owned German shops turned out uniforms, shoes, and other goods for the German army at no labor cost except for some food. The fortune-making enterprise owned by Toebbens paid so much a head to the German Reich for the use of Jews but made it back by cutting down on food rations and demanding an inordinately high production output.[2]

After getting Father's consent to try another smuggling sortie to Lublin, I wanted to leave without delay, but my mother insisted that I stay for the Sabbath. Being home again with my family, sitting at the Sabbath table, was something I had sorely missed during the months at the estate. I scanned the faces around me. Father propped his bearded chin up with his hand, resting on an elbow. This was his thinking pose. His face looked thinner, showing his cheekbones. Mother's hair had grayed, but her facial expression tried to conceal her sadness. My mother's widowed mother, a small, frail-looking woman with a wrinkled face, was also living with us, and she assumed an appropriately pious expression whenever she heard sad news.

Simon had lost all the color he had gotten during his stay in the country. But my most tender feelings were kindled when I looked at Meir, now nearly eight years old. Quiet, polite, sweet, innocent Meir had stolen my heart long ago, he was the bright little star giving us light in this time of darkness. I loved him very much and could not restrain my emotions at the sight of his pale but serene face and the knowledge that because of nutritional deficiencies his fragile health was suffering.

About this time we heard that America was finally in the war, and we took renewed hope in the final outcome. We did not fully realize that up until this time, the Nazis had not wanted too much adverse publicity to reach the American public, lest this give rise to hostile feelings and hasten America's entry into war. Now Germany no longer had this restraint and could unleash its full reign of terror. We thought this meant the end of food packages from Grandma, but we obviously underestimated her, because she soon arranged to have the packages sent through Portugal with the help of a friend at the American consulate in Lisbon. Whereas another woman her age might have given up, she persevered, and her packages helped pull us through the first phase of our plight.

After some preparation, outfitted with winter clothes, wearing heavy woolen underwear and Father's altered warm black overcoat, I set out on my trip. Because I now carried contraband leather goods, I obviously could not make use of my pass, exposing myself to a search at a checkpoint. As many others had done before me, I had to go over the ghetto's wall to reach the outside. Two of my father's acquaintances, who had experience in smuggling people across, took me to a narrow spot along the wall at the courthouse block near Ogrodowa Street. We listened for strange noises; hearing none, the two of them joined hands; I set my foot in their hands, climbed on the shoulders of our guide, and leaped up to the top of the wall. I crouched low for another look around and then jumped down, unnoticed. I checked my musette bag, carried on a shoulder strap, and took off. A novice at this business, I was afraid of being recognized and caught, but I felt better when I reached busy traffic on Marszalkowska Street. It was easier, I thought, to blend in with a crowd. I boarded a streetcar for the main railroad station, but after only a few stops I began to sense someone staring at me, so I jumped when the car pulled away from the next stop. Walking briskly along the curb, I stepped into a passing horse cab that got me to the station.

Changing trains at the eastern railroad station, I stood on the platform watching hundreds of people milling around, simply waiting for the same train (the German troops, with top priority, put a heavy strain on traffic going east to the Russian front). It felt good to be among the living again. At night I felt safer because under blackout regulations the platform lights were dimmed and the train was dark. So far, so good, I thought, as I settled down in a crowded compartment.

But a woman who must have been watching me on the platform indicated that she knew I was Jewish. I waited awhile, then moved to another compartment and opened the door. Feeling the cold wind blow in my face, I walked on the runningboard to the next car, since this type of European train had no connecting doors between cars. At the end of each car there was a little booth, normally empty; thinking it to be as good a place to hide as any, I opened the door, only to be startled by the sight of someone already in there. Crouching down, the poor soul seemed as scared by the intruder as was the intruder, but finally he said in Polish: "Sir, are you 'am-who' or from Posen?"

The word *am-who* is Hebrew for "the People" or "the Nation." If I had not been Jewish, he would have found out, because I would likely have replied, "No, I am not from Posen but from Warsaw." As it happened, I acknowledged my marked identity by replying, "Am-who."

"Friend," he said, "it's a tough life. I thought you were one of those blackmailers who would point you out to the *yekkes* [Yiddish slang for Germans or German Jews] unless you paid off."

Since I thought it best to separate myself from him, I bid him good luck and got as far away from his car as I could without leaving the train. This was one way to spread the risk.

Arriving in Lublin in the morning, I lost no time in looking for buyers and that same day managed to sell all my goods—except for one pair of fine prewar, custom-made, hand-stitched shoes, a present for Gina's mother from my parents.

After spending a day with the Rosenbaums, I prepared for my return trip to Warsaw. Mrs. Rosenbaum suggested that Gina accompany me partway to the railroad depot. My train did not leave until late at night, but I had to reach the station before curfew. Gina, bundled in a sheepskin-lined coat, remained quiet as we walked down Lubartowska Street. There was snow on the sidewalks, and the whistling of the wind was interrupted by the noise of German vehicles and a sprinkling of horse-drawn wagons driven by Polish farmers. My mood was grim as I reflected on present realities and the uncertain future. As we parted, Gina pleaded tearfully for me to be careful. I promised I would be, thanked her, and walked hurriedly away to hide my pain.

On entering the railroad station, I made my way through the throng of German military personnel and Polish civilians as quickly as I could, trying to attract the least possible attention. The atmosphere was depressing—not only because of the gloom of the blackout but also because of the wounded German soldiers lying on the platform, awaiting transportation to one of the many military hospitals in Lublin. The wounded had been brought in from the Russian front under cover of night, apparently to avoid any contact with fresh troops moving up to the front.

No Jew could leave his place without a permit, much less travel by railroad. The permit I had obtained earlier was still valid because the cashier had neglected to stamp it on my preceding trips; nevertheless, I was uneasy as I stepped up to the cashier's window. I was relieved that after examining the permit, he handed it back to me and sold me a ticket to Warsaw. As I turned away from the window and walked down the crowded lobby, an officer of the SS emerged from the station canteen, unsteady on his feet, and stopped a few steps in front of me. He stared at my armband with the Star of David, identifying me as a Jew, and began shouting insults, attracting the attention of everyone in the lobby. Not satisfied, he retreated slowly, reached for his holster and drew out the pistol, motioning with his left hand for everyone to stay clear of the target. While I stood cornered, aware that my time was rapidly running out, I heard quick footsteps. Two tall German MPs emerged from behind me and flanked my executioner on both sides. They put their hands firmly under his arms and released his grip on the pistol, replacing it in the holster, then led him away quickly and quietly. "Firing of arms in a railroad station is *verboten!*" they told him. (In less crowded places, one supposes, it would have been all right!) This all happened so fast and so unexpectedly that I had no time to react. Still dazed, I barely comprehended how close I had come to death.

Meanwhile, the German station police had taken note of me, and a guard in a black uniform ordered me to follow him to the station guardhouse. Before I could fully recover from the first incident, I was hustled into another. Standing in front of the officer in charge, who sat on the desk with one leg dangling and the other one touching the floor, I observed the rubber truncheon that he held in his hand.

"Let me see your pass," he ordered in a rasping voice.

I handed him the pass and the ticket and, as he picked them up, he placed the truncheon on the desk. He studied my permit for a moment and said, "Why did you not have the pass stamped?"

Before I could reply, he had the truncheon back in his hand and was pointing it at my face. He was eager all right. I told him my pass certificate was not stamped because the cashier at the station had not stamped it. He raised his voice and now angrily demanded, "Why didn't you produce the certificate?"

"But I did," I quickly replied.

"You are lying. Now, tell the truth:—why didn't you have it stamped?"

I repeated my first answer. His patience now gone, he hit me several times about the face. I leaned far back but it didn't help. He turned to one of his flunkies and told him to open my suitcase and the musette bag I carried on a sling.

The guards rifled the contents of my bags and found the butter and bread I was trying to take back to my family in Warsaw. The officer picked up the two-pound (1 kilo) cake of butter and set it aside. The rest of the things he threw back into the suitcase and closed the lid. "Now," he stated, "we will check with the cashier to see whether you are telling the truth." But just as he picked up the phone, apparently to call the cashier, the door opened and a guard brought in a woman with a lot of packages. The chief replaced the receiver and proceeded toward the new customer, a Jewish woman in her thirties. She had the ruddy face of a hard-working peasant woman and was wearing so many bulky clothes that it was hard to say whether she was trying to hide something. She seemed scared but stood erect, protesting the searching of her packages and person. Here again the guards helped themselves to some of the food that this frightened but daring woman was smuggling. When they found that she had no pass of any kind, I began to fear what they would do to her. But she was only roughed up and lectured: "It is against the law for a Jewess to travel on the railroad without a pass and to smuggle large quantities of food," the voice of authority said. Then a tragicomical exchange took place. After being searched and roughed up, fleeced and lectured, she was told to go. "But," she demanded, "you have just told me I cannot travel without a pass."

The officer, shaking a finger in her face, said, "You have broken the law and traveled this far illegally. Don't get too smart or we will lock you up."

"So, what shall I do, travel without a pass? I will get caught again."

"That will be just too bad; you should have thought of this before," said the German. "You will just have to take your chances and continue as you have been doing." Ordered out, she collected her bundles and left.

"And what are you waiting for?" he said, turning toward me.

"Me?" I asked.

"Yes, you. Get out!"

Thinking it best not to remind him that he was supposed to verify the truth of my testimony, I made haste to leave. Later, sitting alone in a blacked-out train in the darkness and pressing a wet handkerchief to my face, I thanked God for my rescue. Fortunately, I did not know then that this was only a skirmish compared to what was to come. For now, I was tired but happy to be alive, glad to be heading home to my family with some of the food I had started with. I felt that the worst was past and looked ahead to easier going, as one feels after an operation. Greatly relieved, I once again contemplated the future with renewed optimism. Before sleep came, the rhythm of the train wheels sounded to me like Karl Maria von Weber's *Invitation to the Dance.* Awakened by a whistle noise, I looked out the frosted window to see that we had arrived in Warsaw's main railroad station.

Trouble developed the moment I reached the ghetto wall: a blackmailer accosted me and demanded money. I kept on walking briskly, hoping to free myself from his pursuit, but it did no good. He now had a uniformed Polish policeman trailing us.

"Hold it there," snapped the policeman. I stopped and so did his accomplice. "Now, you have food and you attempted to go over the wall."

I denied this in vain, pleading with him to let me go so that I could reach my home. But he was a cool "businessman" and said that unless I could suggest something better, he would have to turn me in. When I didn't react as expected, the stooge finally suggested that I turn over three hundred *zlotys* to him to see if he could "persuade" the officer to drop the charges. Three hundred *zlotys* was practically all I had to show for the whole miserable trip—including initial capital—except for a bit of food. Think, man! I told myself and responded:

"If this is what it is going to cost me, better turn me in."

"You wouldn't be lying, would you now?"

I kept silent.

"Well, I may be able to square it for one hundred zlotys." The stooge did not let anything get away.

"I will give you fifty," I said.

He got angry: "I think you underestimate your own worth."

All this time the policeman was standing aside, but now he joined in for the pitch: "Well, what are you waiting for? Come on."

When I reached for my purse, the stooge snatched it from my hand and began to count its contents—150 *zlotys*. I demanded fifty back and was told to flee before the "law" changed his mind. I went, with no bounds to my frustration. All this risk and effort nearly wasted. Had I not kept the rest of the money in my boots, I would have returned empty-handed.

But when I finally got home, my parents chided me for worrying over money when I could easily have been gone too. Grandma, with an air of melancholy resignation, piously rolled her eyes upward: "Oh Lord, let this money atone for us all so that we may all be yet delivered." Mother did not like it when her mother went into these pious spells, which were usually followed by quiet sobbing. The lamentation visibly depressed her.

That evening I related to my father all that happened on my trip. First commenting on how well I had handled myself under the circumstances, he insisted that I give up smuggling, return to the estate, and try to stay there as long as possible. It seemed to me that as a smuggler I was forced out not by competition but by the ratio of profit to risk. If only travel insurance had been available then!

Frania, Ida, and Raisa, my mother's sisters, had been with us ever since they had been ordered out of their hometown of Plock in February 1941. Father had installed Frania's husband as superintendent at our apartment building (in place of Joseph, who as an Aryan had had to leave the ghetto), with Ida's husband Joe as his assistant. They were all living in the superintendent's one-room apartment, including Frania's two small children.

During my childhood we used to visit Mother's family in Plock for the second days of Passover, usually going by boat down the Vistula. These excursions were thrilling for us; we children roamed the deck of the steamer on this day-long trip, happily observing such sights as the fortress in Modlin, slow-moving barges carrying grain to the sea, and scores of fishing vessels. The traditional diet of matzos and hard-boiled eggs constituted the menu until we reached Plock, perched high above the river. My maternal grandfather had been one of the gentlest and friendliest persons I ever knew. Well liked by all who knew him, he had spent most of his later years in study and prayer. Now he was gone, and the rest of the family had had to seek refuge in Warsaw.

Winter 1941–42

But time did not wait for sentimental recollections. I was again outfitted with some things that could be sold when I got back to the country. Mother was sad and Father was in a serious mood at our parting again. Sometimes I wondered what he was thinking and feeling. He always presented a calm and confident exterior; he looked pensive but never gave in to despair. Faith must have sustained him, I thought, and such ideas occupied my mind on this trip.

The snow was ankle deep in Lublin, but I did not mind because I now had winter gear to keep me warm and dry, and my depression gave way to a happier mood at the prospect of visiting the Rosenbaums again. Surely a warm welcome awaited me there; in a hostile world full of unhappy events, their home was a refuge generating warmth and comfort. And so it proved to be once more.

Departing for the country early the next morning, I resorted to the safest mode of transportation and set out on foot, hoping to journey about eighteen miles by evening. Fortunately, on the outskirts of the town there were fewer Germans to worry about. In the open fields the wind was wicked and my face felt numb, but as soon as I reached the dense Dombrowa Forest, I was sheltered by the ancient trees. I could hear my own feet making fresh prints in the snow as I followed the bridle path along the road. Suddenly I heard horses' hooves. I wanted to run off the road into the surrounding woods but decided against it, in case I had already been noticed. A German patrol on horseback was approaching from the opposite direction. Contrary to my apprehension, the riders passed, completely ignoring my presence.

Before clearing the woods and heading for the villages in the open, I rested in the serene surroundings, ate my lunch, admired the quiet beauty of the forest in the winter setting, thanked God for sparing me, and then went on. I let my thoughts wander freely from home to the refuge in Lublin, the long war, and all the misery it had brought. I whistled a tune to keep my spirits up. But the nearer I got to the Bychawka estate, the less I relished the idea of going back to my former quarters, to the lice and the dreariness of life that winter brought there.

I thought of going to live in the nearby small town of Bychawa until spring, for I had a little money and a few things to sell. But first I had some personal business to take care of. So, at four o'clock in the afternoon I knocked on Dobrowolskis' door and was greeted by Joseph and his wife. I had brought him some cigarettes. Next, I paid a call on the squire, who did not seem displeased to see me. I set before him the elegant pair of high-heeled shoes that he had asked me to bring for his wife. When she put them on, she seemed very pleased.

"How much do I owe you?" asked the squire.

"I don't know, but if you can think of anything that might help me get along in Bychawa for the winter, I would appreciate it," I replied.

"Very well. I will give you thirty kilos of sugar. How is that?"

"You are most generous, sir, but I could not carry that much."

"Do it in two trips," he suggested.

The squire more than paid the price of the shoes with thirty kilos (about 60 pounds) of sugar, which sold on the black market at twenty *zlotys* per kilo; five kilos was the reward price the Germans paid for reporting a hidden Jew. I carried half my thirty kilos on my back to Bychawa, reaching it late that same evening. Exhausted, I asked for and found a room with a refugee family from Lodz. My days there were spent idly; at night I learned how to play poker. My sugar transaction brought me enough to lead this kind of existence for a while.

Then the authorities announced a deadline of January 1, 1942, for Jews to turn in all the fur coats they owned; the confiscated furs were to be used to line military overcoats for use on the Russian front. This prompted many to sell or give their furs to their Christian neighbors, depressing the fur market considerably. Of course, some people hid theirs, even though such an offense was punishable by death.

Fresh snow fell on New Year's Eve and spread its clean, linenlike cover over the town. Early the next day I was awakened by a commotion: gendarmes were searching Jewish homes. I dressed quickly and ate breakfast in haste, and no sooner had I gotten up from the table than rifle shots coming from the market square shattered the quiet morning of New Year's Day. From the window I saw people running in all directions away from the marketplace. I could hear wailing and lamentations from bereaved women and crying children. I put on my overcoat hurriedly and went out. As I passed the place of execution, I could see that though the bodies had already been removed, red blood and brains marked the place in the snow where the executed had fallen. I did not stop but kept on running until I lost sight of the town. The contrast of blood and snow at sunrise in the stillness of the clear daybreak made the horror all the more shocking.

On the road I met two brothers who had come with the original group of laborers and who worked at their trade as carpenters. They were also fleeing from the danger of being caught by the raiding Germans, so we traveled on together. As the evening approached, we stopped and turned in to one of the peasants' home for food and shelter. A friendly and sympathetic man, the peasant welcomed us, invited us to dine at his table, and provided a safe place in a barn for us to sleep. In the morning we thanked him and returned to town.

Now that the German police were showing more interest in the area, it was only a matter of time before we would have to leave. Having developed a hunted animal's instinct for danger, I decided to get my things together and move back to the estate, considering it a less likely place for police raids. But this fragment of civilization where I could still enjoy the comforts of a real bed, warmth, and contact with fellow refugees detained me in Bychawa for a little longer.

A few days later, on Saturday, January 17, 1942, though the snow and the cold made walking uninviting, I felt a strong urge to join others in prayer and to hear the Torah reading; I had not attended a synagogue for some time. My landlady told me where services were being held in private, and I proceeded to the apartment. When I entered the place, the handful of Hassidim there (about twelve in all), wearing prayer shawls, seemed startled by the presence of a stranger and were perhaps suspicious of my identity and purpose, since my dress was more like that of a country gentile than of a small-town religious Jew. Once their initial wariness wore off, however, they made me feel welcome, and once again I listened to the soul-stirring reading in the scriptures of Israel's expectation of deliverance. I was so engrossed in it that it did not dawn on me, until I was called to the Torah to recite the *Maftir*[4] which was considered a special honor, and read the selection from the Book of the Prophets, that this was my own Bar Mitzvah Sabbath portion of the scriptures; according to the Jewish calendar, it was the fourth anniversary of my Bar Mitzvah. On this day four years earlier I had stood before the congregation in the great Warsaw Synagogue on Tlomacka Street to accept the "yoke" of our law. I had read then, too, the prophecy that had fortified many suffering generations of our people; it promised the eventual ingathering of the House of Israel "from among the peoples wherein they are scattered. . . .then shall they dwell in their own Land which I gave to My servant Jacob. And they shall dwell safely therein, and shall build houses, and plant vineyards" (Ezekiel 28:25-26).

This day's experience in unfamiliar surroundings rekindled the memory of that other Sabbath. Walking back to my room, I hummed the melody of the rousing march that the Warsaw Synagogue choir had sung for the Bar Mitzvah boy, and I recalled the splendor and the joy of that occasion, which had been shared by my whole family. I felt homesick and longed for the world I had known.

The next day I packed my few things and returned to the estate. At the beginning of February a letter from home informed me that Grandpa had passed away; he had died of typhus before the age of sixty. I was very saddened by this loss. He had died in the presence of his children, but Grandma was far away, and because America had entered the war, it was not even possible to communicate this tragic event to her.

One-Way Ticket

Soon news began to trickle in that gendarmes were rounding up men from the surrounding estates—a signal that the time had come to move on. I said goodbye to the people I had come to know and like. The farmhands seemed sorry to see me leave, though Wladoszek's parting words were less moving than those of others: "It's too bad you have to go; there will be no one to argue with."

When we had arrived at the height of the summer, everything had been green and blooming, but it was a windy and cold February day eight months later when a handful of migrant farm workers from all the surrounding estates set out for home. In order to avoid attention we started by wagon before daybreak and reached Lublin in the morning. We presented our letter from the Bychawa work agency to the official in the German work office in Lublin. "How many are in the party?" inquired the German.

"Six, sir."

"This pass is good for a rail trip and entry into the Warsaw ghetto." It was a one-way ticket.

Not knowing when I would see Gina and her mother again, I rushed to their home to spend the few remaining hours of the day, but they were at the store. Lublin had changed, I noted. Jewish forced-labor gangs were seen marching under guard to camps that had sprung up; the Majdanek concentration camp was the biggest around, and the Lipowa POW camp was one of the first in which Jewish POWs from the Polish campaign were interned.

There was unrest in the Jewish quarter. Of late, raids, arrests, and executions had become quite common. I went to the Rosenbaums' store and was spotted at once by Gina's mother, who turned toward her daughter, who was busying herself in the rear, and said, "Gina, look who just came in! We are going to close early," she added. "Why don't you go ahead with Jurek while I get a few things and we shall eat together."

We had not yet gone halfway to their apartment when SS men pulled their canvas-topped truck to a screeching halt a block away. We fled into an apartment house nearby and ran upstairs. On the fourth floor we stood listening for pursuing footsteps. After hearing nothing for several minutes, we descended the stairs and reentered the noisy street. Gina appeared very frightened and remained unusually quiet for the rest of the time we were together. I could not read her thoughts, but in this small space of time it must have dawned on her how fragile our very existence was. Whatever our feelings of affection for each other and whatever our hopes for the future, they all became unreal, like a mirage fading before our eyes. The gradual but steady worsening of the situation carried with it the foreboding of doom. I remember her saying, "It all seems so hopeless." When the time came for me to go, I tried my best to cheer her up, drawing a picture of things better than they really were. She finally forced a sad smile as I looked at her and her mother, then I turned and left. Unlike all previous occasions, this parting was unrelieved in its gripping sadness.

Our small group of laborers met at the railroad station just before curfew. We had our pass stamped, and remembering my recent experience there, I led my friends to a far end of the platform, where we sat down and waited. There was quite a bit of activity in the station. Trainloads of wounded soldiers were unloaded and ferried to Lublin military hospitals. All were stretcher cases. German nurses wearing black capes busied themselves around the wounded. At the same time, one of the German soldiers waiting for a train in the opposite direction was reading a book titled *Warum Krieg mit der Sowiet Union* (*why the war with Russia*). Presently, however, he was distracted by the procession of wounded.

The train for Warsaw that arrived around midnight was half empty, and we got a compartment to ourselves. As we pulled out into the darkness of the night, my heart throbbed, echoing my sadness at leaving people very dear to me. After what seemed an hour, the wheels came to a grinding stop in Pulawy, the first stop. Despite the cold, I opened the window and looked out. A strange and frightening sight shook me, for on the adjacent track stood a freight train. Its cargo was human. Each door was open, the entire opening covered by heavy barbed wire, and in the faint light we could see men who looked liked bearded skeletons; most wore only underwear and Russian army caps, though some had overcoats on. Obviously Russian prisoners, they looked starved and half frozen.

Some of the Polish people began to throw articles of food from our train into their cars, but the German guards put an immediate stop to that by firing warning shots in the air. The Russians were quiet, their faces expressing only resignation. It was a cruel fate that men who otherwise might have tended the soil to make it yield food were now dying from hunger and cold.

At the next stop in Demblin, where my father had done some of his military service, the gendarmes got on the train, searching for illegal quantities of food and anything else that might be contraband. We sat in the dark and waited, keeping our pass ready.

First there was the beam of a flashlight and then a shout: *"Juden!"* One gendarme held the flashlight while another began beating and kicking us all before we could present our pass. He stopped and shouted at us again: *"Raus!"* (Out!). When someone presented our pass, he held it to the light for a moment before crumpling it and throwing it on the floor, still yelling for us to get out. The other guard picked up the crumpled pass, which carried the stamp of the German authorities.

We were escorted to a place behind the platform and lined up at the wall. The dim station light revealed bullet marks on the wall. A third guard approached. He unshouldered his automatic rifle and cracked the bolt back. No one among us uttered a sound. Then the one with the flashlight said, "Wait a moment," and walked away, while the other two continued pointing their guns at us.

I thought, he is going to check our pass with his superior before they shoot us. After a very long five minutes, he returned and gave us back the pass. The execution was off. My companions' terror-stricken faces surely mirrored my own. How close we had come to the end of life's journey right there! Breathing a sigh of relief, I wondered whether I would be as fortunate next time.

The guards had held the train all this time, and now railroad workmen emptied one whole car of passengers and told them to find room elsewhere on the train. A sign reading *"Jews Only"* was attached to the side of the car, and we were put in it. The engine gave a hissing puff and pulled its burden ahead. Our little group whose lives had just been spared came alive again; in subdued voices we discussed our close call. The rest of the trip was uneventful.

When we reached the Warsaw ghetto gate in the morning, we encountered no difficulty in getting inside. Wishing each other luck, we parted, never to see one another again. As I walked home, I could see a change for the worse. Paper-covered corpses were lying in the streets, ignored by people who by now were well used to them. Beggars, more numerous than ever, were also ignored.

Mother opened the door and welcomed me back. She looked pale. Father was in mourning for Grandpa. Seeing my skinny brothers was enough to make me cry. The packages from Grandma were not getting to us now, and all other sources of food were dwindling. The family was on a strict diet, yet Father was still helping others, regularly taking some food to Abramowicz, the refugee tailor, who had tuberculosis.

In the spring of 1942 the death rate in the ghetto reached unprecedented proportions. Several hundred people were dying daily. At home we tightened our belts once more, experiencing real hunger for the first time. Hunger pains and thoughts of food hours before each meal were things we were getting used to. Once, in a fit of anger against this deprivation, I took a pair of ski pants and sold them to an old-clothes peddler on the street. With the money I bought some bread, butter, and sour cream and ate the little feast by myself. At suppertime that day I looked at my parents and at Simon, then fourteen; when my eyes rested on thin little Meir, I could not bear my own folly. To this day I wish I could rewrite the past without that selfish act.

At the beginning of April, rumors got around that an extermination detail had arrived in Warsaw. Later that month the SS stepped up their acts of terror in an apparent effort to paralyze the ghetto with fear and to discourage any potential resistance against the rumored deportation of Jews. They would come at night, knock on the door of an apartment and call out a name, drag that person downstairs, and shoot him or her. Then they would cross that name off their list. On April 18, fifty-two people were massacred on Nalewki Street.

One evening, while I was helping my father build a hiding place in the attic, we heard the sound of car engines, which then meant one thing: the arrival of either the SS or the SD (Security Service) on one of their nocturnal forays. The ghetto was normally quiet at night after curfew. We moved to a dormer window to see two German cars moving slowly along the street below. Suddenly they stopped, and three SS men went into an apartment house across the street. A light went on in a window of the first-floor apartment, and moments later they emerged with a man wearing only pajama pants and an overcoat. At first I thought it was an arrest, but I was wrong. They stood him up against the wall and stepped back, like a photographer positioning the subject. The man raised one hand and shielded his face. A burst of bullets shattered the silence of the night. He slid down onto the sidewalk, his blood trickling into the gutter.

Father and I stared at each other, saying nothing, but our eyes expressed our sense of utter despair. As we embraced, I cried.

"These are dark days and more lie ahead. You must brace yourself and keep faith to survive," whispered my father. I nodded. It dawned on me that even in his warm embrace, I was no longer a lad but a man who must steel himself to be able to face the ugly reality and go on living. The thought haunted me that our generation was fated to experience the fulfillment of the *Tochecha*, the prophetic warning of calamities contained in the Torah.[5]

We were about to leave the attic when a hearse pulled up to remove the corpse. The driver rang the bell for the apartment house super, who came out, received instructions, and went back in. When he emerged again, he was carrying two buckets and a broom. He flushed the sidewalk with water from one bucket, swept away all traces of the blood, and rinsed the spot with the rest of the water.

When we went back down to our apartment, Mother was sitting there crying. She held onto Meir. Simon had watched the proceedings in the street below, and now he was walking away from the window. Even Grandma was up. It was evening; it was morning; it was another day.

5 The Deportations Begin

My anger shall be kindled against them in that day, and
I will forsake them, and I will hide My face from them.
—Deuteronomy 31:17

One day I received a letter from Gina, revealing that she and her mother had managed to run away from the Lublin ghetto in the nick of time before a massacre took place there. The letter gave the rural address of one Stanislav Uchanski at Cmielow, on whose farm they had found shelter. Cmielow was a long way from their home, and it seemed safe for the moment.

News of massacres in other towns added to the growing pessimism. It was June again, and the sun shone brightly—but for whom? One gendarme, nicknamed Frankelstein, shot a few Jews at random every day in the ghetto before his breakfast.

While on an errand one lovely day near the intersection of Karmelicka and Novolipski streets, I observed a party of SS men forcing a restaurateur to give whatever food he had to a group of people the soldiers had rounded up. While they ate, the Germans took pictures. The opinion on the street was that the Germans were trying to show those back home that some of the Jews had it too good. They went to great lengths to photograph scenes suggesting that theme.

Uncle Ben, during a family conference, had urged the building of an underground shelter to hide in, but the idea was not considered seriously, because no one yet really believed the rumors of an impending evacuation.

The darkest day yet for the Warsaw ghetto was July 22, 1942, the ninth of Av in the Jewish calendar.[1] On that day the Jewish Council published a notice of deportation to the east, where, according to the announcement, the Jews would get work. Anyone reporting voluntarily to the embarkation point on Dzika Street would get bread and jam for the trip. *Judenrat* president Czerniakow committed suicide the next day.

Sadness exceeding anything I had witnessed before was everywhere, but many unsuspecting people, worn out by their wretched existence in the ghetto, actually did volunteer. They went to the embarkation point with their children and luggage, taking even their bedding. Not to arouse suspicion at first, the German authorities tolerated the luggage as a bit of pretense and allowed them to take it.

The morning after the announcement, the Jewish police began to round up all the beggars and those languishing on the streets, using horse-drawn wagons for the purpose. The volunteers lured by bread and work kept coming. The Germans had sealed the ghetto gates to all except those working for German industries.

Within three days, ominous news spread like wildfire throughout the ghetto. One man was rumored to have escaped to tell his brethren the worst that they had yet to hear: Deportation to the east meant, in reality, the gas chambers of Treblinka, where the "final solution" was being put into effect. The tidings were too morbid to believe, too cruel to expect even from the Germans, too sudden and too late to prepare against.

Yet believe it we did, and its immediate effect was faintness of heart. That evening I looked at my parents at home and sensed their grave sorrow. Can you imagine being unable to save your own children from the grasp of death? Can you imagine being trapped like an animal in a cage and marked for extinction? The feeling of helplessness filled us with a numbing despair. But Father still kept his calm faith. And as they did every evening the children watched Mother cut bread and give everyone his or her portion. Hunger is very strong, but no stronger than fear: that evening, we did not feel like eating—except for Meir, who had not heard the news.

A frantic scramble began to obtain work in the German-owned shops; the passes Toebbens and others issued meant exemption from deportation. Passes from various other German agencies carried assorted degrees of authority, so that whereas at first all the passes were honored, later only some were good for one's life. Father managed to obtain passes for everyone in our family except Simon and me; we were already working for the *Luftwaffe*.

Under Escort

When I returned to the ghetto, I had gone back to work for Toporol and had gotten Simon in as well. Eventually, however, Toporol "consigned" us all to work for the *Luftwaffe* in Bielany, a Warsaw suburb. Every day we assembled in the ghetto and were escorted to work, and back at night, under guard. The work consisted of cleaning bricks from bomb-ed-out houses to be reused in building new structures. We also worked in a gas mask warehouse.

Meanwhile, the SS resorted to raiding tenements to fill the quotas of heads delivered for shipment east. They soon abandoned all pretense and started packing people in like sardines, 150 or more to a boxcar. This way they could ship more and gas fewer, because many men, women, and children died of suffocation en route. Volume was the key word, and the SS tried hard and earnestly to meet their quotas, as though they were doing piecework. In the first stages of the deportation the SS men were assisted by the Jewish police.

One morning during those frightful days, Father and I were praying, wearing the traditional *tefillin* (the phylacteries worn by adult men for weekday prayer), when we heard a knock.[2] When Mother opened the door, a Jewish policeman walked in and announced that our apartment building was being raided. The Germans were in the yard; everybody had to come out for deportation; passes would be honored, however. Then, looking surprised, the policeman said, "Why are you wearing *tefillin* today? Don't you know it's the Sabbath?" His conscience awakened, he added: "Stay in the house until it blows over." *Tefillin* are not worn on Sabbaths or holidays, but in the terror of the time we had forgotten to distinguish one day from another.

Soon Simon and I had to hurry to our assembly point, but we got there on time and filled in the ranks. Two guards from the Luftwaffe counted our number and ordered us to march toward the Bonifraterska Street checkpoint. Crossing Zamenhofa Street, I saw scores of people, being escorted by the gendarmes for deportation. The men walked silently; the women cried and lamented so loudly it should have penetrated heaven. A boy of about fourteen jumped on the back of one guard and tried to wrestle the gun from his hands, but he was beaten down by another and shot. (On another day, when an older lad had tried to snatch the gun from his captor and had nearly succeeded by tripping the guard, two other guards had pulled him away and bashed in his head with a rifle butt.)

For our work group, the most trying time was at the checkpoints, now completely manned by the SS extermination brigade. We stood still, waiting our turn while the group ahead of us was being searched. Two young SS men were doing the job that summer morning. Suddenly a man wearing round-rimmed glasses was pulled out by an SS man who had found something he did not like. The timid-looking man had a lad of eight or so with him; he tried to leave the boy in the ranks, but the child dutifully followed his father. The SS man, without wasting a moment, walked them both into the ruins of a bombed-out building. Two rifle shots rang out like thunderclaps, and the SS man emerged alone. He pulled the bolt back and ejected an empty cartridge, swung the rifle over his shoulder, and went back to searching the group.

Frisked without casualties, we marched out of the walled death trap into the area of the living. It is several kilometers to Bielany, and the farther we got away from home, the more we could observe the contrast. Here there were open shops and hundreds of people going about their business in the July sunlight. I began to envy the people whose birth entitled them to live, whereas mine had marked me for slaughter.

Our guard Eric was not so bad, considering that he was the ranking guard. That is, he never hit anyone hard, and occasionally he looked the other way when we tried to buy or swap things for bread with the free Poles. We collected a little something for him and his pal, which kept them happy. Guarding Jews had now become a desirable duty because it offered extra benefits, and it was preferred to guarding installations, to say nothing of fighting. Why, a smart guard could make himself a bundle! The only thing Eric the Westphalian did not enjoy was picking us up and delivering us back in the ghetto. He seemed uneasy, as though afraid that the SS might be rough even on him.

This day was important because a captain visited our place of work and announced that the following day we would be interned there for our own safety. "Bring the things you need tomorrow—you will be quartered here." Then he looked everyone over, picking out the very young; he instructed Eric that these were too young to work and should not come the next day. Among those picked was Simon, my brother. I thought, "Oh, what will Father say? What will happen to Simon?"

That evening Eric escorted us past the checkpoint, and from there on we were on our own. The ghetto now was totally under SS rule and was in a constant state of terror. Not only were people being herded for deportation, but SS men kept shooting at anything that pleased them. We ran home alongside the walls, now and then jumping into vaulted entranceways to dodge bullets. When two SS men appeared, riding a rickshaw, their wooden-handled automatic Mausers at the ready, people ahead of them emptied the streets in a panic. Noticing a head in one window, one of the men fired a volley at it. We hopped into the gate of an emptied apartment house and waited for them to pass. Emerging later, we heard another salvo fired, surprising people at an intersection.

We made it home and related the news about the internment and Simon's exclusion. My poor mother started packing for me again, not knowing whether it might be for the last time. There was not very much to pack; aside from some shirts and underwear, I had two pairs of pants, a sweater, and a jacket. My only valuable possessions were the high riding boots that my father had given me after my return from the country estate. The boots had new soles that should last through the next winter; my immediate problem was for me to outlast the soles! Other than the twenty zlotys I already had, I neither received nor asked for any money, nor did I have anything I could sell.

Despite this development, Father maintained a calm poise. Any fears he might have had he kept to himself. In fact, his poise inspired confidence and ruled out the thought that this might be our last meal together. So, to paraphrase, as it is said in the Bible, "Abraham, my Father, got up early in the morning and went about his prayer as he always did."

Before he was through prayers, the time came for me to leave. I had already kissed Mother and my two brothers. Now my father, still wearing his prayer shawl and *tefillin*, walked over to me and raised his hands to bless me. He laid his hands on my lowered head and began: "May God bless you and keep you from going under. May He gird you with strength to withstand, endure, and witness, but not suffer you to die." He concluded in Hebrew, and when I looked up at his face, he was crying. I had never seen him cry before. His tears fell on my face as I embraced him and held on for a moment, bathed in tears myself. Then, drawing backward until I reached the door, I turned around and left.

As I rushed to our assembly point that August morning, words from the Bible that Father had read so often and that I had so often received with impatience and disbelief haunted me: "Thy sons and thy daughters shall be given unto another people, and thine eyes shall look, and fail with longing for them all the day; and there shall be nought in the power of thy hand . . . for they shall go into captivity" (Deuteronomy 28:32).

Internment at Bielany

While thousands of our people were herded into the *Umschlagplatz*, or point of embarkation, our group of 120 men were escorted out of the ghetto to internment at the Bielany *Luftwaffe* camp. As we left, I watched the terrifying tragedy continue as it had yesterday and the day before: multitudes of people were being led to their doom. The old and the young, the sick, the blind, and the lame were all bound for one place. Treblinka's gas chambers were forced to work around the clock to "process" such volume. Nothing made one's heart bleed more than the procession of undernourished children from an orphanage. The sight of their small feet going to a place of execution instead of to a picnic or a zoo was too painful to bear. (It was known that the famous Dr. Janusz Korczak and the orphanage staff accompanied the children so that they would be with them to the end.)

Leaving the specter of death behind, we were transported to our new home. One large barracks in the middle of the Bielany Woods, surrounded by barbed wire and with a sentry at the gate, would be my address for a while. This *Luftwaffe* camp had installations that served an airfield, but Bielany was also a suburb of Warsaw. It was what the

Vienna Woods were to Vienna, and before the war it had been a picturesque place for picnics and winter skiing.

Early each morning we were awakened by the guards, who would walk through the barracks, turning on lights and blowing the whistle for us to rise. Coffee was brought in from the kitchen in big urns and dished out. Then we would fall into formation and march under guard through the wooded area of Bielany, which by contrast to the ghetto was a heavenly oasis—or so it appeared to us. We had to go far enough to reach the streetcar line for a trip to work on a special car reserved for the prisoners. We were taken to a new place of work at warehouses where gasoline, paint, and other things required for aircraft maintenance were stored. The area had a very strong odor of paint. The streetcar travel to the warehouse was the best part of this everyday excursion because once we were there, they really put us to work—hard work. My first job, with another man, consisted of carrying large drums of paint that had a handle on each side. They had to be carried very quickly; they were so heavy that if you didn't walk fast enough, you'd break down.

The first time they brought the soup at noon, we knew right away what to expect as a diet. The soup was very thin, and I recall that after a few days everyone got so hungry that they watched the man stirring the pot with a big ladle to see if a potato would float in before the soup was poured into the mess gear. It was evident that there would be no additional food rationed out to us, but those among the prisoners who had money were able to buy food from Polish peddlers who hung around the streetcar junction—when the guards looked the other way or when we collected something for them. The peddlers knew that they could get premium prices for their food, and I guess the money compensated them for the risk they took by selling food to prisoners.

Most of the men in my group had some money with them, and they managed to get food from the Polish peddlers on the way to and from work. Having no funds, I began to suffer hunger early in this camp, and I couldn't think of any way to supplement my meager diet. Hard work and hunger do not have a favorable effect on one's strength or morale. Food was very much on my mind.

In addition, the news reaching us from the ghetto was horrifying: evidently the Germans were liquidating the majority of Jews who lived there. However, I kept faith that my family would somehow be spared and, by rising a little earlier, continued to say my morning prayers as I would have done at home. One morning, however, the guard who woke everyone up arrived earlier than I had expected and found me praying. After kicking me once, he tore the phylacteries off my head and my arm, threw them down on the floor, and trampled on them:

"You are crazy—what will this do for you? Nothing!" he said. "You are stupid. Don't let me catch you doing this again."

Looking at the *tefillin* on the floor, I remembered when I had first received them and put them on, while Mr. Szweis, my Hebrew teacher, and Rabbi Rabinowicz, the Torah reader in the big synagogue, prepared me for my Bar Mitzvah. I recalled that cold wintry Sabbath, New Year 1938. The sidewalks of Warsaw had been blanketed with snow. Accompanied by my family, I had ascended the steps of an imposing edifice—the great Tlomacka Street synagogue—still limping from a knee injury sustained in an ice-skating accident. I had been elated by the festive solemnity of the moment. My grandfather, my father, my uncles, all wearing black bowlers for the occasion, had looked so dignified.

The interior of the synagogue, like the entrance colonnade, looked very stately. The elevated *bimah*, or podium, where the cantor stood and where the Ark and the Torah scrolls were situated, was under a high dome with prismatic skylights, which sunlight entered as a shower of light rays. Listening to the beautiful singing of the cantor and the choir, my eyes fixed on the light, I had sometimes felt in that synagogue as though in a trance. At such moments I had thought that since we no longer had the Temple in Jerusalem, this was the holy abode on which bright lights were showered from above.

On this special day, accompanied by the resonant voices of the Eisenstadt choir, the renowned cantor Moshe Koussevitsky had everyone inspired and spellbound by his beautiful singing. When he intoned my Hebrew name—*"Yaamod Yosef Benyamin ben* [the son of] *Avraham Chaim, Maftir Bar Mitzvah"*—thus calling me up to the Torah, the moment arrived for me to ascend the steps of the *bimah*. As was the custom with all Bar Mitzvah boys, two members of the synagogue's ceremonial staff escorted me, to the rousing march sung by the choir, *Behol Libi Uvehol Nafshi* (With all my heart and soul), until I reached the table upon which the Torah scrolls rested. There my father stood, his eyes expressing approval and encouragement. Over the years I had witnessed many Bar Mitzvah boys ascending the *bimah*; now it was my turn.

I first chanted the blessings, over the Torah, then read the passage in which Moses implores God to end the plague of hail in Egypt. But when it stopped, "Pharaoh's heart was hardened and he did not let the children of Israel go." (My father would observe later that the history of the Jews in exile was a long list of promises broken by rulers and statesmen.)

Following prescribed custom, I next faced the congregation and recited my two-page memorized speech, beginning, *"Belev maley herdat kodesh.* . . . With a heart filled with reverence and humility I stand in this holy place before the Congregation of Israel to enter into the covenant of commandments with the God of Israel and his holy Torah," and concluding with the quintessential words from the Torah, the *Shema Yisrael*: "Hear O Israel, the Lord is our God, the Lord is one!" The choir echoed my last words.

Finally, I recited the passage from the Prophets, Ezekiel's prophecy of Egypt's downfall for treachery in its dealings with Israel. Then my active part of the ceremony was over; it was followed, as was the custom, by Rabbi Dr. Moses Schorr's charge to me in words of wisdom, ending with a blessing.

At home there had been a quiet celebration, actually a *kiddush*, a small festive meal with our uncles and other relatives and friends. (Ordinarily, we did not see much of them because our religious observances made them uncomfortable.) Mietek Goldfarb, an able attorney and a relative of ours, toasted Uncle Ben and his fianceé Rose and wished them eternal bliss. From Uncle Ben I received a massive volume of Adam Mickiewicz's poetry;[3] from my grandparents, a wristwatch, presumably to teach me the value of time; and from my dear father a memorable, unscheduled, one-hour *musar shmuse* (admonitory talk) after the guests had left. Father showed me many areas of my personality and conduct that could stand considerable improvement. As he stood there, leaning against the wall, warmed by the big tile stove, he looked at me with what appeared to be a mixture of pride and anxiety—probably pride for this day and anxiety for my future. His deepset, wise eyes had assured me how much he cared that I turn out well.

But now all that was a cherished memory of a world that lay in ruins, like my *tefillin*. From that day on I resorted to an abridged form of prayer.

Another experience of an entirely different kind that stands out during this period was the time when we had worked very hard and came back, worn out and tired, to get some sleep, only to be awakened at midnight and told that we had to get back to work. Loaded on the trucks, we were taken hastily to a place by the railroad yard to unload coal. The German in charge said that every man would be assigned to one car of coal. Anyone who finished unloading his would be returned to the barracks to get some sleep. Standing on that car, it seemed bigger than just a night's work to me, but if I stood there and worried about it, I would never get it done. I began to hoist large chunks of coal and throw them over the side of the car. Eventually, the Germans opened the cars and all the loose coal came out on the bottom, but the big pieces had to be thrown out by hand. I worked at it hard, and after several hours, I had my car cleared. Then they assigned me to help someone else who didn't have his clear. Eventually, when we got back, it was already daybreak.

In the morning when we marched through the woods to the streetcar junction for our daily trip to work, I would hum a tune, usually the march from Aida. It helped somewhat to ease my feeling of estrangement and brought temporary respite from anxiety about the present. This melody also suggested to me visions of eventual victory of the Allies. Sometimes melodies of prayers associated with the Sabbath or a particular holiday reminded me of better days, and filled me with yearning for my family and home—people whose fate I no longer knew.

Once a man escaped from our camp, and the *Luftwaffe* captain thought that the situation was bad enough for him to take a personal look at our camp. He ordered the guards to line us all up for inspection. The captain then asked the Jewish man who was in charge of the entire group to name the man who had escaped. When the man in charge seemed hesitant, someone else volunteered to answer: stepping forward, he gave a fictitious name for the escaped man. When asked for a description, he provided a good one—the escapee, he said, was short, blond, and so on, whereas he was actually dark and stout.

Two days later we prisoners were again standing in formation before the captain, who announced that the man we had described had been caught and "lawfully shot." "Let it be a lesson to all of you not to attempt to escape. Here you will work and get to eat, and you will be safe. If you escape, you are surely going to die, because no one can get away." It was obvious that he was bluffing but trying to throw a scare into us.

September 21 was Yom Kippur, a fast day. When they brought our watery soup at noon, by mutual agreement we refrained from eating, because we wanted to continue with our fast until evening. But that day the Germans worked us around the clock, loading a train of motorized sleds for the Eastern Front. They were really cracking the whip then; even the civilian personnel who were not in the forced-labor camp were kept on the job. Work did not halt until midnight, yet not a single man actually fainted or got sick. We drank our watered soup and were taken back to the barracks.

Once, assigned to a work detail in the surrounding wooded area, I helped load liquid containers aboard trucks. During the lunch break, I wandered within sight of a Catholic cloister, which was apparently still allowed to function. Two nuns were outside the building, washing kitchenware. When they saw me, one of them motioned for me to come closer; the other disappeared hastily behind the door and in a moment emerged with a pot of soup.

"Please sit down and eat."

I took the pot from her hand and ate the best meal I had had in many months. I heard one say, "Lord, they starve you."

I thanked them for their kindness and quickly retreated to my work. It was a rare thing in those dark days for anyone around us to show sympathy. But the nuns had kind hearts, and knowing this let a little light in through the hostile, abysmal darkness around us.

One day, while detailed to work at Mokotow, I was approached by a Polish civilian laborer who offered me one hundred zlotys (about twenty dollars) and his shoes for my high boots. The boots were worth much more, but I was hungry, and one hundred zlotys could buy a lot of bread.

I feigned lack of interest, and he raised his offer slightly. I looked at him and said, "I don't know," but he was not fooled. "Come on," he urged, "who are you kidding? You could do with some food!"

"How do you know?" I protested unconvincingly.

"It's written all over your face," he replied, knowing that he held a winning hand. We went into the lavatory, where he helped me pull my boots off. I looked at them for a moment as the new owner put them on. I felt undressed, wearing riding pants with his ordinary shoes, but except for loss of pride this did not worry me. Extra bread compensated for my loss for a few weeks—what a secure feeling! But after the few weeks were up, I was back where I started, minus the boots. I had parted with my most, and only, valuable material possession in order to buy bread.

6 Escapes and Other Fragile Reprieves

And ye shall be left few in number.
—Deuteronomy 28:62

I was beginning to think that if I couldn't supplement my meager rations, I should try at least to work less in order to balance it out. I struck on the idea that I should become the camp shoemaker and requested permission from the captain to do so. He readily agreed that I could repair shoes for my coworkers. My problem consisted of finding a place for a workshop and obtaining an instant course in shoe repair. The few tools made available to me from the German supply were not sufficient to do a good job, and even if they had been adequate, I knew nothing about repairing shoes! When I finished my first efforts, the men cursed because the nails were sticking up inside. It looked as if shoe repair was not a trade to be acquired by a "do-it-yourself" method. Still, the idea of being a shoemaker was a good one because it enabled me to stay in the camp, and for a while I didn't have to work so hard. I simply sat in the room where I slept and banged away with a hammer, trying to do the best I could.

Then I had another idea—a possible way to escape! I advanced the idea by requesting more tools for my shop. It was not until the end of November that I was allowed to speak to the captain, but when I talked to him, he agreed that going back to the ghetto for supplies was practical; he consented to send me there under guard to obtain the necessary equipment. The following day was set for the trip. In the meantime, even before making my request, I had learned that the deportation action in the ghetto had terminated on October 3, after some 300,000 Jews had been sent to Treblinka for extermination. I was very anxious about the fate of my family.

Early the next morning the guard and I came to the checkpoint at the ghetto's wall. The SS exchanged a few words with my escort and let us in. It was now late October 1942; the ghetto had been reduced to about one-quarter of its original size, even smaller. We came to Zamenhofa Street. I knew of a courtyard on this street that led to several other yards, from which it would be easy to make my getaway. When we came to the vaulted gate, I told the guard to wait for me there, that I would go and bring back the supplies. As I went in, I looked back to see if he showed signs of following, but he was reaching for his cigarette case.

For a few tense moments I couldn't quite believe that I really would manage to pull it off and evade my captors. Everything depended on whether my guard would suspect my intention and come into the courtyard. I pinned my hope on a guess that he would stay outside the building because of the typhus scare widely circulating among German military personnel. It was also the assumption among Germans that after the recent mass deportations to the death camps, we would not consider confinement in the ghetto preferable to internment in a labor camp.

If I were not to fail, it had to be now or never. Walking as swiftly as I could without giving the appearance of running, I reached a stairwell across the courtyard. Once inside, I paused for a moment; had the guard begun to follow me by this time, I would have had to run up the three or four flights of stairs and try to make it through the roof hatch to the roof of an adjacent building. Since he did not follow, I reentered the courtyard for the twenty-yard dash—still walking—to the adjacent courtyard via an opening in the dividing masonry wall. In a few seconds, walking out through the vaulted gate, I emerged into another busy street during the ghetto's morning rush.

Only in the realm of the absurd does one escape from one prison in order to get into another, but that was what I had just done. My next task was to find a way to get to my home, which was now situated outside the perimeter of the reduced ghetto through another checkpoint.

I headed in the direction of the Zemenhofa Gate at the corner of Gesia Street, and finding a group of workers marching out under guard, I joined their ranks. I learned from this group that their job was to remove furniture and anything else that could be used by the Reich from all the apartments that had been abandoned by people taken for deportation. This sort of work was known as *Wertefassung*—seizure of valuables. We passed Pavia Street and turned into Dzielna Street, where the SS men led the workers into one of the apartment houses. Trucks arrived, and the men got busy dragging all sorts of things down: furniture, washing machines, clothing, dishes, pots and pans—anything that was usable. At an opportune moment I detached myself from the group and walked through the deserted streets until I reached my home on Leszno 28.

When I entered the courtyard, I was stunned to find the once lively place an empty ghost house. All the windows were open, mattresses were thrown around, covered by a variety of objects: furniture, dishes, pillows, feathers. I went to the apartment where the superintendent had lived but found no one. I called, "Is anyone here? Is anyone here?"

All I heard was the echo of my own voice. Upstairs, the door to our apartment was wide open and I walked in. Objects were lying on the floor; in the dining room and my bedroom everything was in disarray, as if someone had ransacked the place. In the living room, recently occupied by our subtenant, there was no sign of life either.

At last it dawned on me that not only was no one there but no one had been there for some time. Some photographs showing our family in better days lay scattered on the floor; with tears in my eyes I selected a few and put them in my pocket.

I ran quickly up to the attic, only to find it deserted—the hiding place empty. Going downstairs, I saw that a steel door, the rear door to a grocery store, was the only one closed. I tried to open it, but it was locked. I banged on it hard. Someone was there, for a sound came from the other side. Those poor people probably thought it was the Germans knocking. When asked who it was, I told them my name. They knew me and opened the door. Mrs. Blumensztok, the widow of the owner, and another woman who had worked there when the store was in business, were inside. At first they did not speak but simply stared at me in bewilderment. Looking like ghosts, they learned from me that the deportation activity in the ghetto was now over. They told me that my mother and my brother Meir had been taken away while my father was at work with Simon, during one of the larger raids that took place on that street. But they didn't know anything about my father.

With waning hope, I went on to look for Father and Simon. Outside, I ran into Mr. Bart, whose presence in this vacant, off-limits sector of the larger ghetto was as strange and solitary as mine. He had operated the corner restaurant before the war. Now he was here, an uninvited guest, also looking for someone.

Mr. Bart assured me that he had heard hopeful news from others. According to their story, my father and Simon had managed to escape from the embarkation compound in September. Where they might be now he did not know but "the last place your father was known to have stayed was at the next building on Karmelicka 4 in Torp's apartment," he told me. "Why don't you go in there? Maybe you will find out something."

Torp was an electrician, a slight, friendly sort of man who had serviced our apartment building. In a few moments I walked through an open door into his apartment. It, too, was vacant; the beds were not even made up. Noticing a large book on one bed, I reached for it and knew that Father had been here; it was a volume of Jewish history by Heinrich Graetz.[1] A page was folded where he must have finished reading. I opened the marked place and read a few lines.

The passage followed the disastrous consequences of the four-year revolutionary war waged against Imperial Rome from 66 to 70 A.D.

After the destruction of the Holy Temple, when the flower of Judean youth had perished in battle, were crucified, or sold as slaves, Johanan the son of Zakkai requested the emperor Titus's consent to establish a school at Jabneh. Titus did not object, "for he could not foresee that by this unimportant concession he was enabling Judaism, feeble as it then appeared, to outlive Rome, which was in its vigor, by thousands of years."

I loved my father too much to believe that he, too, had been swept away in the deluge, yet among this multitude of doomed humanity there must have been many innocent souls. What had happened was beyond my comprehension. I lingered, meditating for a while, before leaving with a heavy heart. I lamented our plight, trying not to let myself think of Father's anguish at finding Mother and little Meir gone to the slaughterhouse.

With little hope, I went to look further. I wanted to return to the small ghetto, where there was still some semblance of life. To do that, I had to rejoin the group I had come out with. Hurrying, I reached them just in time to return with them from work. Looking at the faces of the people on Zamenhofa Street was like looking at the faces of those you meet at the cemetery after a plague; there was the pallor of death on each of them.

Eventually, I ran into a person I had not expected to meet: the bricklayer who had built the oven for our illegal bakery. He informed me that my Uncle Mietek was living and gave me directions to his apartment. Sure enough, Uncle Mietek opened the door and was deeply moved to see me: someone from among his kin had survived. He was living here with Irka, a one-time salesgirl in our store who had looked after grandpa; she was now his wife. Uncle Mietek told me another bit of startling news. Uncle Ben and Rose were actually on the Aryan side; she had Christian identity papers, and Ben was hidden in her apartment. Also, unexpectedly, my grandmother on my mother's side and two of my mother's sisters, Frania and Raisa, were alive, and Frania had her two little children with her. They were now living on Muranowska Street. And Sevek—always cheerful Sevek, one of our three orphaned cousins—and his wife Rita (who had also been a salesgirl in our shoe store) were alive, but he did not know where they had gone.

After a meal and some talk with Uncle Mietek, I went to see my grandmother and two aunts. I found them at the address given me and they were astonished to see me. Grandma had miraculously saved herself by hiding in a clothes chest. They were all working in the groups that sorted Jewish belongings and furniture plundered from vacant buildings. They asked me to stay with them, and I decided I would, since I thought they could use a man around the place. The apartment was cold because there was nothing to burn except odd wood pieces found at work to heat one stove.

The next day I went to work with the group. It was there that I struck up a friendship with a young man about my age. His name was Henry, and he invited me to join him in combing apartments in search of valuables. Once outside the confines of the small ghetto, we would separate ourselves from the group and see what we could find in the empty houses ahead of those scheduled for clean-up.

Thus began a rather dangerous rifling operation. Each morning we went to work with the group, but as soon as we reached the designated building and the workers started carrying out furniture, clothing, and other goods, we would climb out onto the roof. From there we would go to adjacent buildings and search for salable items. Often we found an apartment that looked as if the people had just left; even the food was still on the table. Apparently they had set the table for a meal but never had the chance to eat it. Seeing in these homes all the family things—the old piano and cupboard, relatives' pictures on the wall, sacred books, toys—was like being in hallowed chambers surrounded by the fragments of an extinct civilization.

But however profound our thoughts, we were after valuables— items that we could sell for food. Sometimes we found jewelry; once, underneath a table where the spare leaf was stored, we discovered a pair of earrings of some value. Occasionally we would find good leather shoes. We took any objects that could be sold easily. These we would smuggle back to the ghetto and sell to fellows who had contact with the outside. The operation was quite profitable. It brought us food and helped me and my family.

Once when we were in a third-floor apartment, a German patrol stopped in front of the building. Four SS men emerged from their car, went into the courtyard, and yelled for us to come down, as if they had actually seen us. But we knew it was a trick to make anyone there think that he had already been seen; the hunted develop an instinct for these things, and we stayed quietly where we were until the Germans came into the stairway. Then Henry and I immediately ran up the stairs to the top floor, where there was an opening into the attic; we got onto the roof of the adjacent building, went down into one of its apartments, and sat quietly waiting until it was all clear again. After a while, descending to the street, we rejoined our group.

One cold December day the SS guards permitted the burning of some old furniture to let the workers warm up while loading trucks. An important rule in our business was not to become conspicuous. If the guards didn't remember seeing you, they didn't miss you when you sneaked away. We got away as usual and reached a building we hadn't completed on our last visit. As we entered the first apartment, we heard hurried single steps moving toward the kitchen. Knowing it could not be a German, we followed. Standing in the kitchen doorway was a startled man. Thinking that we were SS men, he had grabbed a broom and made believe he was sweeping. If we had been an SS patrol, his act would not have worked because we were four blocks away from the group. Shabbily clad, the man leaned forward and stared at me: "Aren't you George Topas, my former student?"

"Why, you are Mr. Szweis, my Hebrew teacher at Razwilowski School."

Bowing his head as if ashamed, he nodded. "Oh," he sighed, "what has the world come to now? Is this what the school prepared you for?"

There stood a teacher who had nourished children with biblical stories of love, mercy, and respect for justice. The children were no more, and justice and mercy had taken a holiday, and the teacher was scrounging for food in a desolate city. There he stood, holding a broom, looking like a scarecrow—but, alas, we did not have time to reminisce.

When we got back, Henry went to warm his hands by the dying fire. An SS guard asked him, "Where have you been? I have not seen you all day." "I carried everything down to the ground floor," replied Henry. The guard did not look convinced. So I butted in. "That's right, we carried it all together." That did it. With over two hundred people in each group, and with rotating guards, all of us were just so many faceless heads.

New Year 1943 marked a change of attitude on the part of the remaining Jews in the ghetto, then numbering about 40,000 (down from a peak of some 450,000). News was circulating about an organized Jewish resistance movement. One of the first acts that had caused a stir among the surviving Jews at the peak of the 1942 deportations was the assassination of Andrej Szerynski, the overdiligent head of the Jewish police, an apostate Jew and reputed grafter. Jacob Lejkin, who succeeded him, was shot in late October 1942 for his own brand of zeal in serving his masters, As the ferment of resistance intensified, other acts of retribution followed with increasing frequency. It was a time of reckoning for informers and collaborators. The underground was rumored to be several hundred men strong. I wanted to join, if only to give vent to my wrath, but unless you knew someone within, you would not be considered. With informers still at large, security had to be intense. People of means busied themselves building ingeniously hidden bunker shelters, but the worn-out majority had to shift for themselves. With no affiliation or contacts that would help me get into the underground and no means of building a shelter, I found myself on the outside, just existing from one day to another.

At the beginning of January, I was walking on the street when someone approached me and said, "Do you know what I just heard? The *Umschlagplatz* is being cleaned again. There is some activity." As I walked away from him, I didn't try to verify this information. I knew what I had to do: I had to get out of this walled death trap at once. After the loss of my mother and Meir, with my father and Simon unaccounted for, survival assumed paramount importance for me. The rumor that the *Umschlagplatz* was being tidied up for use occupied my entire thinking. I could smell deportation in the air. My instincts told me to get out; I had to get back into an outside camp. Maybe the Jewish work agency could help.

It was a clear cold January day when I entered the courtyard of the work office at Zamenhofa Street. Asking no questions, I just looked around and listened. While waiting, I contemplated the attire collected during my rifling days, for when you look for work, you want to appear presentable. I had never been able to find anything that really fit me, except for a formal evening jacket. In order to avoid a grotesque effect, I tucked the tails inside my pants and buckled my waist with a belt.

The office was a very busy place. A lot of men were either reporting for compulsory work, coming back from camps, or looking for work in camps. The Jewish agency under German auspices acted as an intermediary: when the Germans gave an order to furnish workers it was the agency's responsibility to supply the men. This agency was typical of those in many ghettos—the Germans would demand that the Jews administer their own affairs. When the Jews failed, the Germans stepped in and that was much worse.

As I waited, anxious to get myself hired, a Jewish civilian came in, escorted by two *Luftwaffe* guards. I didn't recognize him as anyone from the camp from which I had recently escaped. He was trying to recruit some workers to supplement those at Camp Okecie, which was just outside Warsaw and was the major airfield on the route from Berlin to the Eastern Front. The original group was interned there; the Jewish camp leader wanted another group to commute every day, under guard, from the ghetto.

I was the first volunteer that morning. When there was a large enough group, we were escorted by the *Luftwaffe* guards to the checkpoint. At the wall the SS guards gave us passage, and there we boarded streetcars and were soon out of the ghetto, which again smelled of impending trouble. The work at Okecie consisted of site work and earthwork around the airfield. Polish workers labored right along with us, but they were paid for their work, whereas we had to do it gratis.

I went to this Okecie post everyday and would try to bring some bread back with me to the ghetto. In order to be on time for the morning departure, I had to get up very early, while it was still dark.

On 18 January, I got up before dawn and started to leave the building through the Muranowska Street exit—but when I looked out, my heart almost froze: an SS guard was standing there, sealing off the exit. I knew what this meant: evacuation. I immediately turned around and went back to the apartment, aroused Grandma and my two aunts, and told them to get up and get the children dressed. Our only chance was to get out on Niska Street, which was parallel with Muranowska. Our apartment building had access to both streets.

So they hurriedly dressed the little ones, and we went down to the ground level, this time trying to leave in the opposite direction. But when I peeked out the gate, I found that Niska Street was divided along the middle of the pavement by German gendarmes and Polish policemen guarding the access to the north side of the street to prevent anyone from getting across. It immediately became evident that *our* side of Niska Street was the one marked for evacuation first. Our problem was how to get to the other side.

The sentry post nearest to us was manned by a Polish policeman. It was still dark and pretty cold. The guards had bonfires in the center of the street and were warming their hands. There was hardly any traffic because the people were still asleep, not aware of what was in store for them when they awoke. I picked up Frania's older boy, Israel; the little fellow, named Aaron, was carried by his mother. We emerged from the gate and decided to make a run for it. The Polish policeman spotted us and drew his pistol. He said, "Halt, or I'll shoot you."

"You might as well, because if you don't kill us, they will," I replied.

But he didn't shoot. He turned his back on me, saying hurriedly, "Well, if you are going to cross, damn it, go!"

And we crossed to the other side. I went to the opposite apartment house and knocked on the first door that I came to; I had to get the women and boys in out of the cold. When the door opened, I could not believe my eyes, for the man who answered was a one-time employee of our firm. Mr. Linder had always been a very friendly person, and he had not changed. When he saw this picture of misery, although by now everyone was used to it, he received us with sympathy and invited us to sit down and get warm. He said we could wait there until things blew over. Whether he realized what was going to happen or not is hard to say.

When daylight came, I went out on the street to look for the *Luftwaffe* guards, in case they were coming to take the workers out. Meanwhile, on the south side of Niska Street the action had begun. I walked toward Zamenhofa to see whether I could find anyone belonging to the Okecie group. As fate would have it, I ran into a fellow named Morris Wyszogrod. He had with him his younger brother Paul, who was limping slightly, and I was struck immediately by the tender way in which Morris was taking care of his brother.

Morris and I picked up others who belonged to the Okecie contingent. One was named Mocny, which means strong. Tall, curly-haired, blondish, blue-eyed, freckle-faced Mocny was true to his name, not so much because of his looks as because of his reputation for successful escapes. Another, who was later to play an important part in our fortunes, was Moshe Kessel. A quiet-spoken man of medium height, blue-eyed with a slightly owlish nose, Kessel was one of the sort who say little, do a lot, and have no particular interest in small talk. Unlike Mocny, who was the movie hero type, Kessel in his circumspect way impressed me by his bearing; his measured, determined way of speaking inspired confidence in him as one who could acquit himself well in nearly any situation where courage, timing, and coolness paid off.

Eventually a sixth man joined us. Now the problem was how to get out. We saw a ray of hope in the fact that Wyszogrod was an artist who happened to be doing a portrait of the Okecie camp commandant, an officer named Schultze. Wyszogrod presented us with a proposition: if we could get him to a telephone, he would get us out. Of course, to make such a promise and to carry it out are two different things. But we had nothing to lose, and we began to concentrate on where to find a telephone. None of the Jewish people were allowed to have telephones any more. We would have to go either to a Polish commissariat (police precinct) or to the Germans. The choice seemed clear, so we went to the commissariat—I believe it was the Fourth Precinct on Niska Street—and pleaded with the sergeant on duty to allow one telephone call to Okecie, explaining that Wyszogrod was an artist who was working for the commanding officer there. If they would permit him to make the call, a few lives could be saved.

There was some hesitation on the part of the police, but the telephone call was made—because our very lives depended on it. We held our breath as Wyszogrod advised the authorities in Okecie of our situation. In effect, he told them if they did not send guards to take us out, we were as good as dead. Surprisingly, the commandant told Wyszogrod to stay where he was, and he would immediately dispatch a *Luftwaffe* detail to get us out of the ghetto. Incredible! But time now began to work against us because the south side of Niska Street was almost empty of people, which meant that the side we were on would be next.

We had to leave the Fourth Precinct after we made the call. There was much commotion going on at the west end of Niska, which was nearest to the embarkation point. Across the street a large group of bearded Hassidic Jews, wearing their traditional black hats, were standing against an apartment building wall with their hands raised. Apparently the SS were not going to bother taking them any farther.

A stony silence dominated the air, and the tension was indescribable. The plight of people who had managed to survive the initial ordeal of the big deportation actions and who were now being taken was more than one could bear to watch. Now and then a loud outcry was silenced by the crack of a rifle shot. Not all of the SS men were so clumsy as to shoot anyone that lingered on, such as an old man or a young child who would not come along; some of them were expert at handling the evacuation with the minimum of noise. They would allow children to cry, but if the crying became hysterical, they often felt an obligation to put an end to it. While we grew impatient, a group was led away past us. A little girl wearing a beret held onto the hand of her resigned-looking mother. In her other hand she held a doll.

Minutes seemed like hours, and hours seemed like an eternity. Finally, we began to doubt whether the *Luftwaffe* guards would come after all. We began to ask ourselves questions. First of all, after talking with Wyszogrod, Schultze might have called the SS authorities to get permission to send the guards in, and he might have been told that it was just too bad if there were any of his Jews left there; they would not make exceptions for him or anyone else. Or perhaps he had either forgotten about us or simply decided that it was not such a good idea for his guards to cross paths with SS on a day when they were so busy.

Then a yell interrupted our anxious thoughts: "Wyszogrod! "Wyszogrod!" We ran out of the courtyard where we had nearly frozen while waiting, and sure enough, two German *Luftwaffe* soldiers with rifles slung over their shoulders were there to escort us out of this ghetto to the Okecie camp. Ironically enough, these were our deliverers.

We now had to clear the same checkpoint through which the doomed multitude consigned to slaughter was passing into the *Umschlagplatz*. The six of us formed a column, two abreast, with one guard on the right wing and the other one toward the rear. At the command "Forward march!" we moved forward in pairs, like kindergarten children, until we reached the gate of hell at Stafki Street. Our hearts were beating loudly; we were so close to the trains destined for eternity that it was only necessary for the SS men to say, "Well, your authority to take these men out is void. We act by a higher authority and these men must join the rest of the transport." The SS might readily have disregarded the fact that we were under guard by another authority of the Reich, because they considered lower echelon everyone who was not Gestapo or SS.

As it was, they were only rough with us; they found a watch on Kessel's wrist, beat him, and took the watch. Except for showing an order, the *Luftwaffe* guards did not say a word; perhaps they were too unnerved to argue. The "Angels of Death" had the death skulls on their insignia, announcing the fact that they were a "funeral" agency—the gravediggers of the Third Reich.

Leaving behind us a most unhappy place, we walked to the streetcar stop. Even here on the Aryan side, the street appeared to be off limits—not officially, but the people did not want to come close enough to see what was happening. Then our streetcar pulled out and turned onto a street where people were walking, newsboys were selling papers, and someone was stopping at a kiosk to buy a pack of cigarettes. There were taxis (horse-drawn cabs); there was traffic—a world of the living. It was like waking out of a nightmare into reality—but I wondered whether the nightmare was the reality and I was now dreaming.

But we were not dreaming when we arrived at the camp and were put into the barracks. Here we would be interned, and this started a new phase in my life at Okecie. I never saw my grandmother, two aunts, and the children again. Perhaps they lived until the final action in the ghetto, marked by the armed resistance, but I have no way of knowing.

By this time I was no longer corresponding with anyone—not with Gina, and not with Uncle Mietek, who still remained in the ghetto. I had to struggle to survive right where I was.

The food at Okecie was good only for losing weight. The diet differed very little from that of Bielany, but the opportunities for trade that had existed at Bielany were not at first appearent to me at Okecie. Being a newcomer, I was assigned to the worst job that the Jewish camp leader had to delegate. I was sent again to work on the airfield. The howling winds on that open area in January were wicked, and again I was without any winter clothing. Gloves were essential to keep your hands from freezing. Any sores on your hands hurt worse in the biting cold.

Even though it wasn't legally permissible, the prisoners would sometimes offer to help pilots carry their baggage and often got something from them. On one occasion I carried a bag for a pilot and when we came to the point beyond which I was not permitted to pass, he astonished me by taking off his fur-lined leather gloves and handing them to me. Of course, I was grateful, but I was afraid that if items of German military issue were found on me, they would be considered stolen. So I took the gloves and covered them with rags.

Suffering from hunger, I began to scheme how I could help myself in this situation. Then I observed what the others were doing: they were stealing coal from the yard at the airfield boiler plant and taking it out in sacks carried on their backs. Our barracks was outside the airfield; once we had cleared the gate, we were able to dispose of our "hot" coal in exchange for food or money. Of course, a "collection" was taken for the guards, which persuaded them to stop in the business district and allow us to dispose of the coal. The transaction usually took place in one of the grocery stores, where we could use the money to buy some food. The cheapest and most sought-after commodity was potatoes. Periodically we were searched, and someone would get whipped. But if we observed that the group ahead of us was being frisked, we would drop our coal right on the pavement as we marched so that when we reached the gate, they would find nothing on us.

After a cold day's work in the open, I really looked forward to returning to the barracks. Once we got there, the lights went on. Soon the crackling of the smuggled kindling wood could be heard in the potbelly stove, and the barracks came alive with the voices of men warming up their bodies by the heat of the stove. On the days we managed to get our contraband past the gate and convert it into food, we felt very fortunate. Those who had potatoes or something else to cook would busy themselves peeling and cooking. Eating, needless to say, was the reward of all these labors.

Men walked from one room to another to see someone, to borrow something, to wash up. Wet socks and wet clothes came off and were hung above the stoves to dry. Someone stirred food in a pot. While all this prenocturnal activity went on, enlivened conversation could be heard about the day's events. From the simple to the intellectual, ours was a spirited group.

"How did you manage to get your coal out?" was a frequently asked question.

"I let him search my sack and hid a few pieces of coal in my pants (tied at the bottom)—and you?"

"After yesterday's shakedown, they doubled the guards—our group got nothing through. My buddy tried to get by with a few horse beets and got clobbered by the guard.

"I heard one of the guards griping about the food rationing in Germany; what do you suppose this means?"

"It means to me that before the fat will become lean, the lean will drop dead—that's us".

The sound of spoons scraping against the metal mess gear was interrupted by animated conversation about the progress of the war and the latest rumors from the Warsaw ghetto.

There were a few pairs of brothers among us and a father and son interned together, but most of us by now were unrelated orphans and we had to adjust to the changed circumstances of our solitary existence. We made do with new acquaintances and comradeship. After all, we had much in common. Besides sharing the same miserable lot, most

of us were young men between sixteen and twenty-five. We were all
Polish Jews from Warsaw, pressed into bondage by the Third Reich,
and we were all in the risky business of survival.

There was something about those men that made them memorable. I believe it was their optimism and their will to live. Mocny's record
of escape from other camps and trains bound for the Treblinka death
factory evoked quiet admiration from most of us.

Adam and Bolek Goldman were a smuggling team. Actually,
smuggling does not accurately describe the activity in which many of
us were engaged, but they did it much better than most. Handsome,
twentyish, with the cheerful good looks of a Warsaw sharpie, Adam
could tell jokes when he was in the mood, but his business was no
laughing matter. Bolek was not as high-spirited as his brother but he
was a good teammate; he lacked a mustache and his brother's flair for
nutty humor, but he seemed to regard Adam as Dr. Watson did Sherlock Holmes. With the help of his obliging brother, Adam could, if
given a chance, steal a wagonload of coal. How they did it was something of a mystery, but it had to involve a cut from the proceeds to the
German wagon driver.

Joel Warszawski, a strapping six-footer, and his equal-in-weight
brother stuck to "retail sales." Licht, the Jewish camp leader, was the
sharp fellow who had recruited most of us for this camp. He was
stocky, of medium height, and justifiably proud of having saved lives
by getting us out of the ghetto without taking bribes. Harry Bronstein
and his inseparable friend "Shorty" Wroclaw had the shoemaking
concession here. Wroclaw knew the trade, making shiny boots for the
men in the *Luftwaffe*, and Bronstein bluffed his way along. They did not
have to worry about food, because Wroclaw's skill and service pleased
his customers.

Bespectacled Morris Wyszogrod, the first-rank artist I've already
mentioned, could make a sharp portrait from a photograph. For this he
enjoyed a privileged existence, and his work enabled him to keep his
lame brother Paul from doing hard work. Freudlich, one of the group
leaders, was true to his name, very friendly and cheerful even in times
of trouble. A sardonic fellow in his late forties named Wierzbicki was a
bon vivant and a storyteller, sometimes relating his own adventures
compiled over the years.

An English teacher named David Grynberg pursued his studies
while most of us were interested mainly in food, and we even had a
young rabbi named Mordecai Glatstein, who every morning with a
friendly manner looked for the tenth man so that the required *minyan*,
or quorum, could pray together. With his brother present, he always
managed. The bunk next to mine was occupied by David Rosental, a
young fellow of about twenty-two with a shock of curly black hair and

matching eyes. Quiet-spoken and friendly, he made a good neighbor and was good to talk with in the evenings.

Sometimes we would sit around and pass the evening in talking about happier days in the past, trying to forget the events in the Ghetto. Three Szeinberg brothers, all of them blond and blue-eyed, were typical Warsaw smart alecks and quite entertaining.

When we gathered around, we sat on beds talking about the war and the progress of the Allies and our own fate in this particular camp, and anything else that came to mind, especially the news from the Russian front. The Russians, after many reverses, forced the issue at Stalingrad where, after savage and heroic fighting, a whole German army surrendered.

Such news forecast their eventual defeat sooner, and encouraged us to fight on, living and hoping to finish this journey on our feet. The duration of war with Russia gave birth to jokes like this: "Have you heard Hitler's written a new book entitled, "Der Zehnjaehrige Blitzkrieg mit der Soviet Union" ("Ten Years Blitz War with the Soviet Union")?

Occasionally we were entertained by singing or by story telling.

As the evening wore on, one could hear talk in subdued voices. Here and there a cigarette glowed; the sounds grew fainter, and the lights went out; it was night.

The thing that I didn't look forward to was the morning, when we had to file out in the cold to get back to work at the airfield. I dreaded this time mainly because I wasn't dressed for the job. As I worked in the cold, my thoughts again turned to some sort of stratagem whereby I could obtain warm clothing. The amount of coal that we could steal barely paid for food; it did not allow for such luxuries as clothes.

On one of the many blustery mornings, as we marched to the Okecie airfield, we saw a large contingent of troops looking different from those we knew. Of dark complexion, rather short, wearing ill-fitting uniforms, they looked out of place here. Oh, these poor devils were really cold! They kept pacing around and slapping their hands against their arms to warm up. The language they spoke was not familiar, but we soon learned that they were Italians, troops whom Mussolini was sending to the Russian front. They had a layover at Okecie airfield en route, waiting to board the huge Junker-made planes. These six-engine planes could carry about 160 fully equipped men. I did not envy these soldiers, for the Russian front was no picnic for the Germans; how much less so for the Italians, who were not used to such a cold climate?

The miseries of war did occasionally give way to lighter moments. I recall that working around the airfield we had occasion to witness the

Germans drilling a battalion of short-statured Mongolians clad in green uniforms, trying to teach them drills, commands, and even the Nazi salute. The poor fellows showed no aptitude for discipline, yet every day they were drilled during certain hours. The rest of the time they worked digging ditches and doing road repairs. These Kalmukies, as they were called, many from Asiatic Russia, had been taken prisoner during the initial onslaught of the German Army. Since they were neither Communists nor Fascists—nor anything political, really—the Germans thought they would put them to practical use and get some work out of them, as well as improve their military style.

Later, to honor some German military brass visiting the base, there was a parade of an assortment of uniformed formations based at the airfield. When their turn came, the Kalmukies came marching before the grandstand with their hands slipped into opposite sleeves in order to keep warm. A few of them were puffing on cigarette butts, and all were out of step. In response to their German leader's shouted "Eyes right!" some ranks broke up, while one man ran to the road ditch and relieved himself for all to see. This of course upset the German sense of order, but the Kalmukies seemed totally oblivious to the effect of their performance on the stomachs of their masters. (Perhaps they had only been putting on an act.)

Aside from freezing at work, everything was going reasonably well when, unfortunately, I was transferred to another department. The new post to which I was assigned had the high-sounding name of *Junkers Front Motoren—Reperatur zerlege Betrieb*, Junkers Aircraft Company—front motors repair, dismantling division. We would go outside to the railroad siding and climb over the boxcars on which damaged German aircraft were brought in from Germany and other areas where they had been shot down. We were dismantling all the parts, but our particular department was concerned with machine-gun turrets. This, of course, meant tighter security; it also meant that there was nothing to steal except guns, and no smugglers—or so I thought. The work in the new department was less fatiguing, but there was no way to obtain food. It seemed high time to try to get back to the ghetto and see what I could raise there.

Again, I requested permission through the ranking Jewish *Lager Alteste* (camp elder) to speak to the authorities and thus got permission to go to the ghetto under escort. This time, however, I didn't intend to make a run for it. I only wanted to see Uncle Mietek and solicit his help, if he should still be there.

A young *Luftwaffe* soldier accompanied me as far as my uncle's apartment building on Zamenhofa Street and consented to wait for me. On my way up I ran into some of my uncle's neighbors. When they saw me, they looked bewildered at the sight of my bizarre attire. I was still wearing the same formal evening jacket, now tattered and dirty. One of them took more than a casual interest in me, and after asking a few questions about my internment camp and my relationship with my uncle, he seemed somewhat upset.

"How come you are wearing rags when your uncle is well-dressed and seems to be doing all right for himself? Isn't he your flesh and blood? Shouldn't he help you?"

"But he will!" I protested.

The man continued: "I will talk some sense into him."

I thanked him for his concern but refused his help and decided to handle this on my own.

When my uncle opened the door, I could see that my coming had taken him by surprise. He said he didn't know what had become of my mother's side of the family; he had serious doubts as to whether they were still around. No sooner had we exchanged a few words, though, when the sound of two gunshots made us rush to the window looking out on the corner of Zamenhofa and Niska Streets. There, lying near the gutter's edge, was the corpse of a well-clad man wearing highly polished riding boots.

"They got another informer," said Uncle Mietek.

I recognized the man as someone I had seen before on our street in the early ghetto days. Someone must have pointed him out as an informer. His conspicuously new, expensive clothing was typical of those who were prospering under the German occupation and set him apart from the rest of us in our shabby prewar attire. At last the day of reckoning had come for him. Strangely enough, the Germans seemed indifferent to this kind of internal purge. Moments later, men surrounded the corpse. Someone pulled off his high boots, others took most of his clothing. The hearse came along and collected the remains. The shooting of informers by other Jews seemed to be an organized effort.

When this episode was over, Uncle Mietek asked what had brought me there, and I told him that I needed some clothes and help.

He said, "Well, Yurek, really I can't give you any help; I am not in too good a position myself." I looked around and saw that my uncle was doing fairly well, and he didn't look undernourished, but I didn't know what to say. So he said, "Have something to eat before you go." Though at the moment it was the safer place, the camp at best was coarse compared to this city dwelling and its few refinements. A thought flashed through my mind: my uncle had been selling the substantial stock of new shoes that my father, at risk to his life, had hidden. I felt a throbbing pain in my chest: I was grieved that my uncle was so detached and unfeeling. He was treating me as if I were a casual aquaintance to whom he had no obligation and for whom he had no feeling of kinship.

Naturally, I felt frustrated, and I was on the verge of crying. Instead, I controlled myself and said, "I know that you have been living off the shoes that my father hid, risking his life. You were the one who survived, and you were the one who brought them out of the old hiding place. Selling this merchandise has kept you going. Now why won't you help me? I feel you should."

This angered my uncle very much and he said, "How dare you talk to me like this! Get out!"

I said, "No, I am not going to get out until you help me."

Uncle Mietek became even angrier. He opened the door wide and shouted, "Get out." But I wouldn't leave. In a highly emotional state, he took me by my shoulders, and we got into a scuffle; I disengaged his hold on me and threw him on the couch. In silence we looked at each other. I felt ashamed that it had to come to this, and my uncle also had second thoughts.

He said, "What is happening? Why wouldn't I want to help you? You are my brother's son. You are the little boy I used to pamper and take everywhere on trips. You were the boy to whom I gave movie money every Sunday, and you were the one for whom I bought the first two-wheeler bicycle. And now you have raised your hand against your uncle. How could you do it?" He sounded hurt.

I stood there in silence and lowered my head; I may have cried—I don't remember. But my uncle was deeply moved. He walked over to his closet and found a leather jacket among the clothes hanging there: "Try this for size."

I tried it and it fitted me well. He also gave me a sweater, another jacket, a cap, and some items that I could sell. I said, "I wish this had never happened. Everything you said is true." Before leaving, I asked, "Why don't you come with me?"

But Uncle Mietek shook his head sadly: "I can't—what about my wife?" Irka had actually stood in a far corner of the room and witnessed the entire scene. (I somehow never thought of her as his real wife because his first wife, Renia, had been killed by German troops in Slonim in November 1941.)[3] He walked over and stretched out his hands toward me; I came closer and we embraced each other. Then I turned around and left.

When the guard saw me downstairs, he didn't even recognize me. In my new leather jacket and cap, I could have walked right past him.

"Well," he said, after making a positive identification, "you certainly have a good uncle who is willing to help you. By the way, did you see the shooting?"

"No, I only heard shots."

At the gate the SS men examined the pass and motioned us to go. With my new "capital" in clothing, things began to look up a bit.

After three years of German occupation; the hardships and uncertainties we had endured had turned teenagers like me into men in many respects, except one: a feeling of loss for the unfulfilled promises of youth, with all the romantic notions that the thought implies. Here we were, most of us compelled to work in forced-labor gangs in order to survive, separated from our families and friends without prospects of ever seeing them again. All that we had left were memories of the different and better life we had once known. But the luxury of reminiscing and yearning for what we had lost was reserved for special moments. My thoughts of home turned into visions of my parents and brothers in the evening just before my tired body gave way to sleep. Often I thought of Gina and Lublin. On Sabbaths and Jewish holidays these reveries stirred painful sensations; I could hear the cantor and Warsaw Synagogue choir singing beautiful psalms while I watched my father, looking thoughtful, engrossed in prayer. The scene of our family sitting together around the table, enjoying the Sabbath meal, singing, hearing my father read portions of the Bible to us about our great heritage had always been a moving one; now, lost, it was more precious than ever.

Rumor had it that the SS extermination brigade had once again arrived in Warsaw, and there was increasing unrest in the ghetto. Something was brewing. One afternoon, while I was at work, I saw the plant guards arresting one of our group leaders, a man named Fulde. A tall, handsome young man, he was charged with stealing a machine gun and was taken to the adjacent department, where a Polish woman employed there fingered him. He did not live to see the light of another day. Unbeknownst to most of us, the ghetto was getting some help from within our camp. Like a battered army scraping its men and resources together for the final stand, the men of the Warsaw ghetto were preparing to die with honor. Very little was known outside about the preparations.

The determination to resist took hold and was first tested on January 19, 1943. On that date an SS detachment was fired upon when it entered the ghetto to start yet another day of "Operation Resettlement." Taken by surprise, the SS men withdrew, taking with them twenty-odd casualties. The news of this incident was suppressed by the Germans at the time, but the deportation action was cut short, netting only about 6,000 Jews.

April 18 was a nice clear day. The scent of spring was in the air, but for some it was a spring of despair. The remnant of the Warsaw ghetto

Jews were about to observe the Passover to commemorate the Jewish redemption from Egyptian tyranny. But where were the children to ask the traditional four questions, starting with "Why is this night different from all other nights?" Ordinarily, those present respond with the story of the Egyptian bondage and liberation, but that night the lives of the celebrants hung in doubt. I thought of my eight-year-old brother Meir. On this Passover of 1943, Meir asked no questions. The Nazis had answered him with their "Final Solution." For most of the Jewish children who had somehow managed to survive the 1942 "resettlement" action, when most of Warsaw Jewry had been shipped to the death camps of Treblinka, this was to be their last Passover. They were doomed.

On April 19, 1943, the Germans launched a full-scale operation to liquidate the remnants of the Warsaw ghetto. We were still working at our posts when the news came. They had struck like lightning, but this time there was something new: the Jews had put up armed resistance, and there were German casualties. With homemade grenades, a smuggled-in assortment of pistols and rifles—often held in the hands of teenagers—the Jews met and confronted their mortal enemies.

In a few days I saw planes taking off from the Okecie airfield to bomb the Warsaw ghetto. I was on a work detail around the airfield when I saw one returning plane land. The moment it stopped, the ground crew ran over to help the pilot out of the cockpit. As he walked across the field, he pulled out a handkerchief, wiped his forehead, and spat on the ground. By that time, I was within listening range.

"Verfluchte noch einmal! Der ganze Platz brent bis der Himmel" he exclaimed (Damn it again! The whole place burns up to Heaven).

That evening after work, even at our distance from Warsaw, we could see billows of smoke rising above the ghetto, and a bright reddish glow hovered over it after nightfall. But the fight went on, and the German-controlled Polish press, which in the beginning had made no mention of this memorable event, suddenly gave it front-page space. Still, the Jews of Warsaw could not stop the might of the German armies any more than their ancestors, nineteen centuries earlier, could prevail against the Roman legions. They fought and died.

If there was to be one ray of hope for help, it had to come from the other side of the ghetto—from our Christian brothers. But that was not to be.[4] While the fighters in the ghetto put up a desperate battle, the Polish underground—according to later unconfirmed reports—delayed sending messages to London for help, lest the fight in the ghetto "overshadow" the importance of their own activity.[5] Nevertheless, the Germans considered Jewish resistance important enough to broadcast the action. Surely, many of us thought, London would support the valiant but desperate effort and would airlift the needed arms and supplies. Most of the fighters were inexperienced youths; even their commander, Mordechai Anilewicz, was only twenty-four years old. Without artillery or a single tank, the Jews held out longer than some countries did during the early blitz.

Finally unable to crush the resistance, the Germans resorted to the incendiary bombing of building after building. As the battle ran its expected course, our people were fighting, burning, and dying in the ruins of what had once been my city. The ordeal that began with the closing of the wall around the ghetto in November 1940 was nearing its final act. After three weeks of fighting, much of the ghetto lay in smoldering ruins.[6] The defenders yielded to the overwhelming preponderance of the enemy.

Even then, individual group resistance continued for some time. The SS men and their dogs marched in, hunting for survivors. The shooting of rebels and the deportations of the exhausted remnants were the last acts before dead silence fell on a desolate heap of rubble. And nothing came from London—no encouragement, not even a box of Band-Aids.

History relates that for all his scorn of the Jews, the Roman historian Tacitus had to admit that the war with the Jews was the most fateful in the annals of the Roman Empire. The conclusion forced itself upon me that the fierce German tormentors were not bulletproof either. The spirit of Warsaw spread among the Jews, who found and joined guerrilla and partisan groups, fighting the enemy wherever they could.

Personally, I was frustrated that I could not be with them; that spirit found its way into my heart and mind, and I felt an urge to be a part of this fight. Unable to do anything at that time, I resolved to live so that perhaps I could fight before all this was over. This was also the time when rumors began to circulate that our own camp would be liquidated in a matter of days.

And the rumors were true. We were told by the commandant that in a few days we would be shipped to "another camp." But we knew better, and some of the men—including Licht, our camp leader—had found places where they could hide. One fellow whose name, I believe, was Goldstein was going to be hidden in a cloister, disguised as a Catholic clergyman. The Luftwaffe guards were very "careless," for they permitted fourteen escapes. Whoever had a place to which he could run, did so.

But most of us had no place to run. As the time grew nearer, the men became more depressed. Whereas we had once been preoccupied mainly with thoughts of food, with the prospect liquidation no one felt like eating. The barracks were now extremely quiet. There was extreme sadness and foreboding, a fear of what lay ahead.

The day before deportation, however, with camp security being tightened, Moshe Kessel—a group leader whom I admired but with whom I had few dealings up to that time—approached me: "I have the money and you know your way around. Let us escape."

I was immediately for it. We planned to disappear that last evening. But the other prisoners, alarmed because they were afraid of repercussions, did something unusual: they took away our shoes until morning to ensure that we would not try to escape. In a way this was their plea that we should share their fate. It now looked as if we were all going to travel together at the Third Reich's expense.

7 A Trip through Eternity

*Though I walk through the valley of the shadow of
death, I will fear no evil, for Thou art with me.*
—Psalm 23

On a cloudless morning on May 10, 1943, a group of eighty-eight men
stood outside their barracks. They took no baggage save some food.
Ordinarily, a beautiful morning in May would have evoked some cheer
even among prisoners, but this group was not going on an excursion or
even to work. We were consigned to the SS authority at the *Umschlagplatz*—destination unknown. Only gloom hung in the air, accompanied by a conspicuous silence.

On the last day of work the *Luftwaffe* guards as well as our volunteer
Belgian supervisors (who had come to work in German industry),
knew what was up; they looked at us as people look at someone just
sentenced to death. Slowly we formed a column and filed into streetcars reserved for us. The guards took positions on the rear platform
and gave a signal to go.

The fearful prospects of this trip should have made me indifferent
to my surroundings, but I could not help being aware of the pronounced contrasts. This beautiful warm, sunny May morning contrasted with the ugly fate we suspected awaited us. The trees along
both sides of the street showed their fresh green leaves. A man was
watering budding flowers on a tiny plot of ground. A woman walked
out of a store with milk and groceries for her household. Life seemed to
be awakening to the promise of another spring day.

As we neared the ghetto, the panorama of the living side of town
diminished in the distance. The streetcar stopped not far from the gate
of the once wall-in city, now a smoldering ruin. Prompted off the cars,
we formed a column, five abreast, and continued on foot to the gate,
where several helmeted SS guards stood brandishing automatic rifles
and hand grenades. "*Viefel?*" ("How many?") the SS man in charge
shouted to the *Luftwaffe* sergeant.

"*Acht und achzigh*" (eighty-eight) came back the reply.

We were briskly counted by the guard and ordered to pass
through. We now saw for ourselves what the ghetto had become: just
brick, debris, and of skeletal remains of burned buildings; there was
not a single tree, shrub, or blade of grass to be seen. Amid the smoldering ruins, helmeted SS men in full combat gear, accompanied by dogs,

were everywhere. Occasionally shots were heard in the distance. The SS were busy mopping up the area; the dogs were used to lead them to anyone still hidden in a bunker. They would either smoke the survivors out or blow them out.

I was unable to recognize the streets we were passing, but as we turned a corner, I could see the *Umschlagplatz*. A large group of Jewish survivors directly ahead of us were entering the compound platform, and we were halted, waiting for them to be processed. They were ordered to turn our way, kneel, and lay out all their possessions in front of them. It was not until they faced us that I noticed their thin faces, their hollow cheeks, and a pallor of death that sent pity and fear trembling through my heart. Several wounded men had blood-stained linens covering head wounds. The women and children were too tired and dirty to bemoan their hopeless predicament. Unlike their predecessors of earlier deportations, these men and women were not lamenting or showing any visible demonstrations of self-pity. Only the children looked frightened and sought comfort in the arms of their parents.

While others were already packed into wagons, the group ahead of us was led into a boxcar. Now it was our turn to walk in. The SS man in charge counted our ranks by touching each shoulder with a looped bullwhip, then transferred the whip to his left hand and signed the receipt for eighty-eight heads. I looked after our hastily departing *Luftwaffe* guards with sadness and wondered if turning us over to our executioners caused them to feel any shame or pity.

Since we had been delivered by another military branch of the Reich, the SS did not bother to frisk us but ordered us to board the boxcar. I took one final look around and thought that after all my breaks and schemes to avoid this dreaded place into which I had seen so many others dragged, my turn had come at last.

Ours was the last boxcar, and since there was no more cargo for this transport, we had it to ourselves. We could stand without pressing against each other. Some of us could sit bunched up. This was not bad; the cars ahead of us had 150 or more people each. Before they rolled the door closed, a black-uniformed Ukrainian guard took a position on top of the train, manning a machine gun. The gun muzzle faced the rear of the train to put the gunner in the line of sight with anyone breaking out.

Once the train began to move and the initial shock wore off, the silence was soon broken. Someone suggested that we take turns at the small windows to get air. Then someone else encouraged us not to despair, at least not until we knew where we were being taken. This opened up an avenue of discussion that led to a resolution expressed in approximately these words: "We know that in the past transports were occasionally shipped to labor camps, of which there are many around. If the train is heading for Treblinka, we might as well try to jump, because there is nothing to lose. But on the other hand, if we are heading in another direction, there is still hope. The thing to do is to determine where we are heading."

Maybe because I claimed to be more familiar with the two lines branching off from Warsaw, it fell to me to make a positive identification. I stood at the little windows and kept looking for familiar sights or the name of a passing station that would provide the answer. The train was now moving at forty to fifty kilometers per hour, and we had been traveling for about a quarter of an hour. Since Urle and Srodborow were both twenty-five to thirty kilometers away from Warsaw, one in each direction, it was a matter of minutes before we would know which it was going to be: Srodborow was on the line to Lublin; Urle meant Treblinka.

I kept looking hard and all I saw were telephone poles moving in the opposite direction and trees. Suddenly I knew we had just passed Otwock. Next I caught a glimpse of a tiny railroad station, and moments later the tall pines gave way to a clearing that exposed a two-story structure. I kept my eyes on it until it disappeared from sight. It was without a doubt my childhood playground; the villa that had once belonged to my grandparents.

"Friends," I said, "we have just passed Srodborow."

"Are you sure?" several voices asked in chorus.

"Yes, I ought to be. I spent many happy summers in that house when I was a child. Besides, you all know that Otwock is also 'on the Line.'"[1] Meanwhile, two men had been cutting an opening in the floor in order to pry open a floorboard as an alternate exit for escape. If we had to jump, using the door would require someone to reach or squeeze out through the small window opening to snip the wire seal so that we could roll the door open. Under cover of darkness, the opening of the doors might not attract immediate attention, but in daylight, when the train was slowing down, the floor seemed to be the choice. Once one board was pried loose, the adjacent boards would go more easily.

But for the time being, all our efforts stopped because our hopes rose again that we were headed toward a work camp instead of the gas chamber. Before noon the train halted outside a station to give priority to another train. I looked out the window and saw an old Polish peasant standing opposite the track embankment. He was shaking his head with a somber expression, as though he were watching the funeral of one of his neighbors. After a good while, a freight train overtook us. Then another train passed before ours resumed chugging along.

By noon the heat in the car had become almost unbearable, and our water supply was all gone except for one bottle belonging to an old man and his twenty-five-year-old son. An hour later the old man reached for his bottle. Everyone stared at him as he was about to remove the cork. The old man slowly turned about, reading the anguish on the faces surrounding him.

"Well," he said, his kindly eyes getting slightly moist, "I see, my son, that we will have to share this water with all our friends. Give me a tablespoon." Holding his spoon in one hand, the old man poured it three-quarters full for each person, as if giving medicine. He started with the oldest men and finished with the youngest.

As the sun set and darkness fell, the train, after stopping several more times, moved along its prearranged course. Men talked to one another in hushed voices because of exhaustion and thirst. My mouth felt dry and I longed for water as I never had before. Drops of sweat were rolling down my face. There was bread in the car, but no one touched it because we were too parched to eat. Our strength was gone, and everyone began to slide down to the floor. By arranging our bodies in such a way as to allow one fellow to lean on the next one's side, curling up a bit, we were all able to rest in a partially sitting position.

I had just dozed off when, with a sudden jerk, the train came to a stop. I stood up and looked out, but I saw nothing except another pair of tracks under a few pole lights. The locomotive disengaged itself from the front car and passed by to the rear on the parallel tracks. Minutes later, the engine was pushing the train slowly ahead.

Someone from the floor spoke out: "Where are we?"

"I don't know yet," I answered.

The engine was very slowly pushing the train through a break in a massive masonry wall exposed by dim lights focused on it. After the train came to a halt, the engine disengaged itself and withdrew. Floodlights went on, surrounding the train platform. The guards took positions at the two far corners of the platform. Two more guards did the same on the other side.

Despite the artificial lighting, it was a dark, depressing view. All we could see was the wall, a wide platform, and boxcars ahead of us, now illuminated. When the train stopped, we began to hear the groans of women and the crying of children, begging for air and water, but the guards were merely annoyed by the wailing and now and then they yelled out "*Halt die Schnauze*" (Hold your snout).

All of a sudden the doors to one of the cars rolled open, and a man ran out on the side opposite the platform. Confronted by the guards, he began to run in and out between the cars, appearing alternately on either side of the train. The guards on both sides started after him, shouting instructions to one another. A shot rang through the air, then another. They chased him like a game rabbit and finally caught him in their rifle fire. Wearing only a shirt and trunks, he lay on the platform, his thin bare legs stretched out, his face up to the direct glare of the floodlights. Blood ran fast from his throat; steam evaporated from his open mouth as though freeing his spirit. His ordeal was ended. The guards ignored him and again took up their positions.

The macabre scene we had just witnessed shattered our hopes that we were headed to a work camp, and a wave of fear reached a new height.

Morning came very slowly. At the break of dawn, panic began to mount. Hanoch, the brother of the rabbi in our group, began to cry, saying that he was only twenty-one years old and why must he die so young. A few others joined this unbearable sobbing. The young rabbi began to say the prayer before dying. As the words poured out of his mouth, the tears ran down his cheeks. The whole scene was so unnerving that it began to sap what little stamina we still had.

Eventually someone reproached this self-pitying choir in unmistakable terms. "Stop it!" yelled those who still had not given up hope. "Enough! Why the devil do you cry about being twenty or twenty-one when there are boys here not yet twenty."

Silence and calm eventually prevailed. The sound of barking dogs and the sight of whip-wielding stormtroopers heralded the new day. We heard the snipping of wire followed by a rolling sound, and the door of our car was opened.[2] Before we got out, someone said, "Whatever comes, let's stick together." I was one of the last to get out, and as I looked back, there on the floor of the car lay two hand grenades. The nearest SS man saw them but made no fuss—a bad sign, because unless we were considered as good as dead already, the possession of weapons was one of the most serious offenses.

A Jewish crew, clinically clean, arrived to drag the dead out of the cars. My attention was caught by the sight of the body of a young woman being hauled out and laid on the stack of other corpses. Slowly we cleared the platform, at which point two columns of SS formed on either side of us, guarding the procession. The Jewish people working here would not talk to us, but their terror-stricken glances were meaningful enough. The heat and thirst were making everyone beg for water. The women outside the doomed column brought us water. It seemed then that water was all I wanted. A young SS guard walking beside us asked me, "How old are you?"

"Eighteen years old."

"Only eighteen? I am nineteen. A pity that you must die," he said quietly. I did not answer. Instead, I tried to control my terror. Looking at the neat, silent, Jewish crew did not help. It was like being a dying patient who sees only glances of pity and fear from the hospital staff.

The more these people subdued their emotions and gave no sign or hint of what awaited us, the more convinced we were of the inevitability of death. I began to pray, and the Hebrew words of one of our most frequently recited psalms came to me: *Ashrey . . . yoshvey . . . beysehah . . .* "Happy are they that dwell in Thy house. . . . They will be ever praising Thee. . . . Happy is the people that is thus favored. . . . Happy is the people whose God is the Lord"—a Psalm of David. Continuing, I simply resorted to Polish prose, pleading for rescue, not thinking of the irony or the significance of the prayer.

While our Okecie group kept together, there were many stragglers behind us. A high-ranking SS officer, the camp's commandant Sturbannfuerer (Major) Florstedt, was standing on the side overlooking the daily haul. He was flanked by SS *Obersturmfuehrer* Thumann.[3] Morris Wyszogrod saw his opportunity and ran ahead, standing at attention before the SS officer, reporting his profession as an artist. With a crack of the bullwhip, the assistant had Morris's neck wrapped in it. A sharp jerk had him licking the dust.

At this precise moment, only ten paces before reaching the spot where the commandant stood, Kessel took the initiative and urged us to close ranks and march in step. He ran ahead and, in perfect German, reported a group of *fein Flugzeug Mechaniker* (first-class airplane mechanics) from the Junkers works. He had a sheet of paper in his hand.

The *Obersturmfuehrer* was raising his whip when the SS chief raised his hand. This not only saved Kessel from the lash but was a signal to halt the procession. The big one took the paper and read its contents. It was a letter from the *Luftwaffe* commandant testifying that this group had worked in the Junkers Aircraft Plant—Dismantling Division.

Pharaoh spoke, and his command was as unexpected as the gesture he had just made: "Separate the Okecie group from the rest."

The two rows of SS men moved ahead, closing behind those in front of us and leaving us behind. So they separated the living from the dead. However, a couple of SS guards were picking up stray women and children from behind us, and something heartbreaking took place. Two little children who had apparently lost their father in the crowd latched on to one of our men, crying, "Daddy, Daddy." The guards ordered all three to rejoin the people ahead of us. When our man complained that these were not his children, the SS man tore them away from him and rushed them to the doomed group where their real father was.

We were then ordered to sit down by a barracks wall. In the confusion we lost one of our men, but his son remained; in addition, about seventy others who had happened to linger behind with us were saved. It was then that the Jewish clinical staff were finally allowed to talk to us. The substance of their information was that we were in the camp of Plage and Laszkiewicz, which was the entry compound to the gas chambers of the infamous Majdanek. Of all the Warsaw transports that had passed through, we were a rare exception, the only ones saved as a group. As they put it (in Yiddish): *"Breedeloch me hot eich arois-qezoygen fun dem oyven."* "Brothers, you were pulled out of the ovens." There was no rejoicing, only rest—and all the water one could drink. Florstedt, a big, beefy hunk of a man, returned to the compound, confronted us, and said in an official tone, "Tomorrow you are going to a camp where you will work in an airplane factory. If you will work, you will eat!" Striking his boot with a swagger stick, he walked away.

The sun was high as I sat propped against the wall of the barracks, squinting at its brightness. All that had just happened was too enormous to comprehend. My thoughts about this miraculous survival were incoherent, except that we, unlike so many others, had been spared. The other people who had just been walking through this square were gone; it was empty now except for some blankets, dolls, shoes, and a walking cane. A cart stopped, and two camp inmates gathered all the belongings into it, leaving only fine dust over the hard-packed dirt.

How strange it was, I thought, while the papers herald great battles, report war casualties, and recount the bombardment of strategic targets—here, away from the noise of war, seemingly hidden from the eyes of the world, stands a monstrous giant of a plant, meticulously perfected for mass human extermination! One had to give the Nazis credit for being so ingeniously practical. As we learned later, nothing was to be wasted: hair was used for stuffing mattresses; gold teeth went to the Reich's bank; clothing and shoes were shipped back to Germany. Fat, if any, yielded soap; bones were crushed and ground for high-calcium fertilizer. The rest was burned to ashes. "Is not modern science wonderful?" I stood up and silently said a prayer.

After what seemed like a long wait, we were given something to eat and shown to the barracks for the night. Besides the inmates who worked here, there were also Jewish POWs from the Polish army. Strangely enough, they were still wearing army uniforms and were working on various details in the city, driving trucks and the like. Rows of barracks divided by bare ground were all I saw as dusk fell on this terrifying place. A mournful, eerie silence pervaded the descending darkness.

Once in the barracks, I took off my shoes, put them under my rolled pants, and used this as a pillow. Taking my place on a triple-decker cot, I covered myself with the jacket I wore. Across the aisle the upper deck was occupied by the former Polish soldiers, and an incredible scene was taking place: an army man was entertaining a guest up on his cot—a woman. He was serving her white bread with butter and a bottled beverage. They ate, drank, and conversed in hushed voices as though in the privacy of their home. Just about then the lights went out. How could they enjoy such frivolity with death lurking about us and the blood of the innocent still boiling in crematorium ovens? I found this *tête-à-tête* utterly repugnant, a desecration of a place hallowed by the daily sacrifices of thousands of innocent lives. Perhaps I did not consider then that people confronting death seek comfort wherever they can find it.

Anger gave way to the sleep of sheer exhaustion. Too soon, I was awakened by loud voices. I opened my eyes and listened to an SS man shouting:

"Pass Maal auf! Pass maal auf!" "Attention!. A woman was seen entering this barracks. Unless she voluntarily comes out and gives herself up, you will all fall out, and we will search the barracks!" Silence was the only response.

In a minute a whistle signaled the emptying of the barracks. Still in the darkness of night, prisoners were lined up five abreast against the wall of the building. While one henchman kept an eye on us, the other two went inside to find the woman. Minutes passed and they were still looking. After a long while the hunters emerged without their prey. Everyone was ordered back to the barracks. I did not know what had happened to the woman. I was too exhausted to care and fell asleep.

When morning came again, I pinched myself to make sure I was not just a spirit. The sun spread its warm radiance to welcome all who had lived to yet another day. For many, this would be the last sunrise; for our small group, this was the first day after the resurrection. We knew that for good or bad we were earmarked for work because we drew bread rations before being herded back into the boxcars—this time only fifty men to a car—and food was not wasted on nonproductive transports.

As the train gained speed, tongues loosened in talk about what we had just experienced, but soon our curiosity grew as to what our new destination would be like. So the old guessing game filled the rest of the traveling time. Although we were worn out from physical and mental strain, we had recovered from our terror-stricken daze. Most of us looked disheveled, tired, but somewhat hopeful. I could not put out of my mind Kessel's cool initiative, which had been instrumental in cheating the Angel of Death, and I thanked Providence for foiling our intended escape at Okecie so that all our friends but one, and about seventy people more, were saved. And there sat Kessel, poised and composed as though not conscious of having done anything extraordinary. His tight-lipped mouth and slightly pointed chin gave his face the look of determination that had struck me during our rescue from the Warsaw ghetto in January. Who but Kessel would have thought of obtaining a letter from the airfield's *Luftwaffe* commander before departure? He could have been no more than twenty years old. Beyond him sat Freudlich, who had emerged from it all with his characteristic grin. It was a smile not of gaiety but of quiet confidence. It was heartening to see, and it inspired the hope that we would live to see our executioners hanged.

8 Camp Budzyn

I will appoint terror over you.
—Leviticus 26:16

When the boxcar doors opened, a welcoming committee of black-uniformed Ukrainian guards eagerly met the new arrivals. Shouting commands in broken German and Ukrainian, then using rifle butts, they hurried us off the train. After a double count of heads, the column set off for the camp some distance away.

Our armed escorts reeked of wickedness and greed; they apparently enjoyed the uncurbed power they held over us and were going to make the worst possible use of it. Sure enough, on the way to the camp they charged into our ranks at will, beating us and robbing us of what little we had. Wedding rings went first. Wristwatches followed. Having the first crack at the newcomers, they were not going to let the opportunity slip through their hands or let someone else beat them to it.

While this terror was going on, we were marched on a dirt road through pinewoods. The country vacation surroundings, the smell of pines, the fresh country air, and a beautiful day in mid-May contrasted unbearably with our circumstances. Still hopeful that the camp might not be as bad as the welcome we had gotten, we looked ahead with apprehension mixed with curiosity.

Before this trip ended, I realized that these Ukrainian guards, in trying to emulate their German masters, were surpassing their teachers in cruelty.[1] En route they asked us to sing. When we met the request with silence, one pocked-faced guard demanded, *"Warum Jude nix singen?"* (In his imperfect German,—"Why Jew no sing?")

They slackened their reign of terror when we emerged from the wooded area and sighted a built-up settlement in the distance. It consisted of several red brick, multistory apartment buildings—not the sort of architecture one expects to see in the country. We soon learned that it was a German-Croatian settlement of people who worked at the camp's aircraft plant. Every time the black-uniformed guards gave an order in German it was followed by a customary curse in Ukrainian. As we reached the settlement we came to a road bearing left, and our guard snapped, *"Links!"* (left), coupled with a vulgar curse in Ukrainian.

Turning, we sighted Camp Budzyn about a quarter-mile distant. It did not resemble the *Luftwaffe* camps; this was a genuine SS camp, a fenced-in rectangle flanked by four towers, one at each corner. Looking out from the top of these were armed Ukrainian guards manning machine guns. Directly ahead was an entrance gate. A guardhouse on our right, across the road from a cluster of young pines and brush, was the last landmark as we stood outside the gates. Beyond the barbed wire stood a row of wooden barracks backed by a large open square. No bigger than a football field, the complex was surrounded by a belt of open country surrounded by pinewoods.[2]

The wooden towers gave this place the appearance of an early American stockade such as we had seen in the movies. Had it not been for the towers and the barbed wire, in this country setting you could easily have taken it for a summer camp.

Looking at us were the faces of earlier arrivals lined up behind the barbed-wire fence. Their curiosity was met by our apprehension as to what kind of treatment awaited us inside. After what we had been through, they couldn't surprise us, I thought to myself.

We foot-weary newcomers were halted at the gate while the sentry signaled the guardhouse of our arrival. The *Wachtmeister* came out and took a count, checking the number of men against a receipt; then he nodded to the sentry, and the gates of the camp were flung open to receive its newest residents. Above the gate there was a black sign on which white letters spelled *SS Waffen Arbeits Lager* (SS work camp), and "Arbeit Macht Frei" (work makes one free).

Once inside, our guards parked themselves around the camp perimeter, and we were met by a German SS noncom accompanied by Jews in Polish army uniforms. "Form a single line," he instructed us. "Put your hands out! Palms up! Run to the center where the *Oberscharfuehrer* [staff sergeant] will motion you to the left or right!"

Oberscharfuehrer Reinhold Feix, the camp commandant, stood in the middle of the empty square, sharing center stage with several guards and uniformed Jews. Along the path of our run stood some civilian Jewish policemen, some wielding whips. One by one we ran toward our commandant, showing both hands, and turned in the direction that his finger indicated. The majority were directed to the left; only a few old men were isolated on the right, one of whom had a few fingers missing.

Every club has its own peculiar way of initiating new members. I was willing to hope that the terror we had already experienced was an admission trial given only to newcomers. After all, we had been sent here to work in an aircraft plant, and obviously we couldn't do so if we were maimed or crippled by excessive beating. But the selection made everyone apprehensive, even though we tried to tell ourselves that the older men were to be assigned to lighter work.

Those of us suited for hard work were assembled on the left and ordered to wait for the commandant to address us. Of medium height, blond, with steel-cold colorless eyes and the glossy gaze of one accustomed to heavy drinking, Feix appeared restless. His expression was one of undisguised rancor, cruelty his strongest facial characteristic. Standing erect with legs apart, wearing polished boots, a pistol in an open holster, and a Mauser hanging from his neck, he seemed ready to make the welcoming address.

"You are fortunate to have come here. This is a good camp. Here you will work and get fed. Of course, if you expect to eat, you will have to work for it and as long as you work, you will get along fine. Now, it is prohibited to possess any silver, gold, money, or jewelry—therefore, if you turn it in now, you will not be punished." Just at this moment, someone moved in the ranks. Feix whipped out his gun and shot him on the spot, then resumed without a pause: "Now, when I finish speaking, I want you to turn in your valuables, such as gold, silver, diamonds, and currency."

"Come on," urged a tall, stooping, red-headed Jewish policeman, speaking in German. "You heard what the *Herr Oberscharfuehrer* said. Hand over the things and don't worry about anything. You will get along all right." Several men parted with some articles and money; then we were all frisked, but nothing more was found. The casualties so far were limited to one, a man who only yesterday had thought himself lucky to be saved from the Majdanek gas chamber.

Delousing and a bath were next on the agenda. Meanwhile, Feix was obliged to order the additional execution of "only" one of those separated during selection—the man with the missing fingers, who would presumably have presented a work problem. The others, we were told by the Jewish policemen, had a really good chance of being spared.

Hanging our clothing on racks in the dressing room, we stood naked. The Jewish crew under the supervision of a uniformed Jewish POW rolled the clothing racks into a steam compartment and closed the door tightly. Then, equipped with soap, we walked under the shower heads in an adjacent room. The POW in charge of delousing blew his whistle:

"Listen! You go under the shower, soap up, give the next man your soap, and get under the shower. When I blow the whistle, you step into the next room for your towels and clothing. You get dressed quickly. When I blow the whistle again, everyone falls out in formation. Get it?"

The whistle hung on a cord around his neck. He had a red face and foggy blue eyes. He wore high boots, and his general appearance testified to the fact that being the boss over the *Entlausung* bathhouse was a "good post" for a Jewish POW.

Those who got the soap cakes first looked up at the shower heads.

APPROXIMATE PLAN OF
SS CAMP BUDZYN

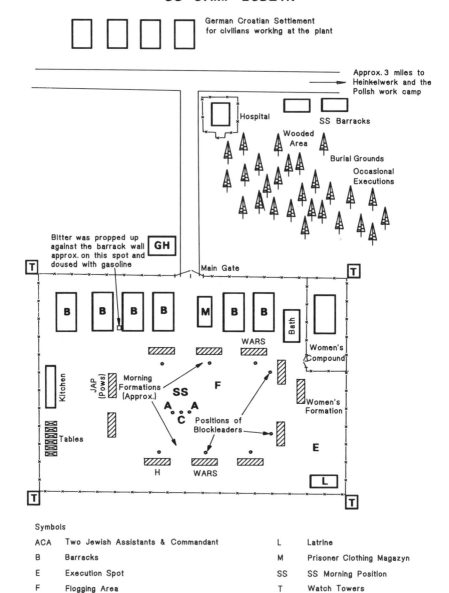

German Croatian Settlement
for civilians working at the plant

Approx. 3 miles to
Heinkelwerk and the
Polish work camp

Hospital

SS Barracks

Wooded
Area

Burial Grounds

Occasional
Executions

Bitter was propped up
against the barrack wall
approx. on this spot and
doused with gasoline

GH

Main Gate

T

T

B   B   B   B   M   B   B   Bath   Women's Compound

WARS   WARS

Kitchen

JAP (Pows)

Morning
Formations
(Approx.)

SS

A   A
C

F

WARS

Women's
Formation

Positions of
Blockleaders

E

Tables

H   WARS

L

T   T

Symbols

ACA	Two Jewish Assistants & Commandant	L	Latrine
B	Barracks	M	Prisoner Clothing Magazyn
E	Execution Spot	SS	SS Morning Position
F	Flogging Area	T	Watch Towers
GH	Guard House	WARS	Warsaw Group
JAP	Jewish-Polish Army Prisoners		

Source: Sketch based on one drafted by the author from memory

When, after a moment of waiting, warm water streamed down, all doubts were swept away. The feeling of the water cleansing my body made me for a moment forget all the cares of the world. At the sound of the whistle, we rushed to the dressing room, where we found our clothes on the racks—still very hot from the steam, which was the method for delousing here. Bathed, dressed, and hungry, we followed the sound of the whistle outside. Although the sun had set, it was not yet dark. The SS and Ukrainians were not visible within the *Appellplatz* (assembly grounds), to our temporary feeling of relief.

Lined up before the bath building, we faced a new personality with the customary whistle and an armband. This thirtyish, oxlike, stocky man with a meaty nose, heavy lips, and a long, drooping chin was our company leader. His armband gave no doubt that his official (inmate's) credentials were in order. Blowing the whistle hard, he called us to attention. "Come on. Stand at attention! At ease! I am your barracks company leader," announced this husky package. He walked up and down the front of the formation, surveying us as he continued: "My name is Majzels and the first thing I want you to know is that when I give orders, I expect you to obey them."

Suddenly he charged through the ranks and warned someone talking not to do so again while still in formation. "I don't want to repeat myself about this. You hear this! Before I show you to the barracks, we will go to the kitchen to get chow."

Facing the company again, he clicked his heels and ordered: "T-t-e-n-*tion!* L-e-f-t *face!* F-o-r-w-a-r-d *march!*" Lifting his knees high, our general marked time in place while his troops passed before him. He must have gotten his job for reasons other than his leadership ability, yet he took it seriously, not aware of his tragicomic effect.

At the far end of the square was the all-important kitchen. Anyone working there was lucky to be near food in this time of scarcity when the measure one received made the difference between life and death. Two lines of men were being served from the kitchen windows while we halted and waited.

"How many have you got?" yelled the chief cook, sticking his plump, red-cheeked face out of one window.

"One hundred and fifty-two, counting myself," responded Majzels snappily. (Yes, sir. A guy dare not rub the major source of life the wrong way.)

The kitchen orderlies received that exact number of identical metal pans and handed them out one by one as our men stepped into the chow line. Each person set his *shisele* on the windowsill under an overhanging roof, and the cook ladled out hot soup, which we ate right outside, standing up or sitting on benches at wooden picnic tables. Two uniformed POWs stood alongside these windows maintaining order. They looked into the faces of the men so that they would know if anyone tried to sneak back in line for a second helping. Majzels, as a company leader in good standing with the cook, could eat twice at the kitchen and take one helping back to the barracks with him. For anyone else to try for an extra bowl of soup was to risk being whipped within an inch of his life by the kitchen POWs. Now and then, they would grab someone in line by the lapels and ask if it was his first time in line that day.

There was something pitiful about us as we stood waiting like whipped dogs for our bowls of soup. But, the cooking odor from the kitchen made me aware of how really hungry I was. Finally it was my turn. The soup was gruel and had more flavoring in it than anything else, but it was hot.

Because we had not relaxed since morning, rest was all we wanted next. It was twilight when we were finally led to our barracks. Majzels, together with one of the POW administrators, walked in first and ordered those already occupying the barracks to vacate the left side. This done, we were let in.

The men who were already in the barracks sat on the edge of their bunks with their legs dangling down and looked at us intently, trying perhaps to see if there was someone they knew. We did the same, and here and there we did see a familiar face. Most of the men in this barracks did not look too bad. The shape of their clothing indicated little wear, as though they hadn't worked very long. After a moment of cautious silence I climbed up to the top tier, and there sat Wierzbicki, our raconteur friend from Okecie.

Soon questions were popping up from both sides of the dividing aisle. "Where did you guys come from?" "What city?" "Warsaw?" "Hey, fellows! They are from Warsaw, too!"

"Don't broadcast that you are from Warsaw," we were told. "The SS guards call the guys from there bandits."

We told them our story and listened to theirs: "Two weeks ago, they flushed us out of our bunkers and we were shipped to Treblinka. There, we were already undressed when they ordered a selection separating younger males from old men and women and children. They told us to get dressed again and shipped us here. Many of us left our women and children in the gas chambers."

"But what is this place like?" was the question most of us asked.

"It's not a convalescent home, but if you have some money stashed away, you can buy extra bread at the plant from the Polish volunteer workmen."

Some men still held on to their bread rations, roughly one-twelfth of a loaf weighing about two pounds. We would get ours tomorrow. Today we hadn't worked.

"But how do they treat you here? What sort of work do you do?"

"Lately it has been quiet," they said.

Some old-timers who came to see us in our barracks had more to say. They had witnessed a lot, and their eyes bore the vacant look of those who have lived through horror. We learned from them about the first selection, which had taken place in the fall of 1942 among the first 1,500 people in this camp. Only a few weeks after their arrival, 105 were segregated from the rest. As the men went to work, they heard salvos of gunfire, claiming the camp's first victims en masse. Afterward, the women were ordered to remove the clothing from the victims. At about the same period, young boys and girls were pulled out of the ranks for execution. When one woman saw that her daughter had been pulled out, she ran after Feix, pleading that he take her instead. Feix obliged by shooting the mother on the spot. The child was spared. A man from Krasnik named Mayer Szazgas and his young son had shown symptoms of scab; they were ordered to undress in the barracks, then led out and shot, standing together.

In the fall of 1942, it had been the practice to make prisoners work at clearing weeds from the inside perimeter of the camp. This work was accompanied by Feix's personal beatings. He would use his whip to gouge out the eyes of a prisoner; then, declaring him unfit to work, and being practical, he would shoot the man.[3]

Those who had been here through the winter also told us that after a group of Jewish ex-Polish army officers who were in charge of the camp had escaped, Feix sought revenge. He and his guards had been outwitted—and after that he was bent on more evil than usual. In the winter of 1942 he ordered the sick to vacate the hospital, situated outside the camp, and moved them to one of the barracks inside the fence. Typhoid patients, stretcher cases, and those able to walk were all herded into this barracks and, except for an attending prisoner staff of two doctors and nurses, isolated there. The next morning Feix ordered that all those who thought they could go to work the next day should leave the isolation barracks. The rest were dragged out, undressed and barefooted, into the snow-covered *Appellplatz* and shot—twenty-six people, including a young boy. The blood froze fast to the snow, so that after the dead were buried, the snow where they fell had to be removed. One POW managed to pull his friend out one moment before the shooting started. So it was that Sidney Engel's life was spared in camp. He had been one of the very first to arrive, and although not a POW himself he was adopted and befriended by two Jewish POWs.

Those who escaped had gone to join the partisans, and when the news spread to an adjacent military POW camp, a similar escape took place there—but three of the leaders were caught and brought to Budzyn to face Feix. Ordered to be hung upside down, they suffered for two days before they expired. Begging the Ukrainian guards to shoot them did no good. To add to their agony, Feix would whip them each morning.

Lately, however, we were told, things had quieted down somewhat except for an execution or a flogging now and then. The Ukrainians still beat and robbed the prisoners while escorting them to the *Heinkelwerke*, the Heinkel aircraft plant (formally, *Heinkel Flugzeugwerke*). But once there the prisoners were placed in custody of the work *Schutz* plant's own police, made up partially of Croatian Germans, who were less rapacious and hateful. Being at work, I learned, was like being in a place of refuge compared to camp.

Since that winter escape, new Jewish POWs from the Polish army had been placed in charge of the camp administration. Most of these had been brought from the eastern part of the country initially occupied by the Soviets. (While most of the Polish POWs had been freed by the Germans after the blitz of 1939, the Jewish POWs from the Russian occupation zone remained interned. Eventually they were turned over to the SS authority and became SS prisoners in camps in the Lublin district.) In Budzyn, approximately fifty of these men were in charge of all the phases of the inner-camp administration, the more ambitious at the top, the less so merely as foremen of various work groups at the Heinkel plant. They all wore their Polish army uniforms and even riding boots.

In addition, some of the civilian Jews who arrived later were able to obtain better work assignments for a consideration. A group of German Jews received their jobs by appointment and for a time enjoyed such privileges as preference in work assignments. For example, a German Jewish doctor named Mosbach had taken over the existing chief doctor's position by having a strong letter of recommendation from the SS authorities at the place where he had last been interned. A tall, elderly man named Schubert had an armband that said he was in charge of a clothing supply room referred to as a *"Magazine"*. A German Jewish former army captain named Bauchwitz was given "command" of one of the prisoner companies. The Jewish camp commandant was a tall, lean, handsome POW named Sztokman, a former Polish officer, but his second-in-command was a civilian named Souberman. Sztokman never carried a whip, and he enjoyed a rare good reputation for trying to avoid trouble.

All this talk finally had to yield to curfew, lights out, and silence. None of the ordinary prisoners were allowed to leave the barracks during the night. Buckets stood at the door for all needs.

I was just stretching out when Wierzbicki nudged me. When I turned his way, he handed me an American five-dollar bill and asked me to keep it safe for him. I was afraid and accepted it reluctantly. Bothered by it, I noted a crack in the wall-board, and after feeling the opening with my finger and looking around to see if anyone was watching, I pushed the bill in. The bedtime stories were not exactly encouraging, I thought, but I was willing to make a try at this place. If the war should end soon, we might have a chance. But I no longer cared about anything except sleep—the only refuge of a slave.

In the morning of the second day the loud shrill of the whistle was a signal to rise. Majzels, standing at the entrance, was blowing hard: "Get up! Hit the floor! On the double! Move! Move! In ten minutes, you fall out and stand in ranks right outside the barracks! Right now, run to wash at the bathhouse. Then you get your coffee. Get moving!"

The sound of metal containers and the rising steam drew our attention. Standing in the quickly moving line, I got a cup of an acorn-smelling brew. It tasted like unsweetened, slightly bitter medicine. But this did not prevent anyone from drinking it. This "breakfast" would have to last until noon.

"Aren't you in formation yet?" fumed Majzels, as the men now made haste to close ranks. "Line up according to height!" We did. "Count off!" Always five abreast, the front rank sounded off with the count. After that Majzels reviewed his troops by passing in front of the column, giving an assortment of orders. "You there, button your coat," he instructed one. "Shorty! Stand erect, not hunched up like an old man!" he ordered another. "Where did you learn to stand at attention?" he rambled on to yet another.

"And you!"

"Me?" I asked.

"Yes, you! And don't answer! Keep your mouth shut when you stand at attention! You a wise guy or something?"

"No." I replied.

"I just told you to shut up," went on the general. "You find something funny?"

I kept quiet this time. "You were grinning before. Don't do it! That goes for all you recruits!"

At this, I could not refrain from grinning, and Majzels charged into the ranks, shaking his fist before my face in apparent anger and yelling incoherently: "Wise guy, eh? I am company commander. Do you hear? What I say goes! When I give you an order, you better do what I say or you will regret it!" He would have gone on indefinitely, but the commandant's whistle outranked his and signaled the time for the morning formation. Majzels ran to face the formation from the center, clicked his heels, took a deep breath, and thundered, "Atten-*tion!* Left *face!* Forward *march!*" He led us into the *Appellplatz* for the morning

ceremony. All companies lined up along the perimeter of the quadrangle, forming a quadrilateral arrangement. It was like the first day of
school—in a paramilitary school, that is. The weather was beautiful,
and the sun was just rising over the eastern horizon. In the center of the
square stood Sztokman and Souberman, with an owlish-looking POW
named Brooks and a sharply dressed POW named Szczypiacki, who
had a black mustache and carried a whip as a sign of authority.

Then the counting began. Szczypiacki walked briskly in front of
each formation to receive a numerical report and a salute from each
company leader. He then stopped before Sztokman, saluted, and
reported the total number of men in the ranks. When Sztokman
returned the salute, the other three POWs stood in line at ease. This
was the cue for Feix and his staff to take the field. Meanwhile, armed
Ukrainians were lining up on both sides of the road outside the camp.

The scene I had just now witnessed, I thought, could have taken
place at a veterans' summer camp jamboree But when the SS walked in,
all illusion vanished. Feix, armed as though going into combat, led the
other two toward the center of the square. The tension in the air was
palpable. From Sztokman to those in the ranks, you could sense
nervousness in both looks and actions.

At a precise moment Sztokman turned his back to Feix and
shouted, "*Stillgestanden!* [Attention!] *Muetzen ab!* [Hats off!]." At these
commands there was a silence broken only by simultaneous heel
clickings as some 2,500 caps were pulled off, and the POW formation
gave their two-finger Polish salute (standing for God and country).
Then Sztokman made an about-face to salute Feix, reporting the total
number of prisoners in the camp. Feix did not return the salute but
made a gesture with his hand and said, "At ease." Continuing with the
ceremony, Sztokman again turned to Szczypiacki, transmitting the
order, at which point Szczypiacki ordered "*Muetzen auf!* [Hats on!]."
Each company leader standing in front of his company awaited the all-
important final count. While Feix stood poised in the center, Brooks
began the count, followed by Szczypiacki, followed by two SS men. As
they approached each formation the company leader would face his
men and order: "Attention! Hats off! Eyes right!"

When this count ended, it was time to switch from company
formations to working battalions, which were not always the same.
Our entire company had been consigned to agricultural fieldwork not
related to the aircraft plant. But as the men began to regroup, a man
suddenly emerged from the crowd whom I immediately recognized as
an old family acquaintance; before the war he had owned a summer
resort hotel where two of my uncles had been guests.

"Jurek!" he said, "Jurek! Did you get here yesterday?"

"Yes, Mr. Luxemburg."

"There's no time to waste. I am taking you with my group. Come on! Look here, Meisels, I am taking him with me," said Luxemburg as he walked away, joining six others. We formed ranks with those designated to work beyond the *Heinkelwerke* in an adjacent Polish volunteer workers' camp.

Soon the slave army was all poised for the march. Feix and the other two SS men took up positions opposite the guardhouse to review the "troops," led by the POW detachment. As they passed by Feix, the whole military routine was repeated. We followed not far behind the POWs. As soon as the lead column turned right at the settlement, the Ukrainian guards moving along on both sides of the road requested singing, and the POWs complied with a medley of Polish army songs that we all knew. The formations behind them picked it up, and soon all of the column halfway back had broken out in song.

At first it seemed strange to be singing, as though there might be gaiety in grief. But after a while the singing made our step smarter, made us feel like prisoners entitled to some measure of dignity, as opposed to hopeless, despairing subhumans constantly in fear for our lives.

As the sound reverberated through the settlement, a perhaps untimely esprit de corps developed among those of us who could march in step and sing in perfect unison. But this synthetic optimism had its limits. At the tail end of the parade the groups not able to maintain a steady pace were often beaten by the guards, who urged them to close ranks or beat them under any other pretext. Occasionally, Feix rode a motorcycle up and down the column, inspecting the ranks.

After nearly half an hour's march, we entered the *Heinkelwerke's* wire gate. The Ukrainians remained outside, and the *Werkschutz*, the factory's security police, took over. A feeling of relief was evident as soon as we all got inside. Led to a square in the middle, the entire procession halted; then every group went to its assigned work.

Luxemburg was in charge of furniture distribution—bunks, benches, food lockers—for the Polish camp, which was still being built but was already partially occupied. The lead barracks was the office and quarters of S.A. (Sturmabteilung, The Brown Shirts) *Oberscharfuehrer* Garbe, the commandant of this so-called Polish volunteer work camp. He had a couple of Polish women doing the housekeeping for him and was our direct work boss. Standing outside in his brown shirt uniform, he cut a handsome figure. On closer examination, I noticed that with his good looks, jet black hair, coal black eyes, and suntanned skin he did not resemble the expected German type. His brown shirt, black tie, swastika armband, and high black boots indicated a military branch I had not run across before. The Brown Shirts, made up largely of Hitler's bully boys, lost its preeminence to the SS run by Himmler in 1934.

"*Guten Morgen, Herr Kommandant,*" said Luxemburg, making an obvious effort at elevating his boss's authority.

"Good morning," replied Garbe, with a smile.

Well, I thought, this was the first time since the Okecie *Luftwaffe* camp that I had heard one of them say good morning to people they had declared as good as dead. Perhaps Garbe was not the typical Nazi.

"I have brought an extra pair of hands to get the new barracks supplied," said Luxemburg.

"Oh," replied Garbe agreeably, without changing expression.

Luxemburg excused himself and took us to the barracks that served as the furniture warehouse. The first thing he ordered us to do was make coffee. It did not take me long to figure out that the small group assigned to this job did next to nothing. Luxemburg took me aside for an hour while we brought each other up to date.

He did not tell me how he had gotten this job, but to me the men in his group smelled of money. Remembering my family as having been well off at one time, Luxemburg naturally might have expected to find some wealth still sticking to me. He questioned me at length, and sensing his interest, I deliberately avoided making any admission— knowing that if I did so the game might be up, and I might be sent off to work in the open fields. Of course, there was the possibility that my lack of faith was without grounds. Nevertheless, I remained evasive on the subject of money, trying to delay showing him my empty hand. When he asked me how I had managed to go through frisking, I answered, "I prepared myself in advance."

To which my boss rejoined, "Whatever you do, don't confide to anyone regarding such things."

"Sometime, when I get used to this place, I'd like to talk to you about it," I threw back to him for whatever it was worth.

Luxemburg was a tall man in his early fifties with thinning blond hair and baggy blue eyes. He always seemed to be holding a cigarette, and when he was smoking, he exhaled two streams of smoke through his nostrils. His left hand was clenched in order to cover part of the missing middle finger with his thumb. A grimace on his face gave it an expression of fatigue, but his walk was brisk. When he talked, his manner seemed indirect. He rarely smiled, and when he engaged in conversation, he always had some specific purpose in mind. He was as shrewd as they come.

It was time to make believe we were doing something, so we carried a few unassembled bunks past Garbe's office to one of the vacant barracks. Garbe, I am sure, was wise to the fact that there was little for eight men to do there, yet he went along with the game because eight men assigned to his care meant that something was going on in his department. In the afternoon he approached me and asked, "What is your trade?"

"I am a gardener, Herr Kommandant," I said, seeing that his grounds could use some landscaping.

"Luxemburg! Have the gardener work around my quarters. Just the man we need to make the place look decent!"

"*Jawohl*," replied Luxemburg. "You see, sir, how I can pick them?" he added, in an obvious attempt to ingratiate himself.

As the time drew near for our return to the camp, apprehension began to creep in. It was relatively pleasant and safe here, and the thought of going back to Feix's domain carried with it the unpleasant sensation of fear—as if we were prospective prey being taken to the hunter. Joining our formation at Heinkel's open square, the *Werkschutz* escorted us up to the gate. Outside, the Ukrainians already waited, and the march back was heavily laden not only with a foretaste of what one might expect in the camp but also with the depression caused by seeing the guards violently harassing the men. Since singing not only reduced the possibility of a beating but also served as a temporary painkiller, we sang the medley of Polish army songs again, then supplemented them with Polish and Russian melodies and even whistled "Stars and Stripes Forever," which was known here as the *Alte Kameraden* march.

As we neared the camp, we saw a figure on a white horse standing by the roadside. It was Feix, who had given up the motorcycle he had ridden that morning. At the guardhouse the German-Ukrainian chief, a drunkard and sadist named Otto, supervised the frisking on the way in; some of the men were severely beaten before the end of the column was within the camp. Then, again switching back into company formations, we stood for a repetition of the entire morning ceremony and the eternal counting. Absurdly, they treated us worse than beasts of burden but counted us with such great care that one would have supposed we were worth our weight in gold.

Following the counting, Feix requested that the men stand in formation and sing the Polish love song, "Mariana." The words of one refrain go something like this: "Tonight, you have promised me for sure that you will become my queen. Tonight, oh Mariana, oh Mariana." When we finished, Feix applauded and then all the men responded with applause that could be heard a mile away. How deceptive was this scene, how easily it would veil for a stranger the sinister character of our prison life.

Shortly before dusk we lined up again for our soup portions, went back to the barracks to get bread rations, and then climbed up on our sleeping tiers to eat slowly in the company of friends. My friends, however, had not fared as well as I had. They worked hard weeding potatoes in the fields under the eyes of guards. Wierzbicki and the older men seemed worn out.

Unexpectedly, two Ukrainian guards walked into the barracks. Silence fell on the place. They looked over our faces as though searching for someone, then called out a name; when an elderly man fled toward the rear of the barracks, they pursued him and beat him mercilessly before removing a gold-capped bridge from his mouth. He sat with a look of utter despair on his face, bleeding from the mouth and holding his belly, where he had been kicked. His missing front teeth made him look pitiful and much older. Some of the others tried to comfort him and suggested he see the Jewish camp dentist the next day.

Wierzbicki than asked me where I was keeping his five dollars (then worth perhaps 150 zlotys). When I told him, he seemed satisfied. Someone tugged at my leg. A young man my age was standing below looking up.

"You are Jurek Topas. Do you know me?" he asked.

"No I don't," I confessed.

"Well, I am Kaufman. I saw you once when you came to visit your Uncle Mietek in the ghetto. I was with him toward the end."

"Go on," I said getting down to the floor. "Tell me what happened."

"We were together in the same bunker when they smoked us out. There was not much hope left. On the *Umschlagplatz*, the Ukrainians dragged people to the basement of a school building and killed them there, taking away whatever they had. When they finally loaded us into the boxcars, your uncle tried to bribe one of them to let him flee with his wife. But the guard took the money away from him, shot them both in the back of the head, and then pulled off your uncle's boots. Had he not tried to escape, he might have lived, as we were in the group who got out of Treblinka. But how could he know that anyone could come through Treblinka to tell the tale?"

"Are you certain you are talking about my uncle, Mietek Topas?" I asked.

He replied, "There are others here who saw it."

I said nothing more, but Kaufman said, "I am sorry, but this is what happened to your uncle and his wife."

"Thanks," I said, contemplating the terrible end they had met. I climbed back up just before the lights went out. I put my finger instinctively in the wall-board hole—but felt nothing. I tried again and again to locate the five-dollar bill, but it must have been taken by someone. With this discovery everything seemed to change for the worse. The events I had witnessed and heard about sank deep into my mind and made me feel utterly depressed. I quietly told the sad news to Wierzbicki, expecting the worst, but he merely chided me for carelessness, which might have been a subtle way of expressing his real disappointment. This was one of the rare times when I was psychologically on the verge of giving up the fight, and I might have, had not exhaustion led me into slumber.

Morning reawakened me to the stark realities of yesterday, but they seemed easier to bear in the daylight. I felt hopeful in spite of the staggering facts stacked against such foolish optimism. As long as the sun shines, I thought, I'll try to hang on. One consolation was that I had an easy job, for a while at least. Knowing this helped me face the days ahead.

During formation that morning someone caught my eye, and there in the ranks, like any other prisoner, stood Mr. Wallach, my high school history teacher. How sad he looked, out of his element, no longer commanding the attention of his students. He had had that rare gift of transposing our classroom into the *Forum Romanum* by the magic of his words. The last time I had seen him was in Warsaw in June, 1940, reading a newspaper headlining the fall of Paris.

A few days later, he took poison—some of the prisoners had smuggled in cyanide capsules—and was buried in a little wooded area in front of the camp where all dead prisoners were buried, whether they had committed suicide, had been shot or hanged, or had simply starved to death.

Back at work, I reported to Garbe. "Good morning, gardener," said Garbe. "Get enough sleep?" It was just a mechanical politeness, but it was politeness nevertheless.

I asked him what sort of landscaping he wanted done and what flowers he favored. But he only shrugged and smiled, saying, "Do as you think it ought to be done," and added as an afterthought, "Whatever you do will make for improvement."

"A good job will take time," I sneaked in, to test the job duration.

"Obviously," answered Herr Garbe and smiled knowingly, shaking his forefinger at me just to let me know that he understood my point.

From that day on, I worked with gardening tools around his residence, making a camp career out of the job. I won the favor of Garbe's Polish housekeeper, and right after lunch she would bring a plate of soup or leftovers to the back door and hand them to me. At first I found this kindness humiliating and pretended not to care for anything she offered, but I soon overcame my pride and accepted whatever she gave me. Hunger was my chief conspirator in taming my pride. On the days when she was absent or did not call, I had to subdue a strong urge to ask, thinking that perhaps she had forgotten. In the course of time, I resorted to many stratagems short of asking, which I never did.

One evening I looked at Wierzbicki and saw that he had aged in the short time we had been at Camp Budzyn. It grieved me to look at his misery without being able to do anything for him. I thought of speaking to Luxemburg about getting him assigned to our group, but Luxemburg had not been happy about my proximity to the "front office" and had already cooled toward me. I had to think of another way.

At the first opportunity, I enlarged the area of the cultivated plots and began turning soil over with the spade. This expansion did not escape the attention of Garbe, who seemed pleased with the improvement I had already made: graded, grass-seeded area had replaced the heap of dirt from the excavation. After the usual morning greetings, he asked what I was up to now.

"Soon the wind will blow and cover the lawn with sand and dust from the surrounding area," I explained, "so I am trying to get the surrounding area seeded as well."

"Oh yes," said Garbe, "but this is a lot of ground to work over."

"Herr Kommandant, may I ask something?"

"Certainly."

"There is a man in the camp who would like to help me. Could you authorize him to be assigned here?"

"Of course," said Garbe.

By then I was not only gardening but had taken over many other chores as well, such as chopping wood for the stove and hauling water from the well. Since my job depended on Garbe's approval, I was always trying to make myself useful. Now Garbe had something special to ask of me. "Come on in," he said, "and help me install the aerial for my radio." This request suggested an opportunity for access to broadcast news after years of doing without it. After I had extended the wire to the top of a nearby tree, Garbe turned on the radio to test it. He grinned approvingly as the signal came in strong. He turned the dial, skipping fragments of march music and official German communiqués, until he heard a foreign broadcast. He looked at me seriously: "Gardener, do you understand English?"

"Not well, Herr Kommandant."

Silence ensued as we listened. My English vocabulary was then limited to the most elementary words, taught to me by a tutor named Szpidbaum. I will always remember his name, not only because of a very refined and depressed-looking appearance but because of his method of teaching. He would say, "I am Mr. Szpidbaum. You are Mr.

Topas. He is Mr. Topas" and so on. Ghetto economics had forced Father to let him go after only a few weeks.

Garbe switched to a German station and raised the volume before asking, "What did they say?" Half-recognizing the similarity of words like capitulation (in Polish, *Kapitulacja*) and half guessing, I tried my best to interpret the news.

"They just announced the capitulation of an island by the Germans."

"What island?" interrupted Garbe.

"An island off the coast of Sicily." (It was the second week of June 1943; a month later over the same radio I heard news of Allied landings in Sicily.) I thought it best then to get back to my work. Garbe remained in his quarters studying maps. Afraid that he would forget about Wierzbicki, however, I ran back to ask again. Less friendly than before, Garbe inquired what I wished now "about this man." I almost stuttered, aware of my wrong timing. "Ah, yes," he said, like one reminded of something in the nature of a bother, "I'll tell Luxemburg. *Gut?*"

"*Jahwohl!*" I said and left to return to work.

At quitting time, when I put my tools away at the warehouse, I said casually, "Another man is needed to help with my work."

"Who says?" asked Luxemburg.

"Garbe thinks we could do with one."

"And you suggested just the right man for the job, I suppose?" he asked sarcastically. "It is not enough that I brought him here; he brings someone else," complained Luxemburg to his companions.

Going back to rejoin the formation, we had to pass by the front office, where Luxemburg turned in the key and reported that we were quitting for the day. Garbe often stood outside, as he did on this occasion, and he addressed our foreman.

"Luxemburg, bring another man tomorrow named—what's his name?" he asked, looking in my direction. I volunteered, "Wierzbicki, sir."

"Right, that's the name."

"If Herr Kommandant thinks it is necessary, I'll bring him," responded Luxemburg. Garbe nodded, agreeing that it was. Old Luxemburg did not like this at all, and his feelings were ill concealed.

Back in camp there was an animated discussion going on in every barracks about the war news "confirmed by British broadcast." I told Wierzbicki about the plan to take him with me the following morning. It was good to see him the next day leaning on his rake. At lunchtime we shared the leftovers. Shortly thereafter I brought Wierzbicki's young friend Abram along so that the three of us could share this comparative oasis—much to the displeasure of Luxemburg, who accused me of "meddling in his business" and "drawing too much attention" to our group. I did not let this bother me much; I wanted my friends with me.

Life at work was going all right; even the nights in camp could have been endured had it not been for a course of events that sent a chill through our hearts. Sunday was always a bad day because we did not go to work, and hanging around the camp was never "healthy." But in order to keep us working, our guards would have had to work, and so also would the Polish civilian volunteers and German supervisors at the *Heinkelwerk*. Thus it was not for our benefit but theirs that on Sunday no work was done. It was especially bad for those who like me depended on scrounging some extra food at work, since one bowl of soup and one slice of bread was all we got at the camp.

On a partly cloudy Sunday in early June, I sat outside against the wall of a barracks talking with Freudlich, who was telling me an interesting story about his youthful adventures. Freudlich, with his indomitable smile, came from Lodz, the second largest city in Poland. Since Lodz was known to be predominantly a textile city, it was no surprise that his father owned a textile mill. After graduating from high school, Freudlich had gone out and bought himself a new suit, before earning any money. Because this was in opposition to his father's philosophy of life, he was rebuked for imagining himself to be a big shot. Young Freudlich's pride was offended, so, contrary to the accepted European custom of a son working in his father's establishment, the young man went to work for his uncle, eventually becoming a manager and then owning the factory. This, however, did not bring about an immediate reconciliation with his father. All this had happened back in the thirties. Since then, of course, his career, his aspirations of proving himself to his father, his plans for the future—all had turned to ashes. There was no father to impress, no wife, no children, and no future. Only the present mattered.

Suddenly, a commotion started: an SS man and two Ukrainian guards came in and headed for the camp office. Moments later, they emerged with Souberman, the civilian prisoner second-in-command to Sztokman. They led him out the gate, turned right toward the camp cemetery, and disappeared behind some young pines. The sound of two rifle shots shattered the Sunday afternoon quiet and echoed through the camp. Someone huddled in the group asked, "Why did they kill him?"

"Why? Did you ask why?"

"Why are you here? Why? Why?" an old-timer kept repeating.

The same day the SS ordered the Jewish administration to make a certain man whom I shall call Dims into a camp policeman. Dims was rumored to have distinguished himself by informing on hideouts during the last days of the Warsaw uprising. Probably they had promised to spare his life in exchange. No one could prove these rumors, but it was strange that he was given this position. A policeman's duties consisted of standing guard outside the barracks at night, maintaining order, and sometimes administering punishment. In return he got separate quarters and free access to the kitchen.

On Monday morning we awakened to startling news. Dims had been shot on the first round of night guard duty and found leaning against a barbed-wire fence, dead. It could have been an inside job, accomplished in accordance with the avowed duty of the Warsaw survivors to do away with their informers.

In mid-June a German civilian made an appearance in the Polish camp. Soon I learned that he was to be an assistant to Garbe. Tall, with a reddish face showing tiny blood vessels, he must have been less than fifty. He was wearing a brown suit the first day I saw him. Working outdoors, I observed him looking sideways. Instinctively, I feared and disliked such changes, anticipating—often with justification—that once we had adjusted to a new but tolerable situation, something was bound to happen to make it worse. Now, here was a "new broom" direct from Germany. Given no specific duties, he walked around the barracks trying to familiarize himself with his new surroundings. He did not look at all happy when he approached me and asked, "Have you worked here long?"

"A few weeks," I replied.

Soft-spoken, he paused for a moment and then resumed in perfect Polish: "My name is Schleswig.[4] I just came here from Stettin, but for many years I lived in Silesia near the Polish border. That is why I can speak Polish."

"You speak the language very well," I said.

"And where are you from?" he questioned, in an unofficial tone.

"I am from Warsaw—the Warsaw ghetto, that is."

"And your folks?" he continued, showing interest.

"My mother and young brother were evacuated for Treblinka's gas chambers. My father and other brother might also be dead, but I don't know for sure."

"*Psia Krew!* [dog's blood]," cursed Schleswig. "The dogs went mad; yes, they are mad to do what they did. My boy, they will pay for it, and from the looks of things, sooner than they expect!"

Stunned by such talk, I asked, "Are you Polish, sir?"

"No, I am not. By the way, what is your name?"

"Georg," I said, pronouncing the name in German with hard G's.

"Georg," said he, "I am a German, all right, and I am sick to see what they are doing to you and to us. Oh, I am telling you, Germany is getting it now." Here his hand made a diving motion, imitating bombs falling.

I could not believe my ears. I had never before heard any German express concern about any German action, least of all for what was happening to the people of the conquered countries. As for doubting the Fuehrer's promise of victory, he seemed to be alone in that, and he could share such views only with someone like me.

"They treat you rotten, don't they?" asked Schleswig.

I only gesticulated with my hand in a sign of resignation.

"Listen, if you had been in Germany in the 1930s and heard him speak of only wanting to provide bread for German women and children, you would have gotten gooseflesh. Why, I thought that anything was better than the conditions we had. But as soon as he got power, man, they went on a rampage and have not stopped since! Believe me, Georg, that is the way it was." When he finished, his face seemed to reflect some inner pain.

"Georg, I will go now to see about the apartment in Siedlung [a settlement for the families of German and Croatian Heinkel employees]. I will try to bring you something to eat whenever I can."

Garbe reacted badly to the arrival of Schleswig. Whenever Schleswig was around, Garbe acted tough. He began to carry a whip and shout at some of the men to get a move on. Why did his conduct change? Did he suspect Schleswig of being a Gestapo man assigned to spy on him, or did he feel that his job was less secure with a civilian around? I remember he once slapped me hard after talking loud and harsh about there not being enough production, but that was when real SS officers had checked around his domain. His behavior before an inferior was different. I never did figure that out, beyond the probability that Garbe was an old party member who trusted no one and was taking no chances.

Marching "homeward" at the end of that day, I marveled over Schleswig's conversation and wondered whether he felt and thought as he spoke, out of a sense of decency and humanity, or because of some personal frustration with the way the party had handled his own career. For my own sake, I wanted to believe in Schleswig's integrity. It was like the promise of an oasis in a terrible snake-infested desert. If there is one like him, I reasoned, perhaps there are others.

Thoughts like these made life seem more bearable than it really was. At such moments I straightened my back, stepped livelier, and sang a bit louder. I endured frisking and the occasional lash.

9 An Endurance Test

It requires more courage to suffer than to die.
—Napoleon Bonaparte

Something was not right one night in midsummer of 1943 when after the count they did not dismiss the formation for supper. A wave of whispering swept the ranks of the assembled. With a sense of foreboding, we received the news of an escaped prisoner whose misfortune of having been caught was the reason we had been detained.

A young man named Jack (Jacek) Eisner was brought into the center of the *Appellplatz* by the Ukrainian guards. There Feix unleashed his whip and cut up his face. Blond, blue-eyed, and slim, Eisner, wearing gray breeches, a bicycle cap, and riding boots, looked to be about seventeen or eighteen. He stood erect before his tormentor. But the fiendish Feix stopped striking him as abruptly as he had started. A wooden post was brought from the guardhouse. One of the Ukrainian guards dug a hole and set in the post; then the ground was packed around it by the stamping boots of the guards. Everything became clear when a piece of wood was nailed on top of the pole to form the letter T. A guard reached into his hip pocket, pulled out a piece of rope, and tied a loop around Eisner's neck. Someone was sent to bring a chair, and Eisner was ordered to stand on it. The other end of the rope was tied over the top of the horizontal piece of wood, making everything ready. Feix pulled the chair out himself. Eisner fell to the ground, the rope still around his neck; the nails in the wooden crossbar had pulled loose. Though shaken, Eisner, unaided, obeyed an order to climb back on the chair. The board was attached to the pole again. When the chair was snatched out a second time and Eisner's body swung in the air, the men gave a loud cry: "Oh God!" But in the moment that separates life from death, the nails holding the upper piece of wood again gave way, and Eisner, surely by now getting tired of dying and living, fell to the ground gasping for air.

The plan to hang him was abandoned. Two guards twisted his arms back, causing him to bend over, and the flogging began. Every time the bullwhip struck his lower back, Eisner shouted out the count. Counting by the recipient of such discipline was mandatory; should he lose the count, the flogging would start over again from the beginning. That was why an older man was as good as dead when they whipped him. Not only was he less able to withstand the ferocity of the punishment; he was more likely to lose the count. If he did, they would whip him until he was dead and then add a few for good measure.

But Eisner was still going strong at forty-eight lashes, administered by the diligent Ukrainians wielding whips with leaded tips that dug into the flesh. (The guards usually administered this punishment, but sometimes the Jewish policemen were ordered to do it for them.) Eisner's voice began to sound weaker at sixty. Every time the whip hit, the men gasped loudly, feeling some of the agony. The count reached seventy.

Eisner's voice was fading rapidly. His pants were cut to ribbons. Blood all over his leggings was splashing on the guards' black boots. It did not look as though he was going to make it. At seventy-five he was barely audible—but here they stopped, letting his skinny bones drop to the ground. There was an unrestrained flood of tears and a look of anguish on many faces. As soon as the guards left the bloody arena, men rushed to pick up Eisner and carefully carry him into the bathhouse. As they turned into the entrance, I caught a glimpse of his face, which was now completely swollen, particularly his lips. But he still breathed, so they would try to patch him up.

Usually I was hungry at this time, but that night I did not feel like eating. All I wanted was permission to speak with God and ask Him whether all this torment was necessary under His jurisdiction. How did it serve His higher purpose? Half dazed, I meditated in a fog, until my mind went blank.

Morning revealed that Eisner's ordeal was not yet over. Feix ordered that he should be dressed and forced to march around the camp's inner perimeter with a load of bricks tied to his body. Helped to his feet by his fellow prisoners, the young man, stubbornly hanging on to his life, summoned some invisible strength and extraordinary courage and managed to oblige his tormentor by what could be described only as a superhuman effort. Along the way, he was whipped by Feix and urged to run, which he did. After a couple of hours he collapsed. The following morning he was ordered to give a repeat performance, and he did, but this time he had to be carried away to his bunk, his life hanging by thread. Feix, apparently assuming that he had finished off his prey, lost interest in seeing him finally expire. Reflecting later on these shocking events, I could not help wondering whether Eisner's survival was in fact a miracle, not solely because he had been able to withstand the immense punishment but also because Feix had not ordered him to be shot and had let him leave the arena still breathing.

Every day we inquired about Eisner's condition, and then one evening we came marching into the camp and saw him walking with a cane. The men let out a yell and a cheer—as though applauding God's saving power. Then came a day that Eisner was able to smile. The "provincials," as we called the men from small towns and villages, later nicknamed him "Iron Behind" (the name "Eisner" means "of iron").

The bitter irony of Eisner's ordeal lies in the fact that he had escaped from the Warsaw Ghetto, after the revolt was crushed, and later happened to be wandering in the woods surrounding Budzyn, looking for refuge. When he saw our columns marching and singing on our way back to camp, he had concluded that it could not be too bad a place and so risked smuggling himself into our ranks—and then risked his life again because of this initial mistake. As we learned later, Eisner and a fellow prisoner from the Warsaw ghetto had decided to escape from Camp Budzyn with two companions who were brothers, using as cover a haystack close to the wire fence in the work compound. Eisner had thought that the nearby woods would also provide good cover. As it happened, one of the two brothers turned sick at the last moment, causing the other one to abort the plan. Apparently the third got cold feet or changed his mind. Eisner was determined to go through with it alone, and he made for the woods, only to find out that they led nowhere, ending in open fields. Missed in the work compound count, he was quickly pursued by the guards. When Eisner heard the barking of the dogs, he knew the game was up.

The only other instance of someone getting so many lashes had occurred in the winter before our arrival, as we learned from the old-timers. Feix was at that time about to execute the sick prisoners, and he had them already undressed near the latrine on the snow-covered ground. Dr. Fenster, an Austrian Jew, then chief physician, pleaded with Feix to spare the life of the first-aid man, Isaak Arbuz. Feix consented but ordered the red-haired Jewish policeman to administer punishment. Dissatisfied with a "mild" application, Feix took over and ordered Arbuz to count each time he struck. Had he not lost the count at twenty-five calling it twenty-seven, Arbuz would have received only fifty lashes, but after skipping the count he had to start from one, netting seventy-five lashes. Arbuz passed out, but he survived.

Who knows why he or someone else was picked for the daily sin offering? Having a spoon with a sharp cutting edge was offense enough to be executed for concealing a weapon. As Freudlich once remarked to me, "They are not going to win the war by torturing prisoners."

In fact, the question of winning the war was no longer the problem for the Germans, who were beginning to "advance to the rear" in order to gain positions of "advantage." A silly joke circulated in the camp: "The Germans blame their reverses on the Jews." "How so?" "The Jewish shoemakers nailed the heels in front of the shoes, causing the Germans to march backwards."

Another bit concerned Hitler's frustrated obsession with bringing England to her knees. "Have you heard?" one would say, "the latest book written by Hitler?"

"No, what did he write now?" asked the one listening, with anticipation.

"*Von den Insel bis dem Pinsel* [From the island to the brush]."

"Oh, he is making an artistic comeback."

One bright summer day I witnessed the arrival of *Luftwaffe* men in the Polish camp where I worked. They moved into several of the vacant barracks and busied themselves setting up housekeeping. They were young men pulled out of the line to undergo an officers' leadership training course. As the days passed, we grew accustomed to their presence. Seeing them standing in T-shirts with suspenders over their shoulders, shaving and washing outdoors, became part of the early morning routine. Later, they would do calisthenics, march, drill, and sing in formation. But most conspicuous was their distinct manner of singing.

One song in particular evoked smiles on the hunger-ridden faces of the prisoners around. The instructor marching alongside the column would first order with gusto: "*Ein Lied!* [a song]."

"*Ein Lied!*" was the choral response.

Then the instructor would count time with the marching cadence, and they would start. "*Wir wollen Marschieren nach England* [We want to march on England]."

"That's the trouble," a prisoner once remarked quietly in the pause between lines. "You want to march—you got to swim!"

Another of their favorite songs with a catchy melody informed us that "the one is called Veronica, and the other is called Marie (three . . . four). Marie, Marie-e-e.

"*Der Stolz der Kompanie*" (the pride of the company)."

Thus, day in and day out, a free concert accompanied our chores. Some of these soldiers let our men perform chores and errands on the sly for food tidbits or cigarettes—when there were no SS prowling around. About one hundred in all, they had been detached from a larger *Luftwaffe* encampment in the area, to which a group of our men were being taken every day by truck. They were rumored to work the longest day, but they were also given more food.

Schleswig, who had occasionally brought me something to eat, was absent; he had gone to see about bringing his wife and daughter from Germany.

One particular Sunday there was unrest in the camp. Feix and a couple of SS men were looking for trouble, and before we even knew he was around, shots had been fired. I ran outside to find out what had happened. I learned that an old man had been pushing a wheelbarrow, doing a clean-up detail. He had happened to attract Feix's attention when he crossed his path. Feix yelled at him that he worked too slowly. The man moved faster. Feix grasped his whip and let him have it right across the back. The old man began to run. He tripped, fell, and overturned the wheelbarrow, spilling all the trash that was in it. Feix put a fast end to this irritation by reaching for his gun and shooting the man down.

Did you ever see hunted animals when they sense danger near? They crouch low, freezing silently in place and thus blending in with their natural surroundings. So camouflaged, they stand a chance. But what can a caged animal do when shot at? What can a starved rag of a man in a barbed-wire cage surrounded by hostile watchtowers do to save his wretched life? What can he do when fired at pointblank by "ungame" keepers?

Not long after they had buried the old man, another one was pulled out from the kitchen line. It was Luxemburg, who had been caught smoking in formation. Feix ordered the rest to watch as Luxemburg dropped his pants to receive his punishment. He was still protesting when they twisted his arms back—but then he had to start counting. Twenty-five was all he got, but after each lash his body shook. It was not only the pain but the humiliation as well. There were women watching, standing outside the compound where several hundred women were housed.

Among these were the wives and mothers of some of the men who had arrived earlier. To have a woman here was a lucky thing. They worked in the kitchens and shops and always managed to bring extra bowls of soup for their men. Even though they lived in barracks separated from the rest of the camp by barbed wire, many a man had been saved from starvation by his woman. Hunger was the main killer here, and the mortality rate climbed every week.

Soon it was our turn again to go to the bathhouse for delousing. Someone feeling good, as one feels while showering, was entertaining the rest. "My friends," he said, beckoning us closer, "if you think you've got it bad, think how our Jewish brothers in America suffer reading about all the atrocities committed against us. I can just imagine a fellow whose name is Joe. He comes back from work, takes a shower, changes for supper, turns on the radio, and sits down with his family to eat. He is pleased to hear the good war news. After dessert and idle talk with the children, he eventually settles down in his favorite rocker and picks up the newspaper. After reading the front page full of military exploits, he looks inside. Reading there gets him all upset. Concentration camps . . . gas chambers. Suddenly, he can't go on. Turning to his wife, he exclaims, "My dear, this is all too terrible! It hurts my heart. Give me an orange!"

"And she probably peels it for him, too," added a listener.

On a hot summer day a new contingent of "guests" came and stood outside the gate. Only roughed up during frisking, they were passed through and, maintaining step, marched toward the kitchen. Looking well and dressed decently, they looked like fresh reinforcements arriving to relieve a battered fort. To think that we once had looked like that when we were at Okecie Camp made me wonder how long it would be before they came to our level—or how much longer we could hold out!

Dress may not make the man, but it certainly helps. The well-clad newcomers were treated with less abuse than we were by the POW at the chow lines. Such were the social conditions in camps that the stronger and better dressed were less likely to get mistreated by camp officials and policemen than were the rag-wearing class on the way down. Before striking someone between these extreme categories, the official first made sure that it was not someone of note or somebody capable of retaliating.

Be that as it may, the men and women who had been brought from their hometown of Hrubieszczow added color to our graying camp. The two most conspicuous men among the new arrivals were also the tallest. A blond, blue-eyed, handsome six-footer was charming Chaim Silverstein, as pleasant in manner as in appearance. Not an inch smaller was Abram Finkelstein, dark-haired, with a black mustache and black eyes. He had served in the Polish navy during the short-lived 1939 campaign and could tell a few stories when he was in the mood. Fred Orenstein, one of a family of five—four brothers and a sister— was tall and a bit hefty, a jovial and talkative physician, who joined the virtually extinct camp medical staff. His youngest brother Henry was lean and slightly stooped at the shoulders. Another member of their group whom I liked was a redheaded fellow named Hak. Of medium height, introverted, always speaking with caution, he had a talent for singing. When this group was integrated into our company, it boosted our vocal power during marches. Hak sang as a *zapiewala* (soloist), and the company repeated each refrain.

When the times of terror relaxed a bit, the pre-curfew chatter in the barracks could be heard once again. A late arrival of a mixed contingent of Russian and Polish Jews from a camp in Minsk, Russia, revived our interest in the progress of the war with their stories of the German retreat. Sometimes there was even some impromptu entertainment. On one occasion a fellow with a gift for mimicry gave the men in our barracks an impersonation of Dzigan and Schumacher, a famous Jewish comedy team of the time who were noted for their witty dialogues in Yiddish. In one scene Dzigan is supposedly sitting on a park bench in Germany shortly before the onset of the war. A German walks by leading a dog on a leash. He looks at Dzigan and says: "Hey, Jew, see the dog; he is your brother." Unperturbed, Dzigan replies in his famous singsong fashion (the way Talmudic students sometimes state their legal arguments): "If he is circumcized, he is my brother; but if he is not circumcized, he is your brother!"

The faces of the young married men, most of whom had lost or were separated from their wives, reflected their melancholy especially during the evening hours, doubtless because they were more aware then of their loneliness. Some did not wish to share their private thoughts with anyone, but others wanted to tell someone of their wonderful spouses. A handsome young man from Warsaw named Frenkel spoke to me sometimes about his happy marriage. Although he had a younger brother with him, he probably felt too embarrassed to discuss the intimacies of his married life with his brother. Appropriately, he was fond of singing "J'Attendrai" (I'll wait for you), a romantic French song made popular on the eve of the war. Occasionally the strains of a song that reminded someone of better days was heard, and the subjects of the prewar world, which had turned to ashes, dominated our private conversations and thoughts, intermingled with pre-Budzyn experiences, rescues, close calls, and war news. We had many hungers, even though the one for food claimed first priority.

It was about that time that I ran a fever, and Dr. Orenstein arranged to have me taken to the hospital, Instinctively, I dreaded the place—who could foresee when Feiks might again decide to liquidate the nonproductive element?—but chills and fever prompted me to consent. Once there, I was put in a real bed; not since my flight from the ghetto had I slept in a linen-covered bed. The hospital was small, and at that time there were no other patients in my ward. A minimum temperature of 38° C (103° F) was a prerequisite for admission. Victims of malnutrition had to die in their own barracks; the hospital could not help them. Others often nursed themselves rather than run the risk of going there. The hospital soup was even thinner, apparently intended for a strict diet, but you could get a lot of tea.

The cleanliness, the quiet, and the tender care of women nurses was a white fantasy that I enjoyed for two days. On the third day the quiet became oppressive, like the lull before a storm. I asked to be released, and since my fever had subsided, my wish was granted. Leaving, I hoped never to have to return; the place seemed insecure. One typhoid patient might have caused a repetition of the previous winter's gory executions. I went back to work, where I felt safer.

Schleswig had come back and had asked about my absence. He had been told about my illness and seemed glad to see that I had recovered so quickly. Soon, however, he began to act with reserve, as though aware of being watched. Meanwhile, the relations between my two gardener friends and me were gradually cooling off. I kept wondering what could have caused it; why this change? But I found no logical answers, because change is not necessarily sustained by sound logic.

The news of Allied landings in Sicily flashed through the camp like lightning. For a second its bright prospect illuminated the darkness of the present. Like a stimulant, it revived hope, but it did not take the patient off the critical list. The Allies had only stepped on the toes of the giant enemy. They would have to strike at his heart before we could hope to be released from his grasp. To endure that long seemed to me like crossing the Pacific to Australia in a rowboat. Still, news of the invasion made you want to go on rowing. The devil must have chuckled at the odds; if the sharks did not get you, the hunger or exhaustion probably would. But in the barracks there were animated discussions about the changing fortunes of war.

"For a while England's position was precarious, if not hopeless," I heard someone from the intelligentsia expound. "After the loss of France, England stood alone."

"Don't be silly! The Jews were with them," kibbitzed a man on the bunk above.

A Trial by Fire

The week passed in a hopeful mood, but Sunday was hot, and again the atmosphere in the camp was tense. Before noon Feix and his entourage had been snooping around the camp kitchen, and this gave us a premonition of trouble. The men began to creep back into the shelter of their barracks, leaving the middle of the camp grounds deserted except for the officials.

Suddenly the sound of a whistle broke the silence and signaled a Sunday matinee performance. Company leaders hurried the men out of the barracks: "On the double! Let's go!" The frenzy was on, and it ran from the top down. All companies lined up in the quadrangle formation. Whispered words passed among the ranks informing us that they had found cyanide on a man working around the kitchen. Accused of having tried to poison food being prepared for the guards, he was marked for capital punishment. It was further rumored that a search had yielded some gold coins, as well as the poison, in a compartment under the false bottom of his mess kit. It was remarkable how fast the bad news traveled.

After the usual sequence of orders, the audience was ordered to stand and wait with the sun beating directly down on the dusty yard and on the men surrounding it. Then a Ukrainian guard emerged from between the barracks. He held a rope, pulling a prisoner with the other end of the rope around his neck. The man soon walked into full view; he was no more than forty years old, pale and naked and barefoot, but he seemed calm and showed no sign of panic. Feix and his SS assistant stood and watched from the center of the yard. Several Ukrainian guards with bullwhips walked behind the victim.

The lead man turned toward the company standing across the *Appellplatz* from ours. The Ukrainians ordered the men in the front rank to slap the face of the naked one. At first there was no compliance with such a revolting order, but the Ukrainians made their point with a whip. "Come on," they urged with guile, pulling the poor man before the first rank. "Slap him! Slapping won't kill him! As soon as everyone slaps him, the show will be over."

The rear guards cracked the whip whenever someone hesitated. So hundreds of palms slapped the prisoner's face in an erratic staccato. By the time he reached the company ahead of us, his face was swollen. A commotion started in the ranks as the men in front tried to shift toward the rear to avoid hitting him. But the guards were in a frenzy, striking at random across the backs of those standing in the rear.

When the man passed before our company, his eyes were practically hidden behind an enormous swelling. From time to time he opened his mouth and begged the men to hit him harder, for he wanted to die soon. In response, a man from the next company broke out from the ranks and hit the prisoner hard on the left side of his chest. He wanted to do it again, but the Ukrainians wouldn't let him; they whipped him back into the ranks.

Before they came around a second time, the man had passed out and fallen. On seeing this, Feix's assistant, SS Sergeant Axman, took command of the situation; he ordered the guards to lay the man against the back wall of the barracks in the shade and prop his head against the wall. Squatting low, Axman took the man's swollen chin and shook it sideways, without results. Reaching in his pocket, Axman brought out a pill. Someone brought water. The pill was inserted in the man's mouth, and water was forced in. Still there was no sign of recovery. The rest of the water in the cup was dashed into his face, but he just lay there motionless.

Not about to give up, Axman sent a guard to fetch a bucket of gasoline. With help from another guard, the sergeant hoisted the victim and arranged him in a sitting position. Then they lifted up both of his arms. Axman took the bucket and splashed gasoline into the unconscious one's armpits. Setting the pail down, he motioned for the guards to keep the arms up high while he struck a match. Flames flashed, and in seconds the burning sensation brought the prisoner to. Before the flames caught in his hair, the guards watered down the fire.

He was helped to his feet and, staggering, half dead, pulled back for an encore. When he fell, the guard's strong hand lifted him up by his choker rope, now shortened to one foot.

Suddenly, the ranks broke loose, making the guards nervous; they dropped the hunk of swollen misery to the ground and reached for their guns to restore order. By the time they got back to the man, he was lying motionless. Someone knelt down to listen to his heart. It was all over for him—Sunday's burnt offering had expired.

Tired by the hot sun and their afternoon amusement, the Germans and their Ukrainian lackeys left. Silently and slowly the men dispersed toward the barracks. What a tragic paradox! The man had hidden poison to spare himself from the eventuality of torture, but as it happened the very thing that was to save him from torment brought it about.

We learned later that the overseer of the *Werkschutz*, a man named Winkler, was in the habit of spying on prisoners with the help of binoculars. It was he who had spotted a man taking a gold coin from a false bottom in a mess kit. Confiscation of the utensil had also yielded the poison. Winkler had reported his find to Feix, thus sealing the man's fate. During his torture the condemned man was quoted as begging for death, expressing the wish to become a "sacrifice of atonement for all Israel." His name was Bitter.[1]

Monday was welcomed like a holiday. We were back at work, away from the camp and its ghastly atmosphere. At work we tried to forget that we were all potential corpses. Preoccupied, the men thought of their jobs as essential and sought in them a measure of dignity. At work we were auto mechanics, lathe operators, riveters, electricians, carpenters, masons, shoemakers, tailors, welders, sprayers, painters, roofers, bakers, and many other things. But back at the barracks, all of us were again a condemned lot against whom the modern Haman had decreed extermination. What was it then that kept us going? Was it the fear of death, being in its immediate presence? Or was it hope against all calculated logic that perhaps by hanging on another week, another month, we might see an end to all this? At no time did these biblical words come to mean more: "The Lord shall give thee there a trembling heart, and failing eyes, and languishing of soul. And Thy life shall hang in doubt before thee; . . . and thou shall have no assurance of thy life. In the morning thou shall say, "Would it were evening!" And at evening, thou shalt say, "Would it were morning!"—(Deuteronomy 28:65–66).

There was little value in brooding, because if you wanted to live, you had first to fortify yourself with optimism; the pessimist was licked from the start. Next, you had to concentrate on keeping body and soul together, which required a bit of luck and some cunning. Otherwise, you might as well have taken the conservative advice of bankers and declared "voluntary bankruptcy." What kept the men going was the habitual urge to live, intensified by the expectation of Germany's defeat. This hope tended to boost my morale to go on, to endure despite the reign of terror that threatened our survival. But each man had his own breaking point.

One day that week, there was an unusually long delay in returning to camp. All the groups assigned to the *Heinkelwerke* were standing in formation outside the plant gate. The guards were impatient; they did not like this delay, but it seemed that the new *Luftwaffe* camp nearby had not returned its contingent of prisoners. Soon Feix arrived on his motorcycle, appearing furious. Suddenly, two *Luftwaffe* trucks pulled up and stopped; the uniformed guards dropped the tailgates, and the men scrambled down. An *Oberfeldwebel* (staff sergeant) from the *Luftwaffe* got out of the cab and lit his pipe. All eyes turned to Feix. The prisoners, the Ukrainians, the *Werkschutz* police within the gates of the plant were all part of the audience. Feix raced to the pipe smoker, stopped within a few yards of him, and began to yell.

"Who gave you the authority to detain these prisoners one hour?"

"Who gave you the authority to yell? Do you think I am one of your prisoners? Man, hold your mouth!" came the cool reply.

"Let me remind you that you are talking to an SS noncommissioned officer, and I won't stand for this!" thundered Feix.

"*Quatsch* [Hogwash]! You are what? You are a hero over old Jews and women!"

Feix, belittled in front of his entire kingdom, surprised everyone by beating a quick retreat to his motorcycle, but not before threatening to cut off the supply of workers to *Luftwaffe*. The *Ober Feldwebel* called after him, repeating, "Who do you think you are? A hero over Jews." Slamming the cab door, he added, "You can kiss my behind."

Feix face was as red as blood. He got on his motorcycle and took off in haste, leaving clouds of dust behind. This occurrence was less remarkable in itself than in having been witnessed by an audience of Jews, Germans, and Ukrainians all of whom had reason to fear the authority of this Caesar. Apparently, where his authority did not extend, he preferred to hightail it in order to spare himself further humiliation. Even though our lives were still very much in his hands and his authority was only momentarily undermined, his stature had been diminished drastically by this argument.

Feix must have had his tantrum at home, because he was nowhere to be seen in the camp for a while. I felt so stimulated by the experience that I overlooked the possibility of retaliation—not against the *Luftwaffe*, who could kick him in his rump, but against us, his helpless prisoners. The next day, as I busied myself around Garbe's quarters digging holes for transplanting bushes, the silhouette of a horseback rider suddenly came into focus. Before I could hide, Feix, astride his white charger, beckoned to me with a finger. My turn has come, I thought. Driving the spade into the ground, I approached briskly, took off my cap, and stood at attention. Towering over me from his mount, Feix looked me straight in the eyes for a moment. I returned his gaze.

"What do you do here?" asked Feiks.

"I do gardening and whatever else I am ordered by Commandant Garbe," I replied.

"What kind of gardener are you?" Feix questioned.

"The best there is, *Herr Oberscharfuehrer!*"

Feix toyed with his automatic, watching me for a reaction. As I stood still and tried to look calm, hoping Garbe would come out, something else must have caught his attention, for he spurred his horse and galloped away. My breathing resumed, and I donned my cap and went back to plant and water my bushes. Perhaps my fear had been unwarranted; Feix had never been known to kill anyone around the *Heinkelwerke*, I reasoned. But then again, he had never been seen here before either.

By the time I joined the formation, I had learned that Feix was up in arms because five Ukrainian guards, among them one of rank, had escaped to join the partisans. Even among the hated Ukrainians, it appeared, there were some who would not buy their relative security by becoming instruments of torture and execution. Some were volunteers from the Ukraine and others recruited from among the Red Army prisoners of war; they were used by the Germans to do their dirty work in the ghettos and SS camps. Whether these five who had escaped were afraid for their skins were the Russians to come, or whether they were prompted by a higher sense of conscience, we could only speculate.

The ranking man among them had been treated for tuberculosis. When the Jewish doctor he had consulted confirmed that his illness had been checked, the escape took place.

As we marched to camp that night, our Ukrainian guards were less belligerent than usual. They could not overlook the fact that this escape, unlike that of any prisoners, had to be reported to Feix's superiors. What would happen? Would those left behind be punished for letting the others run away?

The quadrangle filled up, and the endless counting began, with Feix's presence a harbinger of trouble. Sure enough, he soon picked three men at random, among them a POW named Arnet. Flanked by Ukrainians, Feix paused long enough to explain that these three were to be executed because the guards who had escaped had done so at the prisoners' "urging"! This formality dispensed with, the three were brought to the barbed-wire fence near the latrine and ordered to kneel down. They obeyed, holding their hands behind their necks. As the men cried out, "*Shema Israel* . . . Hear, Oh Israel, the Lord is our God, the Lord is one!" the shots rang out. And it was all over—for them.

That evening the Ukrainians invaded the barracks and went berserk, beating men left and right, apparently trying to prove their loyalty to their masters. The terror reached proportions unprecedented since our arrival. Oh God, would it were morning! There was no singing the next day when we marched out of the blood-stained arena to the refuge of the factory, where you could not believe that there was such a thing as Camp Budzyn. The aftertaste of this most recent outrage was so heavily depressing that even good war news did not seem to mean much to us, and as the workday's end approached, I dreaded the return to camp as I never had before.

In the late July evening the apprehension was evident on the faces of all the men, from the well-clad POWs in front to the ragtag multitude that followed. Each one was wearing some sort of a belt or rope from which his mess-kit or pan hung; all were hungry and tired, all fearful of what lay ahead. Again we refrained from singing. All you heard was the sound of marching feet.

Feix was not to be seen anywhere around the camp upon our return. The count revealed three men missing. In the past, the administration officials had sometimes been able to fake the count and cover up for one missing man by shifting one already counted to close the gap in ranks before the SS man got there. The absence of *three* men was more difficult to conceal. As the recount began, Freudlich, standing next to me, whispered in my ear, "The three are from our company— they escaped from the field."

Sure enough, when the recount ended, our company was singled out. Nevertheless, Axman, in the absence of Feix, dismissed everyone. Knowing that this matter was not closed but not knowing what to expect, we went to line up for soup. In the barracks afterward there was little talk about the whole affair and less conversation than usual. Soon everyone lay down in his bunk. The lights went out and quiet fell over the whole barracks. The night belonged to the slaves. We had risen before the break of dawn, marched miles, stood in lines, worked hard. After a grueling day we fell asleep from sheer mental and physical exhaustion.

A shot fired outside followed by violent shouting woke everyone up. Before I could notice that it was still night, the doors of the barracks burst open, and Ukrainians and Jewish officials urged us to fall out on the double. Szczypiacki and others blew the whistle. I got my clothing on and ran outside with my company, whipped through the door by the guards and by Feix himself.

Feix had someone hold a big reflector spotlight on the half-dazed men coming out while he kept lashing about with his whip and pointing his automatic rifle. We lined up five abreast along the barracks wall in spite of interference by Feix, whose bullwhip kept cracking down over our heads. The worst was the iron ball on the end of the whip that bit into flesh wherever it struck. And to think that I had cried at seeing the picture of floggings ordered by the cruel Captain Bligh of the *Bounty!*

One final count was taken to verify the previous counts. Then Feix bellowed: "Three *Schweinehunde* are missing. I will take thirty hostages and keep them. If in three days the escapees are not back or caught, the hostages will be shot!" Starting at the head of the column, Feiks walked sideways, facing each line of five. Before he came toward the middle, where I stood, he had already picked Bronstein, his buddy Wroclaw, and Matys, all three from the Okecie group. He was in front of our five. His hand pointed to Freudlich. In about five minutes, twenty-six hostages in all had been selected. The Ukrainians marched them to the favored execution spot by the latrine and ordered them to lie face down.

The rest of us were ordered back to the barracks.

I had more than I could stand. I stood by my bunk praying silently for death for myself. "If I may be granted one wish, seeing that we are all dead, please let me die in my sleep, for I don't want to get up to look on my misery and that of these people. All I am asking is a natural, quick death in here and not in the arena."

With the light of another day, I realized that the Chief Architect of this sad planet had not accepted my plea. We were back on the *Appellplatz* for the morning ceremony, but this time it was graced by the twenty-six still lying face down. One was dead; during the night he had asked for permission to urinate, had been told it was okay, then was shot down on the spot when he rose.

Returning twelve hours later, we found the men still lying prone watched over by the black-clad guards. I couldn't eat without feeling guilty, knowing that our friends had not touched food or water in nearly twenty-four hours. The guards made sure that nothing passed from our hands to theirs. The three runaway slaves were still at large, and it was now a question of a small massacre or a large one. Evening came, and then morning—the second day. The faces of the hostages looked bluish. We learned that the guards in their jackboots had danced on the heads and backs of their victims. On our return from work, we contemplated the same sight.

That night I could not sleep, kept awake by the groans of those still lying outside. Evening came, and then morning—the third day. The faces of the victims were by now dark blue and swollen. Three nights and two days without food, water, or motion was more than one could endure, or even watch. Yet the eyes of all the prisoners were centered on this rotting lot of human misery.

The singing during marching had ceased altogether, the men showing indifference to the guards' coaxing and beating. I cursed the day, for it no longer brought a light of hope. The whole world had lost its reason. What good did it do us to know that the Allies would win? What good was it to believe that the retribution would be so severe that it would prevent any possibility of a recurrence? In the meantime, the burning bush to which Israel had been likened was being consumed— though not yet entirely; some were still left.

A Change Of Command

On the third day a rumor spread through the ranks that Feix was to be replaced. If true, this would surely be a change for the better, since nobody else could be as bad. Anxiety dominated our mood on our return to camp. What about the hostages? Would they be able to hold out?

The incredible thing about the hopeless is that against all logic they keep hoping to the end. Here we were worried about the hostages, all along knowing but not admitting that our own days, too, were numbered. On reaching the camp, we were astonished to learn that the hostages had been "released," and that Feix was no longer in command or even on the premises. It was just too unreal to believe, but, sure enough, there was just an empty place of soiled ground near the latrine where the hostages had lain for three nights.

As soon as I got to the barracks, I went to see Freudlich. His black face was swollen like a balloon, and he had difficulty opening his mouth to feed himself, but there he sat on his bunk, eating soup. His eyes were bloodshot and barely open, yet he wore clean coveralls and looked bathed. All the survivors' faces looked alike. I waited until Freudlich finished eating to speak to him. But before I opened my mouth, Freudlich made a hand gesture, begging to be left alone. It was not until the next evening that he would talk again. He still had difficulty parting his swollen lips and could only whisper. Matys, one of the Okecie group, tried to force a pained smile, but he too was still unable to speak.

Feix had been replaced that day by a new commander from the gendarmerie (German police). Sergeant Otto Mohr's first act had been to order the hostages into the bath and to waive their execution. Some were able to get up on their own; others had to be carried. For one man, nothing could be done; in the bath, another man died. But except for those who were personally affected by this ordeal, the rest of us were now preoccupied with speculating on the meaning of the change in command. There was much talk throughout the barracks, all in a hopeful vein. The new boss was businesslike and made it known right from the start that the camp would be run "by the book." From then on, flogging would be administered only for a "reason" and shooting limited to ten men for each one that escaped. These "reforms" did not evoke any signs of joy, yet there was a quiet feeling of relief at being spared Feix's brand of terror.

The first few days passed without any serious incidents, and the tension eased. The sound of song again echoed through the woods around the *Heinkelwerke*. Things were back to what passed for normal. All those in whom there was a breath of life felt as if they had been granted a stay of execution, however temporary. There was interest again in the progress of the war. The Allied landings in Calabria contributed to a feeling of optimism, nourishing the faded hopes for our survival if the war ended soon. Even jokes were heard again in the barracks.

The hopeful mood in the camp was broken by an incident occasioned by an escape. The new commandant, without the showmanship that had characterized previous executions, picked ten men and had them unceremoniously shot. True to his word, he ran this camp by the book—though it is not a good book. Yet when the camp recovered from this most recent bloodshed, the men considered Mohr a better executioner than the SS Feix.

Shortly thereafter, the carpenters began setting up a wooden flagpole-like post. Though there was general concern about this innovation, nobody I knew was willing to guess the worst. Someone said, "They will hang a large bell on it so that the bell ringing will be used for all signals instead of whistles." But what could once have passed for optimism was now subdued.

The following morning *Wachtmeister* Mohr relieved one of the company leaders of his job. His removal delayed our morning departure from camp. Bauchwitz, a German Jew and former captain in the German army, carried himself with military bearing when he was ordered to take his position between two Ukrainian guards, who led him toward the "flagpole." Even as he marched his last stretch, he kept in step with the guards and tried to conceal a limp caused by an old leg wound. Standing by the scaffold, he faced Mohr, who informed him that he must die. There was no further explanation for the execution. Bauchwitz, showing no fear, addressed Mohr for many to hear.

"I am a German officer. I was six times wounded. I have fought for the Fatherland. What have you done for Germany?" His plea, requesting shooting, as befits an officer, instead of hanging, was denied. From the women's compound, Bauchwitz's wife pleaded with Mohr for the life of her husband but Bauchwitz discouraged her: *"Mein Liebling, es ist ganz vergeblich."* ("My beloved, it is all in vain.") He then saluted and spoke briefly, making only one pleading gesture to Mohr, who turned on his heel and left the scene.

As soon as Mohr withdrew, the Ukrainian guards tried to put a sack over Bauchwitz's head, but he vigorously opposed this. With the entire camp watching, a regulation noose was placed around his neck. His hands tied behind him, Bauchwitz took one last look at his audience; then, unaided, he mounted the scaffold's little platform, still hiding his limp, and stood erect, waiting. The platform was rapidly pulled out from under his feet, and his body swung in the air.

Among the men stood his son Rudi, watching. At one moment he had tried to run to his father, but the other prisoners restrained him. For most, it was their first eyewitness experience of a formal hanging, and the event made a horrifying impression. Bauchwitz, a German patriot, a decorated hero of World War I, wounded at the battle of Verdun, had not even been permitted a soldier's death.

All that I could learn about this affair was that there had been a special order from Berlin, with its own sinister logic, reasoning that the existence of Jewish German heroes was embarrassing to a government that had declared its Jewish citizens to be disloyal parasites. Consequently, these heroes had to be declared traitors and subjected to immediate execution.

Those who heard Bauchwitz's plea reported that all he had asked was to be shot like a soldier, not hanged like a thief or traitor; knowing that the order could not be rescinded, he asked only for an honorable death, but even this was denied him. He was not even allowed five minutes with his wife or son. This Jew's only apparent crime had been to serve his country with honor and devotion. In camp he had been a real officer, not merely a company leader for the benefits the job offered. He had cared for his men and had seen to it that the cooks gave them a full share of their meals.

Bauchwitz's cruel fate reminded me of a movie my father had told me about when I was eight or so. Sergeant Grisha, a Russian prisoner captured by the Germans in World War I, was suspected of espionage and interned in an army prison. There, he cheerfully performed various chores, and in the evening he would sing for his guards. The German soldiers got to like their friendly hostage; even a few officers were attracted by his warmth and vivaciousness and believed him innocent of the spying charge. But as a matter of military paper routine, the order came for his execution. The prison officials at first withheld the bad news from the Russian; instead, they went so far as to ask a senior officer to intervene for the life of their prisoner. The senior officer consented to try and went as high as his rank permitted, seeking a pardon for what he termed "an innocent prisoner of war." But the commanding German rebuked the senior officer for his lack of discipline and respect for German military regulations, which he considered more important than the alleged innocence of the prisoner. When the refusal came down the chain of command to the prison, the Germans could only watch Grisha with sadness as he received the news. The next morning, still looking friendly as always, Grisha was led to a stake in the prison ground, where an officer tied a blindfold over his tearful eyes, and, on command, the firing squad loosed its volley.

I had cried when Father finished the story. Mother reproached him for telling his eight-year-old such a heartbreaking tale. My father tried to cheer me up, asking me not to feel sorry for Grisha because, he explained, this episode had not really happened except in the book and on the screen. Ten years later, I knew it could not really have happened. No one ever intervened for Bauchwitz, who was once Germany's hero—nor, for that matter, for anyone else. There would be no taps sounded for Bauchwitz or for the millions of nameless victims of the Third Reich.

10 A New Slavemaster

If there is any pain like my pain.
—Lamentations 1:12

Wachtmeister Mohr's tenure was short-lived. Late in the summer of 1943 he was replaced by SS *Untersturmfuehrer* (second lieutenant) Tauscher. Immediately upon arrival he took center stage to make an opening address. Of better than medium height and heavy-set, Tauscher spread his legs apart and struck a Napoleonic pose, alternately sliding one hand and then the other into his coat opening.

"I am your new commandant and I thought that it would be a good idea to talk to you in order that I be better understood. First of all, let me say that all I am interested in is to see that you work and produce. As long as you work, you eat. If you try to escape, you will surely be shot. But if you stay and work, you may live, perhaps, through the war. After Germany wins the war, you will be exchanged for German prisoners of war who are in England. So let us see real effort in work, to help the war effort. I repeat. . . ." And he repeated nearly everything, then withdrew.

His rank, his controlled manner, and his speech did not resemble those of the brutal Feix, but we held our breath in anticipation, waiting for him to show his hand. Meanwhile, the only comfort we drew from his speech was the admission that there were German war prisoners in England. The intelligentsia debated the matter.

"How do you suppose they treat Germans there?" asked one of them.

"Not half as bad as they treat us here," came the reply.

"If I know what I am talking about," said another one, who thought that he did, "the British probably teach them how to better their soccer game."

"How do you explain that after what they did to their cities?" asked the first one.

"Don't be naive," explained the cynic knowingly. "The generals don't want to treat them harshly. If they do, they risk discouraging war altogether—and to a general, war is as romantic as a kiss to a young maiden. Besides, how else would the people know who is a good general without a war? A general's career without a war is like an actor's career without ever being on stage. Figure that out, boy!"

The rule of the new pharaoh did not change anything. But no

matter how desperate the situation might be in camp, at work I could breathe again. Schleswig, back after another absence, wanted me to come to his apartment at the German settlement. The idea at first seemed preposterous—a Jewish prisoner of the SS visiting a German? But Schleswig insisted; he had already told Garbe that he was taking me with him to "fix something" at his place. Garbe did not object. Luxemburg was told that after my alleged work was finished, Schleswig would personally escort me back to camp before the count.

As incredible as it seemed, here was this German walking with a Jewish prisoner through the open woods, and we were talking to one another like two acquaintances in the park. For a fleeting moment I felt a heady illusion of freedom. The absence of the crowd and the quiet of a late sunny August day made me want to lie down and just hug the earth and cry—cry out to Him Who created it all to look down with mercy. Schleswig must have realized the deep emotional impact that this excursion made on me, because he held his peace for a long while before he spoke.

"Georg, it will not be very long now. The war is going badly for them." I noticed for the first time that Schleswig referred to his Nazi government as "them" with a pronounced emphasis.

"When he first came to power in 1934, he said, 'Give me Germany for ten years and you will not recognize it.' Now, the people know that here he did not lie—another year of war and no one will recognize Germany."

"Did he really say that?" I asked.

"He not only said it but had it engraved on the Munich Reichstag building."

At the settlement, from which our camp could be seen (dampening my illusion of being free), he opened the door of his apartment and asked me to come in. A real home, with rooms, furniture, beds, clean shining floors, personal effects, family pictures (including a portrait of his pretty daughter), knick-knacks—the contrast with what I had been used to in the last two years was too drastic for description. His family was out that afternoon.

Come to the kitchen, Georg. We will see about getting something to eat."

The kitchen was small and spotless, with modern plumbing. He found some bread and margarine and we ate his rationed food. Afterward, he set a bottle of eggnog on the table. Filling two tea glasses halfway, he looked at me and raised his glass; we touched glasses and drank. Schleswig told me something about himself, his family, and his home town of Stettin. The afternoon passed quickly, and soon it was time to get back to the camp. Schleswig escorted me to the gate, where he reported his unorthodox and unusual one-man detail returning ahead of the main body of prisoners.

It was always easier to return than to leave. Back in the camp, I got very hungry again, even though I had had something to eat and drink a few hours earlier. I felt weak and walked unsteadily. I headed for the kitchen to see if I could draw my soup early, ahead of my company. I suspected that this was not going to work, but I was going to try anyway. What harm could it do?

My appearance at the kitchen feeding window attracted no one's attention, nor did it produce any results, so I turned and started for my barracks. But halfway across the empty *Appellplatz* I did attract someone's attention. A voice called, "Hey, you, come here!"

I turned my head in the direction of the voice, and my heart skipped a beat. The man calling me was none other than *Untersturmfuehrer* Tauscher. He stood poised with one hand held behind him, the other rested its thumb behind his belt buckle. The narrow end of a whip was showing from behind his back. When I came within talking distance, I stopped, took off my cap, and stood at attention. The thought of food vanished from my mind. Tauscher, on close inspection, seemed fat.

"What was wrong with your legs before?" asked the commandant, tilting his heels back and forth like one who was going to take his time.

"Nothing, sir. I was just a bit tired."

"Tired?" said Tauscher, moving one step closer. "*Tired?*" He repeated more loudly. "Drunk! Call the doctor," he ordered one of the Jewish policemen, "and we shall find out for sure." He had not yet finished speaking when Mosbach, the pipe-smoking Jewish German doctor, appeared. Without removing his gaze from me, Tauscher asked the doctor, "Is he or is he not drunk?"

Mosbach did not come close enough for me to smell his pipe smoke before he pronounced the verdict: "*Jawohl, Herr Untersturmfuehrer*, he is definitely drunk." This scientific opinion encouraged Tauscher to amplify: "He is drunk as a pig! Who gave you the drink?"

"No one."

After counting fifteen lashes, I felt less pain, except for the little lead ball that kept digging into my flesh every time the whip struck. Twenty-five lashes was all I got. Slowly, I got off my knees and looked at Tauscher.

"How did you get hold of liquor? Who gave it to you?"

"No one, no one." I had resolved not to implicate Schleswig.

"Throw him in the bunker."

The gates of the camp were opened, and I was escorted to the guardhouse where crawl space used as a coal bin served as solitary confinement. I staggered in and was content to be left alone, to lie on the floor and lick my wounds. At that point I did not care about anything except sleep, the only refuge I had left.

When finally I was awakened by the noise outside, I realized it was another morning, and I became aware of the filthy, dark, damp hole I had been in all night. Just then, unexpectedly, the door opened and a guard ordered, "Come on, out of here." Without another word, he led me into the camp just in time to catch up with my outgoing formation.

Garbe stood in front of his office as he often did but he looked annoyed. When he called me to come close, I knew right away that he had been notified about me and probably reprimanded, for he was very angry. He began by shouting:

"Where did you snatch the liquor? You know I don't give you any. Why did you say you found it around here?"

"I did not say that."

At that moment Tauscher and another SS man appeared in the distance. They caught Garbe's attention. If he hoped to impress upon the higher-ranking Tauscher that he was above liking Jews, Garbe soon proved his point: he embarked on a tirade, augmented by vigorous face-slapping.

As Tauscher drew nearer Garbe, still acting furious, ordered me back to work with a finger-shaking warning and words possibly meant for the commandant's ears: "Watch yourself. Next time, I will beat you to death!"

Even though some of his behavior was calculated to absolve himself of any wrongdoing, Garbe really was angry at me for involving him "by association." He did not speak to me for a few days, nor did he later try to explain his violent conduct. His relationship with Schleswig did not change at least to outward appearances, yet he might have guessed that if there was any truth to the drinking charge, the liquor must have come from Schleswig.

Garbe was not a bad guy by comparison with others, but here he drew the line. When a bit of alleged trouble was traced back to his domain, he was not concerned with establishing the facts or pursuing the merits of the case; he was simply content to sacrifice the most vulnerable element as an acceptable scapegoat. He was part of a system that generated this sort of "justice," not only toward its victims but even among themselves, for this was *their* method of survival.

As for Schleswig, he understandably faded from view whenever I was around. In a few days everything had simmered down, but nothing was ever the same again.

Without any formal advance notice, one of Adolf Eichmann's extermination *Einsatz* Kommando units arrived and were quartered in an
empty barracks in the Polish labor camp. Garbe was apprehensive of
them, as were the other Germans, because they knew that the powers
of this group were virtually unlimited. The news of their arrival shook
the camp with sudden fear. The question debated in our barracks was
whether the Germans in the *Heinkelwerke* would be able to stay our
execution in order to save themselves from front-line duty by insisting
that our work was essential.

Garbe ordered me to take hot shaving water to the newcomers'
barracks. Though I was not particularly anxious to see them, I knocked
on the door. A voice snapped, "Come in." I entered holding a large
teapot of hot water, and waited for instructions. These merchants of
death were busy cleaning their automatic guns, shining their boots,
and the like, but they could not deceive me. They were not soldiers—
they were the gravediggers of our people. There was a macabre atmosphere about them as they sang a song that asserted, *"Es geht alles
voreber, es geht alles vorbei."* (Everything goes away; everything goes by.)

"Set the water on the table! And quit staring!" the voice said, and I
was relieved to leave the company of executioners. I knew that their
presence spelled calamity—and sure enough, that evening the guard
was doubled around the camp and the gates were padlocked—something never done before. A hushed, uneasy silence fell over the men in
the barracks. Next morning, we awakened to the startling news that the
prisoners were not to be sent to work. The dreaded thought that our
camp was slated for liquidation came closer.

The spirit of the men was at its lowest ebb since our arrival here. We
had always seemed to bounce back after an ordeal; our hearts had kept
on beating. But as the grim prospect assumed all the signs of impending disaster, there was nothing anyone could do except prepare to face
his Maker. Even then we clung to the thread of hope that perhaps the
German civilian management at the plant was still arguing for the
manpower they needed to carry on—a faint hope, growing dimmer
with each passing hour.[1]

As we awaited our fate, the camp authorities made a strange announcement: they requested inventors, chemists, and engineers to
register in the office. The immediate speculation was that they wanted
to kill the intelligentsia, even if they spared the others. Yet other
possibilities were worth considering. The next step could be very
important, but the wrong choice could wipe you out altogether.
Granted there was virtually nothing to lose either way; one's decision
would simply hasten or delay the inevitable, promised by our foes. I
made my choice instinctively, without lengthy deliberation. Disregard-

ing the fact that I neither belonged to any of the professions they sought nor had I any qualifications related to science, I registered as a chemist.

It was simple enough to register. All you had to do was give your name and profession. I learned later that thirty-six men from the Budzyn camp had registered in the face of impending doom.

But Providence's ways are mysterious. Had it not been for the fear of liquidation, few if any would have registered as inventors or chemists in the hope of escaping their fate. As it was, by the next day I felt like a man regretting the purchase of a stock that was rapidly falling. The whistles blew on time for the morning count, and as we went back to work, everything seemed getting back to "normal." The SS special group had left us on their list of unfinished business, perhaps until we were no longer needed. Being registered as a scientist now became the liability of appearing conspicuous, or so I thought. No one knew what this registration business was all about, and all speculation about what it might mean ran into a dead end.

However, returning to work improved our mood and generally relieved our cramped-up feeling of doom. The German plant authorities must have prevailed on the SS to spare what they called labor essential to the war effort.[2] In reality, the Heinkel plant was a big white elephant. Under the supervision of German civilian personnel some 3,000 Jewish prisoners from Budzyn, together with hundreds of Polish and German civilians, were busy setting up a plant intended to assemble Heinkel HE-111 bombers. Machines displaying French and even Russian labels were installed; parts, blueprints, and paints began to arrive. So even though our labor did not cost them any more than the food they gave us, the German government was spending a fortune trying to get this plant into production.

It was at that time that Garbe dropped me, and I was assigned to work in the plant's blueprint-reproducing office. From the window of the office I could observe the first plane's ribs being assembled and the riveters, with their popping noises, dressing this metal bird with aluminum sheets.

Our office had a blueprint-copying machine operated by two German Jewish prisoners. My friend Hak—the quiet, soft-spoken man from Hrubieszczow—another fellow named Platou, and a girl prisoner constituted the prisoner office crew, under the management of a Polish worker and a young German civilian. No one knew what his job consisted of; our German superior said only that we were "responsible for handling blueprints." To kill time, we would scrounge for food and read whatever came to hand, even German manuals. To read again was a sensational feeling, as though I were learning for the first time.

Talking with Platou, I recognized him as a senior from the Razwilowski School, which we had both attended. He was an accomplished musician and loved music, though his violin had been taken away from him.

The German supervisor was easygoing but always worried about losing his job. He feared being sent to the front and often expressed his concern. Once he said to me, "Look, I am going away for the rest of the day. If someone higher up asks for me, say that I felt sick and went home."

When I looked closely at him, he admitted honestly, "I am not really sick, but this is what you should say if asked; otherwise I could get in trouble." In this way he managed to pile up an impressive number of absences. Perhaps he was involved in another venture, such as counterfeiting, or possibly he was just sleeping off the war.

By the middle of September the first bomber was ready for take-off, but there was no nearby airfield or level terrain suitable for a runway to accommodate its size. Something had gone wrong. A single-engine light aircraft arrived, bringing some big shots from the Reich. Heinkel himself was rumored to be among those who had come to inspect the problem. There was no way of knowing what they had decided except from the new directive issued afterward, according to which the Budzyn plant was going to repair and manufacture aircraft parts only. The finished bomber had to be dismantled, along with all those in an advanced assembly stage, and much of the equipment and machinery that had taken so many months to assemble also had to be dismantled for return shipment. In short, the plant was relegated to the status of an oversized repair shop. Aside from the few small metal parts it fabricated, its main operation consisted of patching wings. But the German supervisors, to save their necks and their own civilian status, made a big show out of it.

At the beginning the wing repairs did keep everyone busy, but soon the Allied bombings began to prevent new shipments; in this winter of 1943-44 the war was going badly for the Germans. The German *Meisters* (foremen) then became partners in crime with the prisoners, not merely tolerating but tacitly agreeing to what could only be called sabotage. Newly riveted patches would be stripped off so that new ones could be put on again, making everyone look busy. Whenever military men came to inspect the plant, the first one to notice them would hiss the concentration camp prisoners' universal password for trouble: *Sechs* (six). In every hall they entered, the word *sechs* would signal a sudden burst of activity. Lathes would begin to turn, hammers to bang, welders to weld, and riveters to pop their rivets. It was the kind of music the military liked to hear, unaware that these were really only the sound effects of a war being lost.

The remarkable thing was that the German civilians were part of this conspiracy—in some sections the same rudder hole was patched as many as ten times!—and knowing this dispelled the myth of German efficiency and made us aware that the end was drawing near. So because all the indicators here were favorable, there was a feeling of relief in the camp that we were back at work.

In spite of this renewed hope, the return prisoners' count showed a man missing one day in early November, and repeated counts confirmed the fact, Tauscher unceremoniously picked hostages, concentrating on the relatives of the missing prisoner, and they were escorted to the favored execution spot by the latrine to await their fate. The commandant announced that he would wait an hour for the missing man to return or to be captured before shooting the hostages. The men were to stay in their ranks surrounding the *Appellplatz* until the hour was up. Then, suddenly, the missing man appeared, walking unescorted toward the camp entrance. He walked slowly and seemed unconcerned about anything except the half-finished loaf of bread he was eating. The guards opened the gate and let him in. There was an oppressive silence as the latecomer was brought before the principal. Since he had not removed his cap, being intent on eating, the guard pulled it off.

Tauscher stared at him but got no attention from the one whose life was in his hands. Abruptly, Tauscher ordered him shot, reaching his verdict in less than a minute. Only then did the man speak. In a Jewish mixed with German he said goodbye to us: "I am going now, but you still have to suffer."

The guards prodded him with a rifle; he did not budge but turned to Tauscher: "You are shooting me now, for which act *you will hang* as soon as the war is lost—*lost*, did you hear?!"

Now the guards pushed him hard. The unfinished bread lay on the ground as the young man walked unaided to the execution spot, already cleared of hostages. Prodded to kneel, he obliged, in the last moment pulling the tail of his coat over his head, as though to use it for shelter or perhaps to say his last prayer. A shot fired from the back cut him down to the ground, face forward, blood running from his head. The prisoners, horrified, exclaimed spontaneously the usual *"Shema Israel!"* Then it was all over, except for the burial.

This poor soul had evidently just wanted, for once, to eat to the full. For this he had paid the highest price. Throughout, he behaved stoically and to the very end showed no emotion or fear. His address to the head butcher, short and simple, conveyed his belief in ultimate justice. He could not possibly have conceived that a Feix might die a natural death long after the war, or that a Tauscher could wind up selling insurance or making money in South America. At that time both the oppressed and the oppressors "knew" that if they should lose the war, they would hang as sure as day follows night. The Nazis expected no less and did not keep their fear a secret—promising, however, to liquidate us first.

11 New Opportunities and New Risks

Thou shall serve thine enemy in hunger and in thirst
. . . and in want of all things.
—Deuteronomy 28:48

After these events I began to experience hunger as I had never known it before. No longer able to scramble for the extra food my old job had supplied, I was existing on rations alone. Those who said our rations were not enough to live on and too much to die on were wrong; the fact was that the men who lived on rations alone *were* dying. The first symptom after you began to look like a skeleton was the swelling of the legs and face. Those who exhibited these characteristics were called in all camps *"Musulmen"* (Moslems). I don't know why, unless this name was inspired by films of hungry and skinny-looking Moslems in India. Once so identified, a man was generally regarded as a goner.

In November, before the frost made its debut, my situation was growing progressively worse. One Sunday I sat outside, leaning against the barracks to absorb the last warm rays of sunshine, but I was not merely basking in a November sun. I was thinking hard, trying to develop a scheme that would improve my lot. Nothing overambitious—just a way to survive by finding a way to get food.

There was hardly any flesh on my bones by then, and I had to think fast before the hunger reached a stage at which it would numb my thinking capacity. This stage is preceded by a lack of vigor, which in turn causes all effort to cease. Aware that I was on the verge of losing my grip on life, I spent the whole day thinking about it. There was no point in contemplating how destitute and low my fortunes had fallen; self-pity serves no useful purpose. So, after much deliberation, I began to concentrate on the clothing storeroom. Schubert, the pipe-smoking German Jew, was in charge of it. New clothing, some of which could be sold, was given out once in a blue moon to a whole company at a time, and our company was not even due. Breaking in could and probably would end in disaster, so something cleverer had to be devised. A legitimate way of getting new clothing, I reasoned, could be found when the company was drawing it—or—or what? Or when someone had no clothing at all on him! And how could someone have no clothing at all on him? By having it stolen at night. What if someone is not believed? Someone could attract a lot of attention from the Jewish officials. That's good. Someone could draw the interest of Tauscher. That's bad. But if someone wants to eat, someone will have to take risks. So, one cold November morning, I got up before the others and stuffed my clothes into the straw sack of an empty bunk away from my own. I dreaded exposure to the cold, but my scheme left me no choice. Wearing only my shoes and my ragged trunks, I went back to my bunk to await the morning whistle.

The success of my stunt depended on the reaction of Sztokman, the Jewish POW commandant, and on timing. From the moment the whistles blew for the morning formation until Tauscher and his SS henchmen entered the camp compound for the morning count there were only a few minutes. In that short span of time I had to attract Stockman's attention and get a favorable reaction before Tauscher and his bully boys investigated the merits of my complaint. The morning rush, I believed, could work in my favor, allowing no time for lengthy questioning by the camp prison administration.

When the whistle blew, I got up and ran outside, complaining that my clothing was missing. I ran slowly, deliberately passing by Sztokman, who always seemed under pressure before the Germans walked into the camp compound. I drew a mixed reaction of smiles and looks of surprise. Shivering in the biting cold, I knew that success or failure depended entirely on Sztokman. Sztokman noticed me all right. How could he have failed? The bizarre spectacle of a half-naked man running in the November chill was enough to attract everyone's attention.

"And where do you think *you* are going?" he asked, stopping me.

"To join my company ranks."

"Like this? What happened to your clothing?" he demanded.

"It was gone when I woke up."

The camp administration assistants gathered around, looking skeptical but amused. Perhaps their amusement influenced the outcome. Just as Szczypiacki, smiling as though he had seen through my scheme, expressed doubts about my story, Sztokman made up his mind and gave his order to the pipe-puffing Schubert: "Get him some clothes before Tauscher sees him and whips him to death!" Whether Sztokman believed the story was not as important as his decision to help me out in a moment of crisis.

When Schubert opened the storeroom and we both walked in, I felt as though suddenly the gates of heaven had opened to let my prayer through. Now I had to take maximum advantage of this opportunity. I did not expect any help from Schubert; he did not strike me as the compassionate type. He treated his job seriously, as though it were a permanent position. So while he busied himself in the back looking for an overcoat in my size, I put on three sweaters and an extra pair of pants. When Schubert returned with the overcoat, I grabbed it and ran to join the formation before he could take a good look at me.

That day at the plant I sold one pair of tweed pants to the Polish employee, who in return agreed to supply me with a quarter-pound of bread every working day for about three weeks. The rest I sold to another employee for cash. (Despite the initial search, some men and women had managed to hide their valuables.) It looked as though I would not starve for at least a month, perhaps longer. With typical optimism, I thought that a lot could happen in one month. And a lot did happen.

Our New Status

The first unexpected occurrence was the replacement of the Ukrainian guard detachment by German Rumanian SS guards. We were certainly relieved to be rid of our Ukrainian tormentors, but as it turned out, their successors were no different except that stricter regulations prevented them from entering the camp at random after hours without orders.

Another event was the evacuation of the Polish volunteer worker camp and its conversion into a regular concentration camp, which became our new home. Now we experienced something new. Hitherto, we had been only "forced laborers," but now after having proved ourselves merely by surviving preceding tests, we were advanced to the new status of *Haeftlinge*, or internees, of a regulation-type concentration camp. Before, we were just statistics without identities; at this stage each one could feel like an individual, distinct from everyone else, because each of us was given a different number, to be worn on his jacket.

Prior to entry, all convicts were "processed" by surrendering their civilian rags for clean blue-and-white striped uniforms, undergoing the customary initiation bath, and getting a funny haircut. The clippers left a two-inch "aisle" in the center of your head, dividing your hair into two even patches. The bizarre appearance had the calculated effect of making us look conspicuous and contemptible. One man would look at another and laugh at his ill-fitting pajama-like uniform and clownish haircut, only to evoke laughter himself. Matching striped round caps without visors completed our new wardrobe.

The new camp was situated opposite the *Heinkelwerke;* that would eliminate the long march to work, and in winter this was a welcome change. The camp was bordered on one side by the factory and on the other by the German *Wehrmacht* noncom and officers' school. We did not know the reason for these changes, but the area had seen many. First it had been a German *Luftwaffe* officers' school, then a Polish camp.

Where I had once worked as a gardener, there now stood a brand-new concentration camp. For us, however, though the scenery and costumes had changed, it was still the same play.

Soon a new commandant relieved Tauscher. Before relinquishing the stage to his successor, however, Tauscher executed two brothers named Seidenberg and their brother-in-law, who came from Zaklikow, for an unspecified offense, although it was rumored that another brother had escaped. Before ordering the execution, Tauscher cynically explained that instead of shooting ten, he would shoot only three, as though trying to win approval.

In another incident, Huna, a boy in his early teens from the nearby village of Zakrzuwek, had been caught eating a stolen potato. When he pleaded for his life, the Germans assured him that it would hurt only a moment and then shot him through the head.

The new SS commandant, a man named Frank, was there long enough to ruthlessly suppress an attempted mass escape at night. Many men were shot while entangled in the barbed wire, and all those trapped inside were machine-gunned. This bloodbath did not discourage a group of Warsaw men from making another attempt on Christmas Eve. Working near the plant guardhouse, they relieved the boozed-up guards of their uniforms and guns and took to the woods. This was apparently more than enough to cause Frank's replacement by still another SS officer.

Equal in rank to his predecessor, SS officer *Obersturmfuehrer* named Josef Leipold was the new ruler. I don't recall anything in his maiden speech or early conduct that would have revealed his character. He had a little dog that occupied much of his time. During morning and evening formations, he would publicly try to train the pint-sized dog, which was indifferent to its master's commands, despite his high rank and undisputed authority. Strangely enough, the dog was then not even disciplined. There was a strong kinship between these two that we prisoners somewhat envied.

Once a prisoner in an administrative post petted the dog and was severely beaten by Leipold for such familiarity. It was a debatable question whether Leipold feared that the dog would be contaminated or whether he was merely punishing the prisoner for his presumption. One among us who was very learned was quoted as saying "judiciously" that no Jew should dare alienate the affection of a German dog. Here the story takes an unexpected twist: the dog, unaware of its master's importance and its own status, bit the hand that fed it. Leipold, in a fit of anger, fired his pistol at the pup in an apparent effort to teach it a lesson, but he missed. He missed the dog, that is, and injured his right toe. Another version had it that he wounded himself deliberately to avoid front-line duty. Whatever the case, to our relief

Leipold, with his right foot bandaged into a large ball, was rarely seen in the camp compound for some time.

Meanwhile, I was given the job of "inspector" in the large hall of the Heinkel plant. They had many lathes on which cylindrical metal parts were turned out, parts allegedly used in the manufacture of airplanes. My job, if it could be called that, was simple enough. Given a micrometer, I had to go from one bench lathe to another to measure the diameter of each piece. Any piece failing to come within the prescribed tolerance went into the waste barrel thoughtfully situated at each machine.

Not underestimating my responsibility, I checked closely for defects and usually managed to find enough *abfaelle* (rejects), as the Germans called them, to give the factory owner his money's worth. Occasionally, though, I would approve a few rejects in each shipment. Eventually I sensed a lack of appreciation for my work and decided to move on when the chance came.

Freudlich, long since recuperated from his hostage ordeal, showed remarkable mechanical ability. He could repair any machine at the plant. The German civilians, aware of the asset they had, treated him with a special respect reserved for no ordinary prisoner. Carrying a small toolbox, he had free access to most of the installation. I am sure that he worked not out of a sense of duty but by natural inclination and curiosity about mechanisms and automation.

Winter 1944

As soon as concentration camp Budzyn was all set up, commandant Leipold ordered the dismantling of the old SS camp. Rather than continue to do nothing and find nothing of practical value at Heinkel, I volunteered for the dismantling crew.

It was winter again, and the countryside was covered in its coat of snow. In January 1944 there was hopeful news about the progress of the war, which was going against the Germans. But it was going more against us. The fifth year under the Nazi whip brought no respite to the handful of people still hanging on in concentration camps. Many would still perish from hunger; others would be worked to death.

I was one of a hundred or so men taking the old barracks apart. What could be salvaged was loaded onto trucks for future use. Anything not salvageable was burned. While our group was working on this old desolate site, bonfires were kept going, solving the problem of disposing of the lumber. The guards had one fire for themselves, and each work group kept one going. It was the only way we could move our limbs in the bitter cold. Because of the cold and the comfort they found by the fire, the guards did not push the actual progress of dismantling very hard.

I had volunteered in the hope of finding clothing; others were eyeing the old camp kitchen for possible leftover food. During the noon break one day I drifted away from the group and wandered into the old bathhouse. The place seemed undisturbed since we had vacated this camp. I found clothing scattered between the benches where the undressing had taken place; it was not much good, which probably was why it had been left. But while scanning these rags of affliction and poverty, my eye caught what looked like a fragment of a banknote. As I bent down and reached for it I heard the sound of footsteps, first squeaking in the snow and then coming in from outside. I quickly examined what to my astonishment were two hundred-zloty notes. I removed my cap hastily and folded the money behind its inner rim before putting it back on.

By then, I had sighted tall SS Sergeant Kleist, who evidently had seen me as well, for he ordered me to come to him. Instead, I ran out through another door, hoping to rejoin my group and fade into the background of other uniforms—you could not tell one of us from another—but he gave pursuit. I heard the click of a trigger, followed by his command to stop or be shot. Taking the obvious alternative, I stopped and turned around, thinking that this might be the last time I would behold the beauty of a winter scene. Slowly he approached, replacing the pistol in its holster, and towered over me. "What did you find there?"

"Nothing."

He did not argue but removed my cap and laid it on the snow, then pulled off one of his gloves and stuck it into his coat pocket. Lifting the cap delicately like something he did not want to spill, he ran his fingers behind the rim and immediately located the money. After examining his find, he neatly folded the confiscated notes and shoved them behind the large turned-out cuff of his overcoat sleeve. At this moment I expected the customary beating, followed by the inevitable *coup de grâce*. The sergeant was not reaching for his gun or whip however; he merely produced a pencil and, not finding any paper, wrote my K.C. (concentration camp) number on his metal cigarette case.

"Your conduct will be referred to the commandant for punishment," he said finally. "Don't worry. You will experience something." (*"Du wirst schon etwas erfahren."*)

With this typically German warning, he ordered me to rejoin my group. I felt momentary relief but began to worry immediately about the punishment awaiting me. There was such a lack of variety in the punitive measures administered to prisoners. It was like a menu that offered duck only; you could have it anyway you liked it, provided it was a dead duck. And what was no longer a consideration, the quantity of bread this money could have bought, still lingered in my mind. Days passed and my anticipated punishment still had not come about. Was it possible, I thought, that Kleist had forgotten all about it? Or had he appropriated the money himself and decided to "forget" to report me?

The days were getting longer now, and it was still daylight as we stood at the regular evening formation for the routine count. There was a wisp of spring, like a thin cloud, in the air. The soil, freed from the winter's snow and frost, sent forth its own scents. Once more the awakening of spring heightened the contrast between its beauty and warmth and the ugliness of our lot. The mass of prisoners in shapeless striped garb stood in rectangular columns. Previously, we had been watched by the noncoms of the *Wehrmacht* who were quartered just on the other side of the barbed-wire fence, but now there were recent arrivals from the Russian front. Word had gotten around that they had been brought here for officers' training to replace the dwindling ranks of the officers' corps. They watched with curiosity the circuslike performances of our morning and evening formations and occasionally showed contempt for the way the SS guards exercised authority over us. Sometimes they even mimicked the stiff manner in which the guards yelled commands.

While we were preparing for the count, one of the onlookers on the other side suddenly yelled out mockingly: *"Muetzen ab!"* "Hats off!"— the command usually given before the SS took the count—and his comrades promptly pulled off their caps and pretended to stand reverently at attention for a moment. Then they burst out laughing. Unnerved, the SS noncoms hesitated. Out from the far end of the camp came commandant Leipold, hobbling on one crutch and a cane. Shaking the cane at the intruders, he shouted for them to clear the area. They replied that they were not his charges. Leipold, now about one hundred feet from them, yelled, *"Haende aus der Tasche venn zu einem deutchen Offizier sprichst!"* ("Hands out of the pockets when you speak to a German officer!") The soldier, unperturbed, kept his hands in his pockets: "The German officers are at the front," he said. "You are a bunch of heroes over women and old Jews!"

At this point Leipold, shaking his stick, became altogether incoherent, but he maintained his barrage of garbled threats, which only seemed to amuse his audience. Eventually one of the soldiers prevailed on the others to leave the area. The scene that we had witnessed would have been unthinkable in 1941 or 1942, but now business was bad and the family was quarreling. For a moment we felt some affinity with these soldiers because we had one thing in common: utter disgust and contempt for this cowardly easy-living elite, who thrived on robbery and cruelty.

The exhibition of mocking contempt for the SS by the *Wehrmacht* soldiers made something of a sensation in camp. Suddenly the whole show, highlighted by the dead-serious routine of commands that had always reminded us of the absolute authority of our masters, was perceived as a grotesque display of overbearing authority over a wretched bunch of miserable men.

It must have been on a day in early March that the Germans decided to frisk the whole camp when we returned from work. They made their intentions known after the evening count in order to prevent anyone from leaving for the barracks. Some outside work groups who had contact with the Polish people had smuggled in food purchased with money they had somehow managed to hide up to that point.

The 3,000 prisoners were ordered to one side of the *Appellplatz*. Blankets were spread on the ground on which to unload bread and eggs. Pots and mess kits were set out to receive money. There was no penalty for the voluntary surrender of contraband possessions. Each man passed by the blankets and dropped his contraband on the way to being frisked. Six guards abreast frisked six men at a time. Some took their chances on getting their contraband through frisking; some had nothing to hide.

As the prisoners maneuvered around, I kept my eyes on the blankets. They were filling with bread loaves and potatoes, and the pots had some money in them; in fact, one deep German army mess kit seemed nearly filled with cash—not a real fortune but worth a few loaves of bread.

Meanwhile, what had begun as an orderly process had turned into two masses of people, one already frisked and the other waiting to be frisked. The two groups drew closer together, leaving between them a crooked dividing line marked by the blankets and pots. The half-dozen guards appeared to be tiring somewhat and functioning less efficiently, apparently trying to get this over with. What's more, darkness was rapidly descending. Making a sudden decision to take advantage of all the elements favoring such a risk, I quickly walked over to one blanket, squatted down as if to surrender something, with my hand in my pocket picked up the mess kit handle through the lining, and disappeared into the milling crowd. All this was done in the wink of an eye. I felt safe and unnoticed.

The outhouse was my immediate destination. Once in there, I examined my catch. There were several ten-and twenty-zloty bills but mostly small paper denominations and a cigarette case. Still, the total was the biggest fortune I had ever laid my hands on. Excitedly, I picked out the large bills and thought about where to hide them. Taking a pin from my lapel, I pierced all the bills through the center, then put my hand through the outhouse hole and pinned this small bundle upward underneath the boards. No sooner had I put the rest of the small bills into my pockets than I heard my name being called.

In fact, it seemed as though everyone was calling my name in unison: "Topas! Topas! Come on out!" It was no use kidding myself. This was it. Someone had squealed. Or possibly the SS had noted the disappearance of the mess kit and ordered a standing formation until the culprit was found. It no longer mattered. I took the mess kit and walked out to face the music.

As well as I recall, I felt resignation rather than fear. Walking slowly out to the center of the grounds where the SS and some prisoner officials were waiting, I noted the hushed silence of all men standing in their regular formations. To my surprise I was again face to face with Sergeant Kleist, who once before had relieved me of my find. This time there was a much larger stake and an audience. I walked over to the blanket and emptied my pockets of the small bills I had retained. Then the towering figure holding the end of a whip uttered his first words: "How do you come by this money?" Before I could answer, I got one lash across my face on account.

"Like everyone here," I began my confession, "I surrendered what I had. But then I realized that my work in the 'construction' is more important than anything else—that in order to do my best work, I must eat. Eat more than rations, which are not enough for hard work. I thought it would be best that I take this money back, so that I can supplement my diet for the best work results!" When I started speaking, my voice was low and unsteady, but by the time I got to the midpoint of my tale, the whole camp could hear my words. Perhaps subconsciously I was making my final appearance more impressive. It was now up to my tormentors to finish and ring down the curtain.

The tall man who was deciding my fate looked at me, then at his entourage, then at the prisoners standing motionless and silent, then back to me, then to his subordinates:

"Give him twenty-five on the naked behind. Did you ever hear such bull?" So I got my second flogging. After the last stripe cut into the numb flesh, I stood at attention.

"He can still stand. Give him another twenty-five."

When I awoke the next morning, I throbbed with pain. My flesh was a bloody mess. The barracks orderly told me that I had passed out and was carried in. "You're lucky to be alive," he said to me. "Others have been killed for much less. Hey, Topas, was it worth it? Tell me."

When the men returned from work, my friends related how the

Germans had threatened to keep the men standing throughout the night without rations if they didn't get the one who had taken the money. Someone volunteered my name; the rest followed. The next day when I went to recover my real loot, I was dismayed to find that only the pin remained. Except for a few bills and a cigarette case that inexplicably remained in my pockets, my ordeal had earned me only pain. And I was still wondering whether they had something else in store for me. I felt that I must try to return to work, if they would let me, because I was not convinced that the punishment I had received was finished. It was too light to fit the "crime" by concentration camp standards, where people were slaughtered for mere trifles or liquidated as useless to the Reich. So I asked to be put back to work, and the following morning before the work group's departure, Szczypiacki asked Kleist whether I could rejoin my group.

The tall one replied: "*Ja, lass dem Gauner arbeiten*" ("Yes, let the racketeer work"), and I quickly rejoined the ranks of my old wrecking gang. It may seem strange, but it felt good to go to work again, to see the outside of the camp, and to keep my mind occupied.

At the outset of the march, a couple of the guards lined up with my rank and engaged me in conversation. It seems that I had become something of a celebrity. My audacity had aroused the curiosity of the guards. Even the worst dog among them, a Rumanian German, spoke to me as though he had been instructed to give me special consideration, while on other occasions he would have used the butt of his rifle whenever something irritated him. This day was different. I was invited during the lunch break to the not-yet-dismantled barracks that the guards used during the day for their comfort. They gave me a sandwich and asked me whether I would like to shoot a rifle at bottles, as they did now and then for target practice.

At first I was afraid to believe that this offer was on the level. But someone handed me a rifle, and I fired several shots, knocking down a few bottles. Pulling the bolt back and ejecting the empty shell gave me a good feeling each time. I was handling the rifle as though I were a free man. The guards complimented my good aim and asked where I had learned to shoot.

"In school and at the Warsaw Zoo shooting arcade, which likewise had only bottles for targets," I replied truthfully, handing the rifle back. This whole episode was a fantastic experience in the annals of concentration camps. Incredibly, for a while, I was treated with special consideration by these guards; then there was a change of guards and things returned to normal.

Soon after these events, all of us who had registered as inventors, engineers, and chemists were ordered to report to the main SS office. Standing outside, we speculated on what was going on. The rumors spreading around the camp were optimistic: we were said to be going to Vienna to work in laboratories, treated as valuable brainpower.

Among the previously registered prisoners were the Orenstein brothers; Henry a slender and cheerful young fellow about my age, had made friends with the men in our group. Tony Feinberg, a Czech Jew, was there, as was Rysiek Krakowski, who had fought in the Warsaw ghetto and had been on the transport to the Treblinka gas chambers. When the able-bodied men there were spared for work instead of being liquidated with the women and children (among them, Rysiek's wife), Rysiek wound up in Budzyn. I remember him as one of the nicest men. Blondish, with blue eyes, he was easy to take a liking to, and we became fast friends—but then, Rysiek was everybody's friend.

When my turn came to stand before Leipold, he glanced up at me and started asking questions: "What is your name?" "Where did you go to school?" This was a question I had anticipated and feared. Not quite fifteen when Poland fell, how could I have received advanced schooling? In the absence of documents I made myself several years older. For my alleged education I picked the Konarski School in Warsaw. The school had nothing to do with chemistry—it taught auto and airplane mechanics—but I chose it because it was not a well-known institution. As kids we had gone there on Sunday mornings to see Tom Mix movies for only ten cents—though at this bargain price we had to sit on the floor. Discipline of the crowd pressing to get in was maintained by the occasional use of truncheons. Now I used this name to bluff my way into—what?

"When did you graduate?" asked my interrogator.

"I did not graduate, because of the war." This seemed to satisfy Leipold, and he placed a checkmark alongside my name. Perhaps he really did not care one way or the other.

After all thirty-six original applicants had been interviewed, thirty-two were selected. So it was that in late March 1944 thirty-two men and one woman were escorted out of Concentration Camp Budzyn and loaded into a boxcar for shipment—destination unknown. I was leaving behind nearly eleven months of internment, which had often felt unbearable. Even without actually knowing where we were being taken, our spirits were high just at the thought of getting away from Budzyn.

Majdanek

After a short trip that gave us a glimpse of the Polish countryside through the barbed-wire-covered windows, the train stopped in Lublin. We looked at people on the streets and in the shops, and it seemed strange to see fragments of civilization again. But our hopes were quickly extinguished upon finding ourselves being taken to the infamous concentration camp of Majdanek. This camp had once boasted close to 50,000 prisoners, but now it was quiet—almost deserted. The specter of death hovered over the crematorium chimney, and a handful of prisoners could be seen here and there doing their chores.

As we were placed between two barbed-wire enclosures, I could read fear and apprehension on the faces of my friends; this place seemed the setting for our execution. Moments dragged on. After a long wait our guards turned over the "inventory" to the camp SS. Any notion of being spared for some special task was soon dispelled by the new SS guards' use of clubs and whips. Under their brutal supervision we were directed to the bathhouse, but first we were subjected to a most thorough frisking—the most humiliating I had ever had to endure. Stripped naked, everyone had to open his mouth, turn around, bend over, and occasionally get kicked. Up to this time I had managed to keep the pictures of my parents and Gina in my possession. Here we were ordered to leave everything before entering the bath. Afterward, we received clean uniforms and Dutch wooden shoes, leaving our last personal effects behind. It was like being separated from our dear ones all over again.

Tony Feinberg had agreed to swallow about twenty gold coins belonging to our doctor; he was to get half the money for his trouble. After emerging from the bath, these two kept close company. But it was not until evening when we were quartered in a compound that Tony had the opportunity to free himself of the indigestible part of his diet. As he did so, the doctor, who was closely observing the process, separated the dropping coins: "One for you and one for me. . . ."

In the compound assigned to us there were also men from other camps. Their presence was unrelated to "scientific" work, yet we had been molded into one group. The next morning we learned from a handful of the Christian prisoners who represented the camp administration that practically all the people in the camp had been liquidated in November 1943. According to their account, people were machine-gunned to the tune of Viennese waltzes that were piped in through speakers to drown out the screams of the victims.

Two of the Poles who learned my name brought me some sugar to eat; they claimed to have known my father.

One morning in mid-April our destiny again took us down a new path. The gates of this dreaded camp swung open, and our group of two hundred men hobbled out in their wooden shoes. Under the supervision of the SS guards we marched through the streets of Lublin toward the railroad station. Women walking on the street stopped and looked at our noisy procession, and many wept. The wooden shoes made most of the noise, like the dragging of chains—and in a sense they were meant to accomplish the same thing, for how fast could you run in those clumsy things?

Not until we received food rations did we actually believe that we were going someplace other than to the gas chambers; we knew that food was not wasted on prospective corpses. The boxcar doors remained open when the train pulled out of the station. Barbed-wire fences made a compartment in the middle of each car for the guards. Since only they had access to the open doors, they had to tend to the emptying of buckets. It was almost comical to see such chores performed by the Master Race, but security dictated that they swallow their pride. Food rations, opening doors to allow air in the cars, and provisions for bodily functions all reassured us that we were slated for work, not annihilation.

The green fields stretched before our eyes for miles as the train slowly chugged along.

Reflecting on the inhuman conditions we had experienced in Budzyn, I felt that we were descending through stages of hell, where the Nazi terror was succeeding, in some instances, in bringing our own people down to that level of indifference where one would close his eyes to his brothers' misery.

12 Concentration Camp Plaszow

There is no wall in the world that a donkey
laden with gold can not get through.
—Attributed to Philip II, father of Alexander the Great

Darkness had descended on the countryside by the time the train came to a halt near Plaszow, a suburb of Krakow, once the proud capital city where nearly all the Polish kings were buried and where the Polish leader Joseph Pilsudski had been buried in 1935. (His heart, however, was buried beside his mother in a cemetery near his birthplace; it was she who had inspired his patriotic fervor.) He had been unique among European leaders in recognizing the danger of a rearmed Germany and had unsuccessfully sought support from France and England for invading Germany in 1934; failing to convince them, he had been forced to sign the ill-fated nonagression pact with Hitler in 1935. Unlike the vacillating politicians of his day, he had foreseen the imminent threat in Hitler's *Lebensraum* ambition, and he would have turned in his grave if he could have seen what had now become of his beloved Poland.

When we stepped out of the train, we found a company of Ukrainian guards on hand to welcome the new arrivals to the Plaszow camp— and I thought we had seen the last of them in Budzyn. With shouting and commotion the group formed ranks, and we started for our new home.

The Ukrainians escorted us to the gates of the outer camp; the German SS took over from there. This place was much bigger than Budzyn. Here you had to clear two gates to get in or out. The inner camp for inmates was separated from the outer camp by electrically charged wires. Surrounded by two sets of guard towers, the outer camp held guard quarters, storehouses, and workshops. At both gates a careful count took place to assure that no one got "lost," and once inside we were greeted by the Jewish "camp eldest," a young man named Chilewicz;[1] Finkelstein, his second-in-command; and assorted officials. Chilewicz's wife, a snappy blonde fashionably dressed and wearing very high heels, was in charge of the women's ward. All the men who came out to receive us, aside from the guards, wore civilian clothes and riding boots. Dressing in civvies was evidently a privilege that went with their station in the camp. They showed no signs of malnutrition. On the contrary, to all outward signs they appeared prosperous.

The natives sized up the new batch of arrivals and clearly showed their disappointment. Instead of the wealthy uncles they would obviously have preferred to welcome, we resembled poor relatives. As seasoned veterans of one of the worst camps, we were neither impressed nor easily moved to fear by the manifest authority of our well-clad brethren but stood wearily in formation, awaiting rations and a place to stretch out and sleep. It was late, and we were very tired.

This first encounter did not seem too unfriendly. Chilewicz engaged several of our men in informal conversation; others asked after the names of people they were related to, helping to locate someone within the group. Finkelstein, taller and heftier than Chilewicz, at one point inquired whether any of us had known him before the war—did he mean before he had become conspicuously successful, by camp standards? Awaiting the answer, he scanned the faces around him. In our ranks was a young fellow from Hrubieszczow who happened to smile at this precise moment. Finkelstein crashed into the ranks and slapped his face hard.

"What do you laugh at?" he demanded.

"Nothing," came the reply from Abram, who took the slap stoically, "except my name happens to be Finkelstein, and we might be related, you know."

In an open fight Abram could have made mincemeat of this bully, but that was not open to debate just then. The official Finkelstein, now curious, quickly started plying Abram with questions, as though wanting to establish whether he was being kidded or not; if he thought he was, it would spell trouble for Abram. As it turned out, they *were* loosely related, which in the present situation at least proved no liability to Abram.

A small portion of bread and two tablespoons of jam were the only items on the menu before we were allowed to shower and given shelter in the quarantine barracks. Plaszow was a big camp; the ground sloped down in one direction, and the main inner gate and the administration guard building were situated at the lowest level. Above this point there was the *Appellplatz*, separated from the gate by the local administration building, the quarantine building, a bathhouse, and a small warehouse. Standing at the lowest point of the assembly grounds and looking up you would be directly facing the main compound of several rows of barracks. Far ahead on the right was the kitchen, far ahead in the center was the latrine, and at the far right was the women's compound. A wire fence separated the outer camp from the inner, and there on the left were the workshops and other warehouses. Far left, outside the wire, was a dreaded hill where most of the executions took

CONCENTRATION CAMP PLASZÓW

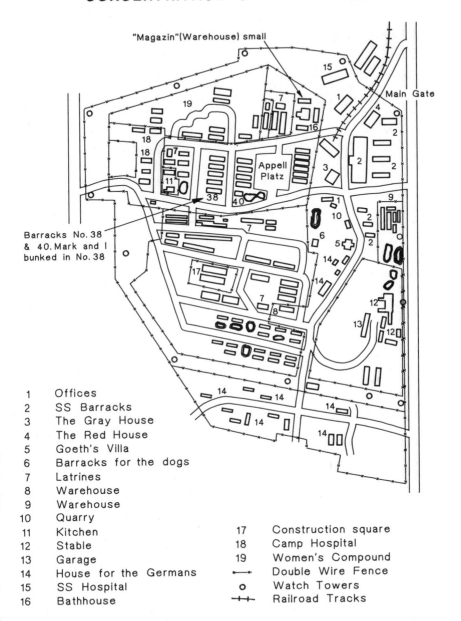

"Magazin"(Warehouse) small

Main Gate

Barracks No. 38
& 40. Mark and I
bunked in No. 38

Appell
Platz

1	Offices
2	SS Barracks
3	The Gray House
4	The Red House
5	Goeth's Villa
6	Barracks for the dogs
7	Latrines
8	Warehouse
9	Warehouse
10	Quarry
11	Kitchen
12	Stable
13	Garage
14	House for the Germans
15	SS Hospital
16	Bathhouse
17	Construction square
18	Camp Hospital
19	Women's Compound
⟶	Double Wire Fence
o	Watch Towers
⊦⊦	Railroad Tracks

Source: Adapted from plan in Proces ludobójcy Amona Goetha
(Krakow: 1947).

place, in full view of the camp inmates. Finally, there were the towers that gave this place its positive identification and the true character of a concentration camp. The towers were equipped with loudspeakers, used alternately for paging the guards and the prisoners, for making announcements, and for broadcasting music.

This camp was quite different from the one we had just left. It also had non-Jewish prisoners. The Poles did not represent more than 5 percent of the 10,000 to 15,000 prisoners, but they were privileged to receive packages and some mail. For the first time, we saw German prisoners, too, who were identified by the letter D (*Deutsche*) next to a green triangle and individual number. The green triangle meant that they were criminal prisoners. Most other nationalities displayed red triangles, meaning political "criminals." Some of these Germans displayed low numbers, and there was a bit of snobbery about these because a low number meant a long tenure—a mark of status among themselves.

A dozen of these German prisoners had been imported here to become *Kapos*, or "heads." They were real German *Kapos*, all right, exercising considerable authority over their various labor gangs, but the often expressed view that they were all cruel and brutal is somewhat exaggerated. To be sure, many were quite vicious, but others were merely trying to get by, as most of us did. The *Kapos* were the German version of the Egyptian taskmasters.

This camp counted among its guests French, German, a few Italian, and even a handful of Greek Jews. SS women were in charge of the women's compound. The commandant was SS *Hauptsturmfuehrer* (Captain) Amon Goeth—a killer.[2] Goeth, we learned, had executed most of the Jews of the Krakow ghetto and its surroundings, confiscating all the possessions of his victims. SS *Hauptscharfuehrer* (Master Sergeant) Schupke, an older man and a mason by trade, was in charge of work assignments. These were the lords who held power over life and death.

The main body of prisoners could be divided into three categories: those who had money were in the minority; those who had neither money, drive, nor opportunity to supplement their camp diet constituted the majority; those who had no money but worked outside the camp and engaged in smuggling food in and clothing out in order to earn their keep made up a sort of "middle class." The men most envied in this camp were the wagon drivers. Their job was to cart waste out of the camp and bring supplies in. Although they were under guard most of the time, nearly every day they had contact with the outside world— a world of families and homes that for us existed only in imagination and memory.

The men who had money were among the 6,000 surviving Jews

who had been brought to Plaszow from Krakow in April 1943 after the liquidation of the ghetto there. A number of them had managed to slip hidden valuables past the SS, whose searches were not uniformly thorough. Having money helped them to secure preferred quarters and indoor jobs in shops within the outer camp. They were also the chief consumers of the smuggled-in food, thus contributing to the improved economy of a camp where there was not as much hunger as there had been in Budzyn. By way of comparison, we had come from a small village to a busy city. Other residents had been brought here directly from their homes and had somehow managed to retain a few of their most personal possessions. It might have looked to all the elite as though our arrival would cheapen the neighborhood and lower the assets per capita.

Kapos

After the customary three-day quarantine, we were assigned to a regular barracks (referred to as a block) and filed out for morning formation. The morning chill accompanied the reveille count and re-grouping, and nearly all of us were assigned to a young German *Kapo* named Toni Fehringer. He was in his early twenties, blond, with small cold blue eyes, of medium build and semiathletic in appearance; he wore a sailorlike cap tilted to one side.

As we moved forward, responding to drill orders, Fehringer aligned himself with the first marching file and counted cadence: *"Eins! zwei! drei! vier! links!—links!"* As he marched, he swung his arms high in the German style of the day. Marching work formations maintained several yards' distance from each other. As ours approached the gate, Fehringer called out: "I report obediently 180 prisoners, all present and accounted for," followed by the obligatory, *"Muetzen ab!"* ("Hats off") and *"Augen rechts!"* ("Eyes right")! The guards scrupulously counted the passing files, recording the number in each formation. Fehringer turned back, marking time until he met the last file, then he called: *"Muetzen auf!"* ("Hats on")!

It turned out that we were to work in the outer enclosure of the camp. We drew digging shovels, and our *Kapo* divided the labor force into little groups, ordering each group to dig excavations that served no apparent purpose beyond providing exercise for the men. It was our first experience with purposely useless work.

Thus far, like an actor offstage rehearsing, Fehringer had not attracted too much attention. Now he came onstage and made himself known to his company. First he yelled for action and speed—*"Bewegung! Bewegung! Tempo! Tempo!"*—as he moved among the men. Then to make his point he walked up to the nearest man and punched him in the stomach. When the man doubled over, Fehringer came back with an uppercut to the jaw, following with another blow to the stomach. The rest of us stirred ourselves, setting up a feverish tempo, but this urge for speed was merely a pretext for abuse. By the end of the day several of our young men had been brutally beaten, and a few had to be carried back to the barracks.

That evening someone urged that we gang up on our taskmaster. The idea was good, but it was given up because the Germans were uncompromising in backing up anyone in authority, from the Fuehrer on down to prisoner Fehringer. In the days that followed, Fehringer carried out similar acts of senseless violence, but he cut down on the number of victims—probably for fear that there would soon be no one left to abuse. Later, to everyone's relief, he left the group to consort with an SS woman.

Under the direction of another *Kapo*, a new work group was formed from the battered Fehringer crew and assigned to level a hill just outside the inner camp storehouse. The new gang boss was completely different from the vicious Fehringer. Quite detached, he kept to himself most of the time. Occasionally he would push the job, and when guards snooped around, he got jumpy, but once they left, he seemed unconcerned with the progress so long as everyone was moving.

Our apparent objective was to cut down the hill and level it off in order to put up a building. Sections of small-gauge rail tracks were laid down for moving lorries similar to the railcars used in coal mines. Equipped with shovels, we kept filling the lorries with dirt and then pushing them to the edge of the hill and dumping their loads. Each day, the tracks were extended over the last day's fill. Each day, the men performed the shovel ballet—digging in, prying the dirt loose, hoisting the fill and depositing it in the heaping lorries. Each day, perspiring whenever the guards observed the progress and merely going through the motions when they disappeared, we continued chopping down the hill.

There was one advantage to such mechanical work: you didn't have to concentrate on it but could occupy your mind with your own thoughts. For instance, when would they call the noon break? What sort of soup was on the menu? Were we eventually going to fare better in this new camp? And the war—would it ever end? And my father—was he still alive? What about Simon? Had he managed to survive the Warsaw ghetto liquidations? Perhaps Father and Simon had been sent to work camps. And what about my mother, my brother Meir? He was only eight years old. And Gina and her mother—had they managed to evade the dragnet and were they still alive? I really did not care to reason too much—reasoning did not lead to happy conclusions, and I had to have faith, faith in the survival of the righteous. Somewhere in this death- and fear-ridden continent there was my father. If everyone else perished, surely he would be spared by the One whom he had served so wholeheartedly, faithfully.

These thoughts, naive as they may appear, never left my conscious mind for long, always returning to renewed hope in the ultimate survival of my father. On his survival hinged much of my faith and belief, nourished on the biblical principle of justice.

But rational thinking was not the main subject taught in Plaszow. The *Kapo* blew his whistle for the end of the workday. Tools were neatly put away. Ranks formed—forward march, and we were on our way to the camp gate, and if there was no execution or other type of punishment, we could hope to stand in line, draw our bread and jam ration, and go back to our barracks. Most men ate their rations sitting on their bunks; others would sit outside with their backs against the barracks wall, enjoying the evening breeze. When the weather was nice, leaning space against an outside wall was scarce.

Until the nine o'clock curfew, the dimly lit barracks aisles were busy with pedestrians going to see friends in another block or a mother or girlfriend in the women's compound. Some would go to the kitchen to look for leftovers or frequent the black market in front of the camp latrine. There you could buy cigarettes, bread, and even butter. Of course, you had to have money to do that, or something to trade. On days when the returning men were searched and not much got through, the prices of those commodities were driven high.

Since newcomers in my predicament could only go window shopping for the time being, I made it my business to scout the camp and examine all possibilities. The striped uniform was not compulsory here, although everyone did wear a number for identification. Too bad we had not brought our luggage with us to change into something less conspicuous than our loud striped uniforms. Among the formations, our group still stood out as the poor relations, still wearing stripes and wooden shoes. Next to food and shelter my first concern was apparel, and shoes figured foremost on my shopping list.

The food rations here were bigger than those in Budzyn, but people with pull got the cooks' job and managed consistently to produce the most tasteless soups. In fact, most of the elite group of prisoners did not bother to eat it, giving their portions to those less fortunate than themselves. The elite lived in block 40, the only barracks that had real beds instead of the three- or four-tiered shelves for sleeping accommodation that the rest were furnished with. Number 40 had an annex: Number 38, which was rated second, was like the lodge of a resort compared to the main building.

Each barracks had a *blockaelterste*. The prisoner with this title divided evening rations for his tenants, appointed the clean-up details, and stood in front of his block's formation during the morning count. After that he returned to the barracks, his only problem being how to pass the time until the men came back from work.

Our block leader was a tall, chunky, strapping Italian Jew who took his task seriously and exercised his authority with loud commands. Since hardly anyone understood Italian, he spoke Yiddish mixed with German. He had Auschwitz behind him—where he must have lost his nerve. Whether out of a sense of fear or because of the extra ration that his job provided, he seemed to do his utmost to advertise himself loudly in order to impress the Germans with his military bearing and discipline. Every time he faced the company he assumed a most serious expression. All puffed up, he seemed to inflate his chest out of all proportion. So comic was his soldier act that he was nicknamed Mussolini, whom he resembled in poundage and expression. The guards who came for the count did not seem to be impressed or even amused, yet Mussolini would not tolerate inattention to his barrage of superfluous commands every morning before the count.

One day in late May at work I was helping to level a relocated section of rail track. The track, I insisted, had to be level. Otherwise, it could cause the filled lorries to tumble over, run downhill, and cause an accident. Some favored a down pitch for the direction in which the loaded wagons would be pushed, but this path led to the edge of the leveled terrace. We set the track level.

During one of these "technical" discussions concerning safety or ease of operation, our quiet German *Kapo* appointed me the foreman of the excavation and another fellow named Rosenberg was made co-foreman. After thus delegating authority, he wandered off the job site every day. The German prisoners could get away with it. Our lot was not altered much by this innovation, except that we posted men at the outer perimeter of the job to keep a lookout for guards. They would warn us with the familiar hissing sound "*Sechs!*" and we would all get busy before we were noticed.

I had some revulsion to the dubious authority that came with my foremanship, but mainly I was really scared. As a rule, whenever the Germans put a Jew in a position of authority, however minor, it was to elect a whipping boy whom they could call on the carpet for whatever they deemed wrong or at their whim.

After several days the German *Kapo* was removed, leaving Rosenberg and me to look after this cartwork. Rosenberg, a young man from the town of Radom, had his brother among our group, and his youthful wife was in the women's compound. He was so thin that he looked taller than he was—about five-foot-ten. He had straight blond hair and blue eyes, and for a prisoner he had a rather cheerful disposition. With one exception, I always remember him smiling. He and I shared the responsibility for the earthwork then nearing completion.

Approximately one hundred men had been assigned to this project, more than enough to do the work in this confined area of about 300 by 150 feet. But we alternated: during the course of an average day only one-fourth of the men would actually work at one time—sometimes not even that many—except when SS men approached. Then we would all work and fake real zeal. We learned early that nearly all SS guards, down to the real bad dogs, would be less inclined to turn on us if confronted with our "busy beehive" routine.

While we were seemingly less oppressed here than we had been in Budzyn, this camp too brought waves of fear; there were executions, repeated floggings, occasional molestations, and confinement to bunkers. Word came from my friend Rysiek Krakowski, who worked at the infirmary, that typhoid fever patients were being given injections of gasoline into the bloodstream—a medication that relieved the patient of his life in a few painful minutes.[3] What a way to check an epidemic!

But life went on, giving each of the living yet another day. And in spite of it all, the sun did not cease to shine upon this miserable part of the planet. The then popular song *"Mattinata* and *Ciantiwine"* (light wine) frequently resounded through the camp from the outside loudspeakers. A young Greek Jew sang a beautiful melody without words to remind him of a better day. Few in number, the Greek Jews had been brought to Plaszow from Auschwitz, to which they had been taken from their native Greece. Unable to communicate in German, they were abused or derided, sometimes by the other inmates. In such instances they called on their "champion," an impressive young man of small stature with dark features and a look of determination and dignity who had been a captain in the Greek artillery; he spoke some German. I wish I could remember his name, but I cannot forget his account of his military exploits in the Greco-Italian campaign. Had it not been for German intervention, the Greek penetration into Albania could have ended in a smashing victory of the Greeks, and the German intercession proved that this possibility had not been discounted.

Mark

A quiet, skinny youth in our work group attracted my attention because he kept almost entirely to himself. Adam looked about my age, and his younger brother Mark worked in the prisoner clothing storeroom inside the camp, directly across the double barbed-wire fence from our project. Adam and Mark too were from Warsaw, my hometown. Casually, I started to talk to Mark through the fence one morning.

"Aren't you the fellow who was selling 'Meva' cigarettes in quarantine?"

"Could be," said Mark.

"Then it was you I argued with about the high price you demanded?"

"One has to do the best he can," said he matter-of-factly. This first contact was not the kind that usually leads to friendship. I reproached him for exploiting the quarantine situation, and he remarked on the virtue of minding one's own business, at which point we were asked to quit arguing by irritated bystanders. "Well, if it will make you feel any better, I am no longer the cigarette king. In fact, I am altogether out of business," Mark concluded.

Still wearing my wooden shoes, I asked whether he could find some old leather shoes in the supply room. In his unhurried fashion Mark walked away from the fence. In the same deliberate way he reappeared the next day with a burlap bag in his hand. "Ready?" he asked. After a quick glance all around, I said, "Ready," not knowing what to expect.

"See what you can do with that," said Mark, hurling the package over the fence. "You will need a shoemaker to fix you up." I opened the bag and found a pair of old shoe tops, sole leather, wooden forms, and accessories. The next best thing to ready-made shoes were custom-made, or perhaps they were even better, if I could locate a shoemaker.

Soon one of my friends, who happened to be a first-class shoemaker, was set up in a shed to work at this trade. The shed was camouflaged by the bushes surrounding the field latrine. There, from the old assortment, he turned out a fine pair of leather shoes—his first pair since his internment. Samuel was really a skilled craftsman and pleased to apply his skill for a change.

Word got around, and Samuel, with my recommendation, picked up some more business. Then—well, you know how it is. First you get a shoemaker, and soon a tailor is needed, and then found. These two shared the outdoor premises, and in their spare time, when no guards were in sight, they were kept humming with work. I got my striped wardrobe hand-altered, the pants cut to size and a rubber strip ingeniously sewn across the back of the jacket to give it a close fit. In time the members of our group began to look as though their uniforms belonged to them. Well-fitting clothing, even of the striped variety, made us feel less awkward and more dignified.

Other activities also flourished around our hill. Some of the men drifted away during the day and tried to "organize" (as the word goes) some supplementary food. Moving about the outer camp and pretending to be working, their activities ranged from stealing from SS barracks to bakery smuggling to working as orderlies. My friend Rosenberg and I knew that we could be a head shorter or at least beaten should one of our men be caught. Yet this was an accepted mode of living at the time.

Contrary to my expectation that when the hill was leveled, our job would be finished, the Germans unloaded all sorts of prefabricated building material and—disregarding Rosenberg's and my protestations that we didn't know the first thing about building—ordered us to erect a hospital barracks. (See the camp plan.) The rationale for building an SS hospital in the outer camp, as best we could figure it out, was that it was an unlikely place to be bombed by the Russians.

Fortunately, there were real carpenters among our men, and the work began. After driving in stakes and drawing a circumference line of the building, they hammered thick, round, pointed wooden piles into the ground. On these, beams were placed to support the prefabricated wall sections. As the building took shape, the SS took a keener interest in this project. As you can imagine, their frequent visits caused a lot of unrest, and the place soon became less popular than before with the inmates.

Early one morning when I was handing out tools, I reached for the last shovel but found it stuck in the ground. Prying it out yielded a paper-wrapped package the size of a shoebox inside a burlap sack. Closer examination revealed that it contained about ten pounds of butter, worth a small fortune in the camp—probably equal to about fifty loaves of bread. It was still fresh and very tempting to anyone who had not eaten butter for a couple of years. It must have been smuggled in from the outside or stolen from the German guards' kitchen, then stashed away because somewhere along the line it had become too hot to handle. I called Mark to the fence and told him of the find. Not giving much thought to the risk entailed, I signaled my intention and after a nod from Mark, who kept an eye on the guard in the nearest tower, tossed the butter over. Mark took it from there.

Before noon, an SS guard paid our outpost an unexpected visit with one of the prisoners. The guard pretended to show interest in the work while his charge looked over the very spot where the butter had been hidden. Unsuccessful, he turned to Rosenberg and me, demanding his contraband. The presence nearby of the SS man put us on guard, and we disclaimed any knowledge of the buried butter. The next thing I knew, I was confronted by the SS man, who pointed his finger at me and demanded to know what I had done with it. I continued to feign ignorance of the matter. Meanwhile, the butter hunter found out that I had a friend on the other side of the wire. He and his SS guard abruptly left for the inner camp.

It began to look bad: the unexpected guests were going to visit Mark and give the impression of being wise to the connection. My observation, which was limited only to glancing over the wire, did not reveal anything to reduce my anxiety. The object was not so much to salvage the butter (a fat-free diet is better than no diet at all!) as it was to avoid admitting complicity in its disappearance and escape the unpredictable consequences. When I found the package, it appeared to have been abandoned—but now the claimants included an SS guard, making the discovery extremely dangerous.

It was not until we were back in the barracks that night that I learned how close we had been to prematurely leaving this vale of tears. But Mark had borne up remarkably well under questioning, giving a good, unexpected, and unrehearsed performance. The guard acting as the whip had stood aside while his scheming prisoner agent opened the dialogue:

"Okay, the game is up. You can now hand over the butter. Topas confessed that he threw the whole bundle to you over the fence."

Unprepared but undaunted, Mark replied: "What butter? If Topas says he has butter, you better get it from him yourself. Someone has been lying to you." Pressed for a good while, he stuck to his story, and his coolness saved the day. But after this episode, our problem was how to dispose of the butter. Whose butter was it, anyway?

Someone wanted to talk to us outside the barracks. The same character again confronted us, but this time he was alone.

"Listen, fellows, give me nine pounds and you can keep the rest."

"Say, if you have a problem, why do you drag the *Yekkes* into it?" I asked.

"Suppose I were to give you two pounds, and you let me have the rest," proposed our uninvited guest.

"Never get the guards involved—it is in very bad taste!" I persisted.

"Oh, him? He was only detached as an escort. Honest, fellows, I work near the stables."

"If you work near the stables, hide your damn butter in the stables and not in our place. We don't want to risk our lives for your butter—if it *is* yours. If your butter had been found on our job site, who do you think would have been punished for it?"

"Oh, well, sure. But now, how about letting me have my butter—that is, eight pounds, friends."

Beginning to feel sorry for him, we asked, "How do we know the butter is yours?"

After more explanations and more bargaining, he finally won us over. We handed him the package, and he was about to leave when we reminded him of his promise to share. Reluctantly, he parted with about one kilo (two and a quarter pounds). Actually, our assistance in smuggling the butter into the inner camp was worth a lot more than that; had it been found, it would all have been confiscated and the smuggler whipped, at least. We never fully learned the man's connection with the SS guard, but using a guard to pressure another prisoner, which could have led to most dangerous consequences, was rare and very low by camp standards.

The butter might have been worth its weight in gold, but it was not worth risking a life for. Yet prisoners did risk their lives by smuggling in bread, which entailed obtaining currency or trading something for it. For either offense, if the ranking guard chose to exercise the authority that made him judge, arbiter, and master over our lives, the prisoner was subject to the death penalty.

Despite the risk, the butter incident not only provided some comic relief but indelibly impressed itself on our consciousness: it showed how two could carry out even a hastily conceived plan, act under stress, and resist pressure, relying on an implicit but unrehearsed understanding to avoid falling into a trap. It was perhaps insignificant in comparison with the daring dynamics of more adventuresome exploits, yet out of this skirmish was born some of the mutual trust and confidence that was essential to our survival in much more trying situations.

Even though I was not fully conscious of it at the time, my friendship with Mark was growing. We just took to each other without bothering to analyze the reasons. He was almost exactly my age— nineteen at that time—and my height and had a stocky muscular build; he had big green eyes and dark hair, curly when it was allowed to grow. Contemplative, self-possessed, and something of an introvert, he nevertheless shared my readiness to take risks. Just before leaving his previous camp near Radom, he had managed to pass for an electrician, actually doing some electrical installations. I laughed when he told me about his first job of installing an overhead transmission, which apparently had undersized wire; it glowed red when the power was turned on.

Nevertheless, he had a genuine interest in electrical work, even though he was assigned to a supply room and registered as a weaver. We spent many evenings confiding our experiences to each other or recalling places and events in Warsaw. Besides being prisoners and Jews, Warsaw was another thing that bound us together.

I recall a story about his childhood in a school whose principal, after learning about some students' misdeeds from an outside source, would look his charges straight in the eye and claim to read the story on their foreheads. The students were so impressed by this see-through method that they cut down on their mischief.

I recall telling him about a childhood experience of my own. After recovering from scarlet fever, then a dangerous sickness, I was allowed to go out for the first time one summer evening accompanied by my governess. We wandered through the Warsaw streets until we came upon the only automat in town, a fascinating place to children. There was one large room for sandwiches and desserts and another for beverages. There was a commotion in the beverage room, occasioned by the beer taps suddenly going full blast. People had only to go up with glasses, and they could keep on drinking beer. The management, unable to stop the flow, urged people to drink, apparently to prevent flooding. But foam was rising on the floor, and there was a large crowd of the curious outside and many free loaders inside. What a time to be too young to drink!

Mark came from a truly religious Hassidic family whose home in Warsaw had been only two blocks away from ours. The youngest of five brothers, he was the special object of his mother's affection and was very attached to her. His father owned a distillery in partnership with a Polish nobleman. The family had a country estate in Pulawy, where they spent their summers. Mark recalled to me the many wonderful happenings of his childhood associated with that place and its surroundings.

The family was stranded in Radom when the war broke out, and Mark and his brother Adam were separated from their parents, who were taken away during the deportation of Jews from the Radom ghetto in 1942. In January 1944 Mark and Adam were on the first transport to reach Majdanek after a massacre of all the Jews in the camp in November 1943. It was there, when our groups were joined for a transport consigned to Plaszow in April 1944, that we met.

Having a good friend makes life richer in any circumstances and is especially comforting in time of trouble.

13 *Steinbruch*

*How long shall the wicked exult? They speak
arrogantly, . . . they crush thy people.*
—Psalm 94

In a few weeks at Plaszow I had learned that even though there was less hunger here, the sword hung over our heads constantly. Hardly a day passed that something terrible did not happen or that rumors of things to come did not prey on one's mind. But in Budzyn there had been only about 3,000 men and women and a few children. There, every beating, execution, and death was taken personally and felt intensely, like the passing of someone that nearly everyone knew in a small town. Here, among some 10,000 internees, as in a larger community, the misfortune of a few did not affect every one of us so personally.

Even from a distance, however, it was hard to ignore the floggings that accompanied the evening count. It was not uncommon to see men being rolled downhill by the cruel and sadistic guards. Then there was the infamous *Steinbruch,* or quarry. A small group of regulars, among them a couple of dynamiting experts, actually did the work there. The guards furnished detonating fuses when the rock had been drilled and the charges already set. But what made the quarry conspicuous was not related to the real work done there. Rather, men sentenced to this place for one day as punishment were doomed to a horrible death or to crippling injuries. For there the guards took special care to make the marked one suffer. Ordered to run with a large rock on his shoulders, the prisoner was beaten along the route with a whip, shovel, rifle, or even a crowbar. Few were brought back uninjured, and fewer recovered ever to walk normally again. It was not an unusual sight at the end of a day to see alongside the standing formation a makeshift stretcher with maimed, bruised, and bleeding human flesh in which the heart was still beating, but the body had all but yielded.

Meanwhile, the notorious Auschwitz doctor, SS *Hauptsturmfuehrer* Blanke, had arrived in the camp—an event viewed with fear and apprehension. Blanke's professional reputation as a doctor was limited to his feared "selections," which consisted of seperating those who were capable of work from those who were not. The latter were disposed of in gas chambers as useless. Blanke's presence in the camp generated rumors about an imminent selection, striking terror in the older and more feeble among us.

It was not very long after our arrival that the weather turned cold, especially for the month of May. On Sunday, May 7, Doctor *Hauptsturmfuehrer* Max Blanke, wearing a military fur-lined overcoat with a turned-out fur collar, stood at the center of the *Appellplatz*, surrounded by his subordinates. What made Blanke's attire stand out was his order that we all strip naked for a major selection.[1] Some of the older and weaker men who had survived earlier selections felt like fish caught in a net, physically unable to pass through the snare set for them.

Everyone rolled his disrobed clothing into a bundle and carried it under his arm, often using it to hide sores and wounds. Mark covered his protruding appendix scar as he walked in line toward the SS overlords who held the destiny of everyone passing before them. A motion of a swagger stick to one side meant an extension of time; a gesture in the opposite direction meant that you were wasting your food rations and would do so no more. Those who no longer merited these rations were released from bondage. Taken to another camp, they were put to their eternal rest with the help of chemistry.

These frightful experiences made unforgettable impressions on the minds and hearts of men. With each one of these victims, part of me died. Yet between these events, there was a life marked by the ever resurging will to live.

It was a rare treat one evening to hear two brothers, accomplished musicians, give an impromptu outdoor concert, surrounded by a most melancholy but appreciative audience. Herman and Leon Rosner, although they were yet young, were reputed to have entertained in first-class establishments before the war. One was a violinist; the other played an accordian in the absence of a piano. The Rosner brothers had been allowed to keep their instruments and were frequently called upon to provide amusement for our captors. Standing there with Mark, I was deeply moved by their performance of Anton Rubinstein's "Melody in F." The simple pleasure of listening to music performed by and for people sentenced to indefinite internment, stripped of almost every semblance of civilized being, was like a momentary breath of life as we had known it before this endless wretchedness.

One morning not much later, an order went out to round up all the children for deportation to Auschwitz. In the formation of the Block 40 aristocracy was a boy of about six or seven. The musician Herman Rosner was his father. Concealed between the ranks, the child had become restless and could easily have given himself away. In order to save his son—Rosner jerked the boy's arm to keep him standing still and hidden from view behind a tall man. I caught an expression of desperation on the father's face during the tense moments when he pleaded with his son to be still because his life hung in the balance. His eyes, on the verge of tears, reflected a mixture of welled-up emotion and strain.

Rosner managed to save his boy that day, but most of the children were plucked out under the watchful direction of SS Sergeant Franz J. Mueller and shipped to Auschwitz, leaving behind a flood of tears and broken spirits. As the children walked to the gate, the Germans cynically piped the Brahms lullaby through the loudspeakers, and the song "Mommy, Buy Me a Little Rockinghorse."[2] Oh, how meaningful seemed the words of our prophet: "Rachel is crying in her grave, for her children are no more."

Toward the end of May the nights grew hot, rather early for our climate, and the guards tolerated our sleeping outside the barracks. Near the storeroom where Mark worked and the fence facing the hospital site, there were bales of straw used for filling mattresses. This made it a good place to bunk out on a hot night. It was a new experience to sleep under the stars. Mark and I would take our blankets to protect us from the morning chill. As soon as we had bedded down, thinking of many things and trying to visit our dear ones if only in dreams we would yield to sleep.

Early one morning, awakened by the noise of vehicles pulling up and car doors slamming, I forced my eyes open. Mark was already awake. It must have been about five o'clock, just about daylight. Two cars bearing the insignia of the SS were releasing their passengers.

The SS officers, presumably from the SD (Security Service) had brought with them two men wearing *Luftwaffe* officer uniforms. Both displayed Iron Crosses around their necks and wore leather flight jackets. The two were tied to stakes that had evidently been prepared immediately in advance of this errand. Blindfolds were put on them, and their hands were tied behind the stakes with their backs toward the rising hill. The attending party withdrew about thirty paces, then two of them turned back and unceremoniously mowed the men down with a shattering burst of Mauser fire, the same as the type used on our boys in Budzyn. German blood spattered all around as their heads fell forward. My heart skipped a beat, and I held my breath. If the SD had realized that their enemies were watching their own disgrace, they would have dispatched us without blinking an eye. One of the party was or bore striking resemblance to Joseph Mueller.

I had never seen anything so ironic. They had just executed, in cold blood, air force officers who had actually done the real fighting for them. What had the men done? Had they perhaps made some uncomplimentary remarks about the conduct of the war? Had they refused to bomb open cities? Or had they perhaps just become fed up with fighting a losing war? It was incredible but evidently true that even

German fighting men were not safe from the absolute authority of the feared SD, which ranked even higher than the SS and the Gestapo. The hospital hill made this an ideal spot because it was out of sight of people on the outside. I never went back there to sleep, but we heard similar morning salvos repeatedly.

We were encouraged by the news of the German retreat as the Russians pushed the front west; they were now not too far away from the old Polish border.

One fine day *Hauptsturmfuehrer* Goeth, the camp commandant, went to the work office and requested that a weaver be sent to his house because his mistress wanted to have woven summer furniture made. In the morning formation, a guard called out a number corresponding to the one on Mark's patch. I watched with apprehension as Mark disappeared with the guard. My friend knew as much about furniture weaving as I did about building the field hospital.[3]

Taking the count and regrouping into work formations always took a good half an hour; in the case of a miscount or escape it took longer. But that morning it seemed the longest. As we were forming our newly named building-trades group, *Bauleitung Komando,* a man told me he had a message for me.

"Yes, what is it?" I asked.

"Your friend Mark sent word that he was assigned to *Steinbruch* for claiming not to know how to weave furn—"

"Never mind," I interrupted.

I left the group at once and while men were still milling around the grounds, I found the *Steinbruch* detachment. Two men had been assigned there for disciplinary work; one of them was my friend Mark, looking calm and perhaps even resigned.

"Listen," I told him, "I've got an idea I must try. If anyone should ask what your real trade is, tell them a tile setter."

I don't recall his reaction; I was already rushing off to look for SS *Hauptsharfuehrer* Schupke, the work boss. He was the only one accessible with enough authority to change "disciplinary" work assignments. I found him surrounded by SS guards and camp administrators. Coming snappily to attention, I attracted his notice. He knew me from his periodic visits to our job site to check the progress of the hospital barracks. "*Herr Hauptscharffuehrer,* we can't finish the bathroom without someone who knows how to lay floor tiles. If this does not get done, the other foreman and I will be beaten and charged with the responsibility."

"What do you want me to do—produce a tile setter?"

"There is one, but he is being taken to *Steinbruch.* Could you get him for the job?"

"Come on. Let's take a look at him." Mark's life hung on a prayer.

Schupke had me point him out, and the guards released him, but they explained his crime to Schupke as we made haste to join our group. I heard Schupke's words following us: "If he is as good a tile setter as he was a weaver, he will be back here. You can rely on that!"

It was no idle threat, but we had gained time to act. On the way I stopped at the Polish group and got an okay to take along the real tile setter—a jolly, fat Pole with a large shaved head. I do not recall his real name, but we had nicknamed him Zagloba, (a famous character from the trilogy by Henry Sienkiewicz (better known for his novel *Quo Vadis*). The fictitious Zagloba was always exaggerating his military exploits, claiming to have been in the place where the fighting was the thickest, while actually he usually was unavoidably detained elsewhere, drinking. But being jovial and witty, he made good company.

Our Zagloba resembled him physically and in his disposition. He could not boast of military exploits, but when it came to drinking, he would have had the original character outdone except for the scarcity of the real stuff. Yet, somehow, liquor had been smuggled in that day.

During the lunch break, after many optimistic predictions by Zagloba concerning the outcome of the war and some appropriate toasts to a most disastrous fate for the Germans, the only immediate disaster was that some of us began to feel nauseated and threw up— except Zagloba, who seemed immune. After an hour or so, fortunately, everyone had recovered—that is, everyone but a visiting German *Kapo*, whose red nose testified to his condition.

As I had good reason to expect a visit from Schupke to check on Mark's work, I suggested to my corpulent companion that he get on with the tile work. Zagloba was soon on his hands and knees and laying tiles, while Mark, his new apprentice, assumed the same working position—just in case. Surveying their progress, it appeared to me that the tiled area might actually be completed that day. Luckily, Schupke did not come until the next day and seemed satisfied with the finished work. The question of Mark's occupation did not come up again.

A different sort of break in the work routine was provided by a crazy SS captain from the building department who wore civilian clothing and became a frequent visitor to the job site. On spotting him, our look-out always gave the signal for activity to resume at an accelerated pace; the people outdoors would get very busy with rakes and shovels, and the hammering noises inside could be heard half a mile away. By the time the captain had ascended the hill, all evidence of inactivity would have disappeared.

Once, noticing our "exertion" at an early stage of construction, he seemed pleased and promised a sack of bread for our group. This unprecedented and much coveted reward was given the same day, averaging about a half-pound of bread per person. On another visit, witnessing the same show, he called Rosenberg and me to come to him, which we did gladly, hoping for more bread. Instead, he got hysterical and whipped us both, alternating lashes equally and complaining of nonproductivity.

I began to have night visions—not dreams—about a tremendous Divine rescue. I let my imagination wander, considering schemes for mass escapes. I had vivid pictures of overwhelming the guards by sheer weight of numbers and, having succeeded, leading the wretched humanity to freedom beyond this death trap. However, when mental exhaustion brought sleep, I invariably dreamed of being chased, caught, tormented, and beaten by the Germans. After such nightmares it was a relief to wake up and shake off the night's experience.

It was an escape in itself to daydream of one, but it was also quite useless. Escapes were not impossible, but finding shelter among the Polish people was very rare. Posted all over the country were signs offering rewards of a few pounds of sugar and a bottle of vodka for turning in hidden Jews, and there was a severe penalty for giving aid and shelter to runaway prisoners. Many prisoners escaped, but as far as was known, few got away. Those who did joined partisan groups or formed their own.

To be sure, when an entire group of ten or twelve men who worked at the plant guardhouse had escaped from Budzyn the previous Christmas Eve, taking with them weapons and supplies, the authorities were so embarrassed that there was not much camp publicity about it, and I recall no repercussions. Also memorable was a successful raid on Budzyn's supply depot by Jewish partisans disguised as German soldiers. The whole job was pulled off without a shot being fired. There had been other successful escapes and raids, but unless you had a well-conceived and calculated plan to reach the partisans in the woods and some Christian people on the outside to help you en route, the idea of escape was a desperate one—at best a temporary relief. Yet desperate and hopeless as this idea was, I never could quite put it out of my mind.

Meanwhile, our camp played host to a large, newly arrived group of Hungarian Jews. Perhaps because they had enjoyed limited freedom much longer than had the other Jews of Europe, the shock of their predicament had not yet worn off, as was clearly apparent from their woeful expressions. For the first time we saw women with their heads totally shaved. Some had kerchiefs to hide their baldness, but others were bareheaded, exposing their naked scalps. This sorrowful procession heading for the customary baths wrung the hearts of some of the most seasoned and hardened men, who were not easily moved by new faces of misfortune.

Later I became friendly with one Hungarian girl and her mother, the only two left of their whole family. The young lady had very short light brown hair and bright, rather childish blue eyes; she showed dimples whenever I succeeded in making her smile. In her late teens, she was remarkably poised, cheerful, and very pretty. Her looks and friendly manner endeared her to anyone who came in contact with her or who fell under the spell of her youthful charm. I would see her on Sunday afternoons, when the women were permitted on the men's compound grounds. The times she spent with me were few and short, but during these brief moments she told me something about her native land. We talked about what each of us would do in the future, if we had a future. She tried in vain to teach me a few Hungarian words, though we used German for our main line of communication. She was like a lovely fragrant flower, and though uprooted, she was now cheering a drab and ugly environment. Her name, I think, was Esther, but I called her Gigi (Dzidzi), which in Polish means "child" or "baby."

In about mid-June the German medics descended on the camp and rounded up a group of young men and women as nonvoluntary blood donors. These blood-sapping raids were repeated several times; afterward, the victims were often too weak to walk and had to be carried back. Cynical from the standpoint of their racist theories, bestial when you think of how they fed and treated their victims, the Germans were desperate for blood for their wounded from the not-far-away front, and they did not hesitate to mix Jewish blood with their "pure" ice water.[4]

But most of the bloodletting in camp was useless. Shortly after our arrival the SS guards somehow heard that the Orenstein brothers had foreign currency. The doctor and his brother Henry were dragged to the guardhouse and beaten until blood ran down over their bowed heads. The two held out and managed to come out of it alive. No money was found on their persons. Admission, of course, would have been fatal; the possession of foreign currency was a capital offense.

A feeling of expectation marked the advent of summer 1944. The Germans were being pushed back and were losing all around, particularly on the Russian front, where they had never recovered from Stalingrad. This news was encouraging but of no practical use to us. We were still behind wire, still marked for extinction, still in the hands of our enemies—still laboring, wasting away, and dying, seemingly to no one's concern. The groans of the oppressed brought no relief. Yet once again, when summer's bright sun bathed the earth in its golden splendor, it brought a feeling of hope, independent of any logic. It made me think that as long as the sun warmed this forsaken planet, the earth and its people would abide, despite the unopposed heinous terror of the day.

One evening in the barracks I stood in line directly in front of Mark for our bread and jam rations. "Mussolini, our block leader, was dishing out our portions, as he had so many times before. The bread slices were cut evenly, but he spooned out the jam into each man's mess kit. Mussolini had a tendency to trim down the portion when a small or weak man held out his dish. I took particular notice of this practice that evening, and something began to heat up inside me. Whenever a skinny specimen visibly showing symptoms of progressive malnutrition came up, Mussolini slopped in only a half-measure, and the cheated ones were usually too weak or scared to complain. As I drew near the rationing spot, I caught a glimpse of a man just being shortchanged. He grimaced but walked away silently. When it was my turn, whether because of my erect bearing or the position I had on the job, I don't know, but Mussolini slapped an exaggerated portion of jam on my tin plate. By this time my anger had reached its peak. With a sweep, I slapped it back in his face, startling him and drawing the subdued laughter of those standing around. Enraged, Mussolini first used his fingers to scoop some of the jam off his face.

I was too angry to appreciate the comical effect of this scene. By the time he had wiped his face, the men had retreated, making room for what seemed inevitable. The block leader looked to me as Goliath must have looked to David. With my back against the three-tiered bunks, I faced a giant sausage with some jam on his meaty face. He came in charging and swinging. I jumped to the side, allowing him to plow his fist into the bunk boards. Then, taking advantage of the moment that it took him to lick his hand, I rammed all I had into his belly. He retreated, but only to gain momentum for another thrust. The spectators were shouting, "Attaboy, Topas! Keep away from him! Duck! Hit him in the stomach!"

This time I hoisted myself onto the bunk. When Mussolini charged again, I swung out feet first, thrusting against his bulging chest. The impact shook him up, and he began to throw wild punches, giving me a chance to land a few good ones. He began to breathe heavily and finally withdrew to his room. (Each block *fuehrer* had his own room.) A self-appointed replacement resumed dishing out even portions of jam.

Whatever satisfaction or relief I might have felt at that moment gave way immediately to fear. Mussolini had put on his raincoat and was heading for the camp administration building with one arm in a sling. Mark surveyed the situation quickly and said, "Don't wait for them to call you. Come on. Let's go!" While we walked, Mark took a rag and made a sling from it, urging me to put it on to simulate being hurt. With this impromptu plan, I quickened my pace to follow Mussolini. When I walked in, he was already there, standing at attention and reporting being assaulted by one of the men. Chilewicz and Finkelstein, the camp elders, together with a couple of SS officials, were listening to the emotional tones in which he delivered his complaint. I stood alongside him and awaited my turn. Disobedience, undermining authority, is serious business with the Germans. I knew I was in deep trouble.

When he finished his report, including the fact of my having thrown marmalade in his face, Chilewicz asked him, "Who did all this to you?" Without turning, Mussolini pointed down at me.

"You don't mean to say that this boy did all this to *you?*" asked one of the SS men. Mussolini replied with the loudest *"Jawohl"* yet.

All of them now looked at him, then at me, reviewing the comparison. Then the SS guards shook their heads and laughed, struck apparently by the contrast in weight. Whatever it was that caused them to be amused was also my saving grace. The Jewish leader, also dismissing this complaint with laughter, told Mussolini that next time anyone attempted to do anything like this to him, he ought to grab him and sit on him.

Late that night, I lay awake feeling sorry for Mussolini. He too was a victim of circumstances, and however distasteful the thought, he was one of us. The next day, the Jewish administration permitted Mark and me to move to Block 38, the annex to Block 40. Block 38 had ordinary bunks, but considerably fewer men than the others, making it a quieter place to rest or sleep after work. A German Jew named Rosenblum was the barracks leader, a quiet-spoken man who was fond of whistling a very pretty tune. Once I asked him what it was, and he told me it was *"Questa o Quella,"* from Verdi's *Rigoletto*.

This was an unlikely place to further one's musical education, yet I had learned another moving melody from Verdi. It was a sample of the finer things of life that made me yearn for more beautiful music, more books, more history, more knowledge. But these were dreams the fulfillment of which belonged to the free. I had to be satisfied with the fragments and scraps of things I had acquired before the camps, and like a poor man who is fond of the very few things he possesses, I was content in the lighter moments to whistle snatches of some of the other beautiful pieces of classical music that I remembered from phonograph records played at home in the "good old days." But even here, I discovered, I could learn—and although I learned considerably less, I appreciated it more.

Though some time had passed, Dr. Blanke was still in the camp. One day, unexpectedly, accompanied by a *Scharfuehrer* (sergeant), he ascended the hill somehow unnoticed by our lookouts, and before anyone was tipped off, he got hold of Rosenberg, my coforeman, and beat him mercilessly. I was waiting in the tool shed that once had been used as a tailor and shoe repair shop. Rosenberg, beaten and bleeding, ran to me crying, "Now it's your turn! Now it's your turn!"

I stood before Blanke and his escort and acknowledged the fact that I was also a foreman on this job. Blanke, already worked up like a bloodthirsty shark, whipped my face back and forth with his bullwhip, while his eager assistant, holding in his hand something like a piece of two-by-four, yelled, "Lie down!" I kept standing until I was cut down by the whip, but when I fell face down, Blanke and his noncom kept striking my back alternately—one with his whip, the other with the board—like two blacksmiths striking an anvil. Every stroke was followed by the groans of the prisoners and the shouting of the two administering the bloodbath, which I finally understood: "*Sage es wird gearbeitet!* Say there is going to be some work done!" I did not speak, not because I was trying to be a hero but because I was simply dumfounded.

The prisoners nearby, trying to save my life, urged in Polish, "There will be work done," and somehow, before losing my senses, I repeated, "*Es wird gearbeitet.*"

"Louder!"

I obliged.

"*Say Herr Hauptsturmfuehrer,*" yelled the second fiddle, "*Herr Hauptsturmfuehrer,*" I repeated. This stopped the beating. A couple of men hoisted me up to stand before my executioner and held me up long enough for me to say once more, "*Herr Obersturmfuehret, es wird gearbeitet.*"

"You should not forget this," said the doctor. I thought, I won't— for as long as I live. The two left, and I was content to lie face down and hug the earth, begging the others to leave me alone and not to look on my disgrace. The back of my vertically striped jacket had horizontal rips; the pants were blood-soaked shreds. God had not forsaken me completely; I was alive, able to withstand more than many who had perished before me, and I had no broken bones. But this consolation did not occur to me just then, when I felt quite willing to join my more virtuous ancestors.

Mark took care of me that evening, and I was allowed to remain in the barracks the next day, to get back on my feet. My worst problem was keeping my clothing from sticking to my drying wounds. My friends wondered how I was able to withstand it all, something I wondered myself. Some of the strokes had reopened old injuries inflicted by Tauscher. The healing process, though, was aided by the summer warmth. In winter, the smallest sore exposed to cold is painful and heals reluctantly.

Meanwhile, the rest of the Budzyn prisoners arrived at Plaszow and were swallowed up in the larger camp. Here, the few big shots of the Budzyn administration were reduced to the status of ordinary prisoners. I had a soft spot for Sztokman, who never that I remember used a whip and who once did me a kindness by ordering that I be given new clothing after my stint of running half-naked in the cold. Mark and I gave Sztokman some cigarettes we "found."

Among events that followed, we witnessed the shooting of Chilewicz, his wife, and Finkelstein—the Jewish camp commandants—right under the hill where the hospital barracks was being built. Their bullet-riddled bodies fell on the same spot where the German officers had been executed. According to rumor, they had been punished for planning or attempting an escape.[5] To replace them, a German who was reputed to have once been a gangster in the United States took charge of the inner camp administration, and another German prisoner named Kramer was elevated to the second place.

Kramer, dark, chunky, of medium height, wearing dark-rimmed glasses, resembled a university student. In reality he was a shrewd, cunning scavenger who would, if he could, have gladly joined the ranks of the Nazis for the advantages it offered. He once said to me, "Just because I am here does not mean that I am not a National Socialist." Nevertheless, as well as I can recall, he never struck anyone; he liked to converse with other prisoners, and by camp standards he was not a bad sort.

One of the most interesting personalities, however, was the camp scribe, a man from Luxembourg named Tiehl. The red triangle in front of his number indicated that he was a political prisoner. Tiehl was a beautiful person. In his early thirties, he had graying blond hair, dark eyes, and patrician features that retained an expression of delicacy and kindness. At a time and place when our captors were trying to reduce men to the level of beasts, Tiehl, a prisoner himself, retained the qualities that mark the best in free men. He was kind and considerate. You could see compassionate sorrow in his eyes when witnessing some of the cruelties that took place before him. His warm personality and good looks evoked a bit of respect even from some of the camp officials.

As the summer reached its height and one event overlapped another, tension and anxiety mounted within the camp. By now we should have been used to a life of constant terror, a life that constantly hung in doubt, a life that we knew was merely a postponement of our inevitable annihilation. Yet the very tension and anxiety were reactions of people who still cared and hoped; otherwise, we would merely have met each crisis with emotionless resignation.

One of the Jewish wagon drivers smuggled his girl out by hiding her under a heap of garbage in his wagon; once on the outside, they managed to escape and were never heard from again. A well-dressed prisoner who was teaching SS *Haupsturmfuehrer* Goeth and other officers horseback riding took advantage of his privileges of free movement and fled on his mount. The expected repercussions followed such events in a wave of terror and executions.

The SS elite continued to lead the life of carefree slavemasters. It was not uncommon for one of them to order a Jewish bricklayer to brick in his friend's door or windows as their kind of practical joke. But then one Jewish craftsman was taken into custody by the all-powerful SD. After questioning him, they released him, but not before they had ripped up the floor in commandant Goeth's home and uncovered the store of diamonds, jewels, and gold that he had amassed by robbing the Krakow ghetto Jews before their execution—massacres in which Goeth himself was known to have participated. Killing Jews was perfectly all right with the SD, of course, but hoarding their valuables was not. Because Goeth had failed to turn over the loot to the *Reichsbank*, he was taken by his cohorts to face his own "final solution," but through his high-powered connections he was spared. Still, we were relieved to be rid of him. He was soon replaced by a lower-ranking officer.

In the first week of June, reports of a large-scale Allied invasion reached our forsaken place. The news caused quite a stir but had no immediate effect on our lot. Since the German defeat now seemed more imminent than ever, the SS men were fond of saying to the prisoners: "There is still time till twelve o'clock [that is, the end of the Third Reich]—at five to twelve, we will put an end to your troubles." Naturally, the SS and all others guilty of murder expected that the defeat of the regime would mean that they would have to face justice themselves, but they were sincere in their intention to destroy all evidence and all witnesses before the end, and this knowledge tended to dampen our enthusiasm about the best news.

Just about that time, a change took place in camp discipline. Previously, any SS man could beat, mutilate, or shoot any prisoner whenever he felt like it. Now, when an internee was found smoking in formation or in possession of a knife or committing any other infraction, the guards reported his offense to the SS administration. A few days later, the various offenders would be called out of formation and the ranking guard would read out their sentences. These ranged from going to a stand-up bunker, to flogging, to time at the deadly *Steinbruch* (quarry). Once, the SS instituted a *Strafkommando* (penal unit) headed by the German *Kapo* who had taken charge of the camp after the execution of the Jewish leaders. The idea, this overseer explained, was to make us work until water boiled in our colons. I was assigned to this group for a very brief period for an offense that I cannot now remember. Red bull's-eye disks were sewn on our backs. These were to serve as easy targets in case someone should attempt escape. All marching was done in double time. The practice of delayed punishment for minor offenses was something new, even though it was disregarded by those who were in the habit of beating prisoners. As well as we could calculate, it was the response to a directive from higher ups: Don't kill them senselessly—work them to death. This revised punitive system was attributed to the shortage of manpower the Third Reich was experiencing. Perhaps for the same reason, the hospital barracks, once a relatively inconspicuous place to work, now drew considerable attention from the authorities.

One bearlike, cigar-smoking SS guard nicknamed *Misiu* (Teddy Bear) began making regular visits to our job site. Occasionally he would beat up Rosenberg and me and even Mark, who had joined our group. What marked him as unique among his own brand of butchers was his emphasis on the job well done. He took his time explaining that his concern for production came before concern for himself and for us. In a quiet way he would tell us that because we had failed to show our best efforts as foremen, he could not avoid punishing us. He did not go for the all-out beating administered by Dr. Blanke but would line us up against the wall and strike our backs with a wooden cane that he carried for the purpose. The trouble was that he always managed to land his cane on the spine. Horsewhipping was painful, but the cane could actually cripple. It was a miracle that we somehow escaped permanent injury.

Whenever we looked mad with pain and indignation or betrayed a desire for revenge, Teddy Bear would say, as others had said before him: "Don't try anything foolish or you will change this camp into a blood-bathed cemetery in an hour's time." Unfortunately, this was not the least bit exaggerated. Electrically charged wires, machine-gun equipped towers, scores of police dogs, an SS company, and a company of Ukrainian turncouts were all we had to contemplate in order to discard any notion of starting a private mutiny.

An even more frequent visitor was the SS *Zahnartz* (dentist). On each visit he grew more impatient for the completion of the dental lab. Frankly, I knew less about the dental lab than it was wise to admit, so it was no surprise to hear him complain about the quality of the workmanship. During one of these sessions Teddy Bear arrived and, surprisingly enough, took our side, arguing with the dentist that materials were scarce and nearly half of the things for "this place" (as he put it) had to be "organized"—the German euphemism for stealing—by us with his own help.

This may have squared Teddy Bear with the *Zahnartz*—after all, they wore the same uniform—but the dentist's animosity toward me was undiminished. On one occasion as we parted, he threatened me with the quarry: "If I don't send you to *Steinbruch,* you can call me Tony!" A word to the wise was enough. Mark promised to replace me for a few days, and I persuaded one of the Jewish work administrators to transfer me to another job.

14 A Daring Enterprise

*In great straits and when hope is small,
the boldest counsels are the safest.*
—Livy

My new job marked a significant change in my meager existence. The work, which consisted of dismantling railroad tracks, was hard, but it was well away from the camp and its depressing atmosphere—and there were smuggling opportunities. For me, the half-hour march each way on the open highway was like window-shopping for freedom.

Marching to work the first day, I felt something fresh: an opportunity to think away from turmoil and the specter of death. My thoughts turned again to hopes of escape—less as an end in itself than as a means to survival. To avenge, to seek justice, to warn against such evil, one first had to survive. My awareness of our helplessness to strike back at our oppressors increased my desire to fight back.

There was something novel about the guards on this new job. Instead of the SS, our escort was a detachment from the gendarmerie. Every morning they awaited our group of 150 or more men inside the main gate; the ranking *Wachtmeister* was responsible for as many heads as he signed out for. Evenly spaced, the guards would line up on both sides of the highway, leaving the center for our column. Equipped with rifles, machine guns, ammo belts, and police dogs, they made the whole party look like a circus. Stealing glimpses at free people, children at play, stores, homes, trees, flowers, and vehicular traffic, we would reach our job site. There the guards would form a wide ring around us to isolate the group from the outside.

Under the direction of brown-uniformed Nazi supervisors from the *Organisation Todt*,[1] our underfed men pried railroad tracks loose, hoisted and carried them on their shoulders, and stacked them.

Polish traders, mostly women, sneaked in occasionally in hopes of doing some business; they would trade bread and fruit for clothing or linens until the guards noticed the commotion and chased them away. Whatever food was obtained by a few men had to be smuggled into the camp, and that was not always easy to do. Personally, I had no worry; having nothing to trade, I had nothing to smuggle either way.

Mark also managed to leave the hospital construction job and became one of the camp electricians, wearing a belt with pliers, screwdriver, and tape as the credentials of the trade. This job gained him access to many storehouse buildings otherwise off limits to ordinary prisoners. So after a while I suggested to my friend that if I could get my hands on some money or some merchandise, I could try smuggling. Mark in his typically unhurried way reached into one of his pockets and produced a 500-zloty bank note, called in Polish slang a "hillbilly." (*Gural*)

"But Mark," I demanded, "where did you get this money? You haven't had it all this time?"

After a moment's thought he replied, "I most probably found it." This was equivalent to saying, "Don't ask."

The next day I managed to buy several loaves of bread and even several pounds of fruit, investing—or, more accurately, betting—all the money. Should they frisk us at the gate, they would take away the foodstuff, but possession of currency could mean death. The guards did not frisk us every day, but at least once a week they would bag everything the outside work groups were carrying. Since all confiscated food went to the guards' kitchen, they had something really good going there and naturally did not want to spoil it. Hence, they treated the surprise frisking as a game. For some of the losers, the game meant bankruptcy; others were severely beaten. Yet nothing discouraged the smuggling activity.

That day we were lucky and got through without being searched. Mark took charge of my first haul and sold the goods to the elite around Block 40. By that evening, our capital had increased, and we were eating bread baked on the outside. It was a good feeling to eat bread bought with one's "earnings." While Mark held on to the surplus, I took the reinvestment capital and kept on smuggling.

I suggested to our foreman that if we could buy the guards off, we could trade less hurriedly and get more for our money and rags. The foreman agreed, provided that I do the "fixing," but he was fair enough to warn me that the last fixer had been executed for trying. Since then, however, the guards had been changed, so I decided to take the chance. I was deliberately allowed to work alone near the *Wachtmeister*, who sat on an embankment. I don't remember much about him except that he was in his thirties and did not appear to be one of the arrogant, haughty, hostile characters that typified that lot. The idea was to engage him in conversation without saying anything for a while that might be construed as proposing a bribe. Our conversation went something like this:

"I would like to say something to you, *Herr Wachtmeister*. May I?"

"Yes, and where did you learn to speak German?" he asked.

"In Warsaw High School before the war."

"For a foreigner, you speak pretty good."

After a moment's pause, while I swung my pick a few times at a stubborn spike, he asked, "What was that you wanted to say?"

"Oh, I merely wanted to say that I was guessing where you might have come from. This curiosity leads me to interesting discoveries," I improvised.

"Well, where do you think I come from?"

"From a city—I can always tell a big city man," I carried on, hoping to score.

"That's right, I happen to be from Berlin. But how could you tell?"

"I watched you a few times and noticed that you seem to be bored by these surroundings."

This led to a conversation in which he revealed that he was a draftee, that he had a liquor store in Berlin and a wife and a "furlough child," and that he was homesick. After a while I asked about the food situation at home, to which he replied that it was bad and that because he had nothing himself, he could not send food packages to his family.

At this point, I showed my cards: if he would allow us to trade with the Polish civilians, we would see that he and the guards got something to supplement their diet every day from the proceeds. There followed a few tense moments. Then he rose and said, "We'll see." Following this vague reply, he went to talk my proposition over with the others. A few long minutes later he returned and advised that it would be all right, but we must be careful not to be seen by the SS or the Gestapo or the higher-ups. He was telling me!

Each prisoner who wished to buy or trade thereupon gave two zlotys for the guards' fund; the guards turned on their heels and kept looking outside the perimeter; and the civilian traders, sensing an opportunity, converged on our outpost. Brisk bargaining began and continued for half an hour or so, until the guards got nervous, which served as a signal to quit trading. The "exchange" was closed.

Our foreman next asked permission for a guard to escort the two of us to a general store known to be nearby, and after a moment's pondering, the *Wachtmeister* sent one guard along. It seemed incredible to be standing in a real store again, even though we were under guard. It was a strange sensation apparently for the shopkeeper as well to see concentration camp prisoners in striped uniforms in his shop, or any-where else. Nevertheless, the money changed hands, the shopkeeper brought forth a large bottle of vodka and sliced Polish sausages and bacon into sandwiches; and we took it all back as a payoff for the guards, who helped themselves to the bottle and cleaned up every-thing else as well. An extra bonus was given to the *Wachtmeister.*

Since this sort of thing made our group prosperous, at least in camp terms, the practice was kept up. Mark, with his access to the storerooms, "organized" items of clothing, which I smuggled out, thus carrying a payload both ways. Carrying stolen government property was, of course, extremely dangerous, but frisking on the way out to work was rare, and I got used to taking chances. On several occasions, we got cleaned out coming back and had to start all over again. Nevertheless, once these smuggling operations got under way, Mark and I and many others began to earn a living, and that meant food.

After one of our unsuccessful returns, Mark decided to fill in for a sick man and joined our group the next day. The idea was to double our bets, but of course it was inescapably risky as well. Mark had liberated some German-issue woolen sweaters from one of the warehouses, where he undoubtedly had located a "serious electrical short."

Emboldened by previous successes, we were not overly concerned as we set out the next morning with our substantial "hot" cargo. I wore one of the sweaters under my shirt and one wrapped snugly around my waist underneath my pants. Mark in addition carried a little canvas bag on a sling suspended over his shoulder and took a position directly behind me in the formation. In a column of some forty ranks of men five abreast, our position was near the tail end. We marched past the first gate and were halted at the outer gate for the regular count. Our escorts were already lined up on both sides of our column and were ready to go—but something was wrong; the SS did not wave us through after the count.

Someone stood up on his toes and reported that they were frisking up ahead. It was being done by the ranking SS man, who quite thoroughly ran his hands down over each prisoner. As he finished each row of five, he ordered them to take one step forward and started on the next row. Somewhere in the middle of the column, he pulled one man out to the side and beat him brutally until the man collapsed. He had found a civilian shawl on him. This did not bolster our confidence, nor did it leave much of a prospect for our future. The SS man in charge had a vile temper and was bloodthirsty. The five men ahead of me took one step forward. It was our turn. My position in the middle gave me enough time to take a deep breath. When I raised my hands for frisking, he looked me straight in the eyes as he ran his hands down my sides all the way to my ankles. He straightened out and stepped over to the next man. My heart must have been beating like a sledgehammer. I was thinking of Mark's canvas bag. At the instant when he ordered our five to move one step forward, I stuck out my left thumb parallel to my shoulder while the SS man stood on our right. Mark, who was able to watch the guard, dropped the sling over my thumb and thus passed the "overweight luggage" to me in the split second that it took the five of us to take a step forward.

The gendarmes had watched this entire show in silence. When it was all over and the gates were opened for us to go, the guard on my left, who had witnessed what had gone on between Mark and me, remarked: "You have more luck than brains." It was certainly close. After that, Mark abstained from going out, but otherwise the smuggling went on.

In the course of my smuggling career, which continued to the end of my stay in this camp, I had several other close calls, but a few experiences bordered on the comical. In order to haul the maximum payload of food, you had to be more enterprising than merely to carry on a retail trade. With Mark's help, I sewed a number of makeshift inner pleats in my coat. Increased volume meant both increased gain and increased risk: bulging like Harpo Marx, I was caught one time loaded to the limit. The guard was not content to let me dump my load into the spread blankets but ordered me into the guardhouse.

As I walked in, several guards rose from their chairs and surrounded me, while one emptied my musette bag. The bag yielded four long loaves of white bread. When they opened my coat, they began to laugh. Six loaves of bread protruded from the pleats like so many rounds of ammo filling a belt. I pressed my luck a bit by asking them to let me keep one of my loaves of bread. Then I was called back from the door as I tried to leave. "Just wait awhile," said the one who had done the frisking. He left the room and returned in a jiffy holding a razor in his hand. Putting his left hand on my shoulder, he made a sweeping move under my chin as though to cut my throat, but actually he did not touch me. Then he shaved off one side of my mustache, which had never been shaved before. This little bit of theatrics drew more laughter.

"Well, what are you waiting for? Go!"

"How about my bread?" I reminded them.

With a sweep of his arm he drew his bayonet. Driving it into the center of a loaf, the guard split it in two and threw one half to me, which I managed to catch as I released the door and hastily left.

On another occasion our group passed the main gate but got trapped at the inner gate, where everyone was frisked and I lost my haul again. Empty-handed, I walked behind the ranks of those yet to be searched. In a moment I noticed and retrieved a package from a man who was holding it behind his back in an effort to unload it. I managed to sneak by without detection. As soon as I got to the barracks, I opened the package. It contained a large bottle of brandy, which was quite valuable; however, it was very dangerous to be caught with any alcoholic beverages.

The man whom I had relieved of the bottle (and of the consequences, had it been found on him) soon came to demand it back in its entirety. Mark and I felt that we were entitled to half the contents for our risk and trouble. After arguing back and forth, we finally agreed to an impartial arbitration (*Din Torah*).[2] A tall baldhead from Barracks 40 consented to render judgment. After listening first to one side and then to the other and asking a few questions himself, he reached a verdict in our favor, basing his judgment on the following reasoning: The "plaintiff" was intent on ridding himself of dangerous contraband, since he did not want to be found with it; he had managed to dispose of if; therefore he was no longer the rightful owner of the package and had no claim to it. Nevertheless, we surrendered half of the bottle to its former owner, and we all parted on friendly terms.

Mark was unable to find a ready market for our salvaged prize, so we were stuck with it. To dispose of the contents we resourcefully had a quiet celebration, inviting our closest friend, one Abram Finkelstein, an old veteran from Budzyn who was residing in the next bunk. When it comes to worry about the future, there is no better anesthetic known to kill pain than the liquid we then tasted; temporary relief is guaranteed.

While we were nipping at the brandy, a typical run-down-looking prisoner came in and observed our tête-à-tête. A feeling of guilt and pity took hold of me. We offered him a drink, but he refused, and casting a sad look at us, he withdrew from sight. On another evening, we were eating some of our imported goods on my bunk when an even less fortunate-looking prisoner walked in and stared at us. We offered him a piece of bread and a tomato. He accepted, thanked us, and leaned against the wall to eat his share. Before he had finished, two SS barged in and began to frisk our uninvited guest. Our astonishment was profound when they found a "hillbilly" note on him. They roughed him up but then left as quickly as they came. It looked as though someone had tipped them off, for our guest seemed as unlikely a specimen to possess 500 zlotys as we were to own a bank. He was lucky that the guards had decided to split it among themselves.

Parting Is Not Sweet Sorrow

More important events began to overshadow our personal experiences. The recent Hungarian arrivals, mostly women, were isolated in quarantine barracks and readied for shipment: destination, Auschwitz.[3] I ran over one morning to an administrative Jewish official—the one who had previously shown some heart when I had asked to be transferred to another job to avoid disaster at the hospital post—and asked him to save Gigi from the transport. Relying on our smuggling profits, I promised to make good any "expenses" he might incur in accomplishing this. After many pleas and much persuasion, I obtained his promise that he would do all he could to get her out. This was the closest thing to certainty there was in such a place, and I thought there was a better-than-good chance of saving her, because she was young.

I had to hurry to rejoin my work formation and could not get word to Gigi just then, but upon my return from work I ran over to the barbed wire of the quarantine compound and asked someone to call her out. Wearing a kerchief on her head, the once vivacious girl looked sad but poised. "I have some news for you," I said. She came as close to the wires as was safe, and I explained to her what I had arranged. I kept my voice low in order not to attract the others' attention. "You see. It's all right. You will not have to go," I said.

She tried to smile and looked at me almost as though noticing me for the first time. Then, softly, she replied: "It's wonderful what you are trying to do for me. It is much more than I could dare expect from anyone I know, but I am sorry, I can't leave my mother. I must go with her."

I must have looked downcast, for she added, "You're a fine boy, George," and started to walk away, again trying awkwardly to smile. Instead, tears welled up in her eyes and began to roll down her cheeks. "Everything will be well yet; you will come out of all this, and someday you will marry some fine young girl. Please don't worry about me."

What a fool I was not to have realized that this gentle soul was so attached to her mother that nothing I could say would separate them. I had tried in vain to help save one life when one life could be saved, but it was no use. Before I departed, I promised to see her the next morning, the last time before they were loaded into the waiting cattle cars.

That memorable morning Mark helped me prepare a package containing food for the journey, and I saw Gigi long enough to pass the package to her. She looked composed and tried to appear cheerful. The morning whistle signaled a hasty parting.

"Goodbye, George," she said.

"Goodbye, pretty flower," I said almost entirely to myself as I made haste to join my formation. That was the last I saw or heard of Gigi. Parting is not sweet sorrow when there is no prospect of reunion in this world.

It was about that time that my number was called out at an evening formation. I came forward and was told by the SS man that a charge of littering had been leveled against me and that the punishment would be forty-eight hours in *Standbunker*. I was to report at eight o'clock that night. The *Standbunker* comprised locker compartments in the basement of one of the guardhouses, each with just enough room for one person standing up.[4] A little opening permitted air to come in. While many had died in less than forty-eight hours motionless standing, a young man could survive forty-eight hours. Seventy-two hours, the maximum ever given, was tantamount to a death sentence.

As nearly as Mark and I could figure out, Mussolini was the only one who might have cooked this up, still angry about the jam fight. After drawing our rations at the barracks, we walked slowly to the offenders' assembly point at the gate. There Mark sat on the ground with me, and we talked a little. At the given time a couple of guards read off the numbers, and we were sorted according to the length of our sentences: twenty-four-hour offenders marched ahead of the few forty-eight-hour ones. This night there were none sentenced to seventy-two hours.

As we came down into the dungeon, the guard released those whose time was up. Some had to be carried. When your number was called the guards assigned you to your cage. You had to walk backward into it. After the door was locked, that was the position in which the tenant remained the whole time there. As soon as all the lockers were filled, the light in the corridor went out, and silence fell over the place, interrupted only by those wishing to talk to one another and by those already there groaning for water.

I wedged myself between wall and door, pressing my knees against the door and leaning my back against the wall. This position took some weight off my feet. While the voices of some grew faint, others' groans grew louder. I was trying to concentrate on something else in an effort to distract my attention from this confinement. I tried to think of the hospital job first. For a while I was preoccupied with the sequences of the building operation. Then I considered all the months that it had taken us to put up the prefab structure, concluding that it could have been done in thirty days flat had they obtained our good will. But there and throughout the camp, if a prisoner could manage *not* to do something right, he always would. It was a part of our instinctive resistance.

I had been warned by graduates of the *Standbunker* that remaining in any one position too long was bad for your circulation. Others had warned that moving your limbs too much tires you out to the point that you cannot find a comfortable position. The trouble was that both theories were correct, as I knew after a few hours.

I had no idea what time it was when the lights came on again. Some SS man was inspecting this quiet torture chamber, inquiring about everyone's name and job. When he came to me I looked out the breathing hole and recognized SS *Scharffuehrer* Eckert, the assistant to Schupke, the SS man in charge of work assignments.

"And what are you doing here?" asked Eckert as though he knew me. His flashlight was still focused on me through the hole when I replied that someone had complained about my littering the *Appellplatz*.

"Indeed? Foreman—you were a foreman, no?" And he opened the door of my stall and let me out. As unusual as this was, it was certainly my good fortune. In parting, he said something about not getting in trouble again.

Eckert was later ordered to the Russian front. The story was told that he was guilty of an indiscretion: an SS woman became pregnant and named him as the father of her unborn child.

One day all the men who had once registered as inventors, engineers, and chemists were summoned to the SS work bureau outside the gate. Some high-ranking German officers were in the office interviewing those who had enlisted. When I reached the place, I found the Orenstein brothers; Baran, a mining engineer; Zylberberg, a newspaperman; and Rysiek Krakowski already standing in line. There were also some who had similarly registered in other camps for this job about which we knew nothing and dared not speculate. Tony Feinberg and Twerski, a Russian Jew who had lived in France before the war, were among the new applicants.

When my turn came to go in, I hesitated a moment, worried that they might get rough—or worse—if they got wise to my bluff about having a scientific background. Several *Wehrmacht* senior officers seated behind a long table confronted me when I walked in. I stood holding my visorless cap, surrounded by glittering high brass. Silver epaulets, jingling medals overlapping one another, monocles dangling on cords were enough evidence that the German army was taking a real interest in concentration camp science material. The man occupying the center position checked my name and number against his list, then used his pencil to point out an elaborate drawing spread on the table. Without preliminaries, he began to follow the lines on the drawing as he explained the function of this unknown contraption, saying things like "The gas enters through this coil; it is cooled or heated; it becomes compressed in the chamber. . . ."

All I saw were piping lines, coil lines, radiation fins, numbers, equations. When he finished explaining, he asked me whether I thought I could work on this project, to which I answered, *"Ja, aber nicht Selbstaendig."* (Yes, but not independently.) He noted my answer, or his own interpretation of it, and nodded, indicating that the interview was over. I left knowing less about this whole business than I knew before I went in.

A Close Call

For a while after this event no immediate change took place in the work assignments of those I knew who had registered as engineers or inventors. My curiosity soon gave way to a matter of more immediate interest. Rumors had spread about selections for a transport to Mauthausen concentration camp, and since bad news could always be believed, there was unrest in the camp. As bad as this place was, no one wanted to go to another Budzyn or to the gas chambers.

It was a hot and sunny Sunday when a train of cattle cars was backed up into the outer camp's railroad siding. Mark and I spent the whole day debating and eventually planning our strategy. First, we pondered the prospect of escape, which on such short notice could not possibly materialize.

A tall, handsome, freckle-faced six-footer from Radom, named Chaim, had become very friendly with us. Considering his size and strength, we thought he was a valuable companion, especially in time of trouble when daring and strength counted. It was no wonder, then, that we took him into our confidence that particular Sunday. After much useless talk about escape, which Chaim was in favor of, we agreed on a less ambitious but just as risky plan.

Because the next day was anticipated as the day of segregation for transport, we had to put our plan into effect that morning. The plan was simple enough: it consisted of hiding in the attic of one barracks throughout the day. We chose the barracks nearest the *Appellplatz* so that we would be able to observe and hear whatever was going on, and we thought it the least likely barracks to be suspected as a hiding place because of its proximity to where the action would be taking place.

The Allies had won in Africa; they were advancing in Italy; they had pushed the enemy back in Normandy; and the Russians had driven the Germans back to the prewar Polish-Soviet border. But to the approximately 14,000 prisoners in Plaszow concentration camp, all this news about the war and the feeling of victory at hand seemed too far away to be real.

On Monday morning the SS, undisturbed about their own future, started the feared segregation for deportation. According to our pre-conceived plan, we waited for our chosen barracks to empty, then entered the building. We located the trapdoor, opened it, and, quickly shoving straw-filled sacks to the side, clambered in. We stacked the sacks one on top of another, providing a barrier between the trapdoor and the front of the attic, where we sat leaning against the wall that faced the parade grounds. Mark took a penknife and began to chisel a hole in the outside wallboards, and we soon were able to observe the proceedings through peepholes.

The Ukrainian and SS guards marched into the inner camp and surrounded the assembly grounds. The first count came up short, and the German *Kapo*, assisted by guards, began to comb the camp and all barracks for hidden men or women. Soon the guards dragged a man out of his hiding place and stood him against the barbed wire bordering the elevated hill on the other side of camp. Shots ripped through the air; they had bagged their first victim.

Chaim got nervous and wanted to give himself up, thinking that perhaps he could save his life that way. We begged him not to, but the big fellow was surprisingly scared and at the moment incapable of making any logical decision. Mark pulled a penknife on him and placed its tip on the side of his neck. It was the only way he could be kept quiet, and the next ninety seconds were decisive, because an SS guard and a *Kapo* were approaching the attic. The trapdoor opened, and the guard thrust his bayonet through the straw sacks several times, stirring dust. Then we heard a voice say in German: "Hey you! Come on out! Let's go!"

Chaim's face betrayed panic but Mark kept the knife against his neck to silence him. We did not stir a muscle, knowing that it was a common trick for the guards to order people out even though they saw no one, thus often fooling people into revealing themselves. Receiving no answer, the two men descended, closing the trapdoor behind them. We all breathed again. Chaim by now was resigned to his predicament and was no longer a "security risk." But our next problem was to withstand the intense heat, which grew worse as the morning wore on and the sun beat down on the roof under which we were trapped.[5]

By midmorning, thousands of men and women had been selected and separated for the transport. Several men had been shot for one reason or another, and a young Jewish nurse had cut her wrist and bled to death in a few seconds. By noon the heat was such that the three of us, exhausted, fell asleep, and it was dark when we awoke. Meanwhile, we had lost track of what had happened. We looked out and saw that the SS were almost finished. They asked for four more volunteers to join the transport, and four volunteers reported, surprisingly enough, concluding the segregation. But the SS and the Ukrainians were still posted, isolating the barracks from the assembly grounds.

I opened the trapdoor and got down under cover of darkness to see what our next move should be. Outside, a large body of prisoners stood nearby, presumably those who had been exempted. A guard pacing past the window of the barracks prevented us from joining this group, but I figured, if we timed it right, we could make a dash for it one at a time. So, using the window as an escape hatch, we managed to join the spectators rather than the passengers.

Suddenly the ranks broke apart to make way for an SS truck loaded with bread. Mark put out his arm and, as the truck slowly moved ahead, swept off three loaves of bread. This much-needed nourishment was very timely. Worn out mentally as well as physically because of our heat-induced sleep in the attic crawl space, we yearned for rest in our bunks. Eventually, late that evening, the men remaining in camp were ordered back to the barracks. Once stretched out on our bunks, we felt a tremendous relief at having this day behind us. By this time we were so hardened by our experiences that for the moment the plight of our brothers confined to the railroad boxcars did not affect us as much as it should have.

When the sun rose over the camp the next morning, the boxcars were still on the railroad siding in the outer camp. When the heat reached its zenith at noon, the SS guards, in response to the pleas of the "cargo," permitted a camp crew to drag out the fire hoses, hoist them over the car roofs, and turn on the water.[6] Such a method of cooling was better than nothing. Nevertheless, for some, the journey came to an end before departure, and they were buried the following morning. The fact that the SS authorities had given permission to use the water was interpreted then to mean that the transport was scheduled for work rather than for a crematorium. After about twenty-four hours, the train with Mark's brother Adam, Harry Bronstein, the youthful Rosenbergs, and many other friends aboard pulled out for its slow journey to its bleak destination. Like Auschwitz, Mauthausen (in Austria) had gassing facilities. Among those who went were many brave people who were to endure another trip, another camp, another ordeal, and another battle for survival. For this stoical endurance they would get no medals, no honor—nothing but pain and many ways of death.

Rosh Hashanah that year came to celebrants in soiled garments, humiliated and bereaved. Nevertheless, it was still for us an awesome time. The People for whom the Jewish New Year had been instituted had seen and survived the opulence of Babylon, the glittering splendor of Greece, and the efficient, triumphant, and barbaric glory of Rome. Now it was being observed by the decimated remnants of our People. The High Holy Day prayers were chanted in a crowded barracks. Unrestrained tears ran down many faces, but when Mark and I wished each other the traditional Happy New Year, the irony of the situation made us smile: here was the eternal Jew with his eternal tradition in his eternal struggle.

During the brief time that it took to conduct the evening service, the chanting was subdued, the voices kept low. There were no outbursts of lamentation. On the faces of the very young there was an expression of quiet sadness. The older men, bereft of their wives and children, shed tears that were immediately wiped off, with nose-blowing and throat-clearing to disguise their silent weeping. On such a solemn occasion the poise and controlled bearing of people who had lost everything can be explained only by our awareness that the slaughter was not yet over, so we did not feel separated from the dead. We seemed to be within the confines of a funeral home, and after facing death almost constantly, we had merely become used to our unbearable environment.

All this time Western advances were being matched by the Russian push. With the Red Army already in parts of prewar Poland, the SS command at our camp ordered all the executed dead to be dug up and burned, and of course the job of destroying the evidence went to the surviving prisoners.[7] It was no small task. The mass graves had to be opened and the bodies stacked on wooden pyres, where they were soaked with gasoline and set afire. The burning went on around the clock for weeks. All the executed Jewish families of the Krakow ghetto had been hastily buried at Plaszow.

I managed to stay on my old job while a considerable number of prisoners were consigned to this gruesome task in shifts. One could see bonfires all around at night, and the stench was strong during that period.

Moving On

Suddenly, in October 1944, the unexpected happened: the inventors and "scientists"—or intelligentsia," as our group was eventually nicknamed—got orders to leave this camp for another place not immediately known. In the early hours of the morning of our departure, I chatted with Mark; I found parting from him difficult. Before saying goodbye, I turned over to him whatever money I had, knowing that Polish currency would be of no value to me in Austria or Germany, where we suspected we were being sent. A package of food passed from Mark's hand to mine. This package, and the powerful memories acquired in this and previous places, constituted my entire luggage. A quick embrace from my friend, a few seconds spent silently looking into each other's eyes, and it was time to join the ranks of about sixty men and one woman grouped for this trip.

As my legs carried me across the familiar grounds, it occurred to me that I was nearly twenty years old; five of those years had been spent under the aggressor, and half of that time as a guest of the Third Reich. The camp we were about to leave was no worse than the one we had come from. Here, at least, I had learned to fetch my own fodder—and since that time I had suffered no hunger pains. Yet my separation from Mark was the only thing that filled me with sadness on leaving this place. It was his genuine friendship that had enriched my experience here and was the only good thing I had acquired in this barren captivity.

We were given rations before embarking in a specially reserved boxcar for our journey—a good omen in those days, since the receipt of food was an indication that we were not yet to be discarded. A slim Austrian half-Jew named Pick, a member of our "faculty," asked me what I thought of the trip and arrangements, to which I replied that it was always a good practice to make reservations, particularly when one does not know where he is going, because there are so many people doing the same thing that there is bound to be a crowd.

It was a comfort to see some of the old-timers among the company. Rysiek Krakowski, two of the Orenstein brothers—Fred the doctor and Felek, and Tony Feinberg, all veterans of Budzyn, were among my traveling companions, and we were in good company. Some of the men actually were real professors and engineers. The mining engineer named Baran was rumored to be one of the brains of the little-understood and less-cared-about scientific project. And it was wonderful to see that Professor Zelmanowski, who had taught biology in my old high school in Warsaw, had made it. The enemy had never been able to strip this man of his quiet dignity or reduce him to the animal level to which some had yielded in their desperation for food. Through the ghetto, Budzyn, and Plaszow he somehow managed to retain his integrity, and his refined ways had not suffered.

The only woman present bore no relation to the work except that she was allowed to accompany one of the men, whose name I believe was Falk—an old-timer from Budzyn. Kramer, the former camp's administrations clerk became a foreman's assistant, while Tiehl assumed charge of the group. One Czech Jew, a few Poles, two French Jews, and one Hungarian Jew made us an international "scientific" body.

There was just enough room in the boxcar for everyone to sit down and lean against the wall, and the SS guards left the sliding door open but kept us away from the opening. After a few hours our car was attached to the tail end of a freight train, and we were on our way. No sooner had the train begun to roll ahead than we were all looking out at the picturesque countryside with mounting curiosity. Later, when mountains were sighted from afar, they must have reminded Pick of his country, for he was inspired to sing the Tyrolean song *"Tirol Tirol, du bist ein schoenes Land."*

Pick may not have been a scientist, but he could sing well. When he sang the famous Viennese *"Wien, Wien, Nur Du Allein"* (Vienna, Vienna, you alone), even the SS guards were moved by its nostalgia. One of them admitted being from Vienna and passed a cigarette to Pick, then also gave cigarettes to others. The sunset moment filled with song reminded both captor and prisoner of their homes. The song faded as darkness descended. The guards sealed the car at a stop and took quarters in an adjacent one. Soon everyone had curled up and was sound asleep.

15 Journey to Germany

*Death and sorrow will be the companions
of our journey.*
—Winston Churchill (1940)

Our train did not make much headway overnight. By the morning of October 8, 1944, as near as I could figure, it had just about reached the 1939 border dividing Poland and Germany. Seeing the stretches of green and brown farmland at the break of dawn had a wonderfully quieting effect on our thoughts. These hills and valleys will abide long after the horrors of war, except in the history books, are forgotten. Seeing the open country suggested the hope that perhaps the death sentence imposed upon us was not imminent.

As the cheerful sunlight burst over the countryside, I envied the people whose lot it was to tend the grazing flocks, to till the soil, to live in relative peace and quiet away from hunger, turmoil, and the horrors of war. It was hard to tell when we had crossed the Polish-German border because the land looked exactly the same on both sides. The first German town of note was Görlitz. Our freight train stopped at the railroad station, which seemed dormant except for some uniformed station personnel and waiting soldiers. But before noon we reached the Dresden railroad yards, and we could see that this large German city had experienced war. Here for the first time was evidence of the Allied air raids. The vicinity of the railroad must have been bombed the day before, and there was a busy beehive atmosphere around the place, which was swarming with POWs.

A pervasive sense of urgency dominated the mood; we heard the shouting of German orders mixed with the clanking sounds of picks, sledgehammers, and shovels. Hundreds of prisoners under the watchful eyes of their German guards were busy clearing debris and repairing the tracks. It was an exciting sight to witness British POWs working to clean up the damage their own air force had probably inflicted only the day or night before.

Until the Allies began to bring the devastating air war back to Germany, the Germans had not disapproved of it or its horror—because they did not feel it, believing as they did in their invincibility. In contrast to the laughter and pride that had followed their relentless attacks on others, there were somber but confident expressions on the faces of the Germans who were supervising these repairs. After having rained destruction on Warsaw, Rotterdam, Coventry, and London in order to paralyze the people's will, the Nazis were now getting a taste of their own medicine. The sight at the train station stirred memories of the 1939 campaign against Poland, of air raids and the screams of the women whose children were suddenly corpses; of collapsing buildings and people engulfed in flames or buried alive under the debris of their own dwellings; of the young man who had held his severed hand in his good one while his life's blood was gushing out; of hundreds of thousands of frightened refugees fleeing from the advancing German armies only to be bombed and machine-gunned on the open roads by strafing planes. All this destruction had been hurled from the air as the German invaders established their own brand of hell on earth with its special machinery for torture and mass murder, as they trampled humanity under their jackboots across a devastated and conquered Europe.

The material damage in Dresden seemed a token retribution; it appeared negligible in contrast with the destruction visited upon Warsaw alone. Here it was, the fall of 1944, the fifth year of the war, but the cities we had seen after crossing the border into Germany had shown little evidence of war. Dresden was a notable exception. Surely our enemies would never learn of the enormity of their crimes except by experiencing some of the punishment they had methodically inflicted on others. Before the Warsaw ghetto's total obliteration, the SS had turned it into a blazing inferno, giving the besieged a choice of burning alive, suffocating from smoke inhalation in bunkers or sewers, or facing their executioners. The German people were only now sharing in the horror of their own doing.

It was a new sensation actually to see British soldiers, even though they were prisoners: they were living proof that there were others fighting. There were other nationalities of prisoners, but the British absorbed most of my attention. I don't know why—perhaps I admired their indomitable spirit, personified by Churchill's courage and determination to "stand alone" after France fell.

It could be that my early reading of English history, written by André Maurois, influenced my feelings about these seafaring people. All I could remember about that book was that the author ended it on an ominous note: he predicted that the invention of the airplane would present a threat to the then relatively secure island. Now England was writing a new chapter in history: from Dunkirk, through the Battle of Britain, to Tobruk and El Alamein, the British had won the admiration of millions of people, many of whom would never see the final outcome.

Unlike most of the prisoners we saw, the British did not seem undernourished. Their uniforms showed little wear, contrasting sharp-

ly with the rags worn by others, among whom I recognized French
POWs. The POWs nearest our boxcar looked in, and their somber
expressions indicated that we had made a frightful impression on
them. Some of us waved to them when our guard was not looking and
received a few faint smiles in acknowledgment. It was a unique moment, during which we felt a sense of oneness with these men.

The freight train resumed its journey, running southwest, and
then it began to climb upward. After a few hours of slow moving,
stops, and occasional air raids, we disembarked somewhere in the
mountains. I recall nothing that could have identified the last station. It
was the dead end of the railroad track. From here we ascended a road
on foot.

When barbed wire, towers, and evenly lined barracks came into
view at the end of the road, the hoping and the guessing games were
over. This was not an institute devoted to the promotion of true science.
It was obviously far away from Vienna, the destination that had
foolishly been rumored, and it did not resemble a haven for scholars or
anything else one might have hoped to see. It was a typical German
concentration camp, distinguishable from others only by its geograph-
ical location and the name: Flossenbuerg.

When the large gates opened, the high chimney of the crematorium became visible as the camp's dominant feature. A level open
field in the foreground, surrounded by an elevated landscape, served
as the *Appellplatz*. On the left side a series of terraces rose one above the
other, and on each level there was a string of barracks. The barracks for
the administration elite—known as Number 1—and the kitchen were
at the bottom of the terrace. Quarantine barracks were at the far end
directly opposite the main gate. To the far right of the quarantine
barracks was the crematorium, and to the right off the *Appellplatz* were
the bathhouse and more rows of barracks, among them the hospital
ward. Outside the gate was the guardhouse, and further secluded from
camp view were guards' quarters and homes.

Even before we reached the gate, our arrival had attracted the
attention of the camp populace. Some of the faces looking at us reminded me of Budzyn. Skin drawn around the cheekbones, making
the eyes look disproportionately large, were positive signs of near-
starvation.

The lone woman in our group was separated from us and taken to
another camp. A German *Kapo* wearing a dark red corduroy jacket and
carrying a whip took charge of the men. To assert his authority, he kept
shouting his orders and using his whip indiscriminately all through
the customary baths. The SS did not bother searching us thoroughly,
possibly because we did not seem substantial enough to warrant it.

A well-dressed prisoner, the designated camp interpreter, offici-

CONCENTRATION CAMP
FLOSSENBUERG

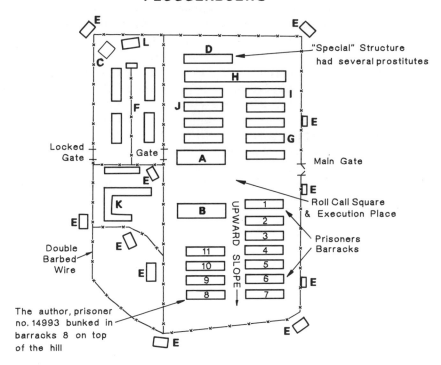

"Special" Structure had several prostitutes

A	Laundry and Bath
B	Kitchen
C	Pit for Corpses
D	Special Structure
E	Guard Towers
F	Quarantine Block

G	Transport Barracks
H	Prison Block
I	Garbage
J	Hospital
K	Construction Office
L	Crematorium - 1943

Source: Adapted from a sketch drawn by a prisoner and used by the U.S. Army at postwar trials in Dachau, 1945-46.

ated during the induction ceremonies. Although most of us understood and spoke German, Voloshin's importance as an interpreter was
due to the large number of Russian prisoners, who as a rule did not
speak German. He and the *Kapos* who were heads of the barracks were
the big shots in this camp. Voloshin seemed outwardly friendly, but his
sly look was not easily disguised by a faint smile.

After the baths, we were allowed into the quarantine barracks and
given bread rations. Every few minutes another camp official came and
looked us over and then left, apparently unimpressed. Among the
visitors was the camp doctor, exercising his professional authority and
appearing not undernourished. My surprise was considerable when I
recognized him as a distant relative from Warsaw named Goldfarb. At
home we had a photograph of my father in army uniform and this
doctor, both on sleds in a typical winter scene. The picture had been
taken when I was still an infant. Far away from a carefree country
winter setting, Dr. Goldfarb in the foreground of a crematorium had
not changed a great deal physically. "You are Doc Goldfarb?" I asked.

"How did you know?"

"My name is Jurek Topas."

"Henry's son?" he said with casual interest. "Well, you don't look
like your father," he said disapprovingly.

I did not appreciate this offhand, inaccurate remark from a relative
whom I had seen perhaps three times in my life, counting the picture
as one—though my prolonged camp diet probably justified his impression.

Dr. Goldfarb's brother Mietek, a very capable attorney and an
amiable person, had lived in our apartment house after his student
days. Mietek's only son, also named Jurek, was my distant cousin and
childhood friend; his mother Stella and my paternal grandmother were
related. When the father rose to prominence, they moved out to
another section of Warsaw, and we drifted apart. My cousin was an
excellent student—something my parents had never failed to remind
me of, if only to encourage similar aspirations and performances from
their son. My uncle had told me that during deportation, Mietek's
parents had helped him jump out of a boxcar headed for Treblinka. He
returned and lived to be deported again at a later date.

The most memorable event that I associated with Mietek Goldfarb
was a celebrated court case that resulted from an assault on my grandfather Jacob by a woman customer who had struck him with a sharp
heel of a lady's shoe. She had been trying on shoes in our main store on
Leszno Street. My grandfather, who normally stayed in his office, was
observing the progress of the sale. The woman, later described as
arrogant and capricious, demanded that the salesgirl bring her every
fashionable style to try on. When our salesgirl turned in despair for

help, Grandpa explained to the woman that she had exhausted the variety the store had to offer. She apparently took this as a hint that she had also exhausted the salesgirl's patience. Offended, she picked up a shoe and struck my grandfather on the side of the forehead, causing bleeding and a scene that attracted the attention of everyone in the store. Police were summoned; my uncle, the first to arrive, ordered the woman to leave the store, and she later accused him of trying to throw her out. She refused to leave. When the police officer came, she announced that she was the wife of Warsaw's chief of police and that she would seek the satisfaction for the "insult" and "rough handling." The police report noted that my grandfather had a bleeding cut on his forehead. The family was concerned about Grandpa, especially because he was a diabetic; moreover, the matter was tainted with anti-Semitic overtones.

The wife of the police chief retained the best criminal lawyer in Warsaw, a man named Szurly. In fact, Brokman and Goldfarb, who represented Grandpa, had at one time been his students in law school. The opening court session was aglitter with the silver stars and medals displayed by the galaxy of police and army brass that constituted the police chief's entourage. As related by my father later at home, Waclaw Brokman, a small, unimpressive man but a brilliant speaker, took issue with the exhibition of authority and declared that this unnecessary display appeared calculated to intimidate the court and tip the scales of justice. He asked that the case be transferred to Superior Court. The request was granted, and when the court convened, the "brass" had disappeared. The presiding judge asked if the parties would consider reconciliation. Grandfather, at first unyielding, finally consented to my father's plea that because we were Jews, we must show a willingness to compromise. But the police chief was unsuccessful in persuading his wife to drop the countercharges. When the matter was tried, the court declared the woman guilty of assault, sentenced her to fourteen days imprisonment but suspended the sentence, and ordered her to pay all medical costs and court expenses for my grandfather. In Poland, that meant reimbursement for the lawyer's fees as well. Considering the delicate balance that existed in regard to anti-Semitism in Poland, this was a remarkably good result.

But here at Flossenbuerg, Dr. Goldfarb simply turned toward the exit and never again spoke to me personally. Had it not been for friends in our group, the loneliness would have been hard to endure in this forsaken place. Many different nationalities were represented among 10,000 or more prisoners, including a black Frenchman who worked as a cook. His uniqueness made him something of a celebrity. German prisoners governed the administration of the camp, and some of them had been there since 1938. Their uniforms bore low numbers, signifying long-term imprisonment. My number was 14,993, registered in Plaszow, but some numbers were even higher.

Anton Uhl, the German camp policeman who consented to become *Lageraeltester*, or camp eldest, in the last days of the camp, had a relatively good reputation among the men. He insisted that every man get his ration, which discouraged cheating by the block leaders (*Blockaeltersten*). Occasionally, though, someone would cry out at night that the slice of bread he had saved had been stolen. The code here was that the thief, if caught, was beaten nearly to death by the *Blockaeltersten* or his assistant.

Even on "full" rations, men were dying from hunger—and the crematorium paid for itself. For the first week we were confined to quarantine, doing cleaning chores within the camp and governed by the *Kapo* in the red corduroy jacket. At first, because of our confinement to the camp, we were classified as nonproductive and were not entitled to breakfast rations. The productive prisoners, in addition to approximately one-sixth of a round loaf of bread after work and soup at noon, were entitled to a slice of bread for breakfast or at ten o'clock. Although the nutritional value of the hot morning coffee, referred to as acorn juice and served without cream or sugar, was nil, it did warm up your body; no one would forgo his early morning coffee, which was drunk before the crack of dawn. According to the existing rules, when the morning lights went on, the prisoners had to hit the floor, and being late meant a merciless beating.

Jointly with other arrivals, we were eventually led outside the camp to work. The first few days must have been a sort of camp initiation. Supervised by guards and *Kapos*, the men in our group had to carry large rocks up and down a steep incline. Just walking would have been dangerous on this high, rough terrain; carrying rocks on your shoulder made the trip extremely hard and hazardous, yet the guards hurried this diabolical work as though the war's outcome depended on it. Inevitably there were fatalities, some from falls down the hill, others from exhaustion and brutal beatings.[1]

After the second day of this tortuous work, I began to doubt whether any of us would last a week. Finally, reassignment to a road-building detail on the fourth day saved the remaining men in our group from a similar fate. Work on the highway consisted of crushing stones with hammers, and we kept this job for what seemed to be an eternity, although it actually may have been only a week or so.

Looking at my friends was like looking in the mirror. Everyone was rapidly losing weight, shedding all that could be credited to our smuggled Plaszow "cuisine." Constant hunger drove me to exert my utmost thinking to come up with an idea, some scheme to alleviate this curse. Hunger was our enemy's cheapest and most potent weapon, for it drained men of their energy to think before they died. The multitudes who perished usually were starved before transport, then packed in boxcars like sardines, and shipped without food, water, or even breathing space.

From the very start of the war until the end we were disarmed by terror and hunger. The ordeal began by our looking upon devastation and havoc, at the ruins wrought by the falling bombs, then into the muzzles of machine guns and rifles. Later, surrounded by the hideous ghetto wall, sealing the fate of thousands, trapped, shocked, and starved, the hunger- and disease-ridden victims were ready for herding to their deadly destinations. At the war's onset, whole divisions of armed Russian troops had surrendered and laid down their weapons. How then could anyone expect starved, sickly men, women, and children, confined within high walls or caged in camps, to fight! Anyway, in order that one may live to fight another day, one must try to live first, and without food that was hardly possible.

This time, no matter how much thinking I put into it, I could not conceive of a way to supplement our meager diet. Unlike the camps in Poland, here there was nothing and no one to trade with; there were not even fields with vegetation—just a barren, rocky mountainside with barracks and barbed wire, dominated by a chimney. If a stray cat ventured into the camp, it never emerged again. The big shots, however, did have access to some extra food from the kitchen. These German prisoners constituted the privileged class, and they dispensed crumbs and leftovers for favors such as polishing their leather shoes, washing their mess kits, or giving haircuts. The tailors and shoemakers among us turned out work for the German *Kapos* and SS guards, for such work would earn them tips in cigarettes, bread, and beans.

In one of the barracks the guards even kept a couple of prostitutes for the benefit of the privileged Aryan prisoners, who could take a number and wait for it to be called. No reason was formally given to explain this special service; perhaps it was to discourage depravity. Some of the long-time German prisoners residing in Block 1 employed young fellows aged fifteen to eighteen as orderlies, called *Kalifactors*. It's difficult to say whether or to what extent these youths were compromised or carnally abused—but it should be borne in mind that hunger can be most persuasive.

16 The Inventors at Flossenbuerg

Ride on over all obstacles, and win the race!
—Charles Dickens

The inventors' group fared better than most; just when everything looked hopeless again, a change took place. After about two exhausting weeks with the road-building gang, we were ordered to the Messerschmitt aircraft-parts plant with the main body of prisoners, though our group was to be kept as a separate entity. November here was a cold and unfriendly month. After marching for about a mile in the striped procession, we were glad to be directed to a closed hall. An SS guard pointed to a heap of books in the corner, instructing our foreman Tiehl that this would be our place of work, and he left after this introduction.

It was incredible and wonderful to contemplate spending the approaching winter months under the roof of this place. As a shelter, it would do; it looked less convincing as a science lab, but this did not bother my "professional" pride. In the middle of the floor stood a potbellied stove, so starting up a fire was our first act of housekeeping. Four long picnic-style tables were set up in the four quarters of this large room, and then we began sorting through the books and periodicals.

These books looked as if they had been dumped off the tail end of a truck after a library raid, and it soon became evident that they were actually unrelated to our "scientific" work, which I had yet to understand. Very roughly, however, we believed that the invention they wanted us to work on was a piece of gas-making or gas-condensing machinery capable of producing concentrated ozone or some other gas. If it could be mass-produced and dropped in quantity over a given area, it would cause all the metal in its environs to oxidize rapidly, and rust would render all moving metal parts useless. Another version had it that the substance would neutralize motor ignition.

Baran and the men at his table began designing the model apparatus for this wonder weapon. Once the drawing was finished, the German mechanics were going to fabricate and assemble a prototype of the thing. For us, of course, the idea was to keep making drawings as long as possible before starting production; on this score, we were unanimously agreed. To the Germans, who viewed it as a secret weapon, it may have been a gas condenser, but to us it was a time expander, heaven sent.

The German high brass, of course, demanded results sooner than Baran and his associates cared to deliver them. They wanted to see something before the end of the war; more specifically, they wanted to run tests on an experimental model before the end of December 1944.

In our pile of books were an old German *Meyers Encyclopedia*, some Polish texts, and English-language biological journals dating back to 1905. Touching books and looking at the printed word again was a novel sensation. After a while we stopped sorting them and merely stacked them on a bench pushed against the wall. We divided our group into four teams, and each team occupied a separate table. There was the construction group, headed by Baran, the mining engineer who was rumored to have sold the Germans this bill of goods. The botanical group, headed by no one in particular, included the Orenstein brothers, Tony Feinberg, and Rysiek Krakowski. The third team was named the interpreters, and their job was to translate Russian chemistry into German. Finally, there were the chemists; I was assigned to this group.

While the construction group under Baran began drafting a complicated contraption, the biologists were scanning 1905-vintage publications for important data related to our project, and the interpreters were translating voluminous Russian chemistry texts at the rate of nearly one page a day. The chemists, however, had no important assignment; in fact, we did not know what to do, so at first we did nothing. Then Tiehl wisely urged all of us to at least make believe we were working. Obligingly, I began to study the *Meyers Encyclopedia*, but before I got to the letter "B" in Gothic German, I switched to one of the Polish books—a relief after a few days of encyclopedia reading. The new book was a medical text; it was concerned with health—just what we needed. In particular, the author emphasized the importance of good wholesome nutrition, but he offered no substitute for it except a reducing diet for overweight persons. The book also dealt with venereal diseases and their cures. The author stated that in the American army the incidence of V.D. had dropped considerably as the result of a modern preventive approach. After I finished this book, I felt all the symptoms for all known diseases. After several days of random reading through all the scientific books, I got back to *Meyers Encyclopedia*.

The work we were doing here entitled us to "breakfast," and because of the significant nature of our project, everyone got an extra half-bowl of soup. What a break! Being spared from physical labor and this bit of extra food spelled the difference between life and death, at least for the time being. Outwardly, everyone seemed content, but inwardly we were worried. While most people had no idea what this project was all about, nearly all of us believed it was sheer bluff. The Germans were not entirely fooled either, but their investment in this experiment cost them less than feeding so many head of cattle. Yet sooner or later a day of reckoning would have to be faced. Only Baran and possibly a few others knew enough to make the German military go along with the work. The only thing that interested the rest of us interned "scientists" was not what the project really was but how we could use this hoax as a vehicle to ride out the war. All inquiries were discouraged with such replies as "it's too complicated to explain," or "you will know in time."

Inspired, perhaps, by our "scientific" work as well as by the news of V-1 and V-2 rockets, a small joke was making the rounds in the barracks: A guard's suspicion and curiosity is aroused by a strange metal object fashioned by a prisoner. "What are you working on?" he demands.

"On a new weapon I invented—V-7," confides the prisoner.

"What does it do?"

"What does it do? It shoots to London and brings back ten POWs."

Strangely enough, there were a few among us who began to act as though they really were part of a significant research project. I must admit that I was guilty of poking fun at one or two colleagues who took themselves too seriously. I once addressed one of these fellows as "Professor *Mucholapski*" (Professor Flycatcher): "And how does the Professor perceive the current state of affairs in the world? Does he think that our invention could considerably alter the outcome of the war?" and so on. Frankly, the very fact that one could regard the project as a hoax and see putting on professional airs as farcical indicates that when we were in this "scientific asylum" we behaved as though we were on leave from the bleakness of concentration camp—if not from our senses.

The snow had already covered this high mountainside, and winter winds were making their sad, whistling sounds at night. When we arose in the morning, it was still dark; when we returned from the plant, it was dark again. Our only solace and good fortune was that we spent our days, except for a couple of hours at morning and evening head count and marches to and from the plant, in a place sheltered from the elements and bitter cold. Our existence was prolonged by the refuge indoors.

The field latrines at the plant, it's true, were under the open skies and maintained by Russian officer prisoners—a deliberately humiliating assignment—but the Russian orderlies thoughtfully burned fires at each site to keep from freezing. It was one of our lesser discomforts to make the daily trip to this rest area; for the men who worked outdoors, however, such as those who manned the air hammers in the local

Steinbruch, this was a desirable retreat. The latest war news and camp rumors were exchanged here. Despite the humiliating chores and hunger, the Russian officer prisoners kept up their faith in the ultimate victory of the Allies.

I believed at the time that our "lab" was the only place in the whole German concentration camp penal system where scanning through books was permissible. We could legitimately seek information related to our work. Every day an SS noncom would barge in unannounced to check on us, but since he knew less about the nature of this project than the men managing the latrine, his inspection was limited to making an official head count and seeing that everyone was busy. Fortunately, we had all become veterans at the art of pretending occupation with work.

Several days had passed; it was still something of a wonder to be seated at a table in a concentration camp, surrounded by printed matter, and to call this work. It was during this early stage that, quite unexpectedly and seemingly by chance, I found two gems. While replacing the bulky Meyers volume, I knocked a small book off the pile; to my astonishment it was *David Copperfield*, by Charles Dickens—an English-language, primary school edition. An idea immediately possessed me: I shall learn English! I had always been impressed by its sound and the people who spoke it, if only in movies, and my enthusiasm was heightened by the fact that this tongue was the one spoken by men who showed defiance and fought relentlessly against our enemies.

Encouraged by my find, I began a thorough search that further yielded a fundamental English grammar book for German school-children. My English vocabulary was limited to a few dozen words or so beyond my ability to count; however, I vaguely knew the Copperfield story from an American film I had seen in Warsaw before the war.

For a moment, my thoughts drifted into the past. I saw prewar Warsaw as it had looked in the evening, the sight and sound of lively crowds of pedestrians; the bright boulevards bathed in dazzling lights, their colorful beams reflected on the passing red streetcars and taxis; the newsboys calling out the names of the papers they peddled. It was a big evening for my brother Simon and me. Our parents were taking us to the movies to see *David Copperfield*. Mom prepared a paper bag with halvah and tangerines for us. Going to the movies was always a happy occasion. Father frequently opposed our seeing movies—he viewed them as a bad influence—but *David Copperfield* was on his "approved" list. And when Father took us, it meant riding both ways, all expenses paid. "Why don't they make more pictures like this, based on literature or history—true to life's problems, instead of these demoralizing pictures?" he would say. Another picture the family saw together was *Captain Blood*, a real spellbinder with Errol Flynn.

David Copperfield's birth during a torrential rainstorm with hurricanelike wind was followed by an unhappy childhood, until he found shelter from the ravages of poverty and a persecuted orphan's existence in the hospitable home of his aunt. The scene I remember most is when David, played by Freddie Bartholomew, has been bathed, and he sits up looking clean and serene in his clean bed and thanks God for his shelter, pleading that no boy should suffer as he did. So impressed was I by that scene and so sorry for all oppressed children that I sat up in my bed that evening and made a similar prayer, conscious of my good fortune in having good parents, living in a fine home, and leading a secure life. Sitting in the prison camp, I had the ironical thought that unfortunately there were not enough sturdy, stern, but compassionate, cane-swinging good old English aunts to save the myriads of Davids from the grasp of hell.

So, after returning to the reality of the dismal, doubtful present, I began to struggle with the first sentence. Because I knew the story and could anticipate the events, reading was not as terribly difficult as I had at first thought it would be. If I knew two words in a four- or five-word sentence, I could often figure out the meaning of the remaining words. After assimilating more words and better understanding their meaning, words I had already defined had to be corrected. It worked like a crossword puzzle: the more words I learned, the fewer were left to guess at. My pronunciation scarcely resembled anything I supposed an English-speaking native would easily understand, but my enthusiasm for learning was not dampened by either the lack of instruction or improper pronunciation. Hunger, my inseparable companion, had at last found a formidable rival for my attention.

Each day I would memorize a few new words and then use them, mostly in constructing ungrammatical sentences. Marching back to the camp compound, I would quietly recite: "The sky is blue; the snow is white. An Englishman's home is his castle. He eats porridge for breakfast and has a pine tree." My mumbling during marches and talking to myself in the barracks, though, attracted some attention and was obviously taken by the men around me as a sign that I was losing my sanity.

Tiehl cautioned me to be extremely careful and on guard with my English books and notes, and some who feared the consequences if I should be caught asked Tiehl to stop me, but he allowed me to continue my study. Whenever the guards came in I hid my notes and books under the large volume of *Meyers Encyclopedia* and busied myself with a German book that was always open for such occasions.

There were some ancient English periodicals among those at the biology table, but they were "studied" without apparent success, interest, or comprehension—because no one there, I thought, knew sufficient English. At the construction table, however, sat a young man among the draftsmen whose name was Goldfarb (unrelated to the doctor mentioned earlier). Goldfarb had a pair of sad, bulging, blue eyes, light brown hair, a narrow face, and a rather serious expression. He was a quiet sort of man and, except for an infirmity, he was inconspicuous. His unsteady, rocking gait betrayed the troubled condition of his feet: the arches were extremely high, causing the weight of his body to rest on his heels and toes. It was remarkable that he had managed to elude the infamous selections for so long. Besides drafting, Goldfarb had another important skill—a knowledge of English.

I do not recall exactly how I found that out, but I eventually did something very rare in concentration camps: I engaged a tutor. Goldfarb consented to help me with my grammar and pronunciation, and I was so grateful that I offered him a bowl of soup—my lunch. But Goldfarb was no ordinary prisoner. He had pride—an uncommon virtue at the time. Not only did he refuse my gesture, but to my embarrassment, he was insulted as well; his look of sad indignation seemed to say: "Am I a pauper who waits for a morsel of bread or a bowl of soup? Am I so devoid of feeling as to eat your portion of food, knowing that we both get the same?" At a time when one's life hung in doubt and the value of food exceeded the value of gold, there were still proud, noble, and strong-willed men who could refuse food if it was another man's ration. Only after I apologized did my tutor resume his instruction.

Flossenbuerg was a strange camp—the only one I had been in that had an all-prisoner concert orchestra. On Fridays there might be corpses piled up outside the crematorium, but on Saturday nights there was *Entlausung* (delousing and a bath), and on Sundays there were concerts in the bathhouse. These were events unheard of by those who had been in Budzyn. Admission was free, but you had to bring your own stool to sit on.

As I recall now, I would rush to get in early ahead of the crowd and sit there until the orchestra tuned up. After that, I was transported out of the realm of grim reality. The repertoire was restricted to the music of those composers whom the Germans deemed permissible for the "undeserving" audience. A couple of SS men were always present to enforce this censorship or to enjoy the music, perhaps both. Under the baton of a Viennese conductor, these international musicians gave a near-flawless performance every time and won acclaim from the camp intellectuals. A favorite of the prisoners was a very lively Hungarian *chardash*, but the concert usually opened with a march—and the "Gladiators March" was a preferred number. Whenever a Czech vocalist delivered a song in his native tongue, the Czechs heartily applauded; they were noted for the deep bond of solidarity among themselves—a trait not conspicuous among prisoners of other nationalities. The overture to *Maritana* by Vincent Wallace was my favorite. It was apparent that music by German composers was not allowed here.

As the year 1944 drew to a close, several events highlighted that period and made an impression in my memory. One cold morning Rysiek Krakowski, with whom I had been in several camps, was pulled out of the ranks by the guards. They found the pieces of blanket that he used instead of socks to wrap his feet. Accused of tearing his blanket, he was tied to a specially designed beating stool and flogged severely, then released.

It was during this time of colorless and bleak days, when the snow had fallen again and was piled high, that a glimpse of the outside world renewed my spirits. As we had been doing for so long every day, we were returning to camp at dusk one evening, and the marching column had halted. At that moment a most rare sight presented itself. A woman dressed in a black fur coat and hat had floundered in deep snow while walking in the uncleared section of the SS guard settlement. She had rosy cheeks and light hair and seemed young from a distance. Before any of the guards noticed her predicament, one of the German prisoners ran out of the ranks and gave the lady a helping hand. He pulled her out, looked at her for a moment, as did most of us from a distance, and then retreated to rejoin the column. In that instant of seeing a smartly dressed woman, the little gesture volunteered by one of the prisoners was very moving. Seeing her there reminded us of that other world in which there were still pretty, well-dressed women. Her sudden presence stimulated our thinking and awakened our nostalgia. She must have reminded everyone of someone he once knew and now missed. As for the man who helped her, this was probably the only simple courtesy he had had an opportunity to perform in several years. Anyway, he was blushing, stimulated by the rarity of this close encounter. Involuntarily, my thoughts drifted to Gina, and I wondered whether she was still alive.

Other news that winter was reassuring: Allied bombings of the nearby cities of Nuremberg and Weiden were a welcome reminder that despite the long wait the war was finally moving closer. The Russians had reached the east bank of the Vistula and had sighted Warsaw, and an uprising by courageous Warsaw Poles had engulfed the entire city, even though it ended in defeat. Just as the Warsaw ghetto fighters had had to yield because they received no support from the Polish people, so the Poles suffered the same fate without the assistance of the Russian army poised on the other side of the river. The Polish winter of discontent followed the Jewish spring of despair; thus the destruction of the ghetto district was extended to include the entire city. Warsaw, the city of my youth, once proud and vibrant, now lay in ruins. The insurgents were deported to concentration camps, and the rest of the people were shipped off to forced labor in Germany. Warsaw was no more.

But these tidings and the noise of the war, aside from the recent air raids, were far away. In the Flossenbuerg concentration camp, except for the hanging of a few Russian war prisoners for an "attempted escape," nothing changed. A typhus epidemic claimed so many lives as to rival hunger in the number of its victims. The men who were infected were afraid to report to the hospital because they feared being killed by gasoline injections. But once so overcome by high fever that they could not go to work, they were taken away. Men who died in their sleeping berths from starvation were marked on their foreheads with a number made with red markers and checked off the barracks roster.

So far, I had not been really sick in camp, which was something remarkable in itself, considering the fact that back home in Warsaw before the war I had been very susceptible to colds, flu, and the like and that hardly a winter had gone by without my being confined to bed once or twice. Here in captivity, existing on rations less than a minimal subsistence diet, under trying conditions, many of us were not so easily becoming sick—perhaps the harshness of our existence had hardened us. I believed that a watchful Providence had spared me from sickness. But coming back from the work compound one day I began to feel a headache, chills, and shivers. By the time the count was over and we were allowed to go back to the barracks, I knew that I had a high fever; I could not even eat my bread ration. Fearing I had contracted typhus and burning with fever, I climbed up on my bunk and fell asleep. I awakened in the morning in a cold sweat, but the fever was gone, so I got up and went to work as usual, amazed by my swift recovery.

Just before Christmas, the Czech prisoners were called down to the office to receive mail and packages—a privilege accorded only to Czech and German prisoners. I ran down the steps of the terraces to join others who stood at night in the snow outside the office, eager to see what the packages and mail looked like. Through the administration office window, I could see the guards opening each package and cutting in half each loaf of bread or cake before handing the rest to the recipient, who eyed his gift with longing. It was fantastic to see loaves of white bread again. They were reminiscent of home and its comforts and warmth.

Many miles away a family sat at a table with someone missing. The mother or wife had prepared the package with great care, praying that it would reach their loved one. When they gathered for the Christmas meal, they were not joyous—how could they be, when one member had been taken to the abysmal remoteness of hell? This package and a few written words were the only links between them, permitted perhaps once a year. It was rumored that Hitler accorded this privilege to the Czechs for their not resisting his aggression.

Soon thereafter, German technicians were busy constructing the "ultimate weapon" from the drawings advanced by Baran and his drafting staff. An unexpected visit by a group of high-ranking German officers in January 1945 revealed their impatience with the pace of the work, and Baran's plea for more time only provoked their anger. The final word was that they would return within a few weeks to test the invention. No one envied Baran, for he was on the spot no matter how you looked at it. The whole group's future was in doubt, but Baran's was more so: if the plans were not finished, he was responsible; if they made the weapon, his case was even worse, because they would soon know that it couldn't hurt anyone unless it was dropped on his toes.

About this time a mousy-looking German civilian of small stature made an appearance in our shop, sent from the Kaiser Wilhelm Institute in Berlin to supervise and speed up the completion of the project. His presence put an end to our relative privacy and set up a gloomy and silent atmosphere. My English study was the first casualty of the intrusion.

17 Reunion
and Separation

Gold is tried by fire, . . . men by adversity.
—Marcus Seneca

The beginning of 1945 marked the arrival of several hundred Italians; their presence at Flossenbuerg as prisoners seemed strange because they had once been German allies. The large number of newcomers created an acute space problem: there just was not enough room for them. But the Germans could always be relied upon to find a solution in matters that required organizational inventiveness, and so we were ordered to evacuate our barracks and to bunch up with a fully occupied one at a lower level. How? By tripling the number of sleepers in one berth space. The original occupant of a bunk shared a "single" accommodation with Tony Feinberg and me. We had to arrange our sleeping positions like sardines. The fellow whose head was at the opposite end of the berth slid into the center between the other two occupants. Whenever one of us changed his sleeping position during the night, all were affected, and we all usually turned over at the same time. Fortunately, transfer shipments alleviated the overcrowding after a few weeks to the point where only two prisoners had to share one berth.

That period was marked by yet another arrival. When someone informed me that my friend Mark had arrived in camp, I rushed down to the quarantine barracks to find him. Among the skeletonlike faces barely resembling the living, I recognized a handful of survivors from Plaszow. As I embraced Mark, our eyes welled up with tears. We clasped hands, each noting how wretched the other looked. Under cover of darkness I led Mark out of the quarantine compound up to my block to talk before curfew. In the semiprivacy of my upper berth, we sat down to share a fleeting moment, oblivious of the crowded barracks. I offered Mark half my bread ration. As we ate our meager dole, I watched Mark's thin face, which reflected his suffering, while in a hushed voice he related the story of his latest ordeal.

The Russians' advances into prewar Poland had forced the Germans to evacuate concentration camp Plaszow. The prisoners had been marched to the town of Gleiwitz and from there to the dreaded Auschwitz. Then, without drawing any rations, they were herded into open boxcars in the bitter winter cold of early 1945. (In summer the Germans used closed boxcars to suffocate people; in winter open boxcars, to freeze prisoners to death.) The train started on its memorable journey into the winter night, giving priority to regular and troop trains and moving slowly in the direction of the Czech border. The prisoners huddled together to keep warm, but without food or protection from the elements, men began to die. Periodically, the train halted in the woods, and the guards ordered the living prisoners to throw the dead ones overboard. The stench was overpowering, and death seemed welcome. Most had died in the few days it took the transport to reach Czechoslovakia. There, whenever the train stopped, the good Czech people—probably astonished and sickened by the frightening sight— threw bread into the boxcars. Even though it was dangerous to do so, whenever the ghost train stopped during daylight, the Czechs tossed in food.

After two weeks of meandering through Czechoslovakia and Germany with no one allowed to leave the car, this macabre caravan reached the vicinity of Flossenbuerg concentration camp. By then the survivors in each car were few; hundreds had perished. From more than 120 people who had begun the journey in one boxcar, there were two survivors; Mark was one of them. Had it not been for the generosity of the Czech people, probably none would have survived. I was reminded of the scene in Pulawy in 1942, when a few half-clad, starved-looking Russian POWs standing in freezing winter cold were the only occupants of a freight car and probably its only survivors.

"You know," Mark said, "through it all, all that mattered to me was our friendship."

We marveled at the strange twist of fate that had brought us together again in the midst of this terrible war. This unexpected and undreamed-of reunion appeared miraculous to us, and it rekindled our hopes for eventual deliverance from our enemies. As the time for curfew drew near, Mark handed me a small paper-wrapped gold coin. Whispering, he told me that a young man from Plaszow, whom Mark remembered from Radom, had given him this coin and asked him to intercede with the authorities, through me, to keep him off the transport, which was scheduled to move on to an unknown destination the next day. The thought occurred to me that I could use the coin to keep Mark with me in the camp.

One more hug, a handshake, and we parted. To have said to my best friend that here in a real German concentration camp we had no influence whatsoever would have been to betray our mutual belief that we could count on each other to do nearly anything. What a beautiful thought! Two friends trusting implicitly in each other's ability and will to accomplish the nearly impossible, no matter what cunning or daring it required. Such knowledge, even if exaggerated by past experiences, does wonders for a man's self-reliance, to the point where he is capable of daring acts he had never thought possible—even though the bleak reality of Flossenbuerg's isolation reduced such notions to fantasy.

I held on to my friend's image and perhaps for the first time I really felt how much our friendship meant to both of us. The lights went out, but I dared not fall asleep lest I lose the presence and awareness of the one good thing that had happened to me since my arrival in this camp. Memories of all our schemes and somewhat "better times" by concentration camp standards (or by comparison) ran through my mind. By joint action, often by taking risks, we had been able to get by. The talks we had had, the plans and hopes expressed, all came back to me.

But these sentimental recollections did not relieve what was pressing on my mind. Mark hoped that I could somehow arrange for him and his friend to stay here and prevent their shipment elsewhere. Prisoners were often sent to surrounding smaller camps—one of which was Hersbruck, a notorious killer that had claimed thousands of victims. The water there contained lead. Hard-driven, worked to exhaustion in tunnel shelters, the prisoners either drank the poisonous water and died from it or died from hunger. Their swollen corpses were brought back and piled up outside the Flossenbuerg crematorium for disposal.[1]

My first few ideas all led to dead ends. Finally, I decided to approach Voloshin, the privileged Russian interpreter. He had struck me from the first as a cunning conniver and one who should not be trusted, yet he was the only one within the inner administration's higher echelons to whom I had access.

As soon as the electric lights went on announcing a new dawn, I hurried to see Mark and his acquaintance from Radom—a slim, rather tall fellow with a sallow, sad expression. His group, separated from Mark's, was being kept in isolation—a sure sign that it was slated for shipment. The possibility of having anyone released who was already listed by number was nil. But Mark's situation was more hopeful because he was still in quarantine. I hastened to reach the *Appellplatz* early so that I could talk to Voloshin. The snow squeaked under my wooden shoes as I walked down toward the administration office. Clean-shaven, wearing a real overcoat, surrounded by a few German prisoners, and, by the standards of the day, looking prosperous, Voloshin stood joking with his elite camp friends. Standing some distance away, I waited, trying to attract his attention. After what seemed like a long moment, Voloshin's roving eyes caught mine, and sensing that something was brewing, he walked briskly over to where I stood. "If it isn't one of the intelligentsia's scientists," he jovially greeted me, his eyes smiling as one smiles in anticipation at a gift-wrapped package.

"I need a favor from you—a kindness that means a lot to two friends," I said politely. "My friend, whom I will point out to you in a moment, arrived with a transport yesterday. He's in quarantine. He has had a very rough time, and I would be much indebted to you if you could arrange to let him and another fellow slated to go away with the transport today remain here.

"And what are you prepared to do?" asked Voloshin. "You know these things are not easy. If I am to help, I will need something better than words."

"Well, I don't have anything except what I found just this morning—a shiny coin the value of which I don't know, but to a collector it could be worth a lot."

We shook hands, and the coin passed to Voloshin.

"Listen," he said, "let me tell you right away that I can do nothing for the guy in the transport group, but let us take a look at your friend in quarantine."

I felt a shock of pain, visualizing the shy face of the young man for whom there was no hope and for whom I was not making a maximum effort. But I had to depend on whatever good will there was in Voloshin just to save Mark.

We found Mark, and after a few routine questions Voloshin promised to arrange a transfer. I rushed to join my formation. A few days passed, but Mark remained with his original group, now readied for transport. Again, in the morning, I ran to see the interpreter. This time, looking less friendly and a bit annoyed, he tried to dismiss me with a mere assurance that he was working on it. When I persisted, he retorted, "Are you trying to spoil everything?"

I sensed that this foxy character did not lift a finger to help anyone except himself, and my premonition of evil was unfortunately justified. When I returned from work, I went looking for Mark—to no avail. He had been shipped off with the transport at midday. Even though it could not do any good, I confronted Voloshin, reproaching him angrily for not living up to his promise.

At first he tried to pacify me by insisting that he had tried but could not do anything. "Anyway, they did not go to Hersbruck," he said. "Why do you guys imagine that every transport goes to Hersbruck? Don't you know that they are hurting for workers to man their plants all over Germany?"

"Where did they go?" I demanded to know.

"How do I know?"

"You don't even know where this transport went?" I asked, expecting not really reliable information but at least reaffirmation that it was not Hersbruck.

"Look here," he responded, "you'd better keep away from me—if you know what I mean"—or words to that effect. Voloshin was threatening me. There was nothing further to be gained from arguing with this cold-blooded fox. Mark was gone, and I had failed to prevent his going. My only hope was that he had not gone to Hersbruck. I resolved to keep alive our promise that if we survived, we would find each other and be together again. Somehow.

Test Run

Meanwhile, the little German civilian from Kaiser Wilhelm Institute in Berlin was wielding a lot of authority at work. Immediately upon arrival he had set up his desk in the middle of our "lab." We waited apprehensively, and it did not take long to find out what he was up to. The little superman called the prisoners before him one by one and inquired about each man's professional background. He concluded each interview by assigning an essay for that person to write in order to establish his professional competence. Clearly, it was going to take days to interview all of us, and I had some time to ponder my situation.

A chemist at our table had to write about sulfates and war. Each evening before we left, Herr Professor collected all the papers he had assigned that day, finished or unfinished, to be graded by him personally.

All the imposters became worried as this examination continued because flunking could mean more than the loss of a job with a bonus of an extra bowl of soup. Expecting to be called at any time, I realized that I would have to think of something better to invent than merely to uphold my phony claim to being an inventor or a chemist. In this situation, which offered no prospect for job security, I asked the good-natured Tiehl for assistance and got it: he promised to corroborate my newly invented occupation, that of "metal technician."

It was close to the end of the second week of interviews that my number 993 (the last three digits) and name were called. I came forward to the examiner's desk, trying to strike a pose of confidence. First he looked down at the paper, then up at me.

"Your name?" he asked, if only to verify the information.

"George Topas," I answered truthfully.

"Profession?" he asked, routinely.

"*Metal Techniker,*" I pronounced with determination.

My questioner here interrupted his brisk pace, like a bankteller who finds a counterfeit note while counting a stack of bills.

"*Metal Techniker?*" he repeated.

"*Jawohl,*" I quickly replied.

"*Das stimmt nicht!* This does not agree with the record, which states that you are a chemist. Can you explain this?"

"Sir, perhaps this is an error, for I am a metal technician."

"*Metal Techniker ist ein grosses Wort.*" (Metal technician is a big word.) "What do you do?"

At this point Tiehl stepped in to explain that I did the reproductions of all the drawings from the Russian chemistry texts that were being translated into German, particularly those that related to machinery, because a metal technician is more familiar with this terminology and can more readily help translate it. Tiehl's unsolicited explanation seemed to satisfy the little German, and he asked no further questions—nor did he assign me an essay. Had it occurred to him to inquire further into my contributions to this project, he might have found them rather disappointing.

Yet my return to the table did not mean I had passed muster. Thus far no one had been fired, but we speculated that when the exams were over, the purge of those who had gotten failing grades would take place. So, though I could breathe for the moment, having avoided getting shot for impersonating a chemist, I knew I might still flunk as a metal technician.

I observed that our captors were as impressed by bearing, discipline, and good German as perhaps by competence itself. So I emphasized form rather than substance and sensed that this made a good impression on most of them. If it were not true, how could I have gotten this far?

No one had been ousted from the group when the German technicians, working from Baran's drawings, completed the test prototype of the "ultimate weapon." On a clear, cold February morning, an array of German high brass paid us a long-expected visit. All groups working in the vicinity of the test grounds, a gorge chiseled out of the rock, were barred that day from entering the area. The result of months of work was a rectangular, radiatorlike hunk of metal full of bolts, coils, and fins; it sat on the floor of our shop, awaiting trial.

Baran, maintaining his calm, was the only one of us allowed to assist the *Wehrmacht* officers in the bunker, apparently to observe and comment on the progress of the trial run. I watched with apprehension while he instructed the German technicians in handling the "weapon," as they hoisted it onto a flatbed car with rubber tires. Extra security guards bristling with weapons gave the departing parade a sense of reality.

Was there a remote possibility that this was, or could become, a real and menacing weapon? While awaiting the test results, the men left behind in our workroom remained very tense and refrained from much talking. We anticipated the worst. The Germans would not like the idea of being misled or fooled. From a classification of uninsurables, we might soon become disposables. Only a miracle could save the day.

Then the stillness was disrupted by a distant noise—the wailing sound of air raid sirens. Instead of lying down on the floor, some of us were attracted to the window by the drone of airplanes. Against the background of clear blue a silver armada of war planes came into full view, roaring across the sky at high altitude. There were so many of them that they transmitted a sense of awesome, irresistible power. A feeling of elation prevailed for a brief moment as we looked at each other in silent wonderment. Only our eyes showed a glint of renewed hope: oh, if only the planes could finish them before they finished us! But the "All Clear" signal turned my attention once more to the test, and our apprehension returned.

The longer we waited, hearing nothing, the more anxious we became. A long time must have passed before the test expedition was finally sighted returning to the shop. The guards were leading the cart like a funeral procession, followed by the gray-aproned technicians, our black-clad little German civilian, Baran, and the bemedaled German staff. The Allied display of air power had not helped their mood.

When they entered, I saw anger in the German faces. Accusing Baran of wasting time, they demanded an explanation. But Baran, the most important whipping boy of the hour, retained his composure, realizing if they were still demanding an explanation, perhaps all was not lost. Carefully, he explained that the invention as constructed still had a few bugs, which could be eliminated in time. When the Germans heard the sensitive word "time," they became still more infuriated and threatened Baran with execution for his failure thus far. Time was one commodity they were rapidly running out of in the winter of 1945. But these representatives of military authority, instead of killing Baran and the rest of us, got to haggling over the time needed to render the invention operative. The best that the highest-ranking German would allow was one month, and "not a day more." All the others appeared to consider the offer generous.

Not yielding even to this tremendous pressure, and seemingly unafraid for his life, which indeed hung by a thin thread, Baran would not commit himself or agree to any date. So admirably did he handle himself, especially for a man who held in his hand what we all suspected was a pair of deuces, that the Germans finally announced they would return on a certain day, at which time they expected all work to be completed—or Baran could be assured of being shot. They could not threaten him with killing his relatives, for with the exception of his nephew, who was with him, they were all dead already. So the visit ended with a tirade of accusations, ranging from laziness to deliberate delay, and the customary threats.

The officers' departure generated a momentary release of tension. It seemed we had borrowed some time, but how much? Enough to survive this nightmarish confinement? Not likely—yet in this sixth winter under Nazi occupation, with its policy of extermination, a small group of starving men still hung onto their lives.

I had become so preoccupied with thinking about this latest experience that I was hardly aware of our return trip, but finally we were back in the camp, standing in formation according to our barracks for the customary evening count. The floodlights cast shadows of the prisoners on the snow. Snowflakes were falling on the high mountainside. The guards moved from the highest terrace, counting formations on the way down. But there was an unexplained delay; we were still being kept at attention instead of being dismissed. Something was wrong.

Just as I became aware of the delay, word got around that the prisoners' count did not check out: one man was missing from Block 8, which was situated at the top of the mountain. The guards ascended the steps and began the count again. Block 8 was were I belonged! By the time it dawned on me, the guards were angrily discovering that the formation at the next lower level had one too many. One absentminded man from Block 8 must have gotten mixed up in the wrong formation. I thought, when they find him they will beat him to death—"Oh Lord! It's I!"

As soon as the guards passed our ranks and before anyone took notice, I backed out of my position and, running in leaps and bounds behind the formations, rejoined Block 8. The guards noted the commotion and returned to the top, but instead of looking for the deserter they took a final count. For a moment I had been a good prospect for being beaten to a pulp. Had it not been for the unpleasant cold and snow, the guards would not have passed over such an incident without using the opportunity to teach a lesson. But they too wanted to be done with this chore; had it worked the other way, I would have had nothing to say or to write.

It was good to get inside, where body heat in the overcrowded barracks kept us warm. I got my bread ration and listened to the latest war gossip, bits of news gathered from guards and German civilians. The news lately had been electrifying. The Russians had crossed into Germany and were pressing ahead. The western Allies were advancing in Italy and all along the western front.

In a moment of thoughtful soul-searching, I felt it was pointless to hope for survival when most of my people had been murdered. Survival after such a Holocaust would not be joyous. Yet I still clung to the hope that my father and Simon could be alive —and perhaps Gina still lived. Who, I thought, will avenge our people? Who will execute justice for the heinous atrocities perpetrated against millions? Anger, hope, dejection, and hopelessness alternately took hold of my mind. But unlike my desperate prayers for death in the Budzyn hell of 1943, I now yearned to live in order to see this great wrong righted. I believed that the administration of justice would be one of the prime responsibilities of the victors. Knowing that the end of the war could not be far off, inspired and engrossed in my thoughts, I wanted to be alone, alone to utter a prayer to God.

I put my concentration camp wrap on and absentmindedly walked out of the barracks. In the dark of the evening, I looked beyond the double barbed wire and began to put my disorganized thought into words of prayer.

Five Minutes of Twelve

An administrative camp official reached our barracks the next morning and ordered the "intelligentsia" out before the regular shape-up for work.

"I shall read numbers," he said. "When you hear your number called, answer and file into formation on the right. The rest of you stand in formation."

As the numbers were read, many really educated people were called out, generating speculation that they were the ones who would continue with the project. When the last number was called, I was left with those standing in place—but so were Baran and Tiehl. In a moment it was confirmed that the numbers called out represented those who were being removed from the job. Among them were several friends, including Rysiek Krakowski. Though we acted with restraint, it was a tearful time. There was only a moment for a few handshakes and then we were separated. Those who were "fired" expected to be assigned to other work here or in another camp.

The bewildering thing was to see some real scientists sacked, while impostors like me were retained. Our team had been trimmed down from sixty-two men to about thirty-five. Back at the shop, the little Berliner warned us that he would not tolerate anyone whose brooding sentiment for departed friends interfered with his work. Our good or bad fortune was that he too was a dilettante in science; had he chosen to retain only the really knowledgeable men, he would have had to fire himself. It was not altogether unlikely that he was acting to safeguard his own assignment; otherwise he might have qualified for the now shaky front. We had heard from returning German soldiers that the party hacks were the only men who had managed to evade the front-line battle now raging deep within Germany.

In early March 1945 the German Reich was tottering on the verge of collapse. We were still prisoners and guarded with great care, but events now began to move at topsy-turvy speed. The SS commandant called all German national prisoners and Luxembourgers (who were regarded as Germanic) outside our compound for an assembly.

"There will be no bloodbath; the German blood is dear to him," was the word they brought back. But this reassurance excluded everybody except the Germans. Hungarian guards escorted some members of their own government into our camp; then they themselves were disarmed and interned. Several American fliers were brought in and confined in the hospital ward.

One night we heard shots; the next morning, we learned that the American fliers had been executed. The guards were nervous. Maybe they were afraid that the rest of us might be freed before they could get orders to exterminate us.

During all the years under the German yoke, I had had nightmares about Gestapo searches and chases, which always ended with their catching me and getting ready to execute me. Except in my daydreams, I had never dreamed of happier prewar days or anything pleasant. But late in March, in a dream as vivid as reality, I visualized a big flat battlefield on which the Allied army was advancing and crushing the Germans, to the tune of Verdi's march from *Aida*. I reawakened with renewed optimism and shared this experience with my friends to bolster their spirit, but they looked at me with sad tolerant smiles.

The end of March saw the return of several German officers, who hustled Baran off to an unknown but not unlikely destination. Our group was no longer working, but the invention gimmick had not been a bad horse to ride through the most critical time of internment—except, of course, for Baran, who had helped conceive it and had tried to make it look like the real thing.

Soon it was April 1945; a distant artillery barrage could be heard in the camp. Anton Uhl, a former camp policeman but himself a prisoner, took over as the German camp leader and instructed us all to wash and clean up for an anticipated visit from the Red Cross—which never came. Then the SS detachment abandoned the camp, leaving only enough guards to man the towers. The prisoners' spirits and hopes soared. The SS guards dropped cigarettes and food tidbits from the towers. No one went to work outside. On instructions from the camp eldest, white flags were hoisted on the roofs of the barracks.

The next day the SS detachment returned to Flossenbuerg; all the flags were ordered down. No more goodies came from the towers; a prisoner who looked up saw only the muzzle of a machine gun. The

The Topas family on a summer holiday in Srodborow, 1926. I am sitting on my father's lap; seated behind Father is Uncle Mietek and leaning against the wall Aunt Bella Krakowiak. On the right is Uncle Ben, glass in hand, next to him Grandma Sura Etta, then Grandpa Isaak Jacob and Uncle Joseph (Juziek) Krakowiak, who left for Argentina shortly before World War II. Standing just behind Grandma is Cousin Sewek, one of the three orphans brought up in my grandparents' home. (Photo preserved by relatives in the U.S.A.)

Above, Grandma Sura Etta Topas as a young woman and Grandpa Izaak Jacob. Below, my parents, Abraham Henry and Genia Topas, 1928. (Photo preserved by relatives in the U.S.A.)

The street where we lived: Leszno Street at Karmelicka Street in November, 1940, soon after the closing of the ghetto. On the right, standing on the balcony of our second-floor apartment, are my father and my youngest brother. Courtesy of Bundesarchiv, Koblenz, Germany.

A ghetto scene: Street cars marked with the Star of David were for Jews only. A Jewish policeman is directing traffic. Courtesy of Bundesarchiv, Koblenz, Germany.

Forced labor columns at the morning line-up. Courtesy of Bundesarchiv, Koblenz, Germany.

Top left: This picture, taken in April 1945 soon after my liberation and volunteering to serve with the U.S. Army, shows the results of hard marching and short rations; right, a bit underweight but fit to fight, with another infantryman advancing across Germany in May, 1945. Left, on occupation duty in Amberg, Germany, in December 1945.

Right, my best friend, Mark, as he appeared after the war. Below, Mark and I in 1983.

At the Bar Mitzvah of our son Matthew in 1966 in Jerusalem. He stands between me and his mother, Bella; our eldest son Henry is on the right, Meyer and Reuel on the left.

following morning all the Jewish prisoners were ordered to assemble on the *Appellplatz* for "evacuation." I suspected foul play and decided not to report but instead hid in the hospital ward. After all the volunteers were gathered, the guards combed the barracks and dragged out the Jewish sick from the hospital. Pretending to be an orderly, I moved from one ward to another, stopping in a room where there was only one sick prisoner in bed, and he appeared half dead. I tensed up when I heard Germans in the corridor urging the Jewish sick to leave. Then the sick man shrilled weakly, "*Jude, Jude,* a Jew is here." His body was on the verge of dying, but not his hate. In desperation, I pulled the blanket over his face, muffling his voice. The guards left.

While a small number of Jews managed to stave off their own departure, those who reported were evacuated from the camp under SS escort. Some of the German prisoners and *Kapos* were given SS uniforms and weapons and acted as guards to help evacuate the rest of the camp; they fit readily into the role. The men from Luxembourg were also accorded this "honor." The following day, no rations were distributed. The Russian prisoners, gnawed by hunger, staged a mass break-in at the bread storehouse and were repelled by SS automatic rifle fire. Freedom seemed so near, yet innocent blood was being spilled over this already blood-soaked ground.

When the SS finally issued grain soaked in molasses, the clamor and stampede for this new food was so intense that the guards hit the milling, swelling lines of prisoners over the head with clubs and rifle butts.

Next, the evacuation of the entire camp was ordered, and prisoners were hastily herded into formation. When they got about 2,000 together, the SS escorted them out of the camp; an hour later, another group left. It seemed to me that the last group would have the best chance of survival, because if all went well, they would be the first to be liberated. So I was not in any particular hurry to leave. Instead, I paid an uninvited visit to the tailor and shoemaker shops (where the middle-class "camp aristocracy" made clothing and boots for the Germans in exchange for such favors as extra food and leftovers) and helped myself to some half-cooked beans that I found on the stove.

The camp authorities had burned the camp files and with them the names of the untold number of people who had lost their lives here. By midafternoon the camp was down to its last 3,500 to 4,000 men. All the remaining prisoners and guards had to leave, and we did; only a couple of guards stayed on to liquidate the hospital. Tiehl, who had deliberately feigned sickness to avoid wearing an SS uniform, rejoined our formation. So, on a sunny afternoon in April we walked out of Flossenbuerg through the gate, even though we had previously been told that the only way out was up through the chimney as smoke.

Escorted by SS guards and dogs, we began our march down the mountain road leading to the highway. After five and a half years of uninterrupted operation, something in the well-oiled Nazi exterminating machinery had broken down: at "five to twelve" they had a problem finding a way to dispose of us. The Allies must have been getting too close to permit the execution of some 15,000 prisoners. Our captors had to have time to remove the evidence.

As our marching columns moved ahead to an unknown destination (we later learned that the orders had been to take us to the notorious Dachau for extermination), a cool April sun set, and dusk fell. All we could hear were the uneven footsteps of the weary multitude being led away from the advancing Allies to some more suitable place of execution. While many of us were surprised by the recent torrent of events, no one was deceived about the odds of survival: our chances of getting through this last march were dim indeed. Only a sudden and unexpected thrust by our liberators could save our thin necks, and nothing less than a miracle could bring that about. Yet even at this late hour, as we were led away from camp surroundings, saw the open country, and smelled the scent of the fields on an early spring evening, hope mingled with fear and expectation.

18 Evacuation March

Shall the prey be taken from the mighty.
—Isaiah 49:24

The scents and sights of nature reawakening from winter's dreariness brought yet another spring's promise and beckoned us with fresh hopes of the freedom that felt so near but was still hidden somewhere in the distance. So, too, did the haunting reality of death hover over us, waiting to welcome us into her cold embrace. Freedom and death both felt very close—which would it be?[1]

For the present we had to keep pace. This was no spring outing, however postcard-pretty the woods and villages we saw; it was an arduous march, and the guards were urging us on.

"*Anschliessen!*" They shouted. "Close ranks." We had been going for four or five hours; it was dark now, but there had been no indication of stopping to rest for the night. We were tired and hungry as well as anxious. I saw the first man fall down ahead; another prisoner broke ranks to try to help the fallen one up, but the guard ordered him back into place.

About ten yards behind us marched a trio constituting the rear guard. As they passed the fallen man, one shot broke the evening silence. This set the pattern: anyone who fell and could not get up by the time the rear guards caught up with him was dispensed with. The longer we marched, the more often we heard shots, and by now we were stumbling on corpses from the groups that had gone ahead of us. Whatever hope or expectation might have teased our imaginations before this, as night descended, the fear of being shot like a dog set in along with hunger and exhaustion; everything looked as dark as the night. Escape attempts met with rapid automatic rifle fire. Some may have gotten away in the darkness, but their chances of success were slim because the German population, warned about the evacuations, were on the alert to turn them in.

Not until the crack of dawn were we led into a large clearing in the woods and ordered to rest. A fine April drizzle added to the dew and made everything moist, but in a few moments, all was very quiet. The "convicts" were asleep.

It must have been late in the morning when the loud shouting of the SS guards awakened us. No food or drink, just "Fall in ranks!" There were several who did not rise. Although urged by others to get up, they could not and were shot sitting or lying face up looking at their executioners.

A continuous drizzle washed the haggard faces of the marching men. Before noon our column was ordered off the road, and unbelievable as it seemed, we were given rations. Meager as a slice of bread and a spoon of jam was, it was chewed slowly because it had to last indefinitely, as far as we knew.

I saw a friend whom Mark and I had known in Plaszow—Mendelson, a barber from Radom. During the break he spotted me too and, without being asked, offered me some grain that he carried in a small container. His gesture at this time was a lifesaver, for I had not drawn any rations before we left except for those few spoonfuls of half-cooked beans. Slim, stooped, and freckled, he always seemed cheerful and usually managed to have extra rations, because good barbers got food tips from some of the guards. Mendelson also doubled as a dentist. In the Radom ghetto he had obliged anyone who wanted a tooth pulled.

Because I had separated myself from the Jewish contingent, which had been the first to be herded together for evacuation a day earlier, I was among men I did not know. Therefore Mendelson was a welcome sight, and for a while we tried to maintain contact.

After about an hour and a half we were herded back into formation, and the march resumed. Next to me walked a dark-haired fellow, wearing glasses, whom I had not known until then. Whispering to him, I learned that he was from Warsaw. At any other time this bit of kinship could have brightened my spirit, but at this point it did not evoke any emotion; we were drained of normal feelings. Except for mechanically moving our feet, we had such a sense of emptiness that nothing much seemed to matter any more. Occasionally, I would exhort my new friend and myself to continue this seemingly endless funeral procession.

Somewhere among the marching survivors of Flossenbeurg, Plaszow, and Budzyn, scattered among several formations in this silent procession, were the men from the inventors' group. I had seen Tiehl at the time of the assembly, before the last group left the camp, but to my chagrin I lost sight of him. A few other Jews had also managed to evade the SS dragnet in the camp, but each of us tried to lose himself in a crowd to avoid detection. In fact, this was the first time that I did not fear being given away by the other prisoners. After all, the sword hung over all our heads—Jew and non-Jew alike.

Most of us expected our execution at the end of the march. Only thoughts of escape or a sudden, miraculous rescue by the Americans kept up our hopes and gave every soul a reason to hang on. Men who became too enfeebled and weary to continue were being shot with increased frequency. During the second day of the march, some of us hung on simply out of the habit of suffering that concentration camp life had instilled in us. In fact, I thought, it took a great deal of courage not to give in to panic or despair when life all around us was being snuffed out. Death pointed a finger and said with a cynical smile: Hey there, you are next! It took faith to hope to beat the impressively unfavorable odds.

As darkness fell again, we were all soaked from the rain. Body heat can dry your inner rags, but after hours of the same wetness, your body merely keeps the moisture warm. That held good for as long as we kept moving, but when we halted before dawn and fell down by the roadside to sleep, our rags turned into cold compresses. We had to huddle together for warmth, and being wet made falling asleep difficult. I felt feverish and began to think about my family and home. I dreamed that my mother put her hand on my forehead and took my temperature; moments later I was in bed, and Dr. Nelson was at my bedside; he took off his stethoscope, talked to my mother as he wrote a prescription. Father helped him with his overcoat. Grandma came in and brought tangerines. I got a lot of attention. Mother did not leave my bedside except to bring tea, biscuits, cereal, and medicine. Father and my uncles brought toys. All this concern and care made me feel very secure, very much wanted and loved. Half awake, I tried hard to imagine that soon I would be surrounded by family and given good care in the warmth of our home, but my wet clothing dispelled the sublime flight from reality, and the distant sounds of my parents' voices assuring me that I would soon get well faded away.

Then the rasping sounds of German commands to fall in filled the air—and the stark reality of another day put an end to our brief respite.

Our ranks were now much thinner because a number of men had developed chills and high fever and had neither the will nor the energy to rise. The rattle of gunfire put an end to their misery. If I had had any tears left, I would have cried to God, but everything momentarily appeared unreal. The only reality was that it wouldn't take much to break the very thin thread of life to which the living still clung.

By late afternoon our column halted and then, after altering direction, resumed the march. My companion from Warsaw started to have chills and began to limp. Thank God, my feet were all right so far, despite the wooden shoes. Anyone who limped noticeably or began to fall back was usually grabbed by the collar and tossed into a ditch by the side of the road; then a guard put a bullet through his head. I took my friend's hand and put his arm around my neck to ease the side where he limped. Helping a friend in this way was not uncommon, but the guards urged us to drop those who limped, warning that the one who helped another would himself wear out and get it in the end. It all depended on the guard nearest you; if he decided that someone was holding up the procession, he shot the laggard.

Because we did not pass through any towns, it was hard to know where we were. Only small hamlets sparsely spaced and often nameless as far as we could see were in our line of march. Just before we changed direction we had heard distant artillery bombardment, but over the next several hours the noises of war had grown fainter. Before dusk, I stepped out of rank long enough to pull the blanket off a dead prisoner lying along the line of march and wrap it around both my friend and me. It was wet, but having been folded by the previous owner, it did not have any bloodstains. Although it added extra weight to carry, it provided some needed warmth for our shivering bodies.

Suddenly there was the noise of marching feet coming from behind us, and being in one of the last ranks in our thinned-out column, I soon observed a large body of men approaching our rear. When they caught up with us, they could easily be recognized as English POWs under *Wehrmacht* guards, and although it was dark, you could see that they had fared better than we had. Besides wearing their uniforms, they still looked like human beings, with a soldierly bearing. Food alone did not make that difference; treatment did.

Soon an argument for road priority took place between their guards and ours; they wanted the road cleared in order to pass ahead of our funeral procession. The SS, typically obstinate, would not give in until the ranking *Wehrmacht* officer angrily declared that either the SS would get us off the road or he would drive over us. We moved aside and watched in amazement as the English prisoners passed in review, followed by some horse-drawn artillery fieldpieces and an assortment of German cavalrymen. The POWs were close enough to touch, but we dared not. They looked at us with quiet astonishment and sorrow. We resumed our procession and soon lost contact with those who passed us; being much more alive, they moved faster.

Eventually, the guards brought our column to a halt. It was late at night, and we had passed a village called Rötz. We were in Bavaria. It had rained most of the night and kept on raining, but the night was not over yet. We were drenched, sitting on wet ground huddled together in nearly total darkness. Although we were in a large meadowlike clearing, there were clumps of pine trees all around. I went to one of the trees and began to break off branches. The cracking noise attracted the attention of a guard, who soon made himself heard and felt as he kicked me in the lower back and said: "Are you crazy? Don't you know that making a fire is forbidden?"

"I only want to cover the wet ground with these branches," I said, and when he walked away, I spread them out for my friend and me. My companion—whose name I had learned was Grudniewicz, a journalist who had worked for a prewar Polish-language newspaper—was running a high fever, and I feared that he would not last another day. For that matter, who would? This ordeal seemed the finishing blow for those who had managed to survive previous ordeals.

My memory fails me; it was difficult to be fully aware of what was happening. After marching day after day and half the night, your senses are dulled, and all you know is to follow the fellow ahead and not to fall behind your rank. Our weary silence was interrupted by the sound of guns dispatching those who either could not or would not continue. So, all that seemed important was to move your feet. A pair of ill-fitting shoes spelled doom for their owner.

How long could this keep up? Only once had food rations been issued since the evacuation started, and this was the third night. The air got colder, and the drizzle continued. I kept waking up every few minutes. Incoherent thoughts crept into my mind. When the Germans marched into Poland, I was not yet fifteen years old. Now it was April 1945. I was nearly twenty-one. What an age and time to reach the end of the road!

There we were, the breathing remnant of a doomed lot still in the hands of our executioners. All night long we heard rain, muffled noises, uneven steps, ragged breathing. Grudniewicz's high fever showed no sign of coming down, and soon it would be morning. I remembered that time in camp when I had had high fever in the evening but by morning it had been miraculously gone; I was hoping for the same for my friend.

At first light we heard bursting explosives; then the sounds died out. I thought I heard artillery fire. The drizzle continued through the new dawn. When ordered to assemble on the road, many men could not get up; perhaps forty or fifty were carried and laid together in a clearing near the road for the *coup de grâce*. Hunger was taking away what little energy was still left in the men who had survived thus far. What day was it? April 22? 23? What did it matter?

I helped my feverish friend to his feet, and as I led him to rejoin the forming column, we walked reluctantly, caring little to continue. Looking at him was like looking in a mirror. We were both goners, our deaths perhaps only a few hours apart. Even as the column was ready to move, an SS man was aiming his automatic rifle at the sick and lame. At any moment we would hear the burst of fire, but for now there was a stony silence all around us, interrupted by the distant noise of a solitary airplane—coming closer.

The guards ordered us to stand in formation while they jumped into the ditches on both sides of the road with their rifles aimed at us. We all stood looking up at what appeared to be a small observation plane with a strange insignia—something like a star of Solomon, which, unlike David's, is five-pointed.

"It's an American!" someone called out excitedly. The plane circled. Ignoring the guards, the men began to wave their prisoners' caps, and yells went up from many throats. Apparently our executioners were too concerned with the ominous signs that their own moment of reckoning was at hand to punish us for our spontaneous demonstration. Yes, there was a tense sense of expectation. The race for time was down to its final moments.

No sooner had the plane disappeared from view than from a westerly direction German infantrymen were bicycling toward the rear of our column and soon passed us. About platoon strength, they carried on their bikes the *Panzerfaust* weapons (something like bazookas but with a large grenadelike object attached at one end) used against tanks and armor. When they got well ahead of us, they hastily dismounted and made for a patch of woods on the right of the road. A moment of quiet ensued. Our guards hesitated about their next move. I sensed that the big hand of the clock was fast approaching twelve, and we were still in the clutches of the SS.

The guards again ordered us to close ranks, and again a couple of them pointed their guns at the sick lying on the ground, but before they got started, we heard a loud rumbling noise some distance to the rear of our column. As the noise grew louder, we could feel the ground tremble. All eyes turned toward the west. Tanks emerged on the horizon, moving in a broad line, and soon they burst into full view. Someone hollered, "Don't get excited; they are Italian!"—although Italy was out of the war. But the sight of the white star brought shouts: "American! American!"

At this magic word the ranks broke up. The guards began to run, leaving forty stretched-out, would-be corpses—some still hanging on to life, though no one really knew how many. The excitement bordered on pandemonium. Soon the tanks were all over the place. When those following the road slowed down and stopped, our men began to kiss them and to kiss the hands of the crewmen, who were tossing out food rations for the starved.

In this state of excitement I stopped the first or second tank and addressed the American, who looked to me like an angel; and in my best English I pointed out the woods where the Germans had fled with their *Panzerfausts*, explaining my fear that they might be used against our liberators. I was amazed and elated when he said, "Thank you very much." Moments later all the tanks cleared the open field and followed one another on the road. When they neared the woods, the turrets turned to the right opened fire, and soon the wooded area was ablaze.

After so many years, it had all happened so quickly—and at the last moments of our endurance! I stood at the side of the road watching the American columns, which were now moving uninterruptedly like a tidal wave. As I bent down to pick up one of the many boxes tossed to us by the Americans, it dawned on me that I was still covered with a wet blanket, which I promptly discarded. Chewing on a cracker, I watched the breathtaking sight, and as in a dream the drizzle stopped and the sun broke out to welcome this longed-for day—our day of liberation.

I lifted up my head and scanned the clearing sky; then, instinctively, I bowed and said a short prayer.

19 The Slaughter Is Ended

God bears with the wicked, but not forever.
—Miguel de Cervantes

The ecstatic feeling of the moment of liberation lingered for some time. Some of the Jews from Flossenbuerg's first evacuation group, I learned, had overpowered their guards and held them prisoner until the anticipated arrival of the American troops. Their courage in the last moments of their captive existence served them well.

I still wanted very much to have an active part in this war, and the opportunity presented itself when I expressed my wish to an American officer before whom I was brought by the friendly, sympathetic GIs. After hearing me out he asked: "George, after what you have been through, do you still want to go into combat?"

"More than anything else," I answered.

My wish was granted. Possibly because of my knowledge of English and German, I was allowed to join an infantry unit of the 26th Yankee Division and lived to fight the remaining days of the war.

While riding in a truck to the then rolling front, I was equipped and taught the use of such weapons as the M-1 rifle and hand grenades, and I learned general orders. The tour with C Company of the 104th took me through Bavaria, across the border into Czechoslovakia, and into Austria. It ended in Aigen-Schlegel, not far from where the Russians and Americans had met. All this in less than three weeks time, on trucks, on tanks, and on foot.

Besides some skirmishes with the retreating foe, our unit ran into some trouble at Passau (on the Danube River). The Germans hoisted white flags and hung them from their windows, but when we approached the outskirts of town, we were fired upon and our advance checked until the air force flushed out and silenced the resistance.

On the first day of May there was a bit of snow, and we were bivouacking in a broad meadow. Suddenly hundreds of GIs were running toward the road, and the fellow next to me yelled, "Hey George, come on, let's go and see our boss!" In a moment several army vehicles passed us, and then one emerged in which a soldier was standing up, wearing a helmet with stars on it and what looked like a pearl-handled revolver at his side. When he saw his cheering troops, his face broke out in a grin; he raised his arms and said, "Heil Hitler with both hands"—the sign of surrendering Germans. It was George

Patton, the "boss" of the Third Army and a crafty fighter in whom the German warlords had found more than a match.

A whole *Panzer* (armored) division wearing black-labeled patches that said *Berlin* on their coat sleeves surrendered to us as did a horse cavalry unit with many Russians in it. I was called to come and act as interpreter. I stood next to a high-ranking American officer beside a microphone, on a rigged-up platform overlooking a broad expanse where several thousand German POWs, their tanks and vehicles halted, were surrounded by American GIs. They looked disheveled and beaten. One officer was soaking his feet in a helmet filled with water. I was reminded of my father's words in Lublin, that I would live to see the conquerors defeated, their arrogance and pride gone.

I faithfully translated the American officer's orders to the German POWs—except at one moment when I could not resist injecting a sentence of my own. When the officer said that "German officers will be responsible for turning in their own weapons and for turning in all the weapons of their enlisted men," I added, "and if you fail, *ihr wird standrechtlich erschossen.*" "You will be lawfully shot"—those were exactly the words that the Germans had used for the most trivial offense during their reign of terror, and I wanted them to taste a little of their own bitter pill. But the Germans probably did not see anything unusual in the victor's issuing the same orders they had when power was in their hands.

Then came V-E Day, the day of Germany's surrender—May 8, 1945. The jubilant mood was marred only by the thought of the war's great slaughter and the fact that for many of us there was no family or home to return to.

Soon after the hostilities had ended, when the division I had joined was scheduled to return to the United States, I traveled to Germany from Austria and presented my letter of recommendation—my only credentials—to Lt. Col. Frank W. Norris, commander of the 90th DIV-345 F.A. Battalion. He assigned me to the Counterintelligence Corps, (CIC) unit in his district, with which I joined in many raids in search of escaped SS men and in investigations of captured SS and other Nazis.

Later, while still attached to a CIC unit stationed in Germany, I had an opportunity to meet two Jewish officers of the Palestine brigade, which was part of the British Eighth Army, who were traveling from Italy to Poland in search of their own relatives. I wrote two passionate letters, one to my father and one to Gina—care of Stanislav Uchanski, in Cmielow, Kielecki, Poland, the last address I had for Gina and her mother—and gave these letters to the two men who were going to Poland.

Two weeks passed and I heard nothing from these messengers. A returning refugee from Prague, Czechoslovakia, however, did claim to have heard that a man by the name of Topas was residing in a room at the Roxy Hotel, which was then filled with refugees. Further questioning revealed that this was my Uncle Benjamin, who had managed to survive with the help of his brave and devoted wife Rose, who had passed as an Aryan. He hid in her apartment on the "Aryan" side of the wall and later fought with the Poles in the Warsaw uprising of 1944, organized by the Polish National Army and directed from London. Overjoyed, I tried to find a way to get in contact with him but mail and phone services had not yet been fully restored for private use.

Then one day, when I returned from one of our postwar raids in search of hidden SS men, my friends told me that a young man with curly hair was looking for me; he had left no name but said he would come back later.

It was June again, and the standing grain was ripening in the fields under the bright sun. The flowers were in full bloom, and the birds, ignoring the calamities of the war, were chirping as though nothing had changed. Shortly before sunset a man on a bicycle pulled up before our headquarters and looked around. At first slowly, he approached; then he drew closer, and I began to make out the facial features of the stranger. The face was rounder and he had a shock of curly hair, but the green eyes gave him away. I was moved to tears when Mark opened his arms and we embraced. Choked up, we could not speak at first.

Courtesy of our American cooks, we sat at the far end of the garden eating our first meal together as free men. Mark was surprised at my American uniform and command of English. The light in the guestroom burned late into the night while we related our experiences to each other.

After we parted company in Flossenbuerg, Mark's group of several hundred men had been transported to the city of Platling in southern Bavaria. Platling was an important railway junction and had a military airfield. The prisoners were dispatched daily to various military installations and were housed in a barn that had been temporarily converted into an SS prison. One day in early spring Mark was assigned to a fifteen-man detail that was sent to do maintenance work at the airfield, sweeping runways, doing general clean-up and digging drainage ditches along the shoulders of the runway. Parked on the field among the fighter planes were several strange-looking planes without propellers—evidently jets.

Before the wailing sound of the air raid sirens could be heard, the drone of airplane engines filled the air. The *Luftwaffe* pilots scrambled out, running to the parked planes, but before any of them could get aloft, bombs began to fall. The few SS guards ran to the parked jets and dived under their wings, where they were incinerated in a matter of seconds by the flames of the exploding planes. Mark and his men had run for the drainage ditches, from which they excitedly viewed the air bombardment, forgetting that they themselves could be harmed by the friendly American fliers. Miraculously, they all escaped injury.

"Seeing the Allied planes in action," said Mark, "was something I will never forget. There were about fifteen of them. The noise was deafening, and it was impossible for us to be heard, so we kept on cheering and rooting for the Americans, which we thought they were. Let me tell you, it was a fantastic sight. It shattered the notion of German invincibility. Here, all of a sudden, we could see with our own eyes that the war was being brought back home to them. It gave us a big boost and the feeling that if this could happen, our situation could not be hopeless forever. The next day we were assigned to the Platling railroad station, which had received its share of the bombs. There were twisted rails pointing upward, and many soldiers had been trapped and killed in a troop train and in and around the station. We were told to pull the corpses out of the wreckage while others were busy clearing up the debris."

Mark told me that in mid-April his group of three hundred men were taken from Platling and marched for two solid weeks without rations. "I would have perished from hunger during the march," said Mark, "had I not been put to work the last day in the home of the mayor, who was well stocked with provisions and chocolate stolen from Red Cross packages. In his cellar I found large cones of sugar. I chopped one up and put it in my pants, tying the pants bottoms around my ankles. This kept me going for two weeks. Some lived on what they had before we left; others dug up whatever they could find in the fields."

By the end of April they were down to forty men. One of Mark's three companions bribed an SS guard with a diamond ring taken off a German officer killed in an air raid in Platling. This took place outside the entrance to a pigsty where the prisoners were sleeping, and the four fled while it was still dark. The guards fired after them but missed.

Mark and the others ran into another pair of prisoners who had managed to escape the same night. The men agreed to split into three pairs and to say, when stopped by Germans, that the SS had ordered them to go back and report for work at the nearest town or camp: that way, no matter what happened, their stories would be the same.

Mark and his companion started marching through a wooded area paralleling the highway north of Traunstein. It was May 1, 1945, and light snow was falling: "It was a miracle, for it reduced visibility and covered our footsteps." Everything went well until the wooded area ended and the two, wearing their striped concentration camp suits, were exposed in an open field. Then the road turned sharply around a natural obstruction, and when they came around the turn, they sighted a roadblock consisting of two German MPs (*Feldwache*) and an officer seated in a military vehicle equipped with radios and antennas. Mark realized that it was too late to do anything except approach and tell their "orders." One of the MPs reported their story to the officer in charge, and the fact that this was the second pair giving the same explanation. The officer, without showing much interest in the matter, noted that the first pair had been shipped out by truck for verification to the SS authorities, but he said they had no more trucks or men to spare for "this business"; since it seemed that their story checked out, let them continue on foot, he said. The third pair got through as well and proceeded some distance before a friendly French POW farmworker offered to hide them in a barn, where he also gave them food, and water to wash up.

The rumbling of tanks the next morning awakened the runaways to the realization that they had been liberated by the Americans. The elation of survival was dampened by the death of Freiman, one of the three who had escaped together with Mark. He had subsequently died of typhus and was buried not far from where he was liberated in Trostberg.

For some of the inmates left behind, the rescue had come too late. Mark later returned to the place of his escape, only to find out that most of the men remaining there had been shot the very morning following his flight, as were the first two whom the German MPs had delivered back to their group.

Even some prisoners who survived those death marches died within hours or days after eating their first real meal because their systems could no longer accept food. For all too many, the long-awaited liberation came too late. Now, I looked at Mark and was grateful that his life had been spared. To have a real friend is a blessing; that we had both survived and were together again was a great consolation. We had been relatively fortunate that throughout our ordeals we had been spared the more notorious death camps, where the gassings, removal of corpses, extraction of gold teeth, castrations, fiendish medical experiments, torture, and executions were commonplace.

Mark consented to go over to Prague in the Russian Zone to try to persuade my uncle to come and join me. A week later, jumping off a freight car with two pieces of luggage (one of them a phonograph), Uncle Ben, still looking pale and undernourished, arrived with Mark. Dear Uncle Ben. Seeing him brought back a wealth of happy memories from the pre-Holocaust world, the world that had vanished in a deluge of blood and tears and was no more. Looking at him gave me the reassurance that such a world had once really existed and that we once upon a time had been a normal, happy family. But I felt the excruciating pain of loss. All the emotions that had been stored up in me for so long and silenced by the realities of the hellish confinement suddenly burst forth with a flood of tears in a torrential, emotional release.

After a week's rest in an apartment in a former Nazi's villa, Ben went wandering through Germany looking for Rose, his wife, and Mark left in search of his brothers. There was still no word from Father, Simon, or Gina, and with each passing week my hopes dwindled. Letters and traveling acquaintances brought back nothing to offer any hope that they were alive. Letters that I sent to my grandmother in New York, hoping to make contact with her, produced curious results. Even before the end of the fighting my name had once been called at mail call. My heart pounding with eager anticipation, I seized the letter, only to find that it was my own, returned with "No such address" marked on the envelope. I had addressed the letter to Mrs. Etta S. Topas, Fifth Avenue, New York, and wondered why the post office couldn't find her! Next I tried Fifth Avenue, the Bronx, but got that letter back, too.

Eventually, I wrote to the U.S. Postmaster of New York City, and my hopes were fulfilled when I received a letter from him informing me that he had located my grandmother and that I would hear from her directly. Good old Grandma sent a letter, package, and money. The letter, aside from reflecting her emotionally excited state, informed me that Aunt Rose was in Kassel, in the British zone of Germany, where she had been sent to do compulsory labor on a farm (as a Gentile).

At the moment Grandma was happy to know that at least one of her children and his wife and her oldest grandson had survived. But she was inconsolable when she was told, eventually, that these three and one of her sisters (who had emigrated to the United States after World War I) were indeed the only survivors of her whole family; that she had lost a husband in the typhus epidemic; two sons—one shot and one unaccounted for—and a daughter; a granddaughter, two grandsons, two daughters-in-law, and all her brothers and other sisters.

I immediately arranged to send a refugee friend who worked around our kitchen to bring Aunt Rose from Kassel, and after nearly a week she arrived. We met with tears, tears of mingled joy and sadness; how happy I was to see her!

"Jurek, you survived!—" she exclaimed. "You are grown up—a man—and you look like your father." Dear Aunt Rose, her beauty and charm remained intact even after all she had endured.

I took her to Uncle Ben's one-room apartment, unbeknownst to him, and introduced her to the German hosts. Frustrated, Ben had returned a day earlier than he intended without finding his wife, and at the moment he was away from the apartment. After locating him, I walked my uncle to his front entrance, where I said goodbye, leaving him unaware that he would find Aunt Rose inside.

I was not playing games. I simply felt that my uncle should find his wife alone, as he had set out to do, and that their moment of reunion should be a very personal, private one. I came back later with a bottle of champagne to share in their joy, happy in the knowledge that bringing my Uncle Ben here had prevented his departure for Warsaw, which would have delayed this momentous reunion. I was elated at their good fortune in having both survived—a rarity among the survivors, who were made up mostly of widows and widowers and orphaned youths. My aunt and uncle would be able to rebuild their lives with less difficulty than most of us.

The term "displaced persons" had entered the vocabulary to designate those who had been freed from camps away from their homeland. The DPs wandered all over Germany and the previously occupied lands in the hope of finding someone dear. In fact, it was high season for wanderers, as the relatives of the remnants searched for their next of kin. The Red Cross and various welfare agencies helped, so that by the time the summer drew to a close most of the living had been put in contact with their relatives, and there was a period of reunions.

But it was then that we first learned the full enormity of the crimes our enemies had committed against us and against other people, even their own. They were, to paraphrase Sir Winston Churchill, "the most lamentably heinous crimes in the catalogue of inhuman acts known in the annals of man."[1]

Epilogue:
Elation and Sorrow

The Jew has made a marvelous fight in this world in all ages and has done it with his hands tied behind him.
—Mark Twain

Letters and packages from Grandma soon beckoned me to come to her in America. One letter mentioned that there were some outstanding young ladies interested in meeting me; I took that as a subtle hint to protect myself from any attention in that direction until I got safely to the States.

I took her invitation to heart and asked Dan DeVries, a fellow CIC agent, to accompany me to Frankfurt to see the American consul. Because of my service with the U.S. Army and several commendation letters attesting the fact, the consul cut the red tape and processed my papers in short order.

In June 1946 I said goodbye to the friends with whom I served and set out for Bremerhaven, the embarkation point for the U.S.A. As I walked up the gang-plank, I began to realize that just as my liberation by the American troops had brought a dark epoch of my life to an end, so too leaving Europe and my exciting service in the U.S. Army was another ending, and a new postwar epoch was about to begin.

Ben and Rose had left for the States a few weeks earlier, and Ben had already found a job. Grandma, accompanied by Rose, was at the dock in New York to welcome me in her arms. You can imagine the torrent of tears as she held me in a warm embrace. Her face had a few wrinkles, but she still exuded the strength and energy that I remembered.

I marveled at the great metropolis and the fast rhythm of life in the big city, where I stayed with dear Grandma for a few days before going to work as a busboy in a resort hotel that summer. After that there was a short stint with an export firm. But I was beginning to feel very estranged; the pain of losing my whole immediate family began to affect me like coming out of anesthesia affects a man who suddenly realizes that his limbs have been severed.

The only family I knew besides my grandmother and uncle and aunt was the army, and I decided to return to it. So in April 1947, at the Whitehall Building in Manhattan, I was sworn into the U.S. Army. The recruiting officer, looking up from my commendation letters, said to me, "These are very good commendation letters, but unfortunately the Army cannot give you any credit for your experience in combat because though you were an Army volunteer, you were not then officially a GI."

I remained in the army for eighteen months but realized that permanent service in the military was not for me. After discharge I did all the "normal" things: I married, raised a family, went into business. But for me as for many survivors, life has never been quite "normal" again.

With the coming of peace, frustrations began to creep in. The twenty-odd apprehended leading Nazis got the benefit of a trial at Nuremberg, conducted by the Allies, with results ranging from acquittal to the death sentence. But soon the worsening relations between erstwhile allies, the United States and Russia, benefited the one-time enemy, who was now coaxed by both sides, each trying to win his favor. The application of justice commenced at Nuremberg by the Allies was soon relegated to the native German administration, where at times Nazis sat in judgment over Nazis. This frequently led to a mockery of justice in the courts; light sentences were imposed, and there were numerous acquittals. A case in point was a well-publicized trial in which a German judge acquitted fourteen women responsible for the murder of 800 retarded and physically deficient German children to whom the accused had administered lethal injections and poisoned marmalade. Testimony showed that those who resisted had stomach tubes forced down their throats, or were given lethal enemas. The judge concluded that the nurses were "simple-minded persons" who did not comprehend the criminal nature of their acts.[1]

I was saddened by this irreverence and disrespect for the past, characterized by a contempt for justice among the German jurists. Hundreds of Nazi war criminals emigrated to South America, where they continued to live undisturbed and seemingly beyond the reach of justice. I felt a sense of outrage and ominous foreboding that this monstrous atrocity had been allowed to go unpunished, tolerated by the same world indifference that produced this unspeakable reign of terror in the first place.

I refused to accept my father's absence as positive proof of his annihilation, and I kept faith in his survival for twenty-two years, likening my waiting to that of biblical Joseph, who was snatched from his father at the age of seventeen, as I was, and who was not reunited with him until he was thirty-nine. Finally, a letter from the International Tracing Service informed me that my father, Prisoner No. 14135, of Lipowa Street Camp in Lublin, had perished on September 25, 1942, on the eve of the Succoth holiday, as shown by the crematorium records.[2]

For many years I tried to trace Gina and her mother, and at last reconciled myself to the thought that they too had perished in the Holocaust. Their last known address was with the family of Stanislaw Uchanski, but my repeated attempts to obtain information from the Uchanskis had no result. Then, thirty-five years after the end of the war, I received a letter from Wanda Uchanska, the second wife and widow of Tadeusz Uchanski, son of Stanislaw. She sorrowfully revealed what she called the "bitter truth," that Gina and her mother had been robbed and murdered, not by the Germans but by thieves who took them from the Uchanskis' house at night, carrying their valuables in two suitcases; the victims were shot and buried in the nearby woods. Mrs. Uchanska did not identify the perpetrators by name, but she commented that there was no lack of "vile people," especially in wartime. She also indicated that in that same woodland near Cmielow Kielecki, where Gina Rosenbaum, age eighteen, and her mother Raisel lie, other innocents were buried during the war years, victims of the Germans and other predators.

My teacher Nachum Sienicki, the agricultural engineer, survived and remarried; he now lives in Israel. Morris Wyszogrod, the artist, survived; his younger brother Paul did not. Morris and his family live in the United States. Rysiek Krakowski also survived and lived with his family in the United States. When he died a few years ago, he was mourned by all who knew him. We shall remember him as a noble soul. Moshe Kessel survived to fight in the wars for Israel's independence and survival; he and his family still live in Israel. The "young" Rabbi Glatstein from Okecie and his brother survived and live in the United States. Fred, Sam, and Henry Orenstein survived; Felek and their only sister did not. The Orenstein brothers live in the United States. Jack Eisner survived and lives in the United States, and I was told that Freudlich also survived and lives here. My friend Mark married my wife's best friend. They live near us, and our families are very close. Mark's brothers also survived; Morris lives in the United States, Adam in Canada.

A Trip to the Past

On our journey to Poland in August, 1989, among the places that bound me with the past was the little village of Urle, where my family had spent the last three summers before the outbreak of the war. After some difficulty in finding the road, we finally located the very house where we had stayed. I was astonished, after more than fifty years, to meet Mrs. Lewandowska, the landlady, who when we knew her had been in her late twenties.

"Do you remember who occupied this apartment the last few summers before the war?," I asked, pointing to it.

She looked at me for a moment as though trying to recall something stored in the recesses of her memory.

"The father was a Polish pilot," I said.

"Oh yes, Mr. Lasota."

"And who occupied this apartment?" I asked, pointing to it.

"Mr. Topas, a very sympathetic man," she said, taking me completely by surprise.

"They had two boys," she continued, "the older one was Jurek and the younger was Shymonek [the endearing term for Simon]."

"Didn't they have another boy?"

"Yes, a little one, Majorek." This referred to my brother Meir. "Mr. Topas was very kind. He brought presents—shoes for my children."

She still did not seem to know who I was, but probably sensed that I was a relation. At that point I thought that except for taking photographs and leaving a little present, the visit was over. But it was not over as far as Mrs. Lewandowska was concerned. Looking pensive and sad, she seemed to want to unburden herself of something that had been on her mind for a long time.

"Shymonek," she continued, "such a nice boy, ran away from the ghetto when the Jews were being shipped off to Treblinka [summer of 1942] and asked me to hide him, to save him. I would have gladly done this. Shymonek was a well-built boy, did not look like a Jew, but I was afraid for my family. . . . He told me that he had a grandmother in America. I never knew what happened to Mr. Topas and Jurek. Yes, I would gladly have kept him but I was afraid. Jews were jumping off the trains going to Treblinka [the railroad track ran through Urle] and a gendarme named Stein was looking for them. I said to Shymonek: 'If I keep you here, we will all be killed.' I said to him: 'Look, my husband will take you to the next village, about five kilometers away. No one knows you there.' He was about fourteen years old. He could have been a shepherd and taken care of the cows there. But Shymonek did not want to go there. He said that he did not know anyone there." Mrs. Lewandowska sat quietly while I tried to control myself and wipe away my tears.

"Please tell me what happened then?"

"I kept him here three, maybe four days and then he left."

And this was all that we learned about my brother. I could not help feeling that she was telling the truth, painful as it was, and that my brother Simon perished, perhaps not far from this place.

"Mrs. Lewandowska, do you know who I am?"

She looked up into my eyes.

"I am Jurek, Shymonek's older brother. I escaped death, joined the American Army toward the end of the war, and went to America.

She smiled faintly, as though pleased.

Before I left, I asked whether they had any old photographs taken before the war. An old album with many loose photographs was brought to me. As I looked through the pictures I came across a photograph of Adolf Hitler.

Justice and History

From the very beginning of the German onslaught on Poland in September 1939, I viewed that event and the cataclysmic period that followed in terms of good and evil—believing that though evil may triumph for a time, it cannot vanquish good.

This outlook was shaped by my upbringing; it was based on belief in a righteous Providence, on the indestructability of the Jewish people, and on the special relationship with God that placed the burden of responsibility for the observance of His Law, the Torah, upon us.

I recall that my father, reading the scriptures to us on the Sabbath, often stressed that justice and righteousness are the very foundation, the underpinning, of world order. With them, there is security, stability, and well-being; without them, anarchy, or tyranny and oppression.

Though all that the Jewish people experienced during the war dwarfed in the enormity of its evil everything that had preceded it, I felt that we, the Jewish people, would survive this too—the greatest catastrophe we had yet had to bear. I was at times confused about these matters, but my mystic belief that my father's blessing protected me and that I would somehow be helped to get through the war sustained me—though at times I felt I was losing my grip on life.

Hitler's proclaimed thousand-year Reich lasted only twelve years. He vowed to destroy all the Jews; he did not succeed in that either. The Nazis thought they could get away with their heinous crimes against the Jews because they counted on the cooperation of other nations with a long history of anti-Semitism. In the end they did destroy millions—both Jews and other innocent people as well.

The Jewish people in their arduous march through history have survived rising and falling civilizations. It seems to me phenomenal that the unending succession of tyrants, despotic rulers, and ruthless opportunists have disregarded the lessons of history of over three and a half millennia and sought and still seek to delegitimize the right of the Jewish people to live unmolested. (Israel is a case in point.)

Are we to learn anything from this experience and apply it for the good of mankind? If not we must expect many trials and tragic lessons yet to come. And if the world is still embroiled in continued strife decades after the end of that terrible war, it may be because this great wrong has not been righted.

The failure to deal with the perpetrators of the Holocaust constitutes a flagrant disregard for justice and for the victims. Also disturbing is the growing trend of distorting the truth about the monstrous crimes, which casts a menacing shadow on the future. During his visit to Poland, Bernard Cardinal Law of Boston, speaking at the site of Auschwitz (1986) had this to say: "The Final Solution of the Jewish Question, itself a euphemism, was originally termed an evacuation in view of the possibilities in the East. Those responsible for Auschwitz invented such euphemisms to mask their evil doing. . . . Confronted with the devastation wrought in this place by human malice, we seek to minimize crimes and to diffuse blame. Victimizers are treated as victims, and victims as accessories. The persistence of the human capacity for evil, demonstrated here, must eliminate the fantasy which inspires these evasions." [3]

I believe that the last chapter of the epoch of arrogance and cruelty has not been closed and that justice has not been served.

For all the suffering by our people in this Holocaust, it poses no new challenge to our faith as I see it. Though unique in its ferocity and magnitude, the Holocaust was not without precedent, but was rather an overwhelmingly exaggerated expression of a recurrent phenomenon in Jewish history. The first indiscriminate slaughter and starvation of the Jews occurred 2600 years ago, in 586 B.C.E., at the hands of the Babylonians during and after the fall of Jerusalem. This butchery was repeated by Imperial Rome 19 centuries ago. The slaughter of Arabian Jewry, the Crusades, the Spanish Inquisition, Chmielnicki's massacres claimed hundreds of thousands of victims.

But scripture not only predicts calamity—it also promises consolation: "And yet for all that, when they are in the land of their enemies, I will not reject them, neither will I abhor them, to destroy them utterly, and to break My covenant with them; for I am the Lord, their God" (Leviticus 26:44).

As for those who inflicted such brutal pain and misery on mankind, history's inevitable verdict is foreshadowed in the words of the nineteenth-century historian James Froude: "Opinions alter, manners change, creeds rise and fall, but the Moral Law is written on the tablets of Eternity. For every false word or unrighteous deed, for cruelty and oppression, for lust or vanity, the price has to be paid at last. . . . Injustice and falsehood may be long-lived, but doomsday comes at last to them."

Like our ancestors, we shall continue to place our trust in the ultimate victory of divine law and justice over arrogance and guile, of light over darkness, and of freedom over tyranny.

Appendix

For the Record

Headquarters Company "C"
104th Infantry
APO 26 U.S. Army   18 May 1945
TO WHOM IT MAY CONCERN:

This is to certify that George Topas joined this organization when we were advancing across Germany and fought with us until the war ended. He joined in with our men serving the same as any of them did. His character has been excellent and his presence has been an inspiration and a morale builder to our men. I take pleasure in giving him this letter.

/s/ Walter E. Garrard
1st Lt. Infantry
Commanding

29 May 1945

The above young man has been a great deal of help to me in conducting an official investigation. He is keen, capable and absolutely trustworthy. I would desire him to serve under me at any time.

/s/ G. H. Allen Jr.
Lt. Col. Inf.
Hdqrs. Third U.S. Army, J A sec.

A TRUE COPY

NAN M. EVERHART
1st Lt., WAC
Acting Adjutant

Headquarters
Third United States Army
APO 403   16 October 1945

Subject: Commendation.
To: Whom it may concern.

1. Immediately after the cessation of hostilities on 9 May 1945 the 345th Field Artillery Battalion, 90th Infantry Division, took over the Kreis of Neunburg as an occupational area. The undersigned was at that time the command-

ing officer of the 345th. The conditions in Neunburg Kreis were not good. Approximately 4,000 displaced persons and 3,000 prisoners of war were roaming about the area. There was no established control over these people and the situation was becoming worse.

2. Soon after our arrival, George Topas, the bearer of this note, appeared at my office with a strong letter of recommendation from a unit of the 26th Infantry Division. I accepted the services of Topas as an assistant to our CIC team.

3. Throughout his five months of service with my organization Topas proved himself worthy of every trust and confidence. He was an invaluable asset to the organization in the reestablishment of order in the Kreis. His complete and intimate knowledge of the problems of the displaced persons in our county permitted us to solve many difficulties with considerable ease. He displayed admirable tenacity and great personal bravery in hunting down the many SS men who were at large in the area. He was the leader of many security raids and he was personally responsible for the capture of more dangerous men than all the rest of the battalion combined. He had learned the English language by self-study in the concentration camp and he was also fluent in Polish, German and Russian. He was used as chief interpreter for the battalion in all our contacts with displaced persons and prisoners of war. He performed this difficult task with tact and ease. His abilities and trustworthiness became a by-word throughout the battalion.

4. In addition to his soldierly qualities Topas demonstrated high moral standards in all his contacts with us and with the displaced persons. His mind was quick and alert at all times; his intelligence was of the best. He continuously strove to improve his knowledge of the English language and American customs. His personality was most winning and he readily established many firm friendships among our soldiers.

5. In view of the remarkable qualities of courage, intelligence, character and personality demonstrated by George Topas, the undersigned recommends him as being worthy of many considerations. In particular I feel that he would make an excellent citizen of the United States for he repeatedly demonstrated his fine characteristics which have made the United States what it is. He is certainly deserving of any assistance which can be given him in his efforts to attain that citizenship.

/s/ Frank W. Norris
FRANK W. NORRIS
Lt. Col, FA
Secretary General Staff

A TRUE COPY

NAN M. EVERHART
1st Lt., WAC
Acting Adjutant

A Letter from the Past

Dear Mr. Topas,

Before I explain why I'm taking the liberty of writing to you, let me tell you a certain story:

It was the summer of 1941. For little Stefa, shut inside the walls of Warsaw Ghetto, summer had one great attraction: work on a small plot of "land"—the site of a bombed out house at the corner of Ceglana Street. With other children—members of a Toporol group / the so called Society for Advancing the Agriculture / she cleared the site of bricks and debris, planted, watered and weeded vegetables, and from time to time proudly brought home her share of "the crop".

Then one day the woman instructor of the group got sick; in her place came a young man. He could have been any age from 16 to 25; in the eyes of the children he seemed very grown-up, very important and very mysterious. There was a lot of guessing: "who is he, what is his name?" After a while the young instructor sent the children to a near-by yard to get some water from the pump, but he told Stefa to stay. He probably felt sorry for the skinny girl with a green pallor in her cheeks and thought her too weak to carry a heavy pail of water. During the short time they were alone he talked to her, asked her questions, and then said: "My name is Jurek Topas. Remember. Don't forget."

It is hard to tell whether he really stressed the word "remember" or was it just Stefa's imagination. In any case she was very proud that he singled her out and that she was the first one to learn his name. All day long she felt elated and superior to other children—a feeling she very rarely if ever experienced.

In a few days the woman instructor returned. Stefa did get a glimpse of Jurek Topas once again when the children went to help picking tomatoes at the cemetery, or perhaps it happened in the church garden on Plac Grzybowski. But he either didn't notice or didn't recognize her; and she was too shy to do anything about it.

Stefa could be considered very lucky: she had an "aryan" uncle who managed to smuggle her out of the Ghetto in the critical summer of 1942 (by that time both her parents had died). She changed her name to Anna, and owing to her "good appearance" was able to attend normal school. Next summer she went for a vacation to the country and practiced her Toporol-acquired skills in a real garden, which seemed more like a paradise to her.

Strange enough, although she soon forgot the names of many people she had come into contact with during her Ghetto days, and they were people whom she had known more intimately and for a longer time at that—the name of Jurek stuck in her memory. She often wondered whether this fact had any significance. Right after the war she absurdly hoped that she might meet him somewhere although she didn't even remember what he had looked like. Nothing except that name and the question: "Why did he tell to remember?"

It must be obvious to you by now that the sender of this letter is little Stefa vel Anna. You may still wonder why I should bother to write to you. Even if you are the person I am thinking you to be one can hardly expect you to remember a ten-year old girl with pigtails who caught your attention or pity or whatever it was for few brief moments over twenty years ago. And yet I would have no peace of mind if I didn't try to clear this up having at last a chance to do so. I hope I've given you enough details to enable you to confirm or deny my supposition.

Strange, but only a few months ago I told the story to my two very close friends, adding that I am deeply convinced this man must be alive. They were of course a bit sceptical, but also quite moved.

And another thing I consider a coincidence: Although I read the Time magazine regularly (I'm a journalist by profession) I hardly ever glance at the letters to the editor page. This time it was the very first thing that caught my attention. That is how I've come upon your name, and your letter about the Wall has led me to believe you might be the very person.

I suppose I could have written this letter in Polish, but of course there is a chance that I am completely mistaken not only in the case of your identity, but also concerning your war experiences—your contact with the Ghetto Wall could have been incidental and you might not know Polish. In that case I would be left completely in the dark.

Please, forgive me my curiosity. I can only hope that considering the circumstances you will understand it and will let me know, whatever the answer may be.

Very truly yours
Anna Piasecka

P.S. Since I don't know your full adress, I'm sending a copy of this letter to the Time, asking them to forward it to you. AP

The War Criminals

SS Oberscharfuerer Reinholz Feix, the dreaded commandant of the Budzyn SS camp, first reported to have been killed, actually died in 1969, while under indictment. Report of his death confirmed by the Justice Department in Ludwisburg, Germany (3/3/89).

SS Untersturmfuerer Tauscher, commandant of Budzyn SS camp (later period) hanged himself in his cell before the writer's scheduled appearance in court to give testimony at his 1967 trial.

SS Hauptsturmfuerer Amon Goeth, the brutal commandant of Plaszow concentration camp and its chief "hangman", was sentenced to death by the Supreme Tribunal in Cracow in 1946 and was hanged.

SS Hauptsturmfuerer Blanke, the "doctor" remembered for his selection in Plaszow, who established his credentials in Auschwitz, initially reported to have been killed, according to German court records committed suicide on 27 April 1945. (Dept. of Justice, Ludwisburg, 3/3/89.)

Toni Fehringer, the brutal Austrian *Kapo* at Plaszow, was found by Simon Wiesenthal in Micheldorf, Austria, in 1948. Sentenced to seven years in prison, he died while serving his sentence. Information was furnished and confirmed by the Vienna Documentation Center.

SS Hauptscharfuerer Franz J. Mueller, sentenced to lifetime in a disciplinary prison by the court in Mosbach, Germany, in 1961 for the crimes he committed in Plaszow camp, was resentenced in Kiel (see the trial at the beginning of the book) to six lifetime terms in 1967.

Notes

Prologue: Witness against Persecution

1. Thomas Keneally, *Schindler's List* (New York: Simon and Schuster, 1982).
2. *Hamburger Abendblatt*, 8/31/67. The newspaper erroneously reported that the witness said it was Mothers Day.
3. Ibid.
4. *Hamburger Abendblatt*,
5. Reported in the local press 3/20/68.
6. Ibid.

1 The Approaching Storm

1. Tarbut maintained schools in eastern Europe promoting biblical and modern Hebrew studies and pioneer settlement in Palestine. *Encyclopedia Judaica* (Jersusalem, 1972), 15:810.
2. The term *Anschluss* came into general use to describe Nazi Germany's annexation of Austria in March 1938; euphemistically, it implied a union between the two countries.
3. The recorded date of the Soviet entry into Poland is September 17, 1939, but it was anticipated a few days ahead of the actual incursion.
4. There is disagreement about this: according to postwar records, the controversial orders for all able-bodied men to leave Warsaw "before the bridges over the Vistula River were blown up" were actually given by Polish Army Colonel Umiastowski from general headquarters over the network of Polish Radio. Another source has it that "there were frequent cases of order—counter-order—disorder, the most serious of which concerned the defence of Warsaw. On 6 and 7 September Warsaw Radio appealed to all men capable of bearing arms to cross the Vistula before the bridges were blown to make their way east and join in the new lines of defence. Many obeyed, but within a couple of days the Mayor of Warsaw, Stefan Starzynski, was calling for just the opposite, for every man to stay in the city and defend it to the last." Nicholas Bethell, *The War Hitler Won* (New York: Holt, Rinehart and Winston, 1973), 103. See also Robert Goralski, *World War II Almanac: 1931–1945* (London: Hamish Hamilton, 1981), 92.
5. Polish tenor Jan Kiepura and his German-born wife, Martha Eggerth, were celebrated singers and actors in prewar Europe whose fame reached the United States and Canada, where they eventually settled.

2 Return to Warsaw

1. The gendarmerie, German rural police, acted as police in occupied Poland.
2. The Russians did not officially discriminate against Jews, so at the time

the Russian zone was perceived as a refuge. Technically, the border was closed between the zones of Poland occupied by Germany and Russia (then allies after the signing of their August 23, 1939, nonaggression pact). Nevertheless, people tried to smuggle themselves across in both directions. Many made it; some were caught. Crossing became progressively more difficult as border security increased.

3. A joyous Jewish holiday, the Feast of Lots, celebrated on the fourteenth day of the Jewish month of *Adar* (about the middle of March), Purim commemorates the miraculous deliverance of the Jews from a massacre in the ancient Persian empire decreed by Haman, its prime minister. The involved plot in this 2,500-year-old story (told in the book of Esther) ends with the hanging of Haman.

4. *Spitzbube*—rascal—in this context probably implied a petty thief.

3 The Closing of the Ghetto

1. Some sources report even greater disparities. According to the *Encyclopaedia Judaica*, 16:342, "The ghetto population received a food allocation amounting to 184 calories per capita a day, while the Poles received 634 and the Germans 2,310. The price per large calorie [1,000 calories] was 5.9 zlotys (about $1.00) for Jews, 2.6 zlotys (50 cents) for Poles, and 0.3 zlotys (six cents) for Germans. The average allocation per person in the ghetto was four pounds of bread and a half-pound of sugar a month. The dough was mixed with sawdust and potato peels."

2. Each Sabbath derives its distinctive title from the portion of scripture (*sedra*) read that day, usually the key verb in the opening sentence. The word *Bo* ("come" or "go") is from the command given to Moses: "Go in unto Pharoah" and demand that he "let my people go."

3. A *Sefer Torah* is a scroll containing the Torah, the five books of Moses. A *Shtibel* is a small place of worship, sometimes a single room.

4. The Jewish Community Council, or *Judenrat*, was not an elected body, but it did count among its twenty-four members dedicated Jewish leaders who consented to serve in the internal administration of the Warsaw ghetto under the authority of the SS. Czerniakow was an outstanding example of such service.

5. "A row of plots where the prison used to stand has been seeded on Gesia Street. Twenty agronomists are employed." Emmanuel Ringelblum, *Notes from the Warsaw Ghetto* (New York: McGraw-Hill, 1958), 188. The Gesia prison yard conversion to farm produce was the work of my group. The youngsters who took Toporol's courses in basic gardening and worked the plots ranged from eight to fifteen years of age. See Appendix for a letter from a survivor who had worked in my group as a young girl.

4 Excursion to the World of the Living

1. The *Volksdeutsche* were ethnic Germans born and raised outside the Reich. Their status was lower than that of the *Reichsdeutsche*, citizens of Germany proper.

2. The ethnic German firms of Toebbens and Schultz moved in and set up their shops in the Warsaw ghetto in order to exploit cheap Jewish labor and thus ensure enormous profits. Bernard Goldstein, *The Stars Bear Witness* (New York: Viking, 1949), 88–90. See also *Krakauer Zeitung*, September 3, 1941, p. 5;

April 24, 1942, p. 5. In fact, the profits these private ghetto-situated companies were raking in were so high as to irritate Himmler. He ordered Toebbens's books examined "with a microscope. . . . If I am not mistaken" he said, "a man who had no property three years ago has become a well-to-do man here, if not a millionaire, and only because we, the state, have driven cheap Jewish labor into his arms" Raul Hilberg, *The Destruction of the European Jews* (New York: Harper, 1979), 339.

4. The *Maftir* is the paragraph-length conclusion of the scripture reading for the Sabbath or holiday.

5. After promises of abundant blessings for faithful fulfillment of the law, the Torah predicts dire calamities as wages of disobedience. In prewar times this seemed an unimaginable nightmare. Such phrases as "I will appoint terror over you. . . . that shall make the eyes to fail and the soul to languish. . . . I will send a faintness into their hearts in the land of their enemies" (Leviticus 26:33,36) did not sound real then. I asked my father, "Did this ever happen?" and Father answered, "Yes, once during the Babylonian conquest and fall of Jerusalem in 586 B.C. and again after the Roman destruction of the Temple of Jerusalem." Yet the chapter ends characteristically on a note of hope: God's anger may be severe, but it is not everlasting; He will grant his people every opportunity to renew the ancient Covenant. Israel is "a people who have been overthrown, crushed, scattered; who have been ground, as it were, to the very dust, and flung to the four winds of heaven; yet who, though thrones have fallen, and empires have perished, and creeds have changed, and living tongues have become dead, still exist with a vitality seemingly unimpaired" (Henry George, quoted in Joseph H. Hertz [late Chief Rabbi of the British Empire], *The Pentateuch and Haftorahs* [London: Socino Press, 1967], 546–47.

5. The Deportations Begin

1. *Tisha B'Av* is a day of mourning that commemorates the Babylonian destruction of Jerusalem, the burning of the Temple, and the slaughter of thousands in 586 B.C. The Romans destroyed the Second Temple on the same day in 70 A.D. Incredible cruelties and massacres followed, leading to the eventual exile of the Jewish people.

2. The phylacteries are two small leather cases containing slips of parchment inscribed with passages from the Torah. Observant Jews fasten one, with leather straps, to the forehead and the other to the left arm during weekday morning services, in fulfillment of scriptural commands (Deuteronomy 6:4–8) that are obligatory for all males from the thirteenth birthday on.

3. *Mickiewicz* (1798–1855) was Poland's foremost poet. During his exile in Paris, when he came upon Jews observing *Tisha b'Av,* he said that a nation that remembers the destruction of its glory and state for such a long time would some day rise again.

6. Escapes and Other Fragile Reprieves

1. Heinrich Graetz (1817-91), Jewish historian and Bible scholar (*History of the Jews,* 1870), is not recognized as authoritative by observant Jews because he took liberties with historical facts, probably to dramatize his prose.

2. The number of 40,000 is taken from Ringelblum, *Notes From the Warsaw Ghetto,* 307.

3. On November 14, 1941, during the second round of deportations, Jews

were rounded up from Slonim and vicinity. "Germans, Lithuanians and Be-
lorussians [White Russians] murdered 9,000 Jews in nearby Czepielow" (*Encyclopaedia Judaica*, 14:1672).

4. A Jewish observer, Dr. Isaac I. Schwarzbart, who was a deputy in the
Polish legislature in exile, has described Polish help as "negligible, insignificant." Several hundred pistols were purchased from the Polish people at
extraordinary high prices. (Hilberg, *Destruction of European Jews*, 323.)

5. The fight in the Warsaw ghetto began on April 19; it was not until May
that a radiogram asking for help was transmitted to the Polish government-in-
exile in London. Ringelblum, *Notes from the Warsaw Ghetto*, 345. Ringelblum was
one of the three signers of the radiogram.

6. "On 16th May, 1943, the Nazis blew up the great synagogue on
Tlomackie Street. This feat of wanton destruction was regarded by S.S. Gen.
Jurgen Stroop as an 'honorary salute,' after which he hastened to report that 'es
gibt keinen Judenbezirk in Warschau mehr' (there is no Jewish district in
Warsaw any more). This was not true. The Ghetto insurgents continued to fight
for several weeks." Stanislaw Poznanski, *Struggle—Death—Memory 1939–1945*
(Warsaw: 1963). Council for the Preservation of Monuments of Struggle and
Martyrdom.

7 A Trip Through Eternity

1. The suburban summer resorts predominantly frequented by Jews
from Warsaw were found along this rail route and were referred to as being *na
linji*, "on the line."

2. Some car doors were secured with wire; others were not. Most often,
the small windows were used for escapes.

3. These SS men are identified in a recent book about Majdanek. "In the
morning Florstedt assisted by Thumann and Musfeldt chief of the Crematorium commenced selection of prisoners. . . . Without . . . registration he
sent transports directly to the gas chamber. . . . This took place in the spring
and summer of 1943 when many Jewish transports were arriving at Majdanek."
Florstedt was later charged by an SS court for personally stealing Jewish
valuables and was fired from his position. Josef Marszalek, *Majdanek Concentration Camp in Lublin* (Warsaw: Wydawnictwo, 1987), p. 9. Florstedt was later
executed for this crime by an SS court. Heinze Hohne, *The Order of the Death's
Head* (New York, Ballantine, 1971), p. 437.

8 Camp Budzyn

1. The Ukrainian guards, generally recruited from Soviet POWs on a
voluntary basis, were regarded by the Russian authorities as traitors and were
later held accountable for their collaboration with the Germans.

2. Labor Camp Budzyn, a satellite camp of Majdanek, had been established in the fall of 1942. Prisoners interned there worked in the Heinkel aircraft
factory. "In the spring of 1943 there were about 3000 prisoners who were
perishing due to inhuman living conditions." Marszalek, *Majdanek*, p. 52.

3. "SS Oberscharfuehrer Reinhold Feix . . . distinguished himself with
[his] particular brand of sadism." Marszalek, ibid.

9 An Endurance Test

1. I later confirmed with Sidney Engel and Morris Wyszogrod, who were both in Budzyn at the time, that this man's name was Bitter.

10 A New Slavemaster

1. According to Marszalek, the resistance movement of Jewish prisoners, including a revolt in Treblinka in August and in Sobibor in October, prompted the liquidation of SS camps in the Lublin district on orders from Himmler. Jewish prisoners totaling some 42,000 were shot on November 3, 1943. The Budzyn prisoners, who worked in the aircraft industry, were spared, apparently because of the needs of the Air Force. Marszalek, *Majdanek*, pp. 50, 52.

2. "It was hazardous to depend upon labor that could be withdrawn by the SS without a moment's notice," as illustrated by an "unexpected and complete withdrawal of the Jewish workers by the SS from Toebbens and Schultz in the Lublin district and their massacre in November 1943 in the Majdanek concentration camp" (Hilberg, *Destruction of the European Jews*, 342, 345). Also: "The conditions of work for the foreign laborers, the POW's and the concentration camp inmates were reported by reliable witnesses after the war. It is well known to all that the inmates were literally being worked to death. They were forced to run while unloading heavy cement bags weighing 100 lbs": *Trials of War Criminals before the Nuremberg Military Tribunal* (Green) (Washington, D.C.: U.S. Government Printing Office, 1949), 7:53, 54.

12 Plaszow

1. *Proces ludobujcy Amona Goetha* (Trial of Mass Murderer Amon Goeth) (Krakow: Central Jewish Historical Commission, 1947), spells the name Chilowicz, but in camp it was known as Chilewicz, pronounced Hilevitch.

2. Ibid. The postwar trial of Amon Goeth, at which he was charged with mass murder, provided overwhelming testimony of his cruelty and greed. Another witness's account in a report of the U.S. Third Army War Crimes Branch, dated 12/19/45, describes Goeth as "a beast in human form who has murdered hundreds himself and has the death of thousands, perhaps of tens of thousands, on his conscience. He was the executioner in the Jewish Labor Camp near Lublin."

3. At Goeth's trial in Krakow on September 31, 1945, Dr. A. Biberstein testified "that which is known to me and what I had seen—the *benzynowe* [gasoline shots] were injected by SS *Obersturmfuehrer* Jaeger, a German doctor. It was used on seriously ill tubercular cases" (ibid. 287). All translations from the *Proces* are mine.

13 *Steinbruch*

1. Although the statement that Blanke's May 7 "selections" took place on a cold day rests on the testimony of several witnesses, one witness—Dr. A. Mirowski—described the day as being very warm. In any case, the selection doomed 1,400 people, who were shipped to Auschwitz for liquidation (*Proces*, 32, 65, 310, 311, 485). Another witness recalled that "Blanke was wrapped in a very nice, fur-lined coat for although it was May it was bitterly cold. The prisoners had to stand naked waiting for hours. As they went by, Blanke would

nod gracefully to the right or left" (Report of U.S. Third Army War Crimes Branch 12/19/45.)

2. "At the time of removal of children from the camp to Auschwitz, Goeth ordered the band to play a children's song *"Mammi, kauf mir ein pherdhen,"* while the mothers of the children had to look on as their children were being shipped away to die" (*Proces*, 33).

3. When Mark gave his occupation as a weaver upon arrival in the camp, he meant basket weaver; in his previous internment he had been employed weaving baskets to cradle bombs. He knew nothing about weaving furniture.

4. "It took place in the following manner: that girls were caught (in the camp), they were taken to the dispensary and blood was taken in large amounts—500 to 800 milliliters" (17 to 27 fluid ounces), or well above the safe donation level (testimony of Dr. Alexander Biberstein and Dr. A. Mirowski, *Proces*, 287, 314).

5. Planning an escape was one charge leveled against Chilewicz, but in reality, he knew too much about the amount of jewelry, confiscated from the Krakow ghetto Jews, that Goeth had kept—in violation of strict rules that all of a Jew's valuables were to be turned over to the *Reichsbank*. Goeth apparently decided to get rid of incriminating evidence. Chilewicz, his wife, and his second-in-command were shot on August 13, 1944 (ibid., 71, 489).

14 A Daring Enterprise

1. The *Organization Todt*, named after engineer Fritz Todt, was responsible for building the "impregnable," western Siegfried line; it also constructed German military highways and installations. See William Shirer, *The Rise and Fall of the Third Reich* (New York: Simon & Schuster, 1960), 378; *Encyclopaedia Britannica* (1958), 8:451a.

2. *Din Torah* is a judicial procedure based on the laws of the Torah, but here it merely meant that we agreed to abide by the decision of arbitrators chosen among ourselves.

3. "At the beginning of September (1944) a transport of Hungarian women was sent to Auschwitz" (witness Kopytecki, *Proces*, 486).

4. "There was a punishment consisting of standing in a small cell in which one could not sit down" (witness Pamper, ibid., 68).

5. This transport to Mauthausen took place on July 27, 1944 (witness S. Hollaender, ibid., 32, 264). It is not recounted in its chronological place here, because my original recollections were written in this order.

6. In a TV documentary shown in the U.S. about Schindler, the German contractor (*Schindler's List*), witnesses claimed that the water hoses were turned on at his urging.

7. "According to the testimony of the witness Grunwald, together with the [gradual] liquidation of the camp in August and September 1944 the [authorities] ordered the opening of mass graves and exhumations, and without identification the corpses were burnt in the open field" (*Proces*, 486).

15 Journey to Germany

1. Treatment of prisoners at Flossenbuerg is described in a report of the U.S. Third Army, War Crimes Branch, 6/21/45, which states: "Flossenbuerg concentration camp can best be described as a factory dealing in death. Although this camp had in view the primary object of putting to work the mass

slave labor, another of its primary objectives was the elimination of human lives by the methods employed in handling the prisoners." Many of the incidents and circumstances recalled in this and the following chapters are also described in that report and in *Trial of the Major War Criminals before the International Military Tribunal* (Nuremberg, 1947).

17 Reunion and Separation

1. Flossenburg had under its jurisdiction 47 satellite camps, of which Hersbruck was considered to be one of the worst. Prisoners there were engaged in underground construction work. (Report of U.S. Third Army, War Crimes Branch, 6/21/45.)

18 Evacuation March

1. A well documented account of the evacuation from Flossenbuerg was compiled by Toni Siegert in *Das Konzentrationslager Flossenbuerg*, in *Bayern in der NS-Zeit*, Vol. 2 (Munich, 1979). A report of the slaughter of prisoners was also issued by the headquarters of the Third U.S. Army under date of 5 July 1945; that report names George Topas among the prisoners who escaped death.

19 The Slaughter Is Ended

1. Address before the House of Commons, May 13, 1940; quoted in Winston Churchill, *Their Finest Hour* (Boston: Houghton Mifflin, 1949), 25-26.

Epilogue: Elation and Sorrow

1. *Time*, 19 March 1965, 25.
2. The letter from the tracing service states: "TOPAS Abraham, born in Warsaw on 14th November 1904, died in prisoner-of-war camp Lublin on 25th September 1942, Prisoner's No 14135. The date of issue of the prisoner's number 14135 is not known to us. The prisoner-of-war camp Lublin was under the command of the Reichsführer SS/Inspekteur der Konzentrationslager im SS-Führungshauptamt and on and after 3rd March 1942, the SS-Wirtschafts-Verwaltungshauptamt/Amtsgruppe D (Konzentrationslager). From 16th February 1943 on, the prisoner-of-war camp Lublin was designated as "Konzentrationslager" (concentration camp) Lublin." They had found no information regarding my brother Simon.
3. Quoted in *Martyrdom and Resistance*, Nov.-Dec. 1986, 15.

Acknowledgments

As this book goes to press, I wish to thank those who have graciously afforded me the benefit of their time to encourage, inspire, read, comment, and correct my manuscript in the course of its lengthy preparation.

First and foremost, I wish to express my gratitude and thanks to my wife, Bella. I cannot adequately pay tribute to her for her assistance with every stage of my work, for her sorely-tried patience, and for putting up with me through all the difficult phases of working on my manuscript. Thanks also to my children who pleaded with me to get my work published.

And to my friend Mark Heering whose friendship sustained me throughout the ordeal we were destined to share, and to his wife Bea.

And to Rav. Eliezer Simcha Wasserman for his inspiration and personal guidance.

My thanks to Adele Moskovitz for graciously reading my early draft and making corrections and suggestions and to her husband, Irving Moskovitz, for his counsel. To Betty Corson, who was senior editor of Lippincott at the time, for her early recognition of the potential of my story and for her encouragement and eventual copy editing assistance. To my friend Eric Freudenstein for his help with the correction of the German words and to our friends Hannah and Charles Kletzki for their thoughtful suggestions on abridging the prewar recollections. Also to the author and movie critic Michael Medved for his appraisal of my manuscript and for helping to strengthen my resolve to have it published. I also remember with gratitude Professor Lawrence R. Fishman, Vice-Dean of Rutgers University, for his valuable advice while I was transforming my work into publishable form.

My special thanks to Jerome Crouch, the editor-in-chief of the University Press of Kentucky for his genuine interest in bringing my work to public light and for his sound counsel; also to the staff of the press and especially to Evalin Douglas and Patricia Sterling.

Last, but not least, I give thanks to the One who spared me from countless perils and planted within me the will to endure and survive so that I might bear witness to this epic tragedy of our People and so to forewarn our and future generations against complacency and appeasement.

Index